Risky Business

Risky Business

INSIDE CANADA'S $86-BILLION
INSURANCE INDUSTRY

Rod McQueen

Macmillan of Canada
A Division of Canada Publishing Corporation
Toronto, Ontario, Canada

Reprinted 1985

Canadian Cataloguing in Publication Data

McQueen, Rod, date.
  Risky business : inside Canada's $86-billion
insurance industry

Includes index.
ISBN 0-7715-9693-6

1. Insurance—Canada.   2. Insurance companies—
Canada.   3. Insurance—Canada—Finance.   I. Title.

HG8550.M26 1985   368'.971   C85-098877-2

Design: Don Fernley

Macmillan of Canada
A Division of Canada Publishing Corporation
Toronto, Ontario, Canada

Printed in Canada

Contents

Foreword

B EFORE I began this book, I swore an oath to myself not to buy any insurance while I was researching and writing other than from insurance relationships I already had in place. This was simply a protective device, because I knew I'd be pitched by some super-sellers. Even with that shield, I've nearly bought more coverage several times. One agent, when I offered my protest of purchasing celibacy, asked, "When is your research finished?" When I told her, she said, "I'll phone you then." And I'm sure she will.

The product, however, was of less interest to me than the people who are in the business of insuring lives and risks of all sorts. Although there have been many Canadian handbooks about how to find the best insurance buys, there has been no full-scale look at the insurance business and the people who make it work. *Risky Business* is such a project.

My thanks to researcher Sharon Illingworth for her unstinting diligence, copy editor Barbara Czarnecki for her deft hand, editorial director Anne Holloway for her patient and professional guidance, and publisher Doug Gibson for his boundless enthusiasm. To them, all the bouquets; any brickbats are mine.

Rod McQueen
Toronto
July 1985

CHAPTER ONE

INTRODUCTION

A T A KITCHEN table in small-town Ontario Ed Maindonald, an insurance agent for London Life Insurance Co., makes his pitch to a young couple. The process is a jousting match, reminiscent of medieval times, where each side tries to unseat the other. Maindonald charges, wielding his patter and his hand-drawn chart, the prospects fight back wearing armour and sour face-plates. Maindonald concentrates on the wife while the husband fiddles with a plastic place-mat and moans, "I hate insurance." He is not particularly interested in leaving his wife a wealthy widow. "If I croak tomorrow," he says, "I don't want some guy coming in here and drinking my beer." By the end of the evening, however, they have both purchased policies.

August 15, 1984, was sunny in big sky country. At Fort McMurray, Alta., 370 kilometres northeast of Edmonton, Syncrude Canada Ltd. insurance administrator George Wilkinson spent the day on the site of the firm's giant oil-sands plant. Both cokers were running at full tilt and the plant was producing the usual daily output, 130,000 barrels of oil. When Wilkinson left about five o'clock, all was well with the world. At 9:20 P.M., catastrophe struck. An eight-inch pipe, one of scores running throughout the installation like string let loose from a ball, suddenly ruptured, and soon a raging fire was under way. The bill for the holocaust that followed may run to $300 million, the largest single insured loss in Canada's history.

The two scenes couldn't be more different, yet they demonstrate the two poles of the insurance business in Canada. Human drama at the kitchen table, human error in the north, the two are linked by a common bond: insurance. In some ways, the two industries, life and general (or property and casualty, as it is also known), are no more alike than oil and water. Because few people really *want* life insurance, it's not so much bought as it is sold by fervent missionaries who believe in the product with the zeal of a born-again Bible-thumper. Property and casualty insurance, on the other hand, has become an essential life-support system. Without appropriate coverage, even a minor calamity can wipe out an individual's wealth; a major catastrophe can bankrupt an entire company.

While the two industries don't really care if a certain client dies next week or if a particular plant burns down next month, they must both wrestle with global ghosts. They care deeply—as they insure or assure against risk—about the total number of forty-four-year-old males who will die next year or how likely it is that there will be a repeat of the 1981 Calgary hailstorm that caused $125 million in property damage in less than twenty minutes. (By way of definition, the designations "insurance" and "assurance" are used in the industry both in the titles of companies and for other descriptions. While they tend to be used interchangeably, the precise definition shows more than a subtle difference. Insurance is coverage against a risk that may not happen, such as fire; assurance is coverage against something that is bound to happen, such as death.)

Winston Churchill once said that insurance "brings the magic of averages to the rescue of millions." The insurance industry runs on such numbers, assessing the likelihood of the risks and setting premiums based on huge samples. The greater the numbers involved, the easier it is to predict next year's horrors or death count and charge enough to pay those who are left behind, cover administrative expenses, and made a tidy profit. As *Fortune* magazine once said about the income of insurance companies: "Those billions in premiums have to be sweated out of the consciences of the people in what is still the most agonizing person-to-person sales duel on the American scene." That's why the business is geared to motivate sales agents into thinking they are God's chosen instruments. "Life insurance was a belief before it was a business; it is a missionary effort," said *Fortune*.

More than 13 million Canadians own life insurance policies—an average of $50,000 in coverage per Canadian household. Per capita, Canadians are the third best insured citizens in the world, after the Americans and the Japanese. Life insurance is the second most common financial investment in Canada. While about half of all Canadians own life insurance policies, only one-third own Canada Savings Bonds and one-quarter have registered retirement savings plans. Only savings accounts, held by 85 per cent of Canadians, are more popular than life insurance. Life insurance is also an important export for Canada. People outside the country buy more than $50 billion of life insurance from Canadian companies. Six million Canadians have dental insurance plans and disability insurance; 10 million Canadians have extended health care insurance plans. Total accident and sickness premiums amount to about $2 billion annually. The property and casualty business is equally pervasive. There is hardly a Canadian household or business without some kind of protection against fire, theft, liability, and all the other tragedies of modern life. Canadians file about $2.5 billion a year in automobile insurance claims. And all those policies, whether life or general, buy more than mere coverage; there's something less tangible as well: peace of mind.

In Canada, there are 170 life insurance companies with $70 billion in assets, and some 300 firms in the property and casualty business with $16 billion in assets, for an industry-wide total of $86 billion. The top twenty life companies (see Appendix A) account for about two-thirds of the total industry revenues. In the property and casualty business (see Appendix B), about one-third of the companies account for 90 per cent of the business. Canadian life companies are among the strongest in the world; they have fully 3 per cent of the United States market even though they are battling against some 1,800 native U.S. firms. Measured by the value of insurance in force, the largest eight Canadian firms are among the top fifty companies in North America. About half the life companies operating in Canada are Canadian; the rest are foreign. The property and casualty business is even more international; about two-thirds of the companies operating in Canada are foreign-owned. In total, the insurance industry employs about 175,000 Canadians, about 60 per cent in administrative jobs, the other 40 per cent dealing more directly with customers, selling policies and settling claims.

Measured by assets, Sun Life Assurance Co. of Canada has been the largest life insurance company operating in Canada since 1908. In 1985, however, Sun's $13 billion in assets was surpassed when The Manufacturers Life Insurance Co. bought The Dominion Life Assurance Co. (legally they remain two separate companies), giving

Manufacturers a combined asset value of $13.5 billion, enough to knock Sun from first place. The fastest-growing company is Crown Life Insurance Co., with a phenomenal 60-per-cent growth rate in individual life insurance sales since 1980. Biggest group life insurance sellers are Sun, The Great-West Assurance Co., and Confederation Life Insurance Co. Among general insurance companies, the market is far more fragmented. The industry leader, Co-operators General Insurance Co., has a mere 5 per cent of the market share and $441 million in annual premium income; Royal Insurance Canada is second with $397 million. As an industry, the general insurance business in Canada is much smaller than the life business. Admits Jack Lyndon, president of the Insurance Bureau of Canada, the property and casualty trade association: "All the property and casualty companies together couldn't take a crack at the big five life companies."

Both arms of the insurance industry are swept up in the sea change that is under way in Canada's financial services sector. Much of the push for change in Canada has been coming from the United States, where corporate activity has been turbulent. There banks, insurance companies, brokerage houses, and the rest all seem to have adopted a strategy worthy of Attila the Hun: when in doubt, invade the other guy's territory. Giant national retailers like Sears now sell insurance, real estate, and securities under the same roof with the usual department store goods: everything from socks to stocks. Prudential Insurance has bought a New York City securities firm and a Georgia bank; BankAmerica owns a brokerage company. Citibank has leased lobby space to an insurance company for sales kiosks.

Until recently, the Canadian financial services sector consisted of four separate, staid, and distinct pillars: banks, loan and trust companies, insurance firms, and securities houses. For the past half-dozen years there has been a blurring at the edges of these four. Companies in each area are scrambling to provide services that in the past have only been offered by members of another pillar. Insurance companies are currently offering a type of term deposit instrument, like that offered by the trust firms; two of the big five chartered banks have actively entered the securities business; brokerage houses have accounts that duplicate a bank chequing account; trust companies are aggressively into commercial lending.

After some initial sluggishness, the insurance industry is scrambling to catch up. "For more than a century, life insurance companies were able to take advantage of a built-in momentum," says Gerald Devlin, executive vice-president of the Canadian Life and Health Insurance Association Inc. (CLHIA), a 117-member industry group. "Their profits were generated by business signed up ten or twenty years before. They lived very comfortably on the surplus created from business on the books. This has now changed forever. The bottom-line pressures we are all experiencing in the 1980s are not a temporary aberration. The public now demands results in the short run, not over decades. We are now thrown into direct competition with other financial institutions in many areas. We have responded by developing an array of new products. All of these forces have eroded the stability of our business in force and have created an entirely new environment for us."

That new environment will include one-stop financial shopping emporiums. Next year Canada's first one-stop centre will be opened by an insurance company, the Laurentian Group, on the ground floor of its new $75-million office tower near Dominion Square in Montreal. Others, notably Crownx Inc., the financial holding company that controls Crown Life, plan to do the same; Crown's venture will be at head office in Toronto. Not everyone in the industry thinks that one-stop is what the consumer wants. "I think the concept has moved ahead of practicalities," says Jack Rhind, chairman of Confederation Life, as he views what Crown chief executive officer Robert Bandeen is doing. "Bandeen is like someone—I won't say a kid—who has gone into a candy shop for the first time. He looks around and says, 'Wow, look at all this. Now, I'll take some of those and some of those and some of that over there.'"

The candy stores, however, are coming. Customers of Crown and Laurentian will be able to do everything from opening a savings account to buying shares in a junior mine. Because Laurentian has a Quebec charter, and because of its aggressive acquisition policy in the last decade, the company has been the first to buy into all four financial pillars. (Crown does not yet own a bank.) A more recent upstart, Trilon Financial Corp., the $55-billion conglomerate run by Peter and Edward Bronfman, has positioned itself with ownership in several financial areas. Trilon's tentacles reach into Royal Trustco Ltd. (trust services), London Life Insurance Co. (life insurance), Wellington Insurance Co. (general insurance), and Royal LePage (real estate). As Canadians demand more products in an ever more competitive marketplace, firms with such links are the wave of the future.

For decades, the insurance companies have been the quiet bankers. Through mortgages, they have financed more than a million Canadian homes as well as 30 per cent of all the Canadian corporate bonds currently outstanding, 17 per cent of municipal bonds, 7 per cent of provincial bonds, and 10 per cent of all Government of Canada securities. Until recently, the bosses at the top, the chief executive officers, have been just as invisible as their corporate assets. "The insurance company top guys in the last twenty years have not been the national figures that some of the bank CEOs have been," says Robert MacIntosh, president of the Canadian Bankers' Association. "That's changing now."

To be sure, insurance has some distance to go before the company names become household words. A property and casualty firm, Travelers Canada, recently carried out a public awareness survey in which one of the questions required the respondent to name an insurance company, *any* insurance company. Thirty per cent of Canadians questioned couldn't. No wonder—the industry seems to be allergic to consumer awareness. For example, only 10 per cent of the 117 members of the Canadian Life and Health Insurance Association do any consumer advertising at all. The rest are content to limit their hype to the company's agents, who in turn beat the drums for the company and its products. The general insurance companies suffer a similar reticence. While most Canadians know who their brokers are, fewer know the insurance companies with which the brokers have placed the business.

Not every company is publicly silent. One of the more imaginative recent corporate image campaigns was conducted by The Canada Life Assurance Co., promoting its tie-in with the World Wildlife Fund Canada. A series of print ads identified various endangered species around the world and sought donations. Ironically, one of the threatened species was Canada Life's own corporate symbol, the white pelican, a bird now reduced to thirty breeding colonies, about half the number in existence at the turn of the century. The bird was chosen to symbolize Canada Life at its founding because the pelican purportedly would shed its blood for its young. In fact, as was later discovered, the white pelican is a terrible parent. If the white pelican is disturbed while nesting, the bird will run about, crushing eggs and young alike. Like the white pelican, all insurance companies these days are battling for their very lives in an ever-changing world of finance.

Modern-day insurance began in London, England, on September 2, 1666, when an oven in the king's bake shop became overheated and caused a fire that nearly destroyed the entire city. More than 640 acres of slums and mercantile houses were gutted. Fire insurance became available the following year. Shortly afterwards, coffee-houses became the gathering spots for insurers sharing various risks. Seamen and merchants needing insurance on a ship or cargo would make their proposal at the coffee-house, to be signed by those accepting part of the risk. Edward Lloyd's coffee-house became particularly popular, and in 1696, he began publishing a three-times-a-week flyer to announce information about sailings and other news of interest to the growing business. Lloyd's of London was born, and it remains the focal point of today's insurance industry. There, on the open trading floor, insurance syndicates take risks on everything from errant satellites in space to tankers in the war-torn Persian Gulf.

The first coverage available in Canada was fire insurance, which appeared about the beginning of the nineteenth century, nearly a century after it was developed in the United States. In Canada, in those early years, the business was carried on almost exclusively by British and other foreign companies; the first to establish an office in Canada was Phoenix of London in 1804. The date when life insurance officially began in North America is a matter of some dispute. Nova Scotia-born Morris Robinson was the first president of the Mutual Life Insurance Co. of New York; according to a tablet erected on New York's Wall Street, he "established on this spot the business of modern life insurance on the American continent, February 1, 1843." In fact a British company, Standard Life, was operating in Quebec City in 1833.

The first Canadian life insurance company was Canada Life, begun by Hugh C. Baker, a Hamilton, Ont., bank manager, who travelled to New York in 1845 to buy a life insurance policy on himself because none was available locally. He made the thousand-mile trip by horseback, stagecoach, and steamboat. For all his effort, he was charged an extra premium because of the "climatic hazard of living in Canada." He started Canada Life in 1847, and by 1868, it was the largest company in the country.

In Canada's early days, as companies were being established, politicians lent their names and reputations to some firms to give them more credibility with the public. Six prime ministers, for example, were associated with life insurance companies in the nineteenth and early twentieth centuries. Wilfrid Laurier was a director at The Mutual Life Assurance Co. of Canada, Charles Tupper and Robert Borden were both presidents at Crown, John A. Macdonald was president at Manufacturers, Alexander Mackenzie was president of North American Life Assurance Co., and Mackenzie Bowell was president of The Imperial Life Assurance Co. of Canada.

In 1875, a superintendent of insurance was appointed to, among other things, protect solvency and ensure that companies had the required assets to pay off claims if they went bankrupt. The office still exists, under the Department of Finance, and the current superintendent, Robert Hammond, is only the eighth officeholder in the 110-year history of the position. In 1877, federal legislation required foreign companies to put up a $50,000 deposit to do business in Canada. Of the thirty foreign life companies licensed at the time, about half withdrew, opening up the market for Canadian companies to gain a foothold. Most of the Canadian companies now in existence came into being during the next twenty years.

The 1877 legislation did not drive out the foreign casualty companies. Companies operating in Canada needed the continued backing of robust international owners to meet the potential catastrophic losses that could bankrupt a smaller firm. All-Canadian companies, operating with a smaller financial base, could not spread the risk by operating in several countries, and as a result, they reeled from a series of disasters. An 1877 fire in Saint John, N.B., for example, ruined three of the thirteen Canadian licensed companies. Fires in Ottawa in 1900 and Toronto in 1904 as well as the San Francisco earthquake and fire of 1906 led to continuing set-backs for Canadian companies and allowed the foreign companies to dominate the casualty business.

In addition to organized corporate selling of insurance, some insurance was sold by tiny local firms. Small mutual fire insurance companies, for example, survived as long as they weren't hit by too many losses. Life insurance was also supplied by fraternal societies. In its simplest form, such coverage meant that when a member died, all the rest were assessed one dollar and the money was paid to the widow. A Mohawk Indian chief, Oronhyatekha, an Oxford graduate in medicine, helped organize the still-active Independent Order of Foresters in 1874 with 369 members. There are currently some four dozen societies selling life insurance, about one-third of them Canadian.

Such early systems generally worked well until the members of the organization began to grow old, the numbers decreased, and the gathered amounts shrank. There were also local tontines, so named after their inventor, Lorenzo Tonti, who devised the system to raise money for Louis XIV of France. Subscribers were put in age classes, and the interest collected on a sum of money was divided among members of that class each year. As the number of survivors decreased through death, the survivors' share of the interest increased until the last survivor received a very large sum. As a form of life insurance, tontines were eventually replaced by companies organized on a sounder actuarial basis.

By the first decade of the twentieth century, life insurance companies were well enough established that a royal commission of inquiry was struck, a sure sign of corporate status in Canada. A 1905 investigation into insurance irregularities in New York state had brought calls for a similar study in Canada. The royal commission reported in 1907 and offered a strong indictment of excessive management expenses and poor, even illegal, investment practices in several companies. Said the report: "Your Commissioners cannot believe that it was ever the intention of Parliament that, under the pretext of investing in the securities of 'public utility' corporations, insurance companies should promote such companies and construct and operate their works. Nor can your Commissioners believe that Parliament intended to sanction the acquisition by an insurance company of the whole of or a controlling interest in the capital stock of a trust company, with the intent of managing and operating it as a subsidiary of tributary concern. These enterprises seem entirely foreign to the very idea of investment." The commission also observed that "insurance companies tend to become powerful aggregations of money with financial rather than insurance aims. The power to engineer these aggregations becomes a thing to be desired." Some things never change.

Life insurance companies were often part of one family's financial fiefdom. One of the leading lights was George Cox, a turn-of-the-century Methodist and prohibitionist who was a director of some four dozen companies as well as president of both the Bank of Commerce and Canada Life. As Canada Life's largest shareholder, he had two sons working at the firm and decided that a third son was too much, so he created Imperial Life (now part of the Laurentian Group) for him to run. Liquor companies were also commonly owners of life insurance companies; the Seagram family, for example, owned Dominion Life. Even with such ownership through the "sin" industries, the stress was always on the godliness of insurance and its protective values. In the 1920s, T. B. Macaulay, president of Sun Life, said: "I think of [a country] rather as a vast group of humans... Over each hangs, by a constantly fraying thread, a sword of Damocles... It falls here, it falls there... The one shield that can protect the family from that falling sword is the life assurance policy."

In a country where public policy has been to allow bigness among companies, it is not surprising that legislation in the early part of the twentieth century focussed primarily on solvency, ensuring that the Canadian public wasn't burned too badly should a company fail and controlling the foreign companies through deposits rather than encouraging competition. Canadian insurance legislation has traditionally fallen between the law of Britain, where there has been very little regulation, and the law of the U.S., where restrictions have been quite detailed. While there was a new insurance act in 1917 and another in 1932, the thrust has been the same throughout: safety for policyholders and a minimum of interference with management.

The current law, the Canadian and British Insurance Companies Act, passed in 1932, has been revised since. In 1948, a basket clause was added so that real estate could be added to the investment portfolio; in the 1960s, when mutual funds were all the rage, life insurance companies asked for and received permission for agents to sell mutual funds; in 1970, insurance companies were given the power to create subsidiaries. Life insurance companies can also own property and casualty insurance companies, but few have rushed to expand in that direction. Little wonder: property and casualty insurance is a bizarre business. From 1970 to 1984, the industry's underwriting losses (claims and expenses paid out in excess of premiums collected) in Canada totalled a staggering $4 billion. That did not mean, however, that the industry wasn't profitable. The underwriting losses were offset by investment income of $8.6 billion earned on their assets, so the net profit in the industry since 1970 has been an equally staggering $4.6 billion.

Still, for all the invoked power of federal law, protection of the public has not been ironclad. Prior to 1981, only four property and casualty firms failed in Canada—two in the 1880s, one in 1920, and one in 1967. In the last four years, five more property and casualty companies have disappeared; in some cases, policyholders of those firms are still waiting for claims that will never be paid in full. No life insurance company, however, has ever failed to pay a death benefit, usually because a stronger company took in the weaker one if it stumbled. Between 1913 and 1924, for example, seven companies teetered and had some $58.5 million in policies taken over by Sun Life alone. Thus while the total number of insurance companies operating in Canada approaches 500 today, more than 350 other companies began business at one time or another, then withdrew or disappeared for a variety of reasons. Indeed, some companies operating today are still in business only because they did not pay all their losses following the 1906 earthquake in San Francisco.

That the insurance companies have been overtaken in importance by the banks in Canada is clear from the skyline of any major city. In Montreal in the 1930s, the largest building by far was the granite structure of Sun Life on Dominion Square, far bigger than the head office of either the Royal Bank of Canada or the Bank of Montreal on Rue St.-Jacques. In the major cities, the banks have been raising their tall tabernacles since the 1960s; life insurance companies are just beginning to match them. Manufacturers, Laurentian, Sun, and The Standard Life Assurance Co. have all recently erected monuments to past policyholders that rival the bank towers in size and luxury. Sun has a $200-million pair of silver towers in Toronto, and Manufacturers Life's ostentatious new thirteen-storey tower in Toronto boasts executive-suite luxury unmatched in Canada, with its cherrywood walls, hand-crafted broadloom, a $20,000 Persian rug, and burled Carpathian elm desks. The tower is attached to the firm's older structure by a new free-standing, copper-roofed rotunda, the first built in Canada in decades. Designer Peter Ferguson told the *Globe and Mail*'s Adele Freedman that such domes have always been associated with funerary monuments and hence made sense for an insurance company. "It's a monument," said Ferguson, "to people who died at the proper time."

The largest life insurance company, however, is only about one-seventh the size of the largest bank, the Royal Bank of Canada, as measured by assets. After the Second World War, assets of both were about equal. "That's typical of what's happened to the life industry over those years," says John Lane, senior vice-president and general manager for Canada at Sun Life. Banks took over the mortgage and personal loan business and continued as the main source of corporate borrowing. Their branches on every corner outdid the insurance business at sucking up the savings of Canadians. Insurance companies stayed in the long-term business: policies for life, not investments for next year. Admits Lane, "We've shrunk in importance."

The numbers tell the tale. In registered retirement savings plans, a key savings area, life insurance companies have steadily been losing market share. From 40 per cent of the RRSP business in 1967, life industry share dropped to less than 30 per cent in 1976, and it is less than 20 per cent today. Life insurance companies did not change their RRSP products when other companies brought out more "user-friendly" types, without the front-end loading charges required by the life companies. The personal savings market has shown a similar decline; while other institutions were rushing to find new products in a more competitive environment, the insurance companies stayed with the traditional insurance policies. In 1970, life insurance companies had 29 per cent of the $45 billion in total personal deposits of Canadians. By 1975, they had 22 per cent of $90 billion; by 1982, only 16 per cent of $260 billion.

Much of the change in the relative positions of the banks and the insurance firms has been forced on the financial services industry by legislation. The laws governing the banks, for example, were fully revised in 1954, 1967, and 1980. In 1954 banks were allowed to make individual mortgage loans; in 1967, consumer loans. In both cases, banks were slow to begin offering the loans, but when they did, they grew to dominate the field. "The decennial revision of banking did lead to social change," says Canadian Bankers' Association president Robert MacIntosh. A federal discussion paper released in 1985 will lead to revisions in no fewer than eight federal laws affecting insurance and trust and loan companies. The overall effect will be to put all financial services on a more equal footing. The banks have had a head start because of the regular review of their legislation. While many of the insurance companies have federal charters and are supervised by the federal superintendent of insurance and the Department of Insurance, which worries about solvency and stability, the provinces have some clout, too. Each has a superintendent who oversees insurance companies operating under provincial charters. The provinces also take a predominant role in supervising the terms and conditions of insurance contracts and the licensing of companies, agents, and adjusters.

The difference between legislative treatments of banks and of the insurance industry has meant a different type of executive in each business. After the Second World War, the bright young up-and-comers went into other fields; the banks and insurance industries became bureaucracies with a non-entrepreneurial generation in charge. Then legislative review slowly altered what the banks did. As the banks became more aggressive, they attracted more aggressive people, albeit more slowly than, say, manufacturing. The insurance industry was even slower to respond to modern management methods. The property and casualty business in Canada was largely run by people trained within the industry with few fresh ideas from outside. Insurance executives became as inbred as a community of backwoods farm folk cut off from the world.

For the most part, the life insurance companies were run by actuaries, professional mathematicians trained in the technical side of insurance who calculate such minutiae as reserves and surplus. They may be good in math but they're weak in marketing and woeful in management. The actuary is the person who is trained in the principles of large numbers and the theory of probability. Equipped with those mathematical concepts, the actuary then calculates the proper premium rates, based on experience. At least that's the theory. In practice, the numbers are often used by the actuary to tell marketing departments that new products couldn't possibly be profitable for fifty years. Because the actuary quashes innovation, he is often jokingly referred to as the "abominable no-man."

Fortunately, not all of the insurance companies have remained petrified. It was Ralph Waldo Emerson who said, "An institution is the lengthened shadow of one man." Groucho Marx put it even more succinctly: "If you want to get a job done, hire a gorilla." With such dictums in mind, some companies have brought in outsiders in recent years to change the corporate culture. Earl Orser, now chief executive officer of London Life, came from the T. Eaton Co. Ltd. in 1978; Andrew McCaughey was hired from the Molson Companies Ltd. to be chief executive officer at North American Life in 1980; Robert Bandeen went from Canadian National to Crown as chief executive officer in 1982. Says Jim Etherington, director of corporate affairs for London Life: "Insurance companies are large ocean liners on extended voyages. We are used to being out of sight of land and we fully expect we will reach port in our own time. Compared with us, the banks are very fast warships that dart over the horizon. It's time we turned on our radio communication networks and set an iceberg watch."

Orser, McCaughey, and Bandeen are the change-masters, men who not only have modernized their own companies, but have set new standards of performance and innovation for the entire industry. "They've come in from the outside and they have some new ideas," says federal superintendent of insurance Robert Hammond. "New blood is always good." "They are market-oriented," says Jean-Pierre Bernier, general counsel of the Canadian Life and Health Insurance Association. "They move with change much better than the others. They are the locomotives of the industry." Claude Castonguay, chief executive officer of the Laurentian Group, is the only actuary and long-time industry officer—in an industry where 90 per cent of the CEOs are actuaries—whom Bernier will put on his list of "locomotives." "Actuaries," admits Castonguay, "are trained to be conservative and to make sure we can provide for all contingencies. It influences your approach to things. The kind of characteristics that make a person like mathematics, statistics, etc. are not necessarily the characteristics that would make an individual a good manager or a good entrepreneur. Why I might be different from the others, I don't know."

Even those companies that have stayed with old-line managers have begun to battle back with new products. Says Sun Life president Jack Brindle, "We have seen more new product introductions in the past five years than during the preceding twenty-five years." Once the parade begins, everyone can join. "There isn't much reward for innovation," says Pat Burns, chief executive officer of Confederation Life. "If a company comes out with a new product today, we can copy it tomorrow." Legislators are scrambling to catch up. "We realize that the traditional insurance markets and products are changing," says superintendent Hammond. "Insurance companies are now issuing contracts that are very similar to the savings-type contracts that are issued by trust and loan companies. Insurance companies call them annuities, but some have daily interest features that correspond closely to guaranteed investment certificates." The biggest in the business is Mutual Life, which in 1984 took in $629 million in annuities from "depositors." "There has been some blurring of the lines of demarcation between different sets of financial institutions, and that's something that's going to have to be considered in the legislation," says Hammond.

The relative decline of the insurance business occurred as the banks grew larger and as the products offered by the companies changed as well. The purest and earliest form of ordinary life insurance is called term insurance; it is an amount payable on death. Coverage is for a specific term, as the names implies, usually five years. The difficulty was—and remains—that as an individual grows older and the likely age of death draws nearer, the chances that the company will have to pay out during the term increase, and so does the premium. Whole life was developed in England in the eighteenth century to smooth out the premiums over the life of the policy. This was done by creating a savings plan that forms part of the policy. The buyer is overcharged in the early years, and the company invests the excess amount and credits part of its gains to the policyholder.

All life insurance is sold on the basis of mortality tables, charts that show the number of people of a given age who are expected to die within a certain period. Similarly with general insurance, statistics are available showing how many car accidents, house fires, or environmental spills are likely to occur in a given period. For example, for a female aged twenty-five, the probability of death within twenty years is only 2.3 per cent; for a male aged twenty-five it is 4.3 per cent. At age forty-five, the probability increases to 12.2 per cent for females, 23.5 per cent for males. By sixty-five, the likelihood a woman will die in the next twenty years has increased to 58.5 per cent; for a man it is 77.2 per cent.

Until recently most life sales agents pushed whole life, pointing out that it was "permanent" insurance, unlike term, which has to be renewed every few years. Moreover, whole life has cash value as well as a death benefit—that is, it can be cashed in before the policyholder's death if he wishes. And, they might have mentioned, the commission is higher. For decades, people paid through the nose for whole life, convinced by an army of agents that only with whole life could they be assured of leaving their families financially sound. Those who sold whole life regarded themselves as a cut above those who sold term and called them "termites." The double-digit inflation of the 1970s put pressure on the whole life market. Whole life death benefits were fine, but the cash value of policies was increasing at meagre rates of 4 to 6 per cent. Smaller companies began pushing term policies with a savings aspect. The slogan became: "Buy term and invest the difference." In other words, take what you would have spent on whole life, buy the equivalent death benefit in cheaper term, then take the rest of your money and put it into some more lucrative investment vehicle.

Consumers began to respond, and moved away from whole life. In the 1920s, only 5 per cent of all new policies were term; by the 1960s, term accounted for one-third of new individual insurance sales; by 1980, about half. Frank Santangeli, president of Aetna Midland Doherty Finsco Ltd., put it this way: "The consumer is more interested in the here and now and less in the hereafter." People were still buying life insurance, but increasingly term was demanded. Because term was cheaper, however, the total amount of life insurance premiums stagnated. That meant that life insurance policies were no longer the savings vehicles they had once been. Banks, with their 7,000 deposit-taking branches across the country, grew; insurance shrank.

The struggle to regain lost market share began in the late 1970s, when variable and universal life policies were introduced in the U.S. Variable life has fixed premiums and a separate investment account; universal life has an investment account, but policyholders can vary the amount of protection and the size and timing of the payments. In the U.S. universal and variable (and various combinations) have reached half of all new sales. In Canada, variable and universal have grown from nowhere to about one-third of the market. With the growth in this area, term has fallen to about one-third of the market for new insurance; whole life retains the remaining third of the new insurance market.

For many firms, however, this newest form of life insurance was slow to catch on. The reason is simple: agents don't like to sell it. The commission is lower than on more traditional policies. Where most insurance policies yield commissions beginning at 80 per cent of the first year's premium—and growing, with volume performance bonuses, to 130 per cent and higher—universal offers the agent only 50 per cent. Now you know why you haven't heard of it. If you have $500 to spend on a new policy, wouldn't you expect to hear about the policy that pays the agent $600 in commission rather than $250? And if the agent wants to sell you a policy on a child, ask about the commission rates, just out of curiosity. At Crown Life, for example, a $400 annual premium on a child's policy until recently yielded an immediate commission to the agent of up to $1,200.

Agents and brokers in the general insurance business, those selling auto, fire, and theft insurance, earn a more modest 12.5 per cent on car insurance premiums and 20 per cent on house policies. The difference, explains the industry, is that everybody needs general insurance; clients seek out the sellers. But less than 10 per cent of all life insurance purchases are initiated by the buyer. That's why life agents sell so aggressively. "People do get disabled, people do die, people do reach sixty-five with no retirement fund," says Derrick Newhook, division manager of Confederation Life in St. John's, Newfoundland. "It's my job to get out there and tell them. Very few people just phone up to buy insurance. You play on emotions, sure you do, but you're not a table dancer. You don't park a hearse in front of the door, but you do present the cold, hard facts."

Even with hefty commission payments, insurance companies remain very profitable. One way they do so is by taking money in through premiums and investing it in other instruments at higher rates than they pay to customers. Because the firms need ready cash to pay death and other benefits, they can't put too much in risky ventures. Typically, 85 per cent of a company's investments will be in bonds, mortgages, and revenue-producing real estate. Only 7 per cent is in common stocks; tiny fractions are in more venturesome stuff such as oil and gas drilling. Many policies sold stay on the books, bringing in premium income. Many other policyholders cancel coverage after a few years, and the company doesn't have to pay out a death benefit. And if an agent leaves, the commission reverts to the company. As an example, one life company began 1984 with 1,760,721 individual polices. In the following twelve months, death benefits were paid on only 20,460 policies, costing the company $43.8 million. After taking account of policy surrenders, expiries, and lapses, the total pay-out was $1.6 billion—a figure that was more than adequately covered by new individual policies written during the year, which brought in $1.8 billion.

Until recently, profitability in the life insurance business has been a snap: sign on more new bodies each year than drop dead during the same period. Charles Dickens's incurably optimistic Mr. Micawber explained it this way: "Annual income twenty pounds, annual expenditure nineteen nineteen six, result happiness. Annual income twenty pounds, annual expenditure twenty pounds ought and six, result misery." Colour the life insurance companies happy. By the same token, however, life insurance companies don't put up much of a fight on a death claim from a policy that's been in force for at least two years. The law says that fraud can void a life insurance policy, but few companies go to court. A similar laxity exists in general insurance claims. Everybody knows there is fraud—a scrape that wasn't caused by the accident repaired using the car insurance, a ceiling repaired that was damaged before the rainstorm in question. Estimates vary, but it is assumed that the cost of repairs claimed under insurance is at least 10 per cent higher than the cost of the same repairs if there were no coverage.

At times, however, the companies will go to great lengths to fight claims. At London Life, for example, director of consumer service George Tingey ferrets out scams from the 12,000 death claims the firm processes each year. With the help of private investigators, he's tracked down faked deaths and phoney death certificates. One 1982 death claim for $506,443.86 particularly caught his attention and, later, that of the media. A man filed a death claim on his wife, claiming she had been killed in an accident in India. The claim came complete with death certificate, cremation certificate, police report, and doctor's statement, much of it written in Hindi. It was all too neat for Tingey, who sent an investigator to India and had the man tailed in Toronto. His wife, police discovered, was still alive. The man went to jail; London Life kept its money. Tingey's nose and a $4,000 investigation had saved the company more than half a million dollars.

Companies can and do regularly go to court on everything from small arson cases to major media events. In 1983, three companies went to court to prevent Peter Demeter from collecting about $3 million in total proceeds and interest as the beneficiary of insurance policies on the life of his wife, Christine, who was found bludgeoned to death on the garage floor of their Toronto-area home in July 1973. Although the killer was never found, Demeter was convicted of second-degree murder for arranging his wife's death and sentenced to life in prison. In 1983 the Ontario Supreme Court ruled that he could not collect the amounts he claimed from British Pacific Life Insurance Co., Dominion Life, and Occidental Life Insurance Co. of Canada. "To permit these actions to go forward," said Justice Osler, "would result in a travesty of justice and would bring the administration of justice into disrepute."

During the next few years, the attention of the industry will be focussed as much on Ottawa as on the courts, as legislation is updated amidst the roiling change. "Everybody's very excited about what's going on in the United States," says federal superintendent Hammond. "With deregulation, everybody's getting into every-thing all of a sudden. That gets people agitated and they think the same thing should be going on here. I'm a little nervous about how quickly things are changing in the United States. We have to evolve and the companies have to be able to respond to the public's needs, but I think we have to do it carefully."

In 1984 the federal minister of state for finance of the day, Roy MacLaren, set up an industry committee to advise government. It met throughout the year and survived an election and a change of government. The information from the group—including represen-tatives of banks, trust companies, securities firms, and life insurance and general insurance firms—was soaked up by officials in the Department of Finance, and in April 1985, a discussion paper was issued. One of the problems the legislation will deal with in the next round of revisions is the different legislative treatment of mutual companies and stock companies.

While the two main types of life insurance companies, mutuals and stock companies, sell the same types of products—life insurance, annuity and savings-type products marketed to individuals, and life and health insurance and pension plans marketed as employee benefits to businesses or associations—they are organized differently. The eighty-one Canadian companies include twenty-six mutual companies and fifty-five stock companies. A mutual company has no shareholders and is owned by its participating policyholders. A stock company has both shareholders and participating policyowners and each group participates in the profits of the company.

While some companies began as mutuals, most of the big mutual companies were created in the late 1950s and early 1960s. At the time, U.S. and other foreign interests were buying Canadian stock insurance companies; control of twelve of Canada's fifty-eight

Canadian-owned companies left the country. Mutualization was seen as a way to maintain Canadian ownership. If there were no stock to buy, no foreigner could gain control; as a result, Sun, Confederation, Canada Life, Manufacturers, and Equitable were mutualized.

To date, stock companies have had an organizational advantage and have been able to own other financial services companies, while mutuals could not. According to the federal discussion paper, new holding companies could allow mutuals to compete equally with stock companies. Such a solution is far more likely to succeed than the one that some were considering—demutualization, or turning mutuals back into stock companies. Says Jack Rhind, chairman of Confederation Life of Toronto, "To recreate shareholders in a company that has been totally owned by policyholders is akin to putting the ketchup back in the bottle. It is messy, to say the least."

While they may look similar to the consumer, the two types of life companies, mutual and stock, have caused bitter debates in the industry. Those at stock companies look down their noses at mutuals, charging that because they are owned by the members, they are somehow socialist. Robert Bandeen, formerly president of CN and since 1982 chief executive officer of Crown Life, a stock company, is one of the most vociferous critics of the mutuals. "They say they are honourable men and have boards that keep an eye on them. I know that argument. I used it when I was at the Crown corporation. In their minds they are the bastions of free enterprise, but they're not. They're socialist. They're run by the policyholders. They get messianic about their work, but there are no financial controls."

Others in the financial community are equally virulent, particularly about the mutuals' management being answerable to no one. Says MacIntosh of the Canadian Bankers' Association, "Mutualization was a disaster. I'm opposed to mutualized insurance companies. There's no ultimate accountability of management. Who do they answer to? They don't have a board. It's a self-perpetuating monarchical regime." "One of my dreams is to be president of a mutual insurance company," says David Atkins, whose audit firm, Coopers & Lybrand, handles many insurance companies. "There are no shareholders, the number of participants is so great that they have no control, and then there's the board, and they have no idea what's going on." For their part, the mutual companies have been returning the insults with their own shots for years. At an annual meeting of the Ontario Mutual Life Association Co. (the precursor to the Mutual Life Assurance Co. of Canada, which was established in 1878), someone said: "The stockholders of a life insurance company are no more use to the company than are barnacles to a ship."

By contrast, the property and casualty industry is better behaved in public. "The P & C industry is very clubby," says auditor Atkins. "They all take in each other's dirty linen through reinsurance. It's far more international than life insurance. They all know each other. The Canadian economy is not big enough to handle big risks. That risk tends to go to places that are exporters of capital, London, Zurich, and New York." As well, Atkins finds the property and casualty business more interesting than life insurance. "We're all going to die, but in the property and casualty business you have a risk—you don't know when or if the event will occur or how much it will cost."

The property and casualty insurance companies are finding it more and more difficult to predict their exposure and the ultimate cost of a policy. A recent court decision in the case of *Borland* v. *Muttersbach and Royal Insurance Group* has caused the industry further concern. The judgment shows how sympathetic courts are becoming to claimants. Royal was the insurer of a motor home struck by a car near Harrow, Ont., in 1981. There were eight passengers in the self-propelled motor home, all related. They included the Borland parents, their two daughters and two sons, as well as Mrs. Borland's sister and her husband. The brother-in-law was killed in the accident and the others suffered varying injuries. The two boys had extensive knee injuries, one of the two daughters received back injuries and still wears a brace, and the sister of Mrs. Borland still walks with a limp after eight leg operations. In addition, the Borlands lost the family electrical business because of time off work. The driver of the other vehicle had only $300,000 in insurance coverage. The camper coverage was $1 million, a figure Royal regarded as the limit of its liability. As the case went to court, Royal knew that the settlement could reach beyond the $300,000 coverage of the driver at fault. Royal assumed that it might have to pay out the $700,000 additional amount to bring the total pay-out to the $1-million coverage limit.

The Ontario judge, however, saw it differently. He saw the $1-million coverage not as a limit per occurrence, but as a limit per person, and he awarded the family $3.5 million. Royal has appealed the ruling.

The Borland case is not the only high-value settlement in Ontario. In 1978, a twenty-four-year-old Ottawa mother, Nicole Suitter, was admitted to hospital for routine surgery. At one point during the operation, she received insufficient oxygen and, as a result, suffered irreversible brain damage that made her a mute paraplegic. After a four-month trial in 1985, during which fifty-seven witnesses were called, an Ontario Supreme Court judge ruled that the injuries were caused when an anaesthetist "took strictly inadequate steps in the face of an emergency." The court awarded her damages of $1.9 million. Ron Griffiths, president of the Insurance Brokers Association of Ontario, says that the growing number of large settlements is turning Ontario into the "California of the North." The Ontario awards, however, fall well short of some U.S. claims. One Pennsylvania man filed a $5.76-quadrillion lawsuit, later dismissed, against the state transportation department. He claimed that he was owed the money for a decade of grief that started when the department charged him twice for the same offence and suspended his licence ten years ago.

With that level of settlement, insurance companies will soon be lords and masters of all they survey and much that they don't survey as well—because no one will be able to do anything without insurance. Asbestosis, for example, has already bankrupted Johns-Manville. The explosion at a Union Carbide plant in Bhopal, India, has brought claims for US$15 billion. What will be the asbestosis of the 1980s? PCBs? Nuclear spills? No one knows, and if the disaster is big enough and brings enough claims from injured parties or the relatives of those who are killed, the international insurance system itself could be bankrupted. An earthquake today in Montreal of the same strength as the one that occurred in the days of Samuel de Champlain would stagger the system.

If there is a single serious failing to be charged to the insurance industry, it is this: neither the life industry nor the general insurance industry is truly prepared for tomorrow. The general insurers are so fixated on past underwriting losses that they have not made sufficient provision for a future catastrophe. The life insurance executives have been so interested in placing blame for their shrinking share of financial markets that they have failed to find solutions. Many executives in both the general and the life industries are staid and stuck in their ways. Those who are falling short are easy to identify; this book points a few fingers. Measured on a return-on-equity basis, some insurance company results are abysmal. Even a well-run company such as North American has a return on equity that is about half what it should be. Management isn't the only problem. Part of the responsibility rests with the boards of directors, who must cease being passive spectators, take a more active role, become more independent of management and more knowledgeable. Too many directors really don't understand what they're overseeing. Says George Clarke, former president of Sun Life: "I don't think that board knows very much about the life insurance business."

In twenty years, the big financial services players will be quite different from those of today. Those who are fleet of foot will still be alive and growing. The dinosaurs will be dying. Niche marketers, those who find a spot in specific market segments because of particular expertise or because they offer particular services and products, will thrive. The vast middle ground, at the moment, is up for grabs. There will be more mergers, more networking of products among associated companies, and more conglomerate ownership of various elements of the business. Right now, there are few insurance CEOs with the vision to see over the horizon and the savvy to take their companies forward along a shrewdly chosen path. Some of those in the vanguard are profiled in this book; others who are less ready are also held up to scrutiny.

Nothing less than a revolution is required to propel the industry into tomorrow. First, the actuaries need to be thrown out of the boardroom, where they've been trying to run companies, and put into the back room, where they belong. With very few exceptions, actuaries have too narrow a background, too few people skills, too little marketing know-how to be running insurance companies. Any company that is currently being run by an actuary—and has an actuary coming along as his successor—risks being left behind in the continuing scramble for consumer dollars. In both life and general insurance, fresh outside thinking on how to price and market the product is needed.

Second, planning must become a more regular, ongoing affair. A few days at a lodge once a year is not enough. Third, companies must stop listening only to the agents and brokers who sell their products. The firms must become more market-driven, more customer-driven, and more responsive to the needs of customers. Fourth, companies must stop grumbling about Ottawa and the other regulators. A timetable exists now to update the legislation; the politicians can't be blamed for the reduced market share. Fifth, insurance sales methods, both casualty and life, have to change. Automated teller machines, self-serve gas, and warehouse-size food stores demonstrate that consumers want convenience and adaptability. Consumers might not want to buy insurance off the shelf without explanation, but does the pitch need to be the offensive duel that it now is, filled with mystery and mumbo-jumbo?

In the future, argues auditor David Atkins, Canadians must be better served with information directly suited to their financial circumstances. One route to achieve that would be by blending products through a variety of company associations, employing networking and cross-selling. "That will be done through a microcomputer run by an agent, not by an automated teller machine," says Atkins. "The agents are particularly good at the person-on-person approach. We all hate the life insurance agent, but he'll come to you at home in the evening. Banks want you to come to them—and they close at three." The insurance companies, he notes, are beginning to be more aggressive. Mutual Life agents are selling mutual funds along with annuities and life insurance. Allstate Insurance Co. of Canada is after new business through direct mail brochures to credit card holders.

Insurance company executives are, for the most part, lazy. While the agent or the claims clerk is still toiling away at the end of the day, the executive is long gone. Any insurance executive who is still in his office after six is probably meeting his wife downtown for dinner. In any other corporate head office, an executive gone by six is gone the next year. At the distribution end, the agent or broker is a harried soul who's trying to juggle a complex array of products with too little support from head office. While property and casualty insurance is a little more straightforward and people buy what they need, life insurance is just the opposite—people often buy just what they don't need. There are few businesses that are more inefficient, more tipped against the customer, more geared to sales instead of service than life insurance. The drop-out rate alone among agents is phenomenal. Of every ten people who go into insurance sales, eight leave after four years. That means a lot of insurance buyers see an agent once and then become orphans.

Worse, the commission structures are outrageously high. With first-year life insurance commissions often over 100 per cent and pay-outs that can continue for up to ten years, insurance agents should offer better service than most now do. In the property and casualty business, the first sale and all renewals receive the same commission. Surely the effort diminishes after some years of simply renewing the same coverage, perhaps with little extra effort. In such a sales system, the agent is king or queen; the customer is both pawn and rook.

I've spent a lot of days, evenings, and weekends over eighteen months with insurance company executives and employees, sales agents, and independent brokers. For the most part, I liked the folks out on the firing line more than their foes back in head office. The people in the insurance business who deal directly with customers are generally more alive and more entrepreneurial than the sleepy gents who people the executive suites. Admittedly, insurance agents and brokers who push products are not easy to love. Brian Wrixon, superintendent of agencies for training and development with Confederation Life and a former agent himself, even had difficulty convincing his own mother that his role as an insurance salesman was a worthy one. "My mother," he says, "took nine years before she was convinced that I was not some kind of a thief."

Well, read on. You may not learn to love insurance agents as only a mother can, but you will learn that you can't live without them. That would be the riskiest business of all.

CHAPTER TWO

THE SETTING SUN
Sun Life Assurance Co. of Canada

I T WAS October 5, 1983, the meeting day of the board of directors for Sun Life Assurance Co. of Canada, the bluest of the blue-chip boards. Among the cardinals of the business world serving on the board: Peter Gordon, chairman, Stelco Inc.; Ian Sinclair, chairman, Canadian Pacific Enterprises Inc.; John Tory, president, the Thomson Corp. Ltd.; Jock Finlayson, former president of the Royal Bank of Canada; and Alf Powis, chairman and chief executive officer of Noranda Mines Ltd. The lone woman was none other than Kathleen Richardson, director of James Richardson & Sons Ltd. and the doyenne of Winnipeg.

Towards the end of the board's regular two-hour conclave, Sun Life president George Clarke was asked to leave the room. As president since August 1978 and a director since February 1978, Clarke thought the request unusual, but if he'd learned anything in his sixteen years with Sun it was this: everything has a purpose that can be revealed only in the fullness of time. He left the boardroom in Sun's King Street headquarters in downtown Toronto and returned to his office. He assumed, since he was excluded, that the board was discussing succession, a problem for Sun because the three senior executives were all so close in age. Clarke, then sixty-two, was less than three years away from normal retirement. He was six months older than the chairman, Tom Galt, and twenty-two months older than the executive vice-president, Jack Brindle. The rest of the top echelon was younger, and none was ready for any of the top jobs.

Sun has a history of longevity at the top. With the consent of the board of directors, Galt could remain chairman well beyond age sixty-five. His predecessor, Alistair Campbell, was chairman until the venerable age of seventy-three. Arthur Wood, who replaced T. B. Macaulay during the Depression, did so when he was sixty-three after forty years of working for the Sun. In 1983, however, succession plans seemed stalled. Tom Galt, not one to make up his mind very hastily on any matter, seemed to be particularly secretive about any plans he had to pass his mantle along. The board of directors had been pressing Galt for some time to bring in a specific plan. At last, he was ready to reveal the first step.

After the board had been informed, Galt strode into Clarke's office to tell him the decision. There were no preliminaries, no niceties of conversation. "It's been decided," said Galt, "that in order to ease the succession, the board has asked that you take early retirement at the end of the year." Galt explained that Clarke's benefits and annual salary of $280,000 would continue until his normal retirement date in 1986. After that, his pension would begin just as if he had worked at Sun right through. Without further comment, Galt rose and left.

Clarke was dumbfounded. The announcement had caught him so much by surprise that he hadn't asked a single question. Galt had offered Clarke nothing more than the basic information, leaving the decision sitting in the room like a bone picked clean and brought into the house by a dog for inspection. As Clarke gathered his wits, the questions began to form. Why now? If he was going to be eased out, why not name him vice-chairman, thus leaving his honour intact?

The next day he met with Galt. "I think this is a bit abrupt," Clarke said. "I'm surprised that there wasn't any discussion." Galt's reply was nothing more than a mumble. The topic was forever closed. No board member sought Clarke out to explain; none of them so much as offered Clarke best wishes at the time.

For the past fifty years, Sun's forward progress has been crippled by a series of similar painful incidents. Only its sheer size has given the firm any momentum in the marketplace. The recent brouhahas include the stormy departure in 1971 of president Anthony Hicks over policy disputes. The fall-out from his requested resignation sapped Sun's energy for the first half of the decade. The second half of the 1970s was spent in paralysis as Sun was buffeted by the politics of Quebec. In 1978, Sun moved its corporate head office from Montreal to Toronto, fleeing the inhospitable climate and regulations of the Parti Québécois. The firm was pilloried in the press and responded ineptly, explaining itself through a paltry few printed statements. The image of the Sun that many carry with them still is the television footage of Galt at the end of a meeting, bending over, putting on his rubbers, his back symbolically turned on the Quebec audience.

As most other companies prepare for tomorrow, Sun takes a unique corporate stance. The firm is not just content with today, it worships yesterday. While others chase business in the streets, Sun hunkers in its hallways. In the financial world, where clout comes with size and class with seniority, Sun acts as if it is on a life-support system, awaiting a miracle cure that may never come. Even its number one position in Canada's life insurance hierarchy was lost this year when Manufacturers Life's assets (with its purchase of Dominion Life taken into account) surpassed Sun's $13 billion. After being number one since 1908, Sun has been eclipsed.

The Sun's comatose response is a mystery to the industry. With its internal cash and assets, it could be an acquisitive force. Instead of a steamroller, it is a stalled handcart. Rather than buying into related financial services in Canada, so as to lead everyone in product development and growing market share, it is content with internal committees and eternal studies. Says Drew McCaughey, president and chief executive officer of North American Life, "I'd love to get my hands on Sun Life. They've got a $1.5-billion surplus. I'd buy a trust company, among other things. They're a great company, but their position has made them smug." Any current power comes largely from history, not from anything modern or creative. "The strength they have inherited from the past," says Claude Castonguay, chairman and chief executive officer of the Laurentian Group, "gives them a certain momentum and rate of growth." In the financial herd, Sun is an ageing bull.

"The Sun could be the Esso of the 1980s," says Paul McCrossan, currently the Progressive Conservative member of Parliament for York-Scarborough and a former insurance company employee and consultant. "There is a time in industries—whether Carnegie with steel or Rockefeller with oil—when one company can use its financial clout to climb over everyone else in the industry. They haven't deployed it yet. There are any number of people who could turn Sun into the terror of the industry—but they're not at the Sun. That is not their corporate culture. Entrepreneurial people tend to go elsewhere.

The Sun is the sleeping giant."

Sun's executive officers don't disagree. "The company tends to undersell itself," admits John Gardner, senior vice-president and executive officer. "Most people feel we're not very innovative." Even when people inside suggest that Sun go out and flex its muscles and grab market share, president Jack Brindle rejects the strategy. "You mean loss-leaders?" he asks. "We can't do that. Underpricing means losing money. We lost money a few years ago in group health [insurance]." How much better it is to stay the course. "It's a wise organization that knows when it's strong and knows when to sit and watch," says Cam Leamy, senior vice-president for marketing. "We will not be stampeded into different directions because some other companies are. I look around at London or Crown and what people are attempting to package. I think they would be wise to stick to their knitting."

If numbers meant everything, Sun would be unstoppable. The firm has $13 billion in assets and $107 billion worth of life insurance in force, and it ranks among the twelve largest life insurance companies in North America. There are 3,000 field representatives and 4,900 staff in an organization that stretches across Canada and into the Philippines, Hong Kong, Bermuda, Great Britain, Ireland, and the United States. In the 1940s, Sun had more business in force in the U.S. than in Canada. Today about 25 per cent of life insurance sales are in the U.S., 30 per cent in the U.K., 40 per cent in Canada, the rest in the Far East.

Sun's real estate portfolio runs to about $1 billion and includes office towers in Toronto, Calgary, Edmonton, and Vancouver. Its most venturesome investment is through a company called AT&S Exploration Ltd. AT&S is a consortium of Sun, Texaco Canada Resources Ltd., and Atco Ltd. It was formed at Texaco's initiative to use grants under the National Energy Program, and the three companies invested a total of $50 million. AT&S is looking for oil in the Beaufort Sea and drilling for oil on the Banquereau Block off the east coast.

Few Canadians are untouched by some ray of the Sun. There are 1.6 million individual policyholders and 5.2 million certificate-holders under various group plans. The largest chunk of Sun's assets, however, some 38 per cent or $4.4 million worth, is tucked away safely in bonds, far from the wildcat world of oil exploration. A further $4.1 billion is in mortgages and stocks. Sun manages another

$2.4 billion for other pension funds. About 100,000 Canadians are pension clients of Sun. Further, Sun manages pension money for eight of the top twenty pension funds in Canada, covering 500,000 more people. For the Sun, however, high noon is well past and the long afternoon shadows are beginning to stretch across the executive suite.

Thomas Maunsell Galt is the Sun King. At six-foot-four, Sun's chairman and chief executive officer is a man of bearing, but he lets a room possess him rather than trying to dominate it or those around him. There is a funereal cast to his suitings, an upper-class ring to his accent, which has been described as "Montreal mid-Atlantic." "He's a bit of an aristocrat," says Cam Leamy. "He's a member of the Canadian establishment. He values his position there." His blood-lines are rich. Great-grandfather John Galt, an agent of the Canada Company in the nineteenth century, established and populated southern Ontario with new towns such as Guelph and Goderich. A great-uncle, Alexander Galt, was a father of Confederation. Grand-father Sir Thomas was a chief justice of the Ontario Court of Common Pleas.

A hereditary condition has given Tom Galt's hands a slight tremor. He is a handsome man and his chiselled face, with its high forehead surrounded by greying hair, is a cross between the rough good looks of Jack Palance and the forbidding countenance of Clint Eastwood. In public, he is cold and austere; only in private does he thaw out. "He isn't the person most people think he is," insists Sun president Jack Brindle. "He has a good sense of humour. He's got a lively sense of the ridiculous." When Sun moved into new offices in downtown Toronto in 1984, not everything was quite in order. In the chair-man's office, for example, the floor was uneven. A block of pine had to be put under one leg of Galt's desk so the desk wouldn't wobble. Someone asked him why the floor was askew. "Apparently," Galt dead-panned, "the floor was built on a slant so that if the sprinklers came on, the water could run off."

He was born in Winnipeg in 1921 into one of the city's wealthy families. His father, George, was in the tea and coffee importing business with a cousin. The firm, G.F. and J. Galt Co., handled the Blue Ribbon brand and was eventually sold to Brooke Bond. Tom was the product of his father's second marriage, the only son amidst five daughters, four of them from the first union. His father died when Tom Galt was six. Tom, his sister, and his mother moved to Ottawa, where Mrs. Galt had been raised. There she remarried, and Tom attended Ashbury in Ottawa and Lakefield, near Peterborough, Ont., both private boys' schools where the chapel, the playing field, and the classroom filled up a young man's time and fitted him for the world.

In 1941 Galt joined the Royal Canadian Air Force and was stationed in India as part of the radar watch guarding against the Japanese in the Indian Ocean. After the war, he attended Queen's University and the University of Manitoba, then followed actuarial studies. He graduated in 1948 and was hired immediately to work for Sun Life in Montreal. "In the summer of 1948, before I joined Sun Life, I was asked by a family friend why I was going to the company," Galt told Mark Witten for a 1982 article in *Saturday Night.* "I told him Sun Life was the largest life insurance company and the president had always been an actuary." The older man was amused. "He thought it was dumb," said Galt. "It turned out not to be so dumb." For the first ten years, the Galts, now with a son and daughter, lived in the Town of Mount Royal, then moved to a five-bedroom stone house in snooty Westmount in the late 1950s, as Galt worked hard to be noticed. The Sun had not done much hiring during the previous two decades. There were few ahead of him on the corporate ladder to the top.

Most summers the family went to their home in Métis, on the south shore of the St. Lawrence River. The family's first cottage, a rambling frame structure, burned, and Galt now has a two-storey frame house with a cedar shake roof and screened-in veranda that overlooks the river from a high cliff. A local golf and tennis club supplies the recreation in a town much favoured by Anglo-Quebeckers. In the old days, the electricity at the Seaside Hotel invariably went off at four o'clock as everyone plugged in the electric kettles to make tea. Other Galt holidays have involved trips to the vineyards of France to add to his already encyclopaedic knowledge of wines.

"He's a very private person," says his son, George, a Toronto literary and travel writer, "but he's not the hard-bitten tycoon type who locks himself away in his study at home and has no time for his family." Says long-time friend Gordon Osler, chairman of Stanton Pipes, "He is bright, thoughtful, and articulate. He is truly a *gentle* man." Among his personal pursuits, Galt most likes to play golf. In

Montreal he belonged to Mount Bruno; now he plays at Toronto Golf, but not as much as he used to in the days when he scored consistently in the respectable eighties. He plays at tennis, has done skeet-shooting at the Montreal Skeet Club, and has bagged the odd deer, although he enjoys walking in the woods with the gun more than actually shooting game. His house in Forest Hill, in central Toronto, is decorated with antiques and often resounds with his beloved classical music and opera; before attending live opera he will often study the music and libretto. He sees performances at the Metropolitan Opera in New York as well as those done by the Canadian Opera Company, of which he is a director. Once he saw *Aïda* performed in Rome, complete with live horses and elephants.

His favourite indoor sport is brain-teasers of all sorts: riddles, puzzles, and quirky problems that require not just intelligence but a nimble mind. Even his reading, when it does turn to fiction, has in the past run to mysteries by John Le Carré and Agatha Christie. Although he has a chauffeur-driven Cadillac at his beck and call, he often prefers his own automobile, a beige Checker.

While Galt is quick to grasp others' ideas, he is sometimes slow to share his own around the office. "You don't always know what he is thinking," says George Clarke. "That can be a problem when you want to know what a chief executive officer wants for the company." He is more likely to communicate his ideas after things go wrong than to lead others in directions that he thinks are right. "Tom's ways," says Sun chief actuary Don Gauer, "are mysterious to behold." For his part, the departed Clarke sees current chairman and CEO Tom Galt as a "passive and part-time chairman." He adds, "In the current environment, no other company can be run that way, so I don't know if it can run that way or not. It's a wealthy company, it's going to do well for years. It's not going to go broke, but it needs modern management methods. The status quo is not satisfactory."

To say Tom Galt is shy, as everyone does, is to underestimate the depth of his distaste for public performances. Tom Galt makes Howard Hughes look like a gadabout. His only regular public speech is given at the firm's annual meeting and can go through four careful drafts before delivery. He served as chairman in 1984–85 of the Canadian Life and Health Insurance Association, but was rarely in public view. As a major spokesman for the industry, he might have been expected to take the industry's case on the road at a time of ferment in financial services. In fact, he made no public speeches, rarely even represented the CLHIA at a head table, and regularly declined interviews. He was the only insurance executive who refused to be interviewed for this book, although he freely granted approval for any other Sun executive to talk.

His one recent news conference, after being designated CLHIA chairman in 1984, elicited some morsels of information but showed that he had few fresh initiatives in mind. He worried, for example, about the growing reliance by the public on deposit insurance, charging that "there is no incentive for the consumer to look at the company he is dealing with to see how ably it is managed." He called the rush towards one-stop financial shopping "overstated." Public appearances and speeches, he need hardly have pointed out, would be rare. "It's not my strength. It takes me a long time to prepare a speech."

Even his brief acceptance remarks that day had been carefully written out, something that Galt himself joked about in front of his peers. He had long planned the route to the chairman's spot by working his way up the association executive ladder during the preceding years. As he arrived at the podium, he waved his notes to the gathering and said, tongue in cheek, "I took a chance and made a few remarks in case my lobbying was successful." Once in the chairman's role, however, he did little. It was as if he took his turn because it was expected of him, not because he had any views or visions to share. Galt's low profile was in marked contrast to the previous year's CLHIA chairman, Mutual of Canada's chairman John Panabaker, who gave five speeches, met half a dozen provincial superintendents, and lobbied countless politicians. As Galt took over the job, Panabaker predicted: "Tom Galt will be more laid-back than I was. He will be more conservative." Referring to his successor's non-existent speech itinerary, he said drily: "Obviously, there is a difference of opinion."

There is a difference of opinion between Panabaker and Galt on how to run a company as well. "From the outside," says Panabaker, "Sun appears to have a strong culture. It's by no means *our* culture. I'm not sure I could operate under it. It may come out of their Montreal background. Tom is a product of a lifetime in that environment. It's a very formal kind of company. It's also a very complex company with a variety of world-wide areas in which they operate. Maybe you can't keep [Mutual's] informality when you've got that kind of complexity." There is something else that marks Galt's firm.

"The Sun," says Panabaker, "has always been very conscious that it is the largest life company in the country." Now that Manufacturers has surpassed Sun, however, there is only one area remaining where Sun can claim first position: paternalism. More than the other large financial services companies in Canada, it handles its employees as all companies did decades ago. Says vice-president for human resources Doug Lang, "We probably are the last bastion of paternalism."

Sun Life was founded in 1865 by Montreal businessman Mathew Hamilton Gault (no relation to current chairman Tom Galt). Gault was the Canadian representative of Mutual Life of New York, the firm that then dominated North America. In 1868, Canadian legislation demanded that $50,000 be placed on deposit with the government by foreign insurance companies operating in Canada. Many foreign-owned companies objected and withdrew from Canada, including Mutual Life of New York, and Gault began The Sun Mutual Life Insurance Co. Thomas Workman, who also served as president of the Molsons Bank, was Sun's first president. His duties during his eighteen-year term seemed to consist entirely of showing up at the office every day to sign policies personally. Directors were drawn from the business community and included Alexander Buntin, a sailor who had become known as the "paper king of Quebec." His accent was Scots, his wealth inexhaustible. The story is told that someone once remarked to him: "They tell me, Mr. Buntin, that you are as rich as Croesus." "Weel," came the reply, "I dinna ken who Croesus is, but for ivery dollar he'll pit doon, I'll pit doon anither."

In 1874, Robertson Macaulay joined the Sun; his son, Thomas Bassett Macaulay, joined three years later; and so began a dynasty that would run Sun for sixty years. Canada's market was too small to support burgeoning growth, so emissaries were sent to travel extensively to the U.K., Europe, and the Far East, thus establishing the international scope of the current business. By 1914 Sun required a new head office, so a cornerstone was laid for a building on Dominion Square. Nothing—not even Knox Church, which was demolished—could stand in its way as it grew to become a twenty-six-storey structure, the largest building in the Commonwealth, in 1933.

Sun planned to fill the building with busy clerks approving

applications. There was room for 10,000 people, but during the Depression and after, floors remained empty and were used for annual new car displays and the city basketball championships. Outside, there were fluted Corinthian columns, inside more columns of syenite, a dark green stone. The bases were done with black Belgian marble, the capitals of terracotta covered in dull gold. The walls were surfaced with selected Italian rose tavernelle marble, the counters were carved from Levanto marble, the doors, railings, and grilles outfitted in bronze. The executive offices were finished in oak panelling, and roll-top desks were everywhere to be seen.

Those were heady days for the Sun and for T. B. Macaulay, who had succeeded his father. T. B. was seen as one of the more aggressive businessmen of the time. Unlike many insurance companies, which ran very conservative investment strategies, under T. B. Macaulay the Sun leaped into the risky world of common stocks. Fully 52 per cent of Sun's assets were in solid companies, such as Canadian Pacific, International Nickel, Radio Corporation of America, International Business Machines, and American Telephone & Telegraph. Macaulay became so notorious for his views that his last name was twisted into "Make-all-you-can" by his detractors.

Gordon Beatty, a retired actuary with Canada Life, recalls meeting Macaulay in the 1920s. Beatty had the temerity to say that if he were in Macaulay's position, with capital gains on the stocks amounting to several millions, he would cash in and take a million in profit. Macaulay was indignant. "No, you wouldn't," said T.B., "because you would never have reached that point. You would have cashed in everything at $100,000." Recalls Beatty: "I was a small man. When the Depression hit a couple of years later, T.B. may have wished at times that he had been smaller, too."

When the stock market crashed in 1929, Macaulay's dream to fill the building with Sun employees was ended. Allegations were made in Parliament that Sun was technically bankrupt, as sales dropped, surplus disappeared, and policy loans skyrocketed, with people borrowing against cash values in their policies. In 1931, the government of the day saved Sun with legislation to allow the company to give special values to securities holdings. The building, erected to be a monument to the future, became a mausoleum for the past. A shattered Macaulay retired, saying, "I could save myself but I can't save the company, so I'll have to go down with it." Sun survived, but to this day Macaulay's ghost remains in the boardroom, urging investment caution and a low corporate profile. Stock ownership, for example, today runs at a mere 7.8 per cent of assets, even though the legal limit is 25 per cent. If a company can be run from beyond the grave, Sun is it.

In 1984, when Sun opened two new office towers in Toronto, it looked as if that cautious past had finally been purged. The buildings sit like gates straddling University Avenue and cost about $200 million, Sun's largest real estate investment in dollar terms if not in square footage. At the opening they were only about 45-per-cent leased. Sun itself, with seven of the twenty-eight floors, is the main tenant in the building on the east side of University. The west tower is named the Merrill Lynch Tower because the Canadian subsidiary of the U.S. brokerage house signed on for seven of the twenty-four floors.

The towers are the Sun King's castle and reinforce the smug fortress mentality of the firm. Although only 200 Sun employees actually work in the tower, the buildings were hailed at length during the 1984 annual meeting by an audio-visual presentation that required fifteen projectors to flash its multiple images. The slide show cost $50,000 and included, among other images, exterior shots of the building's growth taken by a camera permanently positioned in director Peter Gordon's nearby office for the duration of construction.

Outside Sun's tower sits a twenty-six-foot bronze sculpture by Canadian Sorel Etrog. Sun and Galt may have spent more time planning that sculpture than plotting any reorganization or strategy for the future. Etrog prepared close to twenty different studies, including a five-foot model, the most he has ever done for any commission. Galt visited his studio regularly, and board members once trooped in *en masse* to inspect progress. One day, nine people from Sun showed up. "They drove me crazy," says Etrog. The finished work took fourteen months to create at a metal-fabricating plant near the Toronto airport. The collection of rectangles, circles, and other modernistic shapes is called, not surprisingly, *Sunlife*. Its cost was a staggering $350,000.

Inside the building, the appointments on Sun's floors are luxurious. A second-floor fitness centre features a universal gym with eleven stations, each accommodating up to eight people, dancersize rooms with stereo equipment, and three examining rooms; there is an outdoor jogging track on the cafeteria roof. Even the wallpaper is in keeping with the fitness theme: the design shows a heartbeat as it would appear on an oscilloscope. In addition, there is a staff training room and a lounge equipped with playing cards, cribbage and backgammon boards, and a pool table complete with balls for both snooker and boston.

The twenty-seventh-floor boardroom is done in rosewood, travertine marble, and fabric-covered walls with acoustic batts behind to muffle sound. One wall is all glass with a view of the CN Tower and Lake Ontario beyond. Even a small storage room off the main boardroom offers the same breath-taking view. The boardroom itself is wired like a NASA launch site. A mobile control panel packed with buttons operates a reverse-screen projector for slide shows, three co-ordinated slide projectors, a fifty-inch screen for video presentation or computer graphics transmitted directly from personal computers in the investment department. The mahogany table is in the shape of a closed U and was built in modules to fit the size of any meeting. In its longest configuration the table stretches thirty-six feet. It is surrounded by leather armchairs, and each place sports a leather binder in a colour known within the company as Sun Life ochre. In addition the binder is tricked out with a gold Sun crest and imprinted name.

The art on the twenty-seventh floor was chosen by Galt, aided by Toronto art consultant Lonti Ebers. "He didn't want a collection," she says, "he wanted works. He did not want an ongoing commitment to art." The choices include a huge Jack Bush painting for the boardroom that cost Sun $40,000 and a $60,000 Jean-Paul Riopelle in the directors' lounge, both bought from private collections. For his own office, Galt chose a Lynn Chadwick sculpture, a $20,000 three-foot-high figure with a triangular head. Galt was open-minded but careful about subject matter for the purchases. Among those he considered was a group of six works on paper by Sandra Meigs. Rejected as inappropriate for the Sun were any that showed people sitting on bar stools or smoking. His selection process, according to Ebers, was "a bit ponderous about how it would reflect on Sun Life's image and what the policyholders would think."

He was equally involved in choosing signs for use in the building. Usually such contracts are dealt with at levels well below the chief executive officer and approvals are given on the basis of a few mock-ups. Not so at Sun. Galt had to see and personally approve most of them. "He's always treated me like a plumber," says Paul Arthur, a principal at Newton Frank Arthur Inc., the design firm that handled the signage. "I have never felt so useless as I did standing on a wind-swept plaza with Tom Galt. I have never seen a place where approvals were more difficult. Do you know that we had to have all signs *full size* for approval? At one point, I said to someone in the architect's office that somewhere in [the Toronto suburb of] Mimico there is another Sun Life building—full size. His reply: 'You're only half joking.' Galt is like God, he pays attention to the sparrows."

The brouhaha over signs paled by comparison to the competition suddenly ordered by Galt once the buildings were open. He decided he wanted a new logo and possibly a new name for Sun. Seven design firms were invited to appear before a Sun committee in December 1984. Hours of preparation, with no compensation, went into the presentations. For Newton Frank's Allan Stormont, Galt's decision to have a new logo was "capricious." Stormont's message at the presentation was the same as it would be for any company consider-ing such a major change: "You could destroy the culture of your company. We will only consider this as a phase one study of whether you *need* to change your name and your image in the shifting sands of financial services."

"I have never participated in such a curious exercise," says Arthur. "Symbols and logotypes do not a corporate identity make. They should be writing a master plan for the next decade. They will get a new logo, but with no thought for the next ten years." When the committee reported unofficially to Galt that it liked two particular approaches, Galt listened to them, then ordered that the whole process be cooled. His interest had waned. Committee chairman Peter MacGibbon retired a few weeks later and the committee slipped into limbo. In the end, the project just seemed like so much busywork. "The chairman feels we ought to have logos and symbols when the time comes," explained Sun director of public relations and communications Jeffrey Norman, "but the time hasn't come."

Galt's failure to press for change has a long and honoured history at Sun. That's because those who do try to prod new ideas to life have always run afoul of their superiors. Sun's history is littered with the bodies of those who tried to push Sun into such change. They did not survive in the suffocating atmosphere where doing least lasts best. After Macaulay, the next two presidents, Arthur Wood and George Bourke, brought a stability to Sun that carried the company through the quagmire of the Depression. Between the two of them they ran the place as successive presidents from 1934 to 1962, when Bourke became chairman; Sun was then in the final stages of becoming mutualized, as several other Canadian companies had done to prevent foreign ownership.

The new president in 1962 was fifty-seven-year-old Alistair Campbell. Born in Scotland in 1905, he was recruited there as a young university graduate to work in Montreal for Sun as a $1,500-a-year actuarial clerk in Montreal. His presidency was very much a continuation of past executive thinking. During his regime there was more planning done in the investment department, but for the most part, Sun's motto might have been "Steady as she goes."

By the late 1960s, there were two contenders for president, Tom Galt and Anthony Hicks, five years older than Galt. Hicks's background in Sun included investments and administration, a change from the usual actuarial careers of the men who had run Sun in the past. A likeable, quick man, Hicks was interested in modern management methods. As well, he wanted to bring new marketing techniques to the field personnel. He was impetuous and strong-minded, two unpopular traits at Sun. Still, Campbell picked him and Hicks was installed as president at the 1970 annual meeting.

Part of Hicks's duties included visiting the operations in foreign lands, and in 1971 he toured South Africa. He returned to Montreal to find Campbell undergoing treatment for cancer of the larynx and barely able to talk. Campbell spent the summer battling this condition until a clinic in Chicago cured him, and he was able to return to work in September. But three months had passed and Hicks had learned to like running the place on his own. Communications between the two had not been smooth, and Hicks had new marketing and organization ideas that he wanted to put in place. Campbell wasn't so sure he wanted to move that quickly. Recalls senior vice-president and secretary Jim Gowdy, "Mr. Hicks was going ahead along a track. In September things came to a head. The chairman wasn't quite ready for all the things Tony was anxious to get ahead with."

Hicks was particularly anxious to reorganize the company regionally. Except for British operations, everything had been run out of head office for decades, so the separate U.S. office planned for the following year was a major step. Hicks, however, wanted more, specifically a separate Canadian organization away from head office. Recalls Campbell, "You can't do too many of these things too quickly. There is a demand for additional people that has to be filled." Campbell favoured the separate Canadian organization, "but it was a question of how quickly it could be done." (It wasn't done until 1979.) It was all too much for Campbell, and he did not back Hicks's plans. Hicks was left isolated in his ambitions, a sure corporate sign that he was no longer welcome. George Clarke says of Hicks, "He expected more support than he got."

In the end, the board agreed with Campbell that young Hicks wanted decentralization too quickly. Peter MacGibbon, then company secretary, puts the problem in equestrian phraseology: "The board felt he was trying to rush the fences." Word of the end came when Hicks was travelling in New York. As president of the Canadian Life Insurance Association (as the industry association was then known), Hicks was attending a U.S. association meeting with association vice-president Jack Rhind, then president of The National Life Assurance Co. of Canada. Hicks got word that there was to be a Sun board meeting that week at which he would be asked for his resignation. "I felt very emotional about it," Rhind recalls. "He had made such an effort to be bilingual." Rhind saw this and other traits in Hicks as indications that he was a modern executive, with a social conscience.

Rhind, who is an intense and caring person, decided to step in. Once he returned to Toronto himself, he began telephoning members of the Sun board. The first he contacted was John Tory. The Hicks resignation had occurred at the first meeting Tory had attended, so there was little he could do about it. Next, Rhind telephoned another director, James Sinclair, a former cabinet minister in the government of Louis St. Laurent. The conversation took a bizarre turn.

"Well, who are you?" demanded Sinclair, after Rhind had stated his concern. "I'm the vice-president of the association," Rhind said. "Tony's the president."

"Yes, but what company do you work for?"

"Well, I work for National Life."

"You mean to say," said Sinclair, "you're phoning me and you're the president of another life company?" Rhind realized the naive futility of his effort and ended his short crusade on Hicks's behalf.

Effective December 31, 1971, Tony Hicks was gone, at fifty-five. He told friends he just planned to take a year off, but he never really worked again. He continued to receive an annual income from Sun that was less than his salary but more than his pension for the next ten years, until his Sun pension kicked in at sixty-five. Hicks, now tending the orchard on his property near Franklin Centre, southwest of Montreal near the New York state line, has spent the years since trying to forget. "I was going to write something at the time of my demise," he says, "but I never did. I threw what [papers] I did have into a pile, then I threw most of that out. I haven't been through what's left. I'm not sure I'd be a reliable witness," he says, laughing. "There is a tendency for the human mind to forget the unpleasant memories."

Former president George Clarke, who also remains on the payroll, went as quietly as Hicks and airs no complaints about Sun. The officers are expected not to muddy the waters, neither while they are there nor after they leave. While Clarke and Galt did not have the same communications problems as their predecessors, Campbell and Hicks, it did not do George Clarke any good to be head of a strategy planning committee called the Directional Planning Task Force. He came up with a variety of new ideas, none of which gained much support for quick action from either Brindle or Galt. Brindle's reaction is typical, repeating the Sun Life gospel: "We've got plenty to do at the moment by tending to our knitting." Clarke had fallen into the Tony Hicks role of man-on-the-move and Sun just didn't brook such impatience. "We like to be innovative," says Brindle, "but we're in no hurry."

After Clarke's departure, those left behind closed ranks to suggest that Brindle's ascent to the presidency had always been planned. At sixty-one, when he was appointed, he could expect a full four years in the chair rather than the two years he would have had if Clarke had retired at the normal time. Waiting for Clarke did not sit well with Brindle. "I would not have accepted a two-year presidency. Everybody would have been very conscious that the next bus would be coming down the road." According to Brindle, the plan was in place when he moved from Britain to Canada. Galt, he says, told him: "If this works out, and you settle in, it will give us a couple more years for succession."

Clarke, who had joined Sun in 1967 after seventeen years with Manufacturers, soldiered on bravely in his office even after Galt had announced his early retirement. The next month he carried out his duties as president at the grand annual occasion known as the President's month dinner. October traditionally is President's month at Sun, a time when all the agents try to reach high sales targets. Come November a black-tie dinner is held, and the various divisions report their success to the president. Those division heads who are reporting results below their targets are expected to try to hide failure with bombast and badinage. The president, for his part, is expected to be light-hearted and spontaneous. For everyone, that night's performance during the evening is almost as important as what happens during the year.

Some sixty of Sun's directors and management élite watched as Clarke replied to the division reports that November 8. Everyone was aware that Clarke was on the way out, but no mention was made of it. At the Sun, such events are like an unwanted pregnancy in a Victorian family or an uncle who drinks a little too much. Everyone knows that problems exist, but they are spoken of only obliquely. After Clarke had talked about the sales figures, he spoke in more general terms. "I would like to observe," he told the group, "that the company has many fine, talented, and capable people. There are major challenges. I hope these challenges are met and overcome. May you have the wind in your sails." Then, in a nod to bilingualism, he translated the phrase into French: "Le vent dans les voiles." Next came an Irish saying: "May the road rise to meet you, and may the wind be always at your back." Only in his closing sentence did he finally allow himself the slightest remembrance of times past, the most glancing of remarks that spoke to his departure. "The President's month dinner has always been a special occasion. I will always remember it as such."

Since everything at the Sun is done at its proper time and everyone knows his proper place, there was a quiet lunch for company officers in December, where Clarke was given a boxed pair of decanters. In April, he was honoured along with two other board members who were taking normal retirement. Each received a silver tray engraved with a depiction of the new building. The system that had spawned him then spurned him. Clarke has set up an insurance consulting business, but he sees none of his former colleagues from Sun.

From the outside, it looked as if Clarke and actuary Alex Robertson were being forced to take the blame for disastrous results the year earlier. Net income of $73 million in 1981 had plunged to $797,000 in 1982. There were two reasons. First, as Brindle puts it: "We had lost sight of common sense in pricing on group life and health [insurance]." Competitors thought that Sun was trying to undercut the market. "Sun just bought its way in," says Charles Kimball, vice-president for group insurance with London Life. Second, the heavy strain of new business coming from the U.S., with Sun's acquisition of Massachusetts Financial Services Co. (MFS), meant increased administrative expenses and additional actuarial reserves, thus reducing net income.

Although the actuaries set prices, Robertson wasn't to blame for the mistaken deep discounts on the group life and health insurance, Brindle insists. "Alex had had enough. He was ready to resign. We have always felt in Sun Life that when you pass sixty, you can retire—as indeed I felt I could go back to England." A new corporate office structure was being formed, an amalgam of the previous corporate and national divisions. Corporate took overall corporate responsibilities while national looked after domestic operations. The officers, explained Brindle, needed to work together more closely rather than in separate empires. Robertson no longer fit. "Alex is extremely able as an actuary, but the feeling in the company was that a pulling together of the corporate and national operations was required rather than a splitting apart." After the bad results and the differing views, both Clarke and Robertson were gone, apparent scapegoats. For his part, Tom Galt took no blame. Crown's Bob Bandeen, amazed by the drop in profit, notes that there is no retribution for bad performance in a mutual company. "If that was a publicly owned company," says Bandeen, "the stock would fall by half."

MFS, the cause of the drop in net income, was Sun's first major diversification under Galt. Purchased in 1982, Massachusetts Financial Services Co. was a Boston-based firm that had been selling mutual funds since 1924. As a result of a legislative change in the U.S., MFS found itself unable to sell one of its popular products, accumulation annuities, as a tax shelter unless MFS were owned by an insurance company. Lawyer David Horn, then vice-president and company secretary for Sun Life in Toronto (he now heads the U.S. division), heard about MFS and told Clarke and Brindle. Within two weeks, MFS senior partners were in Toronto and the deal was struck, subject to valuation by First Boston Corp., the merchant bankers. Sun paid the fifteen MFS partners $50 million and kept all but one, who retired. As part of the deal, there was a bonus arrangement for the partners to assure continued growth. Under the deal, Sun would pay an additional $15 million to MFS employees in 1985, if growth was good. The targets were met in 1984, several months early.

The continued success was due to a variable annuity sold by MFS that proved to be particularly popular. The annuity allows an investor to contribute money regularly to one or more of a number of funds available. In 1982, interest rates were high and U.S. consumers were looking for money-making vehicles. The MFS funds, then sold through 3,000 insurance brokers and 24,000 securities sales representatives, reached US$200 million in new business in 1982. During the first two years with Sun, MFS assets under management rose from US$4.7 billion to almost US$8 billion.

The sheer size of MFS sales demonstrates both how the business works for the company and how it cuts against the bottom line. The increasing business put a drain on Sun's balance sheet. Since the bulk of the sales were in five-year annuities, Sun had to make provision to repay the amounts deposited, plus interest, at the end of the term. In order to be sure that the money owed would be available to the investor, Sun had to set aside funds known as reserves. Because of the huge sales totals, reserves were sizeable. From MFS sales alone, Sun put $60 million into "surplus strain" to back up the sales. On the books, in the weird world of insurance accounting, the amount appeared as reserves, not as net income. Between the high strain and the poor health insurance pricing, 1982 was a disaster for Sun. The success of MFS had become something only an actuary could explain and a blot on the balance sheet.

To make matters even more curious, when year-end results were released the following year, the 1982 net income had been restated. What had been a net income of $797,000 at the end of 1982 had actually been $5 million, according to the 1983 annual report. It was the fourth year in a row that Sun had restated earnings to put them on the same footing as the current year. "It can all be quite disconcerting. The lesson, I suppose, is that we must at all times beware of false profits!" Galt joked to an industry group. He explained what had happened by saying, "We lost sight of the importance of having profit accompany growth. In 1981 and 1982 we were being aggressive in our group life and health pricing, just when health claims were rising. We also sold a large volume of high-surplus-strain annuity and pension business in Canada and the United States. We found our growth had outstripped our profitability. In other words, we did not manage our business to give the right balance."

Jack Brindle was chosen to help Tom Galt restore that balance. Where Galt is cerebral, Jack Brindle is physical. Says Doug Lang,

Sun vice-president for human resources, "Jack's got everyone jumping higher; everyone is more excited." John Arthur Brindle is sixty-two and was born in Manchester, England. He fought during the early years of the Second World War inside the tanks of the Royal Tank Regiment in the Middle East. He rose to sergeant and, as such, was either in the lead or in second position when the tanks were on the move on European roads, the prime target for an enemy shell. After a few tanks were hit, the corps learned to have someone moving with the advancing column, armed with a flame-thrower, working the ditches ahead. His tank regiment was the first to reach Belsen, one of the infamous death camps. German doctors outside persuaded them that it was a hospital for infectious diseases such as typhoid. The tanks rolled on, the men not hearing until later of the atrocities within.

Brindle's company commander, Jack Kempton, an Imperial Life insurance branch manager, urged him to work in London for a Canadian insurance company. Brindle was not keen at first. After the war, he recalls, "England was a drab and battered place." Instead, he stayed in the forces and, because he spoke German, remained in Germany to help with the establishment of a civil government there. In 1947, he took his commander's advice and joined Sun Life in Manchester. His training consisted of hearing about one of the company's policies for twenty-five minutes. After that, he was asked, "You understand the policy? Well then, go and sell it." After four days and ninety calls, he finally found a buyer in a builder's yard and left with a cheque in his pocket for £89, 1 shilling. About half the premium was his. Brindle could only think, "If I can do this well knowing as little as I do, I should do very well when I've learned something." In his first year, he made £1,200.

He became a branch manager in 1953 and was manager of agencies by 1959. During the mid-1950s, as he moved through management, he could see that the training program in Britain was not much better than what he'd been through. Any support material was of pre-war vintage. On a visit to Canada Brindle was amazed by the training material available. He filled a steamer trunk with it and dispatched the trunk to England, where it was adapted into three levels of courses for agents. In the 1950s and 1960s, all the Canadian life insurance companies had good growth in Britain because they were selling something most British insurance companies were not: life policies with guaranteed cash values, as well as guaranteed loans and loan interest amounts. Sun was doing particularly well and was twice as large as any other Canadian company, with about 2 to 2.5 per cent of the market share. The six Canadian and four Australian companies operating in Britain had about 12 per cent of the market, about the same as they have today.

In 1973, Brindle was named general manager for Great Britain and Ireland, overseeing 900 agents and 1,000 staff. Because of his experience in running operations for an entire country and region, Galt called him in 1979 to beef up head office staff in Toronto. Brindle, who'd spent his life in Britain, was not pleased with the prospect. "I didn't volunteer," he confesses. In 1979, the decentralization Tony Hicks had sought was finally to be applied to Canada. Galt wanted Brindle close at hand because of his experience at running British operations. He was made senior vice-president in charge of marketing; he retained his title of senior vice-president and general manager for Great Britain and Ireland and agreed to share his time between Britain and Canada.

"There was a lot to leave to come here," he says. Although both he and his wife became Canadian citizens in 1985, retaining their British status as well, he intends to retire to Britain and misses such unique institutions as the Canada Club, for example, the oldest continuous dining club in London. Founded in 1810, its members meet three times a year at the Savoy Hotel. By 1980, however, his tour in Canada was looking lengthier. He was executive vice-president and had picked up increased duties in Canada. Of the next seven officers immediately below him and Clarke, four reported to Brindle. In the corporate world, where control is achieved through such relationships, Brindle was a powerful man.

Although Brindle had Britain on his mind, the presidency was an appealing thought. "There was no palace revolution, no ultimatum," he insists. "Sooner or later I was going back to Britain. The question was when. I was a couple of years younger than George. It was felt that in the run-up to the next generation, we didn't really need the three of us, so George decided to retire early." There was no point in making Clarke a deputy chairman and keeping him in the executive. Says Brindle, "It would have fudged the issue. People would have seen it as musical chairs." Also, Galt wanted to retain his power. If Clarke stayed on, what would Clarke actually do all day? Tom Galt wasn't prepared to give up any duties.

Little wonder. The Sun has always taken a rather grand view of itself and its staff. In 1967, chairman Alistair Campbell described the typical Sun Life representative this way: "He invokes worthiness; he appeals to prudence, to right conduct, to human consideration, and to love. He asks men to take thought for the morrow; to make present sacrifice for future comfort—for the comfort of others. In an extravagant age, his call is to thrift."

The officers relish the secrecy allowed by operating a mutual company. Specific salaries, for example, need not be disclosed. Says corporate secretary Jim Gowdy, "It gives you a comfortable, almost private company protection. You miss all that newspaper publicity [about salaries]." The salaries, in fact, for vice-presidents are $70,000 to $100,000; senior vice-presidents earn up to $175,000; the three general managers, $200,000; the president is in the $275,000 range and the chairman around $400,000. The principal officers have additional perks; about twenty have cars supplied. The officer selects the car he wants (usually in the $15,000 range), the company buys it, then the officer buys it back from Sun over three years, paying no interest. The five top men (the chairman, president, and general managers) have chauffeurs as well. The forty-five vice-presidents are allowed two club memberships paid for by the Sun, one club with dining facilities and one recreational, such as a golf club. Initiation dues up to $3,600 are covered, as are $1,200 in annual dues. Business entertainment at either, of course, is also paid for by the company.

Although Sun claims to base executive salary on performance, there is no bonus system such as many other firms have introduced to reward excellence. There are fewer staff following the recession. From the beginning of 1982 to the end of 1984, world-wide staff decreased from 5,358 to 4,684, a 12.6-per-cent reduction over three years. At those rates, however, Sun employees didn't see the kind of wholesale cuts that many other firms suffered. By comparison, it is a safe haven from the hazards of the world—if one doesn't rock the boat. "This is a long-term business," says Peter MacGibbon, former vice-president for corporate affairs. "A more deliberate style is more fitting. This is not like the toy business, where product life is short."

That deliberate style was what Tom Galt, then fifty, brought to the position of president when Hicks departed in 1971. Unlike Hicks, who had been moved around a bit in the company to gain experience in various areas, Galt had a background that was almost totally actuarial. He was seen as a cautious captain after Sun's brief flirtation with change. In Alistair Campbell's mind, Galt and Hicks were equally talented. "Hicks was more at ease on a platform," says former chairman Campbell, "but Tom had the essential qualities." For Campbell, the Hicks episode was just a brief management flurry. "We're all different," he says. "You never get the perfect man. And sometimes when you think you have found him, you've made a mistake. That's how I look back on it."

"There was a return to normal," says Gowdy. "It became like insurance business as usual. We had been on a new ventures program." Clarke was appointed executive vice-president, the number three man. "It was steady as she goes," says Clarke, "carrying on with the way it was before Hicks became president." Although the new threesome were quickly ensconced on the executive floor of the Montreal head office, it took a long time for the firm to recover. Hicks's departure sapped the energy of the place for the next five years and removed any adventure that might have lurked in anyone's soul. Campbell began to peel off more and more of his duties and give them to Galt. In 1973, Galt picked up the additional title of chief executive officer; Campbell continued as chairman for another five years, to August 1978. While the U.S. division was established during that time in Wellesley Hills, Mass., outside Boston, little else was accomplished. "It took two or three years after Hicks left for us to get going," said Gowdy. "We treaded water. By 1975, the U.S. had settled down and we began to look at long-range planning."

Planning, however, became overshadowed by another problem that began to take up more and more of the executive thinking time: language. Even before the election of René Lévesque and the Parti Québécois in November 1976, Sun was grappling with how to deal with the changes in Quebec as the francophone majority flexed its muscles. After Lévesque came to power, Sun's cocoon was forever split. Moving Sun out of Montreal, where it had issued its first policy in 1871 and been a landmark since the 1920s, was fast becoming a probability. Campbell quietly began to poll the three or four most senior officers for their views.

Although specific language requirements were set only slowly by the government, there was unrest at Sun head office because only about 15 per cent of the staff was bilingual. Recruitment was becoming increasingly difficult; actuarial graduates from outside Quebec refused even to visit for interviews. Anglophone employees were constantly being lured outside the province. During the two years after the election, Sun lost 130 people, including about 10 per cent of the datasystems department. Although specifics on missed sales opportunities were impossible to total, word kept coming in to head office from western Canada and the U.S. that prospective policyholders were leery of doing business with a company head-quartered in a province that they feared might become a foreign country. A survey of staff in 1978 discovered that a majority were willing to move out of Montreal if it was required. By year-end, some other numbers were becoming clear: individual insurance business had fallen by 2 per cent from the previous year. Quebec unrest was blamed. Sun concluded that it had become a leper in the industry.

"Language became such an issue," says Campbell. "If you're an international company you've got to have a strong and stable base to operate out of. You can't do business in the U.S. in French. That's what it was coming to—for both the U.S. and the rest of Canada. We would have had to write and do everything in French, then have it translated for everyone else." Through 1977, the possibility of leaving Quebec was discussed at the meetings of the executive committee of the board, chaired by Campbell. "I favoured the move," says Campbell. "There were responsibilities to policyhold-ers. I looked on those responsibilities as uppermost. When it came to the nitty-gritty, the decision was made by the [board] executive committee and also the board. It wasn't something that came in a day. It was building, building, building." And all the while, the company was nearly paralyzed, thinking of little else.

Not every life insurance executive in Quebec understood or sympathized with Sun's difficulties. Claude Castonguay, president of the Laurentian Group, wondered at the time why only Sun was having problems. "Look at Montreal Life, Prudential, and Standard Life—they're all doing well," he told the *Globe and Mail*. "They're not suffering because they're here." Nor was there an anti-Quebec backlash in the rest of Canada, as Sun claimed. Castonguay's Que-bec-based firm sold in Ontario through Imperial Life. "I haven't heard any complaints about our ownership." Castonguay feels no different today. "[Sun] became a very negative symbol in Quebec. When you look at the explanations, it was a situation that was badly managed. There was a lot of emotion; you can't explain the move on a strict rational basis. They didn't want to face tensions in Montreal. They took the easy way out."

On January 3, 1978, the board decided it could wait no longer;

Sun's head office would move to Toronto. Staff was not informed for three days, when a half-page memo was distributed to every department. It read: "The president has an important message which he wishes to communicate personally to as many members of the head office clerical staff as possible." No one needed to be told what the message was. Word that they were to assemble in the seventh-floor auditorium at 2:45 P.M. travelled the corridors faster than the inter-office distribution system could carry the printed memo.

More than a thousand people gathered to hear the news on January 6. "Ladies and gentlemen," Galt began. "I have called this meeting to acquaint you with a very important decision the board of directors took at their meeting on Tuesday, January 3." He told the gathering that notices would appear in newspapers, that the decision was difficult and made with much regret, but that it was "essential for the long-term good of the company." He was thirty seconds into his speech and he still hadn't told them what the decision was. His next sentence revealed it, but only by implication. "We hope to be able to offer positions in Toronto in due course to all those fully satisfactory clerical employees who wish to move."

There was no cheering, but there was some applause. Assurances were made about house appraisal and guaranteed sale agreements as well as financial assistance to offset higher house prices in Toronto. Staff were informed that few functions would be moved that year. As well, they were told that Sun planned to maintain a strong presence in Quebec and would not sell the building. Galt urged them not to talk to the media, asking them to refer any queries to the corporate relations department. There could be no questions, he said, and departed the room, ten minutes after they had assembled.

Word spread instantly throughout the business and political community of Montreal, to Ottawa and beyond. One of the telephone calls went from vice-president and actuary Don Gauer to his brother-in-law, Jean-Luc Pepin, then co-chairman of the Task Force on Canadian Unity, a body charged with binding the country's wounds. The Sun move was not helpful to that process. When Pepin heard the decision, his first question was: "Have any of the members of the board resigned?" "No," was Gauer's reply. "Well," sighed Pepin, "they must have felt it was the only thing they could do."

The board met again on January 14 to discuss the reaction and to plan for the special meeting called, as the law required for federally chartered mutual companies, to allow policyholders to vote on moving the head office. At first blush, after the move was announced, there was much relief within the organization. The staff had felt embattled and were glad of an escape hatch out of Quebec. At least 50 per cent of them wanted to move to Toronto, if only for the chance to expose their children to another city and a different culture, according to estimates by Doug Lang, who took over the personnel department six months after the announcement. In the end, only about 500 out of the total 2,200 corporate staff moved to Toronto. Many of those left behind were unhappy not to move. Says Lang, "There was a backlash when a lot of them realized they weren't moving."

The bigger backlash was outside. The politicians, among others, were quick to pounce on the decision. Finance minister Jean Chrétien arranged a meeting for Campbell and Galt with Prime Minister Pierre Trudeau for an hour one evening at the prime minister's residence, 24 Sussex. Among the arguments put forward by some of the politicians of the day was that as a federally chartered company, Sun should stay as a symbol of Confederation. Campbell saw the realities of doing business in the world differently. At the time, ardent PQ supporters thought it was just fine for Sun to go. They argued that once independence came, Sun and all the other fleeing head offices would have to return to be able to carry on business in the new "country." For Campbell, there was no choice. "Looking back, I don't see how we could have done it differently. We knew we would be the centre of attention." Perhaps Sun had little choice; the only door out of Quebec was through a special meeting of policyholders. Still, Sun's actions remain baffling when there was a quieter route. Over the next half-dozen years, the Royal Bank of Canada and the Bank of Montreal moved key staff and whole departments to Toronto while nominally retaining their head offices in Montreal.

While Sun focussed on the legal requirements and talked to politicians and employees, the media were not fed enough information from Sun to satisfy their cravings. It was decided that the company would comment mainly through written press releases. As a result, Campbell did not meet the press himself, and the anti-Sun headlines raged without much offsetting comment from Sun. "It got out of kilter," admits Campbell. "I wasn't available for interview because of this," he says, touching his throat. What about Tom Galt? "That was the obvious question. I can't answer that. He dreads these things." The media, says Campbell, treated Sun unfairly. "The media treat insurance in general unfairly because they don't see it changing, changing. The media never got to grips with the Sun Life move. All they wanted was headlines." And headlines they got. Even the usually straightforward *Financial Post* took a few whacks. Screamed one headline: "Sun Life stumbling with Quebec sales force defecting."

Trudeau's request for a delay could not halt the move; he had only slowed it down. He succeeded in having the special general meeting of policyholders, originally called for January, delayed three months. By April 25, when the meeting convened in Toronto, strong feelings were ready to erupt. One outspoken policyholder at the meeting was none other than Robert Bryce, a former deputy minister of finance. He termed the announcement "abrupt and inept" and said that he hoped that other firms "will not feel compelled to follow." He urged that competent French Canadians, wherever Sun was headquartered, be able to advance within Sun.

Bryce realized, however, how little say he as a policyholder had in the decision. The board of Sun Life had spoken; there would be no turning back. "As a former member of the Ottawa bureaucracy," Bryce said, "I must respect the entrenched strength of the management and staff of the big mutual life companies who have no shareholders, face no take-overs, and are subject to no effective control except by those whom they select to serve on their boards."

Another critic who acted as a focal point for opponents of the move was Richard Holden, a lawyer with the Montreal firm of Geoffrion and Prud'homme. To him, management was governing as if by some "divine right." Holden charged that Campbell, a director of Asbestos Corp. Ltd., was using Sun as a weapon to stop the Quebec government from taking over Asbestos Corp. In the end, none of the arguments mattered. Neither Holden nor Bryce nor Chrétien nor Trudeau could stop the Sun. The policyholders approved the move by voting 84 per cent in favour. With the initial hullabaloo over, Campbell, who had been with Sun for fifty years, turned over the role of chairman to Galt in August, and George Clarke was named president.

While there may have been criticism in Quebec, outside the province there was a positive response. Sun's individual insurance sales in Canada outside Quebec increased in 1978 by 20 per cent. Within Quebec, however, just the opposite occurred. Thirty per cent of the 400-member Quebec sales force (half of them franco-phone) left. As a result, sales plummeted 27 per cent. Overall, individual sales in Canada rose by 4 per cent in 1978. On balance, at year-end, the executive could congratulate itself on the financial results even though the move ranked as one of the worst public relations fiascoes in modern-day business.

A small marketing group moved to Toronto in 1978, and about 220 people, including the datasystems department, moved in 1979, as did Galt and Clarke. About 300 more transferred in 1980, leaving 1,500 people behind in Montreal. In all, only twelve people who were offered a move refused, usually because they were near retirement, with grown families and paid-up mortgages; fewer than five whose functions moved were not offered a move themselves. House sale prices in Montreal were guaranteed after appraisals, mortgages in Toronto were based on lower-than-market rates (staff paid 8.25 per cent rather than the going rate of 12 per cent), one month's salary was paid for expenses such as new rugs or drape refitting. Each staff member was allowed two fully paid house-hunting trips to Toronto and up to five days off with pay. In the end, the total cost to Sun to move the employees was more than $5 million. The firm regarded the move as a success. Only two employees who moved asked to return. Recalls Doug Lang, then vice-president of human resources, "It was tougher on the wives who didn't work."

Today the move can be regarded with some distance and even a little humour. The times were testy and anglophone Sun executives were being castigated outside the office for other reasons in addition to the move. Vice-president Lang, for example, was president of the Quebec Association of Protestant School Boards at a time when the government and school boards couldn't agree. Meetings he chaired turned into placard-waving demonstrations. At one point, he was hanged in effigy. On his office wall today is a framed copy of an Aislin cartoon published in the Montreal *Gazette* in 1977. It shows a Quebecker being bitten in the leg by a British bulldog. The caption reads: "Sit, Protestant." The overall corporate stance is now equally self-deprecating. When Sun opened its new building in Toronto in 1984, the company assembled an exhibition of archival material—old machines, policies, and photos—and among the items on display were blow-ups of newspaper stories and unfavourable editorial cartoons scourging the company for the decision.

After moving to Toronto, Galt continued the management style begun by his predecessors forty years earlier. The main management meeting was that of the officers' executive committee (OEC), a group that included about eighteen senior people, all executive officers who originally met weekly; the schedule eventually changed to every other week. It was a forum where items could be tabled, information communicated, approval assumed. It was not really a consultative body; the move, for example, was never discussed by the OEC prior to the board decision.

While there had been much talk about forward planning, little concrete work was done until 1978, when a two-day management meeting was held at Hovey Manor in North Hatley, in Quebec's Eastern Townships. Originally built as a summer home for a Georgia gentleman, Hovey Manor has been an inn since 1950. Its most famous artifact is a Gothic-style clock said to be haunted. It will chime only when the name of Plumley LeBaron, a local whose odd ways included wearing a coon coat in summer, is invoked. Little was invoked at the Sun planning session. Galt offered no vision of the company for the others to follow. The group tossed up none, either.

Next the consulting firm of P.S. Ross & Partners (now Touche Ross) was hired to advise Sun on direction. A team headed by Sandy Aird made some recommendations, including splitting the Canadian and corporate divisions. The least popular suggestion was to disband the officers' executive committee. It disappeared in 1979 to be replaced by the senior advisory committee (SAC), which is scheduled to meet but four times a year. SAC consists of the heads of the three national offices, four corporate officers, the president, and the chairman. Some Sun employees still lament the demise of the OEC; while it was too large a body for decision-making, at least it was a good place to communicate. Others disagree. Says secretary Gowdy, "Now it's so much easier to implement things. We had to wait for OEC to approve almost anything."

Forward planning continued to evolve so slowly as to be imperceptible. A planning officer, Bob Mifflin, was hired in 1980 as vice-president for planning, but it was 1981 before George Clarke drafted a statement of intent of corporate direction, something that could be used as a guide to planning. Clarke produced a four-page memo, an outgrowth of a letter he had written to Brindle when the latter was transferred from England. Even that memo was not the final version; it simply formed a framework setting out the need for planning and some possible directions. Explains Clarke: "The company had always done long-range planning, but it had always been in some-body's head. It had never really been put down in writing. In the 1970s, we just kept doing what we had been doing before—with some response to competition. But in the 1980s it became obvious we were into a new ball game."

Sun did not join the game already in progress until the fall of 1982, when the Directional Planning Task Force was set up under Clarke. It was to produce written recommendations on operations in the entire company. In order to gather raw material and data, several dozen employees were interviewed. The turbulent financial services environment was surveyed and by the spring of 1983, ideas were beginning to flow to Clarke. He was urged by his colleagues to show the task force's thinking in draft form to Galt in order to hear Galt's views. Although Clarke did discuss aspects of the findings with Galt, he decided not to give Galt any written recommendations until the project was complete. Finally, in mid-1983, fully five years after the first planning session at Hovey Manor, Clarke presented Galt with three one-inch-thick black binders, one for each area (Canada, the U.S., and Great Britain and Ireland).

The reports were brutally honest. They demonstrated the frustra-tion of many in the firm with the Sun's slowness to respond to changing times. One agent was quoted as saying: "In today's market, I am upset, scared, and confused, and I get little or no help from my company." The report pointed out that the four-year retention rate (the number of agents recruited who are still there after four years) was not much better than the 1983 industry average of 18 per cent. That is, of every hundred agents brought in, after four years only eighteen were left. In contrast, Manufacturers had a 22-per-cent rate, London Life had 32 per cent, and Mutual Life was an industry leader with 44 per cent. As one branch manager said in the report, "We run body shops." The persistency rate (policies in effect after thirteen months) was declining. While once it had been over 90 per cent, the report noted that it was falling and had reached 85 per cent. In other words, of every hundred policies sold, fifteen lapsed after thirteen months.

Recommendations were numerous and far-ranging. One possibil-ity suggested was a walk-in branch where the public could buy Sun's products. Another was to use letters already being sent to policyhold-ers to sell other products. "We must make better use of the 32-cent stamp," the report urged. Most important, however, was the need for leadership from the top. "Senior management must take the lead in 'setting the tone'."

While some things at Sun take time, when Galt gets his hands on something he can change, he does. In 1984, he received a letter from a Sun mortgage-holder complaining that he could not understand what Sun was saying in a three-page letter he had received. In this case, it helped that Galt knew the complainant, but he swung into action with a campaign that affected five Sun departments dealing with the public. In each, video training and written material told employees how to use the telephone to find out a policyholder's specific complaint, then instructed them in writing clearly.

Important as customer communications are, they are only one aspect of Sun's response to the market. How any change will be accomplished, except by default, remains unclear. Sun does not keep the entrepreneurial employee challenged. If those with ideas—like Hicks—are not rejected, they very often flee. One who worked with Clarke, for example, was Frank Santangeli, now president of Aetna Doherty Midland Finsco Ltd., a new firm created as a joint venture between Aetna, an insurance company, and Midland Doherty, a stock brokerage firm. Finsco has accumulation and mutual fund products for sale by both companies. Sun could have been the insurance company involved in the plan, but Santangeli left and shopped the idea around. "Sun Life for many years has never reached its potential," says Santangeli, who departed Sun after fourteen years. "That's been the frustration of any bright guy who's gone in there."

The next generation is even now moving into place. Early in 1985, two appointments were made that indicated who might be the next president and, in time, the next chief executive officer. The two are executive vice-president John McNeil and senior vice-president John Gardner. They have joined Galt and Brindle on the executive floor, where two offices had waited empty for a year. In the early going of these corporate sweeps, McNeil, who had run the U.S. operations, was half a step ahead of Gardner, who had been in charge of Canada. In McNeil, Sun has the only candidate for president since the first president, Thomas Workman, hardware merchant and banker, who at least comes equipped with experience outside the insurance business. McNeil spent ten years at Sun, then thirteen years elsewhere, including the Bank of Montreal, before returning in 1979 as vice-president for securities investment.

Until Galt chooses between them, probably sometime in 1987,

there will probably be little change in either the Sun's corporate culture or its consumer contact. Then the new man will need to pick his direction amid a framework that was set during the Depression. While the Sun has not been totally eclipsed by the succession of high-level departures and by a continuing low profile, its prospects have certainly been dimmed. In fact, as other financial services move into new positions and adopt new plans, it is very likely that the Sun will never shine as brightly again. "I think we will become more sensitive to the fact that we are involved in a more competitive product," says vice-president for human resources Doug Lang. "From the big player in the life business, we'll become a small player in the financial services sector."

That's a long way down from number one.

CHAPTER THREE

RUNNING AGAINST THE WIND

The Maritime Life Assurance Co.

IN THE HALIFAX boardroom of The Maritime Life Assurance Co., overlooking the Northwest Arm of Halifax harbour, hangs an evocative Jack Gray oil painting of Canada's best-known sailing vessel, the *Bluenose*. Under full sail, she is crashing through the Atlantic waves, overtaking another schooner. For the internationally acclaimed schooner, it is a typical position—moving into the lead. Like the *Bluenose* when it was first launched, Maritime Life started life as a mere regional institution, content to be confined to the Maritimes. But just as the *Bluenose* gained growing fame as the winner of the International Fisherman's Trophy Race every year from 1921 to 1938, so too did Maritime become widely known beyond its boundaries. In fact, for a few years in the 1970s, it became a corporate maverick, a notorious ne'er-do-well shunned by the rest of the industry, running, as the *Bluenose* did so well, against the wind.

From a sleepy seller of ho-hum coverage, Maritime remade itself into one of the industry's innovation leaders. It threw out the old-fashioned notions of permanent protection, where cash values grew as slowly as moss in the deep woods, and replaced them with quick-sprouting new money policies in the sunshine of high interest rates in the 1970s and early 1980s. In so doing, Maritime leaped from being a tiny firm all the way to tenth position out of 170, measured by new individual insurance. There are currently 465 employees, with 373 of them in the mirror-clad head office on Halifax's Dutch Village Road and 92 in the field. Business is done through seventy-six general agencies across the country and about 1,200 individual sales agents. As growth came, assets exploded from $264 million in 1978 to $1.4 billion in 1984. More importantly, however, through its maverick ways, Maritime single-handedly and forever revamped the way Canadian life insurance companies do business, changing how consumers are treated and how they are rewarded by their policies.

Maritime Life was founded in 1923 by a group of Nova Scotia families. With head office in Halifax, branches were opened in New Brunswick, Newfoundland, and Prince Edward Island. Because traditional trading patterns on the east coast were north–south, agencies were opened in Bermuda, Nassau, and the West Indies. The firm grew slowly through the years, owned by various Atlantic Canadian interests. By 1948, when it celebrated twenty-five years in the business, Maritime was still a small player, with $37.3 million in life insurance in force. Today, the top few agents will write that in a single year.

Starting in the 1950s, Maritime began the speedier growth that would mark its coming days. President from 1954 until January 1970, when he became chairman, was W. C. (Bill) Schwartz. In 1960 Maritime enjoyed a record year. It saw the greatest increase in new premium income in the company's history. For the first time, strong agencies outside Atlantic Canada began adding to the totals; 40 per cent of all new business came from Ontario and Quebec. By 1966, the expansion rate in both sales and business in force exceeded that of any other life insurance company in Canada over the previous ten years.

Maritime then set out to go after specific captive markets. In 1961, Maritime began a special services division to sell insurance to personnel in the Canadian Armed Forces. Today, with agencies near most bases in Canada and the one in Lahr, West Germany, Maritime is the largest supplier of life and health insurance to armed forces personnel.

While no individual or family ever had control of Maritime, among the latter-day shareholders were Reuben Cohen, of Moncton, and Leonard Ellen, of Montreal, the low-profile magnates who control Central Trust and Crown Trust. But in 1969, ownership of Maritime left the local collection of Maritime interests when the John Hancock Mutual Life Insurance Co. of Boston purchased Maritime for $6.85 million. Under successive presidents Orville

Erickson and Michael Hepher, the company, which had started small and regionally oriented, began to make waves across the country. From 1970 to 1979, individual premium income increased by 1,198 per cent; group insurance premium income grew by 2,450 per cent. There were 300 employees, and assets had increased at an average of 38 per cent per year, compounded annually. From $50 million in 1973 (fifty years after its founding), assets had reached $427 million by the end of 1979, when Hepher was wooed away to England to become assistant managing director of Abbey Life and Maritime went looking for a replacement.

The interloper who arrived was a bearded and cowboy-booted American who set not just Maritime but the whole Canadian insurance industry on its ear during the three years that he ran the firm. At thirty-eight, Ray McEneaney was hired at $65,000 by Hancock to run Maritime. He asked for a free hand and was given it, even though not everyone at Hancock was convinced that he'd had sufficient training or possessed enough talent in marketing. Their doubts just fuelled his determination to succeed.

McEneaney was born in Dover, N. H. He graduated in aeronautical engineering from Notre Dame University in 1963, at twenty-one. Rather than become just another rivet on the airframe at a place like Boeing, McEneaney chose a work-study program at Northeastern University and John Hancock. Actuarial work appealed to him because he could see it brought higher positions on the corporate ladder, and he became a fellow in the Society of Actuaries. By 1969 he was second in command of a department of 300 employees.

The pace wasn't quick enough for McEneaney. He knew he had to carve out a spot for himself and make a name within it. The paper-shuffling around him cried out for more efficient methods. As the fifth-largest life insurance company in the U.S., Hancock was a huge place—6,000 employees in Boston alone and some 15,000 agents and support staff in the field offices. Like any big firm, it was constantly being reorganized in the hopes of achieving new efficiencies. In order to learn the most up-to-date methods, Hancock sent McEneaney to the Institute of Social Research at the University of Michigan.

The institute was experimenting with corporate organizational models similar to those that were later called quality circles when imported from Japan. Hancock was one of several firms that served as guinea pigs for the plan, which divided employees into small groups. Employees filled out questionnaires about their jobs and their supervisors. Thirty such groups (McEneaney was in charge of ten) met to discuss ideas that would change the workplace and work methods. As a facilitator—he thought of himself as a change agent—for the groups, he learned early on how to get the most out of staff, using innovative methods. "It showed me that rather than be dictatorial, I could sit back and let people come to their own conclusions through a process." He would later export this revolutionary management style to Maritime Life.

Next step, however, was to become involved in designing the part of Hancock's computer system that handled policy changes. At a time when anyone interested in the area was fascinated with the humming hardware or the jobs that computers would replace, McEneaney looked at the systems from the user's chair. He spent his time ensuring that computer screens and keyboards were, in today's terminology, user-friendly, a concept that would be embraced later by all computer manufacturers and users. Once again, McEneaney was an innovator.

By 1974, he was supervising Contract Services, a Hancock department the size of most individual insurance companies. It did $1 billion in new insurance business annually. He then spent a year in Washington on a government–business exchange program. He found the civil service frustrated his action-oriented methods. Again, he found a way to put his thumbprint on the larger system. "They always wanted me to write white papers," he says. "Instead, I worked with individuals and solved their problems. That made more sense." His specific responsibilities included working with the Pension Benefit Guarantee Corp., ensuring pensions for employees of firms that had gone broke. That, however, was only part of the learning process. He also benefitted from working with the other thirty-five executives from all over the U.S. in a enriched program, which included sessions with members of Congress and visits to Brussels to see NATO headquarters and meet with the leaders of the Common Market organization.

When he returned to Hancock in 1975, he was handed a troubled department with 110 employees that was backlogged with 1,100 applications from individuals wanting to set up pension funds. He replaced supervisors, applied the University of Michigan problem-solving techniques, and within a year had the backlog reduced to ten applications. A year later he was given added responsibility for another department; he was in charge of both, with a total of 410 employees.

Word of McEneaney's talents was spreading through the organization. In 1977, when Hancock subsidiary Maritime Life was looking for someone to run its operations in Trinidad, McEneaney was tapped. There was a certain appeal to the title—chief executive officer—and to living in Port-of-Spain. Further, the previous CEO had gone on to become minister of finance in the Trinidadian government. On the negative side, it was a tiny division—only fifty-five employees. He and his wife visited Port-of-Spain and he concluded: "I didn't think it was going to occupy me all day." He turned it down. Still, what he was doing at Hancock wasn't sufficiently fulfilling either; he detested being one of the mob. "I was 110th on the Hancock succession list of vice-presidents." There were 110 vice-presidents. "I made them aware I was champing at the bit."

When Maritime Life came back a second time in 1979, this time the top job was open. He would run the company differently from Hepher. "Hepher was hands-on and involved in more decisions than he should have been," says McEneaney. "It was the kind of place where people felt they were all on one floor and could walk around and talk to each other every day."

Right from day one he was pitched into new problems. Someone had the bright idea, before his arrival, that every new employee at Maritime should see a ten-minute videotape of the boss welcoming him or her to the firm. McEneaney was told about the project on his first day and urged to tape it immediately. He was stunned. "*I'm* the newest employee," he pointed out. There were bigger shocks. For all his past eagerness to advance, he suffered a moment of self-doubt now that he'd arrived. He didn't really know how a company president operated, he'd had no role model or mentor and had barely seen the Hancock president up close. "I didn't even know what a president did—and suddenly I was one."

There were few early errors. The owners at Hancock were not watching too closely, anyway. They treated Maritime as an investment in which Hancock had a passive interest rather than as a subsidiary requiring active involvement. Four times a year, at board of directors meetings, Hancock received a full report on Maritime's operations. In large part, however, Maritime had such a free hand that even McEneaney was surprised. It was just the place to try out some of the organizational ideas he had learned at the University of Michigan, some of the bubble-up style of management that invited underlings to dream up new policies and products and encouraged them to voice their ideas and advance their views. What he tried to put in place was a system where each officer had more responsibility, a management structure that could run on its own after he was gone.

In fact, Maritime had a history of innovation. In the early 1970s, consumer awareness about insurance had begun to grow; people wanted choices beyond the two traditional offerings—permanent whole life and term. Beginning in 1974, under president Orville Erickson, Maritime offered "new money" insurance policies; it was the first firm in Canada to do so. No one else followed suit for fully eighteen months. The term "new money" came about because these policies signalled the first significant change not only in how insurance was priced and sold but also in what it did for the policyholder.

For decades both term insurance and permanent whole life insurance had been available, but agents usually pushed the whole life because term cost about one-quarter as much as whole life, with correspondingly lower commissions. Term had become popular with consumers who wanted cheap coverage, but those who sold it were regarded coolly in the industry. New money policies—where cash values actually reflected market conditions—were seen by the venerable institutions as just another step down the slippery slope away from the high-blown ideals and higher commissions of permanent whole life insurance.

Maritime's new money policies offered both death benefits and a high rate of return on the policyholder's money. These high returns could result in either quickly rising cash values or, more often, the purchase of more insurance. Maritime was able to guarantee interest rates for five years because the premiums received were invested in five-year mortgages with fixed interest rates. Gone was the caution of the old-line insurance firm, which set low returns to the policy-holder in case its own returns were low. The new concept was that the policyholder could look at his policy every few years and change it to suit both his needs and his income as well as changing market conditions. It was just the opposite to the traditional approach, in which a policyholder bought a policy and left it untouched for years while the agent earned continuing commissions and the company (once first-year administration costs were taken care of) saw profits.

To be sure, in the past the insurance companies had little choice but to be conservative. Policies guaranteed amounts payable to policyholders for fifty years. The companies had only one opportunity—at the time of sale—to set rates, consider mortality experience, figure in administrative costs, and make investment assumptions. As a result, companies were ultra-cautious; sometimes they were able to pay a policyholder a higher dividend than promised, but rarely were they forced to pay a lower one. But with the new money policies, the issuing company had a chance to make adjustments every five years. The company could match precisely the funds promised to policyholders with the funds invested in mortgages during the five-year period, allowing new money policies to pay high returns to the consumer *and* guarantee the company a profit. Maritime's investments in mortgages with secure returns grew from 42.4 per cent of its assets in 1974 to 76.2 per cent in 1984.

Maritime had two other advantages over other companies. Its independent agency network allowed most administrative costs to be carried by the agents, not by head office. Those costs did not, therefore, need to be taken into account in the cost of issuing and servicing the policy.

Further, Maritime's rates were not as constrained by the standard mortality (or life expectancy) tables as those of other firms. Premiums in the conventional policy are set by the mortality tables of the year when the policy was first purchased. A policyholder who bought twenty-five years ago is paying premiums that are still based on 1960 mortality tables, although progress in medical science has increased life expectancy since then, allowing insurers to set ever lower premiums. Maritime built this gradual decline in premiums into its pricing assumptions. In fact, its first new money products had so many new pricing, interest, cost, and mortality assumptions built in that they looked almost unbelievably inexpensive by comparison with the rest of the industry.

The first policies invented by Maritime's actuaries were adjustable single-premium whole life policies. One example worked like this: a thirty-five-year-old man who paid a single premium of $8,860 for $100,000 worth of insurance coverage in 1974 would have had his coverage increased over time at no extra premium. His protection was then in place; there were no further premiums. Contrast that with the same man who bought a traditional whole life policy for $100,000 with an annual premium of $1,386. Over the next thirty years, until he was sixty-five, he would pay a total of $41,580 in premiums.

New money is a pricing concept that can be used in a number of ways. While Maritime's first new money product happened to be a single-premium product, today virtually all its new money products are the annual premium variety.

By 1980 a good deal got better. Because interest rates continued going up, Maritime's overall investment portfolio had earned more than expected. As a result, policies sold in 1975 were adjusted by increasing the death coverage by up to 20 per cent—with no premium increase. As interest rates continued to climb in the marketplace, coverages were increased in 1981 as much as 65 per cent— depending on age—again with no additional premium. (If interest rates had fallen, coverage would have been adjusted downward or the policyholder would have had to add a further premium payment to maintain the original level.) With rates shooting up, however, the products became more and more saleable and Maritime's reputation as a maverick grew. The old-line firms could only stand on the sidelines and scowl.

The new money policy was an obstreperous child that the industry could not accept. It was McEneaney's challenge to lead the child into maturity. It was his good fortune to arrive in May 1979, just as interest rates were about to shoot up and Maritime's products were about to become the talk of the industry. Even with its dynamism, Maritime was not without its fuddy-duddy employees. Not everyone at Maritime was as gung-ho as the products. In fact, much of the propelling force had come from Hepher. Because it takes some time to develop, price, and market a product, McEneaney assumed there must have been some work in new products going on when he arrived. He soon found out otherwise. A conversation he had with a product actuary went like this:

"What have you got on the drawing board?" McEneaney asked.

"Nothing."

"Well, a new product is due in six months."

"Well, when we get there, we'll develop one," came the sanguine reply.

That wasn't good enough for McEneaney, and he began to pressure the marketing department to produce. The head of the department quit and McEneaney installed a younger man, in his early thirties. He did that in several areas, bringing in young bucks without a tradition to defend to produce new products. One of the new policies was a ten-year term product that allowed the buyer to pay all the premium up front and actually be repaid by the tax-free cash build-up within the policy itself. At the end of the ten years, the policyholder was refunded the amount of the original premium. In other words, Maritime was giving the stuff away—free.

Such no-cost insurance was revolutionary stuff. The old-liners in central Canada were filled with scorn. "In the beginning," says McEneaney, "most of what we got was bad-mouthing from others in the industry." The industry, of course, was worried that Maritime's buyers were convincing holders of traditional policies to cash in old-line company policies in favour of new money products. McEneaney knew that at most only 15 per cent of Maritime's buyers were trading in policies from other companies, but he thought he might as well take advantage of the reputation he was gaining.

In an industry where there are few high-profile public spokesmen, he set out to become one. He took any speaking engagement he could find in Atlantic Canada and visited all the general agents across the country. Such visits in themselves were unusual. Most agents never saw their company president from one decade to the next. Travelling also gave him the opportunity to give media interviews, appear on television talk shows, and do open-line radio spots.

Not only did McEneaney shock his colleagues by his public appearances, his message was scandalous. He told anyone who would listen that permanent whole life insurance was a waste of money. Typical of his comments were these published in the Hamilton *Spectator* after a 1980 interview. "The attitude of the insurance industry to the public has been 'Here is our product—take it or leave it,' said Mr. McEneaney. 'Well, what people have done is left it,' he said."

Looking back on his message on those media tours, McEneaney recalls, "The public had never heard a life insurance executive say that. The rest were too much toe-the-mark companies." He cut quite a swath as he toured the radio stations of the land. Even his physical appearance struck those he met as unusual. Few Canadian executives sported a full black beard like McEneaney, who had always prided himself on his individualistic attire. At the Hancock, he wore cowboy boots and discovered that they irked some of his superiors. That just made him wear them more often. He also favoured denim suits. Once, after a presentation to some higher-ups, he was told that one of them later commented to another: "Who was that guy in dungarees and a beard?" As far as McEneaney was concerned, he could receive no greater compliment.

At Maritime, he bowed to convention only slightly. He stopped wearing the cowboy boots. After a few months of podium presentations, he realized that his delivery could be improved. In a world where too few Canadian executives even come out from behind their desks to see what's going on or to explain their own thinking, McEneaney took a public speaking course so he could communicate better. Nothing stopped him from thumping the drum. Once, in Calgary, just before an interview, he put a foot-long rip in the seat of his pants. He scrounged some straight pins, closed the tear as best he could, and went on with the show like a seasoned vaudeville trouper.

McEneaney seemed to be fascinated by everything he saw and wanted to soak up as much of the country as he could on his travels. He carried bird identification books with him and stalked sought-after species in Vancouver's Stanley Park between appointments. Once, during a particularly busy migratory period, the public relations man travelling with him had to drag McEneaney away from this pursuit in order to get him to the next meeting on time. McEneaney even purchased maps of the countryside over which he flew. While others on the aircraft were relaxing and reading, he was like a kid on his first flight, poring over his maps and staring out the aircraft window trying to identify cities and rivers and other landmarks from 32,000 feet in the air.

While his larger interest was to rouse the public on what a bad deal most insurance had been, that wasn't his only mission; he was also trying to reach his own agents. "I was trying to appeal to general agents, not the end-user. I had to show them that Maritime was not just some small regional company back east." Previously, the company had sold its products through a combination of general agencies (agents who sold Maritime and other firms' products) and traditional branch agency offices (selling only Maritime products). By the end of 1976 Maritime had only general agents. Each was responsible for expenses and overhead costs (including staff) while Maritime provided some supplies and promotional material. The agent, because he was an independent businessperson, could sell products of several firms and grow at the rate he wanted without any quotas from head offices.

Not all of the agents had the financial resources necessary to go out on their own, but Maritime refused to help finance the independent operations with loans. Says McEneaney: "When they asked for financing, we said no. We told them, 'Go to the bank. If you've been successful, you'll get money. If you're not entrepreneurial enough to go on your own, maybe you're in the wrong business.' " The agents in the field responded positively, and their number actually increased, from fifty-five to sixty.

The industry, however, was paranoid. The bad blood flowed openly in Calgary in 1981 at a meeting of the marketing section of the staid industry group, the Canadian Life and Health Insurance Association. While McEneaney was on a panel, charges flew that Maritime was secretly financing its agents and that it was "twisting." (Twisting is the act of persuading a customer to cash in an existing policy and replace it with a new policy from a different company, a practice regarded as unethical, at best, by the Life Underwriters Association. In some circumstances it is illegal.) One question from the floor was typical: "Don't you think that you're ruining the industry?" Another attendee put the charge of twisting directly. He said that Maritime was "taking other people's clothes and remaking them." McEneaney is unrepentant. "Those people thought they were working for the industry, not the shareholders. It is a close-knit industry and there is a lot of feeling that the industry should be preserved in its close-knit state."

By that time, however, Maritime wasn't the only firm offering new money policies. Others included Excelsior Life (now Aetna Canada), Gerling Global, North-West Life, and Colonia. Most of the big boys did not arrive until 1981, after a sufficient logjam of public demand for new money products had developed; then the rest of the industry began to compete, too. Maritime and McEneaney were even welcomed into the inner sanctum: McEneaney was invited to become a member of the CLHIA executive. It was a signal not just that the war was over, but that Maritime had been right.

To this day, McEneaney cannot understand why the big players in the industry let Maritime have the field all to itself for so long. "The mistake they made, as a group, was that they didn't play hard. When you are on the defensive, you play hard and stamp out guerrilla groups like us. But they didn't. They gave us five to seven years. I couldn't believe it." It wasn't just market share that the industry lost to Maritime's aggressiveness, says McEneaney. "They lost agents who decided to leave them to do business with us."

Throughout, McEneaney had done it his way, the way he'd learned at Michigan a decade earlier. "The process we had was to get the ideas out. I'd make the decisions, but I wouldn't make them beforehand." The results came for all to see. "We came from being a small company in the Maritimes to being a major firm." He knew that his own style was unusual. "I was a maverick, but that allowed me to promote Maritime Life. It got me first notice, then I could tell them about Maritime."

But for McEneaney, industry acceptance meant that his time had passed. He was earning $90,000 a year by 1982 and felt he had shown those folks at Hancock that they needn't have worried about any weak spots he might have had. "I proved that I knew something about marketing." Annual premium income at Maritime had risen during his time from $137 million to $190 million, assets from $300 million to $950 million. He had gone to do the job for three years and the time was almost up. Hancock had never wanted an American in charge for more than a short time.

McEneaney had even more important reasons to leave. "I didn't have anything left to prove." In his last year at Maritime, he even shaved off his beard. He departed in September 1982. Today he is a vice-president at the international insurance consulting firm Tellinghast, Nelson & Warren Inc. He works out of the firm's Jacksonville, Fla., office advising others on mergers and acquisitions, strategic planning and marketing. It is a location and a life-style that he sought after the rigours of Maritime. His home, with its atrium, is on a creek leading to the St. John's River. His kids can go sailing from the backyard. With nothing left to prove to anyone, he remains clean-shaven and has hung up his cowboy boots for good.

McEneaney's replacement at Maritime was J. D. (Dick) Crawford. Like McEneaney, he came from outside; he was, however, a Canadian. Crawford was a twenty-two-year veteran of North American Life Assurance Co. and had risen to the position of senior vice-president in Toronto head office when he got a telephone call from a head-hunting firm, Caldwell Partners, in February 1982. He met the four Hancock directors on the Maritime board for a ninety-minute interview in the Four Seasons Hotel in Toronto. His background spanned the various elements of insurance. Born in Montreal in 1935, Crawford graduated from the University of Toronto in math and physics. He had spent four years at Excelsior Life Insurance Co. as an actuarial student, then joined North American in 1960.

Unlike many actuaries, he had left the back-room number-crunching and sold the product for a time. In his student days, he had even sold aluminum chairs door-to-door. "I discovered I was not a natural salesman," he said. "I made some sales, but it was the beginning of my understanding of what selling was all about." At North American, he had gone on calls with the investment department staff and given actuarial advice to pension funds; he had accumulated twelve years' experience in group insurance. Crawford was intrigued by Maritime. "It was an exciting place by reputation," he recalls. Crawford was working under Drew McCaughey, who had joined North American as chief executive officer in 1980 from outside the industry. The way to the top was blocked for a while so Crawford, at forty-seven, welcomed the Maritime offer.

Maritime had always been a place where offbeat behaviour flourished. One unusual employee was W. J. (Jay) Logie, who was general manager from 1954 to 1968. Over the noon hour, he would visit one of his favourite local pubs and order two bottles of beer, one cold from the refrigerator, one at room temperature from the shelf. He would then mix the two in order to create the precise temperature at which he thought beer should be consumed. Most lunch-times, he would order a second pair (again, one cold and one warm) and sometimes a fifth and final bottle, from either the fridge or the shelf, depending upon which was required to maintain his mugful at the requisite temperature.

The individual management styles of Hepher and McEneaney were hard acts for Crawford to follow. Crawford told them when he arrived that there would be style differences between him and his predecessors, but the changes caused no problems. "Because it was a youthful group," says Crawford, "there was less 'This is the way we've always done it.'" He supported the concept of the independent agent. That was an important touchstone because by that time, few wanted to see it changed again. With that reassurance given, he was able to set his goal—a balance between growth and profit. Although assets had grown from $886.5 million in 1981 to slightly more than $1 billion in 1982, net income had fallen from $3.4 million to $736,000.

Crawford had arrived at a most uncertain time, not just for Maritime but for the whole industry. In November 1981, the federal budget had spelled the end to some annuities popular with many insurance companies. But that wasn't the only bad news. Previously, when a policyholder bought a single-premium policy, paying for it in one lump sum, that amount had been tax-deductible. The budget ended that provision, too. "The federal government did a number on us," says Crawford. How it affected Maritime can be seen in the sales totals of single-premium life insurance and non-registered annuities. In 1981, sales of those products amounted to $40.8 million; they fell to $14.6 million in 1982, $5.4 million in 1983, and $777,000 in the first half of 1984.

Crawford's first push, then, was to create new products to replace those killed in the 1981 budget. Success showed by the end of 1982, by which time four new products had been brought out. Half the 1983 sales were in products that hadn't even existed at the beginning of the previous year. One new product, "instant issue," a life insurance policy an agent could write and put in force on the spot, didn't catch on in the field, but even that failure demonstrates Crawford's open attitude. "New product ideas are very fragile flowers," says Crawford. "It's very easy for technical people to crush that flower before it blossoms. I would rather have it the other way— to see how the technical side can support the ideas, to create a place where people have the right to do an experiment that doesn't work."

Crawford's gardening metaphors have their roots in his personal life. When he was in Ontario, he grew a pumpkin that weighed 105 pounds. When he arrived in Nova Scotia, home to champion pumpkin-grower Howard Dill of Windsor, Crawford got some of Dill's seeds and sent them to friends and associates. In 1984 his biggest pumpkin grew to a fifteen-inch diameter, then shrank. Crawford blamed the wet weather. He grows them in his garden at his home, a one-and-a-half-storey structure, formerly owned by the late senator Harold Connolly, facing Point Pleasant Park. Built by a shipbuilder's staff in 1947, it has oak floors, mahogany wall panelling, and a separate stable converted to a recreation area with a five-seat acrylic hot tub. One room houses a Commodore personal computer on which Crawford drafts his own speeches. Maritime pays for his membership in the Halifax Club and the Ashburn Golf Club. The CEO's perks include very little life insurance. When he joined, he had a personal policy for $200,000; Maritime added a further $100,000.

In addition to the new consumer policies produced after his arrival in Halifax, Crawford also oversaw the development of a new concept in pension fund management, called the master management system (MMS). It assumes that pooled pension funds (where the assets of several funds are brought together and invested by one manager) perform better and thus earn more income than a single fund can earn on its own. For small to medium-sized businesses with pension funds to invest, there are really only two choices: try to run it yourself, or join a pooled fund. If the choice is to join a pooled fund, the problem then becomes how to know which has the best track record and continuing investment advice.

The subsidiary running MMS found the best independent pension managers through computer analysis. One hundred funds with $80 billion invested in common stocks, bonds, and mortgages were studied, and the eleven best managers (with total managed assets of $3 billion) were chosen to advise on the investment of funds under MMS management. "We tried to find those that were good," says Crawford, "not just falling down lucky."

MMS is operated by Pencorp Systems Ltd., with its headquarters in Oakville, Ont. Maritime bought a 21-per-cent interest in Pencorp for $200,000 and has since increased its investment to $1 million and a 30-per-cent holding. At first MMS was intended to handle pension funds with $2.5 million to $50 million in assets. Now, however, small company pension funds, with as little as $250,000, can participate in a pension fund that invests in other pension funds. The annual administration fee ranges from 0.67 to 1.25 per cent of funds invested, depending on the size of the fund. For that, each client receives a monthly statement and a quarterly comparison with the competition. According to Maritime, return has been in the 17-per-cent range, compared with an industry average of 11 per cent. The MMS service was first available late in 1982 and had assets of $250 million at the end of 1984, with a goal of $450 million at the end of 1985.

"What we originally did that labelled us as mavericks has lessened," says Crawford. "We were a celebrity company. We're now building a reputation." Part of that has to do with spreading responsibility and dropping the one-man, high-profile style. "A company that has all that locked up with one guy is not developing a culture." Now the culture is to let the chorus of new products sing rather than count on any solo performance, no matter how tuneful.

"The pace of change has accelerated," says Crawford. "When

history is added up, it will be an era where the customer has benefitted. It has a lot to do with small companies like Maritime wanting to grow faster than the industry." In 1982 Maritime Life had a 2.3-per-cent share of the market in new individual policies. In 1983 market share rose to 2.5 per cent and by May 1984, it had risen to 3.1 per cent.

In the end, it was not the ownership switch to Hancock in 1969 that started the forward momentum of Maritime, although certainly the take-off began after that change. Perhaps it was more luck than anything, the right man at the top at the right time. It was under the workaholic Hepher that new money policies were first cooked up. He oversaw the early, entrepreneurial growth phase and put in place the agency system that would make it work. He was followed by the maverick McEneaney, with his modern management techniques, who was able to cajole more products from the actuaries. Stung by Hancock's concern about his marketing capability, he set out to prove them wrong and did, with a grandstanding piece of executive leadership of the sort that can only work at certain growth stages of any company. The current boss, Dick Crawford, has the wider industry background to consolidate growth, reach out for new areas such as pension management, while maintaining the individual character of the place, allowing every voice to be heard. All in all, not bad for a firm whose marketing department used to think that the best advertising it had was that the firm's symbol, the *Bluenose*, appeared on every ten-cent piece.

CHAPTER FOUR

A FLOCK OF EGOS
Inside the Million Dollar Round Table

IT IS EIGHT O'CLOCK on a grey morning in June, and the sidewalks of New York's Avenue of the Americas near Rockefeller Center in midtown Manhattan are a scurry of humanity. Women trip along in Nike runners, their fancier footwear stowed away in tote bags. Men, prepared for rain, sport umbrellas like lances at the ready, the furled colours reminiscent of banners at medieval jousting matches. The streets are gridlocked with the only four types of vehicles that seem to exist in New York: yellow taxis, tired 1969 Chevelles, snooty Mercedes sedans, and stretch Cadillac limos with boomerang-shaped trunk-mounted aerials. The overall noise level is deafening.

This morning amid the high-rise honchos on the corporate climb and the harried office workers are 5,784 life insurance agents headed for Radio City Music Hall. They come from more than 400 different companies in forty-six countries. In most other towns, such a gathering would merit a visit from the mayor. In New York, it is just one more blinking bulb on the marquee of life. Outside the front doors of the famous hall where the Rockettes lift their limbs, a Dixieland jazz band tootles its wares. The agents moving into the theatre take note, but the rest of the passing herd does not. It is not that it is too early for such festivities, it is just that the veteran New Yorker cares not a whit for such hoopla in a city where anything can and does happen on the streets.

The Dixieland sound marks the beginning of four days of sales ideas, motivational speeches, and self-celebration at the world's largest industry-wide gathering devoted to the fine art of convincing people to buy something they don't want. This is the fifty-seventh annual meeting of the Million Dollar Round Table, the *crème de la crème* of life insurance agents and a group that travels in style. Meeting organizers had asked for the thirty-six Rockettes to appear as part of the program. The charge for one six-minute session of the world-famous chorus line of high-kickers was $25,000. To open *and* close a session, the cost would almost double, to something in the $45,000–$50,000 range. Instead, the MDRT bought the house out Sunday evening, saw the opening and closing kick lines—and the ninety-minute musical review running at the time, "Gotta Getaway"—all for only $37,000.

What is being celebrated here in New York, as it is at the MDRT meeting every year, is personal success. The ego feed starts as soon as the arriving agents hit the Radio City Music Hall front doors. There they are greeted—after a quick check of name tags—by name. Equally important, the greeters, wearing black top hats, add a message. "Glad to see you back, Jim" or "Congratulations on another great year, Russ." There is a fraternal feeling in belonging to a circle of excellence that other poor duffers are prevented from entering. They are gathered like knights—with a smattering of ladies—at the round table within the castle. The peasants are relegated to some dusty plain outside the gates and beyond the moat.

The organization's first meeting was held in 1927 at the Peabody Hotel in Memphis, Tenn. There were but thirty-two registrants, and these were attending another meeting, a convention sponsored by the National Association of Life Underwriters, when they declared themselves to be an élite and met for lunch to start MDRT. As the 1930s came, the members numbered about the same. Sessions were expanded, however, to include breakfast meetings and walks at Colorado Springs or wherever else the larger convention was being held. The budget for the meeting was $4,000.

By 1984, the budget had grown to $1.5 million. The sales requirements to gain entry to the circle had shot up, too. At founding, $1 million in annual sales was big stuff. Inflation, however, has meant that increasingly higher goals have been set. Now, to become a member, along with other criteria, an agent must sell US$2.3 million in new life policies (with a minimum of fifteen different lives involved) in a year. In fact, most members do better than that. The average volume for a member is about US$4.2 million. An agent's commission income comes not just from those first-year sales but from the premiums of policies sold in earlier years as well. In all, the average income of an MDRT member with ten years in the business is about US$75,000.

But it isn't just high income that's being celebrated here. This is not a bunch of boys at the bar flashing a roll of bills they won that day at the track. No, there is something else. There is the firm knowledge that 97 per cent of the insurance agents in the world are just not good enough, don't have the talent or the tenacity to break into this élite. The MDRT has 25,000 members in countries around the world from Australia to Zimbabwe. Of that total, 1,820 are Canadian—the second-largest contingent, after the Americans—and 519 of them have come to New York. Canadians have been attending MDRT meetings since about 1930. This year's bunch will be particularly vocal because one of their own, Ron Barbaro of Toronto, has been designated next president of the MDRT, the first non-American president of the international organization.

The importance of attendance to each member is shown by one notable fact: the agents pay their own way. Their companies do not contribute. Among the 1,100 international members who are here from outside the U.S., some delegates claim they spend one-tenth of their annual income just to attend. This is not, then, some reward junket where an agent spends a few hours at meetings and the rest of the time enjoying the local sights and sounds. The meetings are well attended and run twelve hours a day; spouses are not allowed to sit in.

Radio City is an appropriately famous hall for this gathering. Here top performers have strutted their stuff in front of more than 260 million people since 1932. It boasts two Wurlitzer organs, the Rockettes, and a three-ton gold fabric curtain—the largest theatrical curtain in the world. It is not, however, the art deco beauty of the place that has drawn these life insurance agents like moths to the flame. No, for an insurance agent, MDRT could be held anywhere. For them, MDRT is a combination of Harvard Business School, Mecca, and the Blarney Stone.

In the auditorium, the 5,882 red plush seats in the orchestra and three balconies are filled before eight-thirty. There is a full-throated sound in the air as these super-sellers greet old friends, try to impress new acquaintances, and generally just feel good about being there. The vast majority of the attendees are white males in the thirty-to-fifty-five age bracket. There is a sprinkling of women in the crowd, but there aren't many in the organization from which to draw. Of the 25,000 members, only 1,055 are female, about 5 per cent of the membership—but substantially more than the 1 per cent registered as recently as 1975. In the industry overall, women represent about 12 per cent of the sales force; in Japan, more than 80 per cent of the agents are women. There, selling insurance became an avenue of livelihood after the Second World War for the many women who headed single-parent households.

Golf shirts are *de rigueur* with the MDRT crowd. In addition to the ubiquitous name badge, some also sport a white ribbon. That signifies membership in an even smaller circle within MDRT, a group called Top of the Table. To achieve that honour, an agent must sell US$12.75 million worth of insurance in a year—about six times the MDRT minimum. Top of the Table started eight years ago with an admission criterion of $5 million in sales. There were only 300 members. With the requirement now pushing $13 million, there are 670 members. If MDRT members are above the salt, Top of the Table members are the lords in this feudal system. To the other MDRTers, Top of the Table members might as well be gods. To see, to touch, to learn technique from a Top of the Table member is enough to make an MDRTer's morning.

They have gathered to be reassured that the whole process of selling life insurance, their life's task, is not just a job but a *calling*, and they are monetary missionaries to the world and its wants. For the next four days, they will worship success, try to snare some good luck from others, and learn what they call "transferable sales tools." They will also feed on each other's vitality. Here a salesman's fragile ego can be stroked, a year's adrenalin can be stored away. One of the 108 speakers, three-quarters of whom are MDRT members, captures the feeling many share when he announces to the assembly: "I like me best when I'm with you."

Over the stage hang two giant video screens, so that even the onlookers up in the gods can see every grin and grimace on the speakers' faces. Between the screens is suspended a sign with the initials MDRT in flashing lights. At stage right, there is a small television newsroom set where two "announcers" provide continuity. On stage, two podiums are equipped with the kind of word-prompters used by Ronald Reagan when he gives the State of the Union address, twin pieces of square glass on thin stalks. The audience can see through them and gets an unobstructed view of whoever is speaking, while the stage speakers can see the words of their speeches roll by at just the right pace for presentation. In the front rows sit past presidents, resplendent in identical navy blazers. The five members of the current executive flit about the stage decked out in tuxedos.

As eight-thirty approaches, the babble in the hall reaches fever level. People are congratulating each other on their successful return, they wave and point across the rows like politicians on the prowl, bask in the glory of their very presence here at the Million Dollar Round Table, the gathering they themselves refer to as "a flock of eagles," proudly pointing out that eagles—because they are strong individuals—don't usually flock. This is the big league, desperate to keep proving that in the life insurance business people *do* matter. To them the MDRT is proof positive that exceptional people will always make a difference.

The program opens with a video presentation showing clips of international newsmakers and world leaders interspersed with insurance industry leaders. It is a deft, if pretentious, presentation that equates insurance leaders with world leaders. The accompanying audio talks about "taking the cause to the highest levels." The "cause" is insurance, free enterprise, and the freedom of agents to sell products without government intervention. Interview clips show industry spokespersons explaining to the great unwashed the difference between whole life and term life. They go on to defend the industry from unnamed critics and unspecified charges. They see a bogeyman out there somewhere who needs to be constantly fought. There is much cheering from the crowd. The pizzazz closes with a song: "This Could Be the Start of Something Big."

Next the spotlights fall upon forty-six MDRT members rising in formation on an elevator platform from beneath the stage. The music builds to a crescendo. They are carrying flags from the countries represented at the meeting. As the countries are introduced one by one, behind them the seventy-member Boys Choir of Harlem sings. A message is read from the White House, the first one that the MDRT has ever received. "America needs to be told again and again of the message that our free enterprise system has plenty of room for those with unlimited aspirations and determination," Ronald Reagan has written, "and that it offers personal and professional fulfillment to the men and women who are willing to work for it." It is signed with his own hand. There is more cheering. The daughter of current MDRT president Paul Buckley gives the invocation, and Buckley delivers a stem-winder of a speech. "Those who dream most," he tells them, "do most. The most dazzling performances are the ones you've already given." The crowd is really worked up and it's barely quarter after nine.

Time for a little enemy-bashing. First governments, then the banks. The U.S. federal deficit will be $320 billion in 1989. By 1987, says Buckley, it will take half of the personal income tax paid just to cover the interest on the debt. As for the banks—well, spit in their eye. The banks are second only to governments in their attempts to interfere with insurance. Buckley, an agent with New England Mutual Life, has a personal anecdote. He tells how a few years ago he went to a Boston bank looking for personal investment advice. They urged him to put money into a coal mine tax shelter deal. He invested $25,000 and took the $75,000 tax write-off the bank told him was within the rules. "Two weeks ago," he announced ruefully, "I settled with the IRS for $50,000." There is much sympathetic clucking in the hall. "A small-potatoes scam," he continues, "and I paid a fee! And the banks want to get into the insurance business? Can you believe it?" Thunderous applause follows.

Buckley now has the audience's attention and he lays on a chilling line. "Dying is something that doesn't happen just to our clients." Life insurance agents, he says, die younger than the rest of the population. The very people who sell death benefits are themselves more prone to early death. Most susceptible of all are the high performers, those who operate full-tilt, under great stress—indeed, this very audience. Of the ten most recent deaths among MDRT members, he tells them, six were sixty or under. The youngest was thirty-six. Citing the obituary column in the club magazine, he asks, "How many of us will be featured in the next year?" The unavoidable message: while the rewards for the super-seller are high, so are the risks.

The thirty-minute speech winds up with lavish descriptions of insurance agents as "the diamonds of the free enterprise system...a profession whose ultimate purpose is to carry others in their time of need." More cheering. There is no amount of flattery these people find offensive. Over the next four days every technique and tragedy known to man will be rolled from the stage: first-person accounts of failures and how they were overcome; the death of a child and how that changed a way of life; born-again Bible-thumping; supply-side government-bashing; music, dancing, singing—including a couple of songs belted out on the stage by members. Throughout the first morning session, called the main platform, the audience is eager, even agog, for more thrills. They want to hoot and shout, they want to cry and be cradled.

The morning spins along like a well-oiled network production. One of the speakers, Aidan Jones, is resplendent in a pink sports jacket. A Brit, he is a member of the London Philharmonic Choir and one of the thirty-two speakers before the MDRT this week who are not members themselves. His prop is an easel with a giant pad of paper. His style is bombastic. He moves away from the podium equipped with prompter and gives his half-hour diatribe without notes. As he fills a sheet on the easel, he tears it off with great gusto, balls it up, and tosses it at his feet. Soon he is knee-deep in discarded paper.

He is there to teach the audience how to convince a prospect to put 5 per cent of his annual income into insurance—a mere pittance, if only the client would listen. Jones lists the various expenditures people have, and they add up to 95 per cent. He labels the rest "Keep For Yourself." At that point in the presentation, Jones suggests, the agent asks the prospect: "Do you want to give away *more* than 95 per cent of your income?" When the prospect replies "No," Jones claims, the sale is all but made, because the client has agreed he wants to save 5 per cent. "And you didn't say it," he shouts, "the prospect did." Insurance, he stresses, is a savings tool. The prospect is not spending money on premiums, the prospect is keeping some of his income for himself. For Jones, the whole selling process is easily defined. "What closes a sale is not a product brochure, a computer in your briefcase; it's concept, enthusiasm, a felt-tip pen and a piece of paper."

The next speaker, Dr. Barry Asmus, professor of economics at Idaho State, is one of those glib economists whose spiel is smooth, whose phrases are polished. His quarry is socialist politicians. "The mainspring of private ownership is capitalism. When you borrow from Peter to pay Paul, you make Peter a Paul-bearer." He has other targets: "The press is running around blowing out candles, then talking about how dark it is." And Capitol Hill: "The energy crisis was legislated in Washington. Property rights are in jeopardy when legislatures are in session. There's no end to the good that do-gooders will do with other people's money." He points out that 70 per cent of the land in the eleven westernmost U.S. states is owned by the government. If the government sold only 5 per cent of that land, it could eliminate the national debt.

Although Asmus is not passing on any sales tips, he is espousing a philosophy that most of his audience salutes. Every epithet generates applause. For him, the three rules of life are simple: teach your children to work; private ownership is the prerequisite of freedom; God has blessed you materially so give to the church of your choice. In the end, freedom is all. He points out that his parents were born in the Soviet Union and emigrated to the U.S. When he travels abroad today, "I literally kiss the ground when I return." He receives a standing ovation, one of numerous such responses from the 6,000 that morning. It is twelve-thirty, and except for a ten-minute break, few have stirred from their seats for over four hours. Even fewer have left. The morning has been a combination of back-patting, Norman Vincent Peale, and Amway without the soap.

At the end of the morning session, they spill out into the street, scurry back to hotel rooms, grab lunch, and prepare for the afternoon. There is no lack of choice. There are twelve one-hour concurrent sessions from which to choose at two nearby hotels. The topics include such exotica as "Providing Estate Liquidity for Second Death," "Buy/Sell Agreements," and "Philanthropist's Supplemental Income Plan." One of the more interesting is the "Sales Ideas Olympiad," which plays to 236 in a packed, narrow meeting room. A panel of six MDRT members from Wales, England, Canada, South Africa, Jamaica, and the U.S. spend the hour spilling out individual thoughts on how to find prospects, how to close a sale, and how to avoid hearing the client say the dread two-letter word "no."

The prize for the worst or best idea, depending on whether you are the agent or the aggrieved, is put forward by Brit John Mather. He tells the group that, as they all know, one of the best sources of names for possible policy sales is satisfied buyers. Trouble is, there are always a few such buyers who won't pass on referrals or claim they can't think of any names at the time. Mather keeps a list of these people and by year-end, he usually has twenty clients who have given him no sales leads. The week before Christmas he visits them, one by one, at their homes. Again, he asks: Can you think of any people who might benefit, as you have, from my services? Again, they usually draw a blank. At that point, he walks over to their mantel and picks up the first Christmas card that comes to hand. He reads the name, points out that it must be a friend, and gains his first referral. Mather claims that the average home receives thirty cards. His twenty previously reticent clients, therefore, produce 600 new names among them. In January, he telephones all 600, using their friends' names as a starting point for the conversation. Half agree to see him and he sells one-third of those—100 new policies in January he wouldn't have sold without going through client Christmas cards.

Christine Leach, of Wales, is equally aggressive. She approaches strangers in food stores when she shops. "You look familiar," she says to someone. She then goes through a list of schools, clubs, and neighbourhoods where they might have met. Of course, they never successfully establish where their paths have crossed because they haven't—until now. What is happening, however, is that Leach is learning where the person lives, what clubs he belongs to, and what schools he has attended—all information that points to life-style and income. "After a few minutes," says Leach, "I have identified whether or not the person is a good prospect."

The group is all ears for these and other gems, including the suggestion that an agent phone a prospect in the middle of the night to speak to the man's wife. After identifying himself as an insurance agent, he says, "I'm sorry to hear about your husband's accident." "There must be some mistake," the woman replies, "my husband's right here." "Oh," says the agent, "then the accident must be next week." Then there's the line one panellist uses to sell insurance to each of the two partners in a small company: "How would you like to be in business with the next husband of your late partner's wife?"

While finding prospects is difficult, as everyone in the room knows, once they are uncovered, the next hurdle is to overcome their objections to buying insurance. The panel spends a few minutes offering suggestions to the attendees. One panellist shows a way to increase the value of a policy a man buys on his wife when he just wants to have enough to pay for funeral expense. The panellist points out that funerals in 1950 cost $400; today they cost $4,000 and by 2010 they will cost $40,000. The size of the policy that the prospect is prepared to buy has just been increased dramatically. Points out the panellist: "We're not talking about a lot of insurance, we're just talking about enough to bury her."

The Canadian panellist is Frank DeFederico, of Etobicoke, Ont., thirteen times an MDRT member. While he sells life insurance for several companies, most of his business is with North American. He has an idea for others to use when they hear one of the common reasons a man won't buy life insurance—he claims he does not need insurance because his wife could go back to work if he died. DeFederico acknowledges to the client that she might earn $20,000 a year if she were able to get a job, if she did not become disabled, and if she didn't die herself, thereby making orphans of the children. Those are the contingencies one has to deal with, DeFederico argues. By comparison, a $200,000 insurance policy invested at 10 per cent brings $20,000 a year in income—an absolute. His line to the client is this: "What do you believe in—absolutes or contingencies?"

If the prospect is still not convinced, he may try to beg off by saying that he wants to think about the proposal. In that case, DeFederico has a further scheme. "You qualify for our think-about-it plan," he says. He then explains that an application is completed, the first month's premium cheque submitted, and the purchase approved. Then, at the end of the first month, if the client wants to cancel, he can. If the client is not yet convinced and still says he wants to think about it, DeFederico's line becomes: "Mr. Prospect, you mean to tell me you want to think about our think-about-it plan?" As he rolls the line, he looks triumphantly around the room. Those who aren't scribbling down notes on his lines give him an approving round of applause. Such workshops and similar lectures go on until nine-thirty at night. In the city that never sleeps, these are the life insurance agents who never stop.

Everything begins again at six-thirty the next morning, Tuesday, with 1,800 attendees sitting eight to a circular table in another hotel meeting room for what's known as a Sales-A-Rama breakfast. Chairman is Toronto's Ron Barbaro. In 1955, he was a dime-store manager in Windsor, Ont. It was Barbaro, along with the president of McDonald's in Canada, George Cohon, who rescued the Santa Claus Parade in Toronto when Eaton's decided in 1982 to cancel the seventy-seven-year-old event because of the recession. Barbaro and Cohon headed a private-sector fund-raising committee and within three days raised $1.5 million from twenty corporations in $75,000 donations over three years. Barbaro is also chairman of the board of management for the Metro Toronto Zoo. He does radio advertising for the zoo and once, as a publicity stunt, rode a camel round a race track.

This morning, the next president of MDRT is introducing nine fellow members sitting at the head table. Never mind the flock of eagles analogy; Barbaro has a more apt description. They are, he jokes, "a flock of egos." Last year, he says, the nine sold $238 million in insurance among them. The group also boasts insurance in force of $2.5 billion. All of them get full introductions—name, company, MDRT membership history—by Barbaro. He walks with a remote microphone, moving behind each in turn at the table on the stage facing the audience. One man, however, neither needs nor receives any description. Barbaro moves behind him, raises his hands as if in papal blessing, and announces reverently: "The man—Ben." One of the others at the head table places his hands together as if he were praying and looks skyward. There is a standing ovation from the crowd.

Ben is Ben Feldman, an unlikely-looking gnome of a man who, at seventy-three, is the world's greatest life insurance salesman. He lives in East Liverpool, Ohio, and sells for New York Life Insurance Co. His first million-dollar sales year was 1946, and he has been an MDRT member ever since. For most of that time, he has worked twelve hours a day, seven days a week. He has been first among New York Life's 8,500 agents in sales volume almost every year since 1955 and has himself sold more than $1 billion worth of life insurance. He sells more in a week than most insurance salesmen sell in a year. His 1982 volume alone was $87 million, more than most of his peers will sell in a lifetime. His annual income has been estimated as high as $5 million, a figure Feldman modestly says is "too high." He spends more than $1,000 a day in premiums on policies on his own life.

A shy man, he has made his mark selling insurance mainly to partnerships and small businesses in the heavily industrialized area of Pennsylvania and Ohio where he lives. His pitch is basic: his clients need insurance to protect their assets and their investments. When a partner in a business dies, the other partner will need money to pay the estate of the deceased partner so the living partner can continue with the business. Estate taxes could wipe out everything without a life insurance policy. The same with family businesses: a life insurance policy on the deceased will mean that the remaining members of the family can pay death taxes without having to sell the business and lose their livelihood.

Feldman is not the archetypal boisterous salesman. When he first spoke at an MDRT annual meeting, in the 1950s, he did so from behind a screen because he was too shy to face the audience. Feldman was twenty-six in 1939 when he first applied to work for Equitable Life of Washington. A friend was earning $35 a week in insurance, compared with Feldman's pay packet of $10 from delivering poultry for his father in Ohio. Feldman flunked the aptitude test, but being the natural salesman he is, he convinced them to hire him anyway.

Since that low-key start, Feldman has churned out books and tapes on sales techniques, lectured in nearly a dozen countries, and brought two sons into the business with him. Some of his techniques are masterful. If an executive passes word to Feldman that he is too busy to listen to a sales pitch, Feldman has been known to send in the secretary with five $100 bills and a request for five minutes. He has also lost his stage fright. At a recent MDRT meeting, a client of Feldman's agreed to join him on stage—if Feldman promised not to try to sell him more insurance. Feldman agreed. When they appeared together on stage, however, to discuss the merits of life insurance, Feldman promptly tried to sell him more.

The industry's hero-worship of Feldman goes beyond his income. It is not just the monetary success that has made him such a revered figure in the industry and within MDRT. He has a position in insurance history as one who changed the direction of MDRT and of insurance sales in general.

The level of sales required for membership had started at $1 million and rose only slowly as the years passed. Even in the early 1960s, the annual sales quota for MDRT membership was $1.2 million. After qualifying for three years, an agent became a life member. It was an easy pace and some members then went into semi-retirement, played golf three times a week, and earned a comfortable $35,000–$40,000 a year. They serviced their clients, sought few new ones, and watched the commissions from previous years' sales roll in. There were no more goals, no reasons to work ever harder, no value in performing for their peers. They had MDRT status forever; they'd found eternal life right here on earth.

Then Ben Feldman single-handedly changed the rules. In 1966 Feldman became the inspirational focus for the industry by standing up at an MDRT meeting in Boston and announcing that his sales goal for the year was $50 million. *Fifty million.* No one had ever dreamed such a level was possible, let alone made such a public declaration of intent. Since that time, MDRT requirements have been raised substantially, there are no more easy lifetime member-ships, and Top of the Table has set new goals for the top super-achievers.

Feldman is the final speaker this morning. As he stands, there is reverential silence in the room. You can almost feel the anticipation. What will his goal be this year? What tip will he have to double my income? Expectation mounts as he moves to the centre of the stage. Whispers fellow New York Life agent Serge Morel, of Montreal: "I couldn't believe it when I first met him. He was so—" he pauses, groping for the right word, "so simple," he says finally. "He makes more than the president of General Motors." Morel's awestruck face joins the masses turned towards the guru.

Someone drapes a microphone cord around Feldman's neck and he begins to speak. His posture is stooped, his voice low, almost inaudible, his speech afflicted with a lisp, his words halting as he begins by exalting partnership insurance. "If your partner dies," he says, "try going down to the bank to borrow the money [to buy his share]. The bulk of a man's income is earned income. If this stops, his income stops. Doesn't his family have a right to go on living?"

He then rambles on to the contentious issue of one-stop financial shopping and counselling the public. "Financial planning," he says drily. "They tell me it's coming." The hearty laughter in response is soon snuffed out. "Don't laugh. If you get into another man's backyard, you'll stub your toe." The audience, suitably chastised, listens intently again. He launches a series of bullets. "I'm a package salesman. Define the problem. Find the price tag." Then make the pitch. "I'm holding a million dollars for you. I'd like to have you as a client, then I'll look at the problem that you have. I'll serve you and solve those problems."

The members of the audience are not just hanging on his every word, they are memorizing them. They are thinking: *I* can be like him. *I* can make that much money. All that is stopping me is a new routine, some more effective prospecting techniques, just a few more ideas on how to overcome objections, and a little bit of luck. Suddenly, after eight brief minutes, the audience with the Pope of East Liverpool is over. It has been a strangely disappointing speech. Much of it was inaudible, the rest a disconnected collection of one-liners.

His listeners, however, are not about to say that the emperor has no clothes. You can't argue, after all, with results. As the breakfast session ends, the throbbing theme song from *Chariots of Fire* pours out of the room's speaker system. Feldman is mobbed on stage by about fifty from the audience. They look to be at the young end of the attendees, those seeing "the man" for the first time. For five minutes, he cannot move. He is trapped by admirers, a captive of his own success. He can only accept their congratulations and their adulation with a shy smile. He glances around to see if there is yet a clear path to the door, looking almost lost and baffled to be among them. They continue to come, wanting to press closer, to carry home his image, to touch his garments and tap his success like so many spouts driven into a maple tree in the spring.

Outside the hotel and across the street at the Ziegfeld Theatre, the movie *The Karate Kid* is about to open. The marquee announces: "He taught him the secret to karate lies in the mind and heart. Not in the hands." Ben Feldman's message precisely.

Tuesday's main-platform session at the Radio City Music Hall begins at eight-thirty with another heart-pumping audio-visual. As stills of a jogger flash before the audience, the baritone-voiced sound-track talks of blood, sweat, and tears. "The more you achieve, the more you want to achieve, the more you must achieve." The audio-visual is followed by ten dancers on stage in jogging outfits, belting out a song. The theme is "Go for the Gold." The lyrics are meant to uplift:

> This is my day to make it,
> to be all I can be.
> I am a winner—
> MDRT.

Then, just to show that the audience of life insurance agents shouldn't take themselves too seriously, the dancers are followed by flickering clips from a black-and-white Hollywood musical called *Gold Diggers of 1937*. Selected scenes show an insurance agents' convention with various company signs sprouting from the excited audience. The platform speaker in the film is whipping his audience into the same state of ecstasy as this modern audience achieved yesterday and wants to hit again today. "Get him so enthused about what life insurance can do for him," entreats actor Dick Powell, "that he can see himself lying in his grave." The film clip closes with all of them singing a rousing tune. The chorus could be every insurance agent's motto: "There'll be pie in the sky when you die."

Back to live entertainment, with two of the MDRT's senior citizens in a scripted presentation. Ben Silver, a New York Life agent from Oakland, Calif., and George McVety, an agent with Prudential Assurance Co. Ltd. of England, in Calgary. Both are in their seventies. Ben opens the dialogue talking of his father's early death with no insurance coverage. There is much head-shaking and some sympathetic tongue-clucking from the audience. "Eighteen years ago," announces Silver, "I licked cancer. The last eighteen years have been my most productive." There is a burst of applause. McVety leans over, touches Silver's arm, and says, "Ben, maybe we should all get cancer."

McVety then turns to the problem every agent faces, the one that, like cancer when it strikes, must be licked. The problem is the fear of failure. Everybody fails from time to time, he points out. "The Lord himself only got eleven out of twelve right." Ben allows how he wanted to quit six times in his first year of selling. He would be on the telephone or out knocking on the door of a prospect—all the while desperately hoping that no one would answer. McVety offers a piece of advice meant to help make the sale once a prospect has been confronted and the sales battle joined. "Everybody's talking about change," McVety points out, "but until somebody can stop people from dying, nothing has changed." Silver cites some other home truths to reassure the agents that what they do all day really matters: "I've never met a widow yet who felt her late husband had too much life insurance. It's too bad a man has to die before a widow and her children discover how insurance-poor you are. Money properly used is the root of all good."

McVety relates how in 1978 he was attending his company's sales meeting in Hawaii. He and three other agents were moaning to management about the lack of incentives for the top agents. It was July, they already had about $10 million in sales, and they said they would write $20 million if the company would send them on a world tour, fête them at a London banquet, and give them each a Patek Philippe watch. The company agreed until it discovered that a Patek Philippe can cost $6,000. A lower-priced watch was substituted. They met the target; the company paid. McVety goes on to point out that insurance agents don't need to retire at sixty-five. His largest sale came at seventy-two, with a premium of $1.8 million. There are appreciative whistles. (At that level, his commission would have been about 2 per cent, or $36,000.)

But the money doesn't matter, the contests are not relevant, says McVety. He claims what does make him happy is the legacy that he has created. "Hundreds of clients and their families will be provided for because I was an insurance man." Silver agrees and mentions his home in Rancho Mirage, near Palm Springs. It sits next door to Frank Sinatra's place. "How nice it would be," says Silver, "to have Sinatra say he lives next door to Silver." It is a cue for a song. Just then, in the orchestra pit, a pianist strikes a chord. Silver steps out to the lights at the edge of the stage and begins to sing "Young at Heart." His career as a singer, his drive to become better known than Sinatra, has been launched. Soon everyone is singing along with him because they all know that through insurance all things are possible. The auditorium, which has heard the best, resounds to the sound of 6,000 insurance agents singing, "Fairy tales can come true, it can happen to you, if you're young at heart."

The next speaker is Burt Meisel, an MDRT member with Connecticut Mutual Life in Southfield, Mich., who brings to the stage the unquestioned authority for human conduct: the Bible. He turns to the Book of Genesis and reads the story of Joseph. He interpreted the pharaoh's dream that predicted seven years of plenty to be followed by seven years of famine. Because of Joseph's prophecy, Egypt stored up grain in the good times and did not suffer in the bad. For the serious-minded agent, this is proof positive of the value and need for insurance. It is biblical backing for their role. Only a man of the cloth comes better equipped to serve—and all he has to offer is faith. An insurance agent has funds.

The remainder of the morning is taken up with a doctor talking about stress, an insurance company executive who describes insurance agents as missionaries because they sell a product associated with social benefit, self-denial, and even love. Finally, the wrap-up orator is a fire-and-brimstone Baptist preacher from Missouri. His opening: "I love being with winners. You're energizers." He further incites the audience, already at fever pitch from an emotional morning, by taking a few shots at the members of his own faith. "Baptists," he says, "don't make love standing up in case people think they're dancing." He tells the audience that just as they can bring on personal depression by sitting alone in a darkened room, they can pull themselves out of a depression, too. His theme is that they have worth as people, separate from their success. Success isn't the only way that society measures them or that they should measure themselves. He leaves them with this mantra of self-motivation ringing in their ears and raging in their hearts. "I am a person of some worth."

Two high-flying days down and two to come. Some, however, are still waiting to reach nirvana. What they want is a sign, a burning cross within that can keep the heat on all year. As the 6,000 mill about waiting for Wednesday sessions to begin, one Canadian attendee is comparing the New York gathering to recent annual meetings he has attended: "Others build, this one gives the unexpected. It hasn't reached a crescendo yet. It better happen today or it'll be flat on its ass."

If the first performer of the morning can't do it, no one can. Dennis Kelly, a non-member and a veteran of several other MDRT meetings, is a Chicago actor, entertainer, and whip-up artist. Accompanied by a pianist, he spends forty minutes on stage alternately stroking their egos and belting out upbeat songs. His blue suit coat is soon removed and the spotlight focusses on his blue shirt with white collar and red tie. He talks about his own family in a refrain that would be repetitive to anyone else but this audience: the family that buys life insurance finds heaven on earth. "Not only did my father love and care for his family during his lifetime," says Kelly, "he is still doing it after his death because of life insurance people like you." Kelly's father died three years ago. Just recently, his mother bought her second car and a time-sharing vacation arrangement, and—because of life insurance—"she is financially sound."

Kelly recalls an earlier MDRT meeting in 1978 in Honolulu: "There was a big heartbeat in the air." He has come back because, as he puts it, "if you're around frightened people, you'll be frightened, so you go with winners." Even when he gets depressed between meetings he claims that the memories of MDRT meetings have helped him realize that he can overcome disappointments on his own. "I have 6,000 friends who can share that sinking feeling of losing." He breaks into a song, another Sinatra tune, "That's Life." The words have been rewritten especially for his audience. "I'd roll myself up in a ball—" then a quick spoken aside "—make sure my premiums are paid up—and die."

He urges them to live for the future, not dwell in the past. He cites his father, who once told him: "Your past will eat you alive if you let it." By this time, his listeners are not just eating out of his hand, they are all but eating out of their own hands in their excitement. "Hold on to your dream," he shouts. "Tough problems don't last, but tough people do. I can soar like the eagles because of you. You have given me light. I will spread your spirit of commitment wherever I go." Then comes the invocation: "May God reward you handsomely." He closes with a song and receives an extended standing ovation.

The next speaker is from Glasgow, Scotland, and one of the 5 per cent of MDRT members who are women. After a mere three years in the business, Anne Gibbons has reached the pinnacle, Top of the Table, and has her own business with a staff of sixteen, including eight female associate agents. She is a vibrant woman wearing a tartan outfit who hasn't lost either the enthusiasm of her first year or the memory of her first sale, when she got so excited that she ran all the way home, leaving her car at the client's. She sold twenty policies in her first week on the job. She quotes Robbie Burns ("A man's a man for a' that") to show that everyone is approachable because everyone is cast from the same mould, and Henry Ford ("You can do anything if you have enthusiasm").

The next president, Toronto's Ron Barbaro, is introduced to the agents. A life insurance agent for thirty years, he was a success from the start. His first calendar year's sales were high enough to catapult him into the MDRT. He is a life member of MDRT and a charter member of Top of the Table. At the same time, he has travelled widely and addressed more than 450,000 sales people in every province, forty-nine of the fifty states, and fourteen other countries. He is a partner in his own firm, Win-Bar Insurance Brokers Ltd. In addition to the zoo and the Santa Parade rescue effort, his civic involvements include being past president of the Italo-Canadian Club and co-chairman of the Canadian Association of Chiefs of Police Research Foundation of Ontario; he is a board member of Ronald McDonald Houses of Canada Foundation and the Canadian National Exhibition Association. He is married with three children.

Barbaro parks his five-foot-10½-inch frame in front of the double microphone on the stage, glances at the prompter, looks out at the audience, and offers up his opening line after his coronation as their president: "I want to thank everyone who voted for me." His voice is high-pitched, like a night-club comic's. His manner is exuberant and infectious as he points to the reason most members attend: "We draw energy from each other." Making sales isn't enough, he says, urging the audience to spend time in community and charitable work and with family. To make the point, he introduces his father and his wife, who are in the audience.

He touts both life insurance agents and the product. "We have become an indispensable part of our clients' lives. It is no coincidence that life insurance is a product only of the free world. MDRT is the United Nations of the insurance world." He talks about the possibilities of teleconferencing so that international members who can't afford to attend can at least watch the proceedings live. "Let us hang a sign in the member countries," he concludes: "MDRT spoken here."

The previous president, Paul Buckley, who is cool and collected where Barbaro is hot and hurtling, thanks Barbaro. "Ron is Ron is Ron," he says, shaking his head. "Toronto has survived many disasters, natural and man-made. I wonder if it will survive Ron Barbaro."

The next platform guest held up for emulation is a twelve-year-old girl. Markita Andrews of New York has sold the most Girl Scout cookies, as she tells the group, "in all human history up until now." When she was six, she sold 600 boxes. In 1983, she sold 5,000 boxes. Half-way through 1984, her total is more than 17,000 boxes. Walt Disney Productions has made an eleven-minute motivational sales film about her, calling her "the Cookie Kid." She is everything this audience wanted to be at her age. "I'm only twelve," she begins. "I'm too young to drive, but I'm not too young to believe in the free enterprise system."

She is an accomplished speaker and carries off her part with poise. She passes on her sales tips to much applause. "I do what has to be done to make the doing do-able. I know my product, I set a goal, I go where my customers are." She has a rejection rate that would make any grown agent weep: only about one in an estimated 1,100 potential customers says no. "Rejection isn't defeat," she tells them with all the authority of a psychiatrist, "it's a temporary set-back." She commiserates with her audience, telling them that like insurance agents, she suffers the slings and arrows of jokes from her customers. She relates a typical example that she has heard dozens of times: "Are you a Brownie selling cookies or are you a cookie selling brownies?"

Ben Feldman climbs the stairs at the front of the stage. The two shake hands near the footlights and stand looking at each other for a moment in mutual admiration. Their greeting is treated as a historic moment, as if a commemorative postage stamp should be issued to mark the occasion. This is the legend meeting the legacy. The free enterprise fraternity has heirs, selling has continuity, Markita and youngsters like her will be the MDRT members of tomorrow. Feldman asks her, "Have you ever thought of selling insurance?" Then, rhetorically: "Aren't we both in the people-helping business?" Then they get down to the business they're both in: sales. On behalf of the attendees (each has unwittingly paid $2, hidden in the registration fee), Feldman purchases a box of cookies for everyone. It is a new record for Markita—6,000 boxes. (Even that is not enough. Later, in the exhibition area, where attendees are to pick up their boxes, Markita is autographing boxes—and selling more on the spot.)

Thursday. The final day opens with more dancers and singing. The process has become as common as morning coffee. The first speaker is Ty Boyd, a professional motivational speaker from North Carolina. He runs out onto the stage when introduced and gives a rebel yell. "Yeeeeeow!" he warbles. "We're pretty high, but we haven't made the summit yet." He urges more professionalism among agents, saying, "If they arrested you today for being a pro at what you do, would there be enough evidence to convict you?" In his view, religious overtones help. "There's got to be an evangelical feeling about what you do." He warns them of the enemy within, the personal one that causes professional failure. "I look in the mirror and I don't see my best friend, I see my worst enemy." He urges them to make clients feel important, by asking questions and listening attentively. "Lots of salespeople I know only speak in a whisper, ask lots of questions—and cash big cheques."

The next two speakers get deeper into the dark side of the business—defining and dealing with success. Tom Costello, a former football player with the New York Giants and now a manager agent with Home Life Insurance in New York, admits that injuries kept him from success in pro ball. He discovered life insurance while sitting at the back of a hotel hall listening to—who else?—Ben Feldman. Costello even does a more-than-passable imitation of Feldman's lisping whisper. "Who's thirty years old?" he quotes

Feldman saying that day at the hotel presentation. "If you give me three cents I'll give you a dollar." People actually came forward as if he were Ernest Angley out on a crusade to collect money and cure cancer. "Who's forty?" Feldman continued. "Who's got four cents—come on up here." More left their seats throwing pennies and nickels at him. Said Feldman, "I just sell money. That's all I do. Wanna give me a nickel, I'll give you a dollar."

Finally, Costello asked someone what was going on. He was told the speaker was the greatest life insurance salesman in the world. "That's the business for me," he declared. He was a quick success, but he was soon selling to the exclusion of everything else. Holidays were punctuated with phone calls to the office. Even the fishermen in Nantucket, where he vacationed, were prospects. "The higher I got on the roof," he said, "the harder it was to keep on dancing." He discovered that it was too difficult to be number one because there was always someone better coming along. "Don't fret about copping life's grand awards," he concluded. "Enjoy the small pleasures. Live today as if there is no tomorrow."

The same theme is taken up by the next speaker. His presentation turns into the tear-jerker of the week. The speaker is Wayne Cotton, a North American Life agent who works out of Edmonton, with red hair and a neatly trimmed red beard. "We've become a competitive race in so many ways. Ego gratification, competition, and recognition are the driving forces that sometimes push us blindly ahead." Be an achiever, be a leader, he tells them, but "at what personal cost?"

His own personal cost was staggering. In 1980, he had been selling insurance for twelve years. In ten years, he had taken ten days' vacation, once going seven years without a day off. Saturdays he'd work until three, Sundays he'd be back at the office by ten in the morning. He was managing eleven people in three companies, giving numerous speeches, publishing marketing presentations, and serving as president of two organizations. His medical problems mounted. Between 1977 and 1981, he had a series of five stress-related problems: nerves, stomach disorders, blood pressure, headaches, and back problems. "I lived on prescription pain-killers for a year and a half just so I could keep walking." His blood pressure soared to 150/100, a rate that meant a twenty-year reduction in life expectancy for a man his age. All the while, he was receiving plaques and accolades for his achievements.

Suddenly, in November 1980, "I blew a fuse." He ran a two-day meeting and afterwards could not even recall being there. "I was totally burned out." His financial planning was in disorder. He lost $80,000 in investments in 1979, more in 1980. "My plans to be a hero in this business hadn't included any of this." Personal bankruptcy was suggested but he refused. He had no cash flow, so he shut down his business and sold his house. "I had several legal hassles, no real assets, and I owed a small fortune."

He had no choice but to start over. He convinced his creditors to give him more time, opened an office with one secretary, and bought an 1,100-square-foot condominium with a $500 post-dated cheque and a large second mortgage. He and his wife began to go out for breakfast together, talking over problems, seeking solutions. He stopped working evenings. His blood pressure went down, the headaches and back problems disappeared, he spent more time with his family and even wrote some poetry. Meanwhile, his production went up and he was able to pay off his debts. When the second mortgage came due, he was able to retire it with excess cash flow from the business that month.

"Achievement is important, but at what personal cost? Life is for excellence—but excellence is living life fully, having a total experience, not just a superficial high from one part of your life. You can't be number one forever. Everyone must someday walk out of the spotlight. It is those who lead a balanced existence who have the most satisfying lives in the end. The whole-person concept is important." In 1982, he and his family moved to Kelowna, B.C., 800 kilometres from his office in Edmonton. He now works twenty-six weeks a year at his Edmonton firm, Cotton Planning Services Ltd. He commutes to Edmonton by air and spends three-day weekends in Kelowna.

In 1983 he worked 100 days, gave speeches on 85 days, and took 180 days classified as days off for holidays—including thirty-four long weekends and nine weeks off. "If you're too busy to take a holiday," says Cotton, "God'll give you one you hadn't counted on." Kelowna is a place to relax, ski with his family (he hadn't skied with them in seventeen years), and go fishing. "I've got clients and relatives who don't even know I live there. I don't sell any life insurance in Kelowna. I am there to enjoy."

He describes his business life now as one that is on automatic pilot. "I haven't called on a new prospect for four years." His philosophy: try to be better than you are, but at fewer things. "Some say I'm semi-retired—others say I'm semi-retarded. And what do I care—I'm doing my own thing! And guess what's happened to my production? It has gone up and up!" He closes with the story of a man who spent a Sunday morning with his four-year-old daughter as she drew him a butterfly. The child died suddenly within the next twenty-four hours. The child was Cotton's.

A slide flashes onto the giant screen behind him. It is a photograph of the butterfly. Cotton himself wears a butterfly ring. "Practise family time," he says. "They will not always be with you." The tear-jerking tale underlines his message against workaholic behaviour. He has even come to terms with her death. He recalls what his dead daughter gave him: "I could have never loved as much," he concluded, "if you never came."

He receives a rousing ovation. As he joins the honoured guests in the front row of the theatre, there is much back-slapping. Audio and video tapes are available of all speeches. The most popular is Cotton's. It remained on back order for months.

The emotions continue to build as John Amatt tells the audience of the 1982 Canadian assault on Mt. Everest, the mountain where one man dies for every two who reach the top. It is a tale of teamwork, overcoming impossible conditions, and eventual success. Powerful music and a slick slide show heighten the presentation's effect. "When a climber stands on the summit," says Amatt, "all men and women in the world stand with him." But there is a metaphor in all of this for life insurance agents, he says. "Everest is a plateau that, once attained, allows you to see the next plateau. Everest is the beginning of the future, not the end of the past. The answer is to remember what we felt on the heights when we are down in the valleys. We all have the potential to stand proudly on the summit of our lives."

The week closes with a return visit from the Harlem Boys Choir, singing "Climb Every Mountain." Dozens of agents involved in producing and organizing the show are waved onto the stage and introduced. There are handshakes, high-fives, and hugs all around. With the entire audience raised to a fever pitch, the convention ends and the stage empties. As he walks down the aisle, Ron Barbaro greets a friend. "Well," he says, "how do you like showbiz?" All of those swept up in the week's religious fervour could only reply: Amen.

CHAPTER FIVE

OVER THE RAINBOW

North American Life Assurance Co.

A T THE 1981 annual meeting of the Million Dollar Round Table, three dozen special guests were introduced, about half of them chief executive officers from the largest life insurance companies in North America. Among those assembled on the movable platform that would rise to the level of the stage to the tumultuous applause of the 5,000 gathered to honour them were two Canadians, Drew McCaughey, president and chief executive officer of North American Life Assurance Co., and Earl Orser, president and chief executive officer of London Life Insurance Co. As they rose along with the others into the spotlight on the stage, McCaughey turned to Orser and said with some amazement in his voice, "Who'd ever have thought that we'd end up in the life insurance business?" Orser could only shake his head in disbelieving agreement.

Who, indeed. The two had varying backgrounds in finance (including some time together at Canadian Marconi Co.), and both were newcomers to insurance. Orser had joined London Life in 1978, McCaughey had joined North American in 1980. Yet both companies had turned to outside hands for the same reason. The companies had run out of steam and needed outsiders to come in and give them a competitive kick-start. The two were joined in the industry by a third outsider, Robert Bandeen, who left his position as president of Canadian National in 1982 to become chairman, president, and chief executive officer of Crown Life Insurance Co. The three have put the once-sleepy business on its ear. In the industry, the three are still referred to as "the new boys."

Until their arrival, the industry had been dominated by unimaginative number-crunching actuaries who tended to freeze out new

97

ideas. Insurance, critics said, was an industry in a coma, run by museum curators who enclosed products in glass cases and did not allow updating, as if preservation of past methods was sufficient to guarantee success forever. They did not know that they needed to be like gardeners, pruning old ways and planting new ideas to maintain vitality and growth in the years ahead.

Andrew Gilmour McCaughey's fresh attitude towards change and growth was typical of the three new boys. "I've spent my life trying to make Canadian companies compete world-wide. If we don't do that, we'll be a banana republic." One result of his world-wide travel and deal-making is that he can get by in French and Italian. His company, North American, has 900 sales agents and managers in Canada, 362 in the U.S., assets of $2.9 billion, and $31.3 billion in insurance in force. Of that $31.3 billion, fully $7.7 billion is in group insurance sold primarily through direct mail to various industry association members and alumni from particular universities.

His manner, even at sixty-three, remains boyish. At table, with friends, he is an entertaining companion. As befits his Irish ancestry, he can tell a story, often a ribald one, with verve and style, employing dialects and accents ranging from Bronx cabbie through north-of-England housewife to Mafia don. Typical is a story he likes about a man who was going on a world cruise and was told to be sure to try the seafood delicacy scrod. Throughout the tour, he never found it. Finally, after he returned, he asked the taxi driver in desperation as he left the ship in New York: "Where can I get scrod?" "Buddy," replied the driver, "I've been asked that question a thousand times, but I've never been asked it in the past pluperfect subjunctive."

McCaughey's personal motto is: "I'd rather fight than lie." No one need worry that McCaughey will ever be reticent with his opinions. The first year he joined North American, for example, the perk for top-selling agents was a working trip to Hawaii. McCaughey went and was not impressed by the islands. He's been back once but has vowed never to return, as he puts it, "to drink dishwater and eat pork fat at a luau." As a former accountant and financial officer, his assessment of his knowledge of the North American Life balance sheet is equally blunt: "I don't understand the numbers." Even so, McCaughey has reshaped North American in his own image, merged it with another company, and taken it from twelfth to sixth, as measured by value of Canadian individual life insurance sales.

McCaughey was born in Montreal in 1922 and graduated from McGill with a degree in commerce. During the war, he flew Wellingtons and Warwicks out of England, Scotland, and North Africa, usually on convoy patrols or air-sea rescue missions. He knows that the military taught many from his generation the skills for business, but he thinks many were sent home with a misguided view of the world, believing "somebody up there will solve my problem." As a deputy squadron commander, McCaughey learned a different life lesson. He flew with a crew of six and learned organization and self-discipline. "You don't have to like the people you work with, or have them like you," he says, "but you have to have their respect."

He qualified as a chartered accountant in 1950 with Clarkson, Gordon & Co., then spent fourteen years with Canadian Marconi Co., rising to executive vice-president for finance and administration. He joined the Molson Companies Ltd. in 1967 as vice-president for finance, later becoming senior vice-president for finance, with responsibility for strategic planning and corporate development. During his thirteen years there, he put together about ten acquisitions for the burgeoning company, including the purchases of Beaver Lumber and Diversey Corp. He sold companies as well. "Selling," he has often said since, "is harder than buying." Still, there was overall, diversified growth. When he joined, sales were $150 million, all in beer. When he left, the companies he'd helped acquire had pushed total sales to $1.6 billion, less than half in beer.

In appearance, he bears an uncanny resemblance to the actor John Forsythe, one of the stars of the television soap opera *Dynasty*. McCaughey is constantly battling with his weight, which can climb a few pounds over 200 if he is not watchful of his diet. On his five-foot-ten frame, he prefers to keep it close to 180. He is always impeccably dressed, favouring blue suits and blue-striped shirts to match his blue eyes. "My wife," he laughs, "says I was born wearing a shirt and tie."

His home is in the west-end Toronto suburb of Etobicoke, on a quiet crescent. He lives there with his second wife (he was divorced) and three cats. Of the three children from his first marriage, only one, a boy, is still at home. His backyard runs into a ravine with a spring-fed creek so clean and deep that it serves as a swimming hole.

McCaughey's salary is typical of the industry, in the $200,000–$225,000 range annually, depending on the company's performance.

His net worth, however, exceeds that of most of his colleagues. In addition to his North American role, he is also chairman of Canadian Foundation Co. Ltd., a construction company with $130 million in annual sales. He holds shares worth $2.7 million, although a loan to purchase the stock means that it is, in his words, "highly leveraged."

McCaughey has broad interests and hobbies, everything from photography and carpentry to opera and shooting. For years, he used a shotgun that he "paid $15 for when I was eleven, or $11 when I was fifteen, I can never remember which." In 1983 his wife surprised him by asking for a shotgun for herself. He presented her with an over-and-under 20-gauge Browning. While he was scouting the racks for her gift, he treated himself to a 12-gauge Browning. After some trap-shooting practice together, the two of them went after grouse and pheasant in the fall of 1984 at a lodge in northern Wales near Mount Snowdon. He is a sailor and owns a CS27, moored at the toniest sailing club in the city, the Royal Canadian Yacht Club, where initiation dues are $8,000.

The first approach to McCaughey to join North American came when he was at Molson's. A head-hunter had been retained to seek out a successor to president David Pretty, who was nearing retirement. Pretty was a long-time employee who had joined the firm in 1947 as a securities analyst. He had added some new blood to the executive, but not enough. Among the recruits was Lloyd Kirk, now fifty-two, who joined in 1975 as agency vice-president to help boost lagging sales. The company had had five years with meagre or even negative growth. By comparison, Commercial Union, where Kirk had been deputy director of agencies, was expanding at rates of 15 to 20 per cent a year.

Kirk split Canadian and U.S. sales under executives Ted Hill and Dick Crawford respectively, and a new and competitive term policy was introduced. Over the next eight years, branches across Canada were cut from fifty-seven to forty-three. They were also assigned more gung-ho managers. When Kirk joined, the average branch manager was earning only $25,000. Kirk built a fire under all of them. "If they didn't want to double their income, I didn't want them around." Training was improved and the results followed. Over the last ten years, North American's annual sales increases have usually been twice the industry average. Today, a branch manager earns $75,000.

As Pretty was coming to the end of his career, the directors realized there was no obvious heir inside, so they looked elsewhere. For his part, McCaughey responded to the challenge. "I thought it would be a good idea to roll up my sleeves and start over." He had seven years to go before normal retirement at Molson's and because the CEO at the time was three years younger than he was, McCaughey knew he wasn't likely to get the job. As for North American—well, like many firms in that field at the time, "it wasn't a very big company; it wasn't very exciting—but the prospects were."

McCaughey went through three months of interviews, even submitting to psychological testing for the first time since he had joined Canadian Marconi almost three decades earlier. The tester gave McCaughey a high score. "Apparently," quips McCaughey, "I bamboozled him enough." When he joined North American in 1980, his ignorance of life insurance was both an advantage and a disadvantage. "I can't sell something unless I believe in it," he says. "I can't believe in it unless I understand it. So it took a while to get my arms around it and say: do I want this?" As a result, it wasn't really until 1982 that McCaughey began to make the changes he wanted. When he did, his ignorance of tradition was beneficial. "As a new person in the industry, I didn't have any beliefs or understandings of what you can or cannot do."

At first, McCaughey was not universally welcomed. When he joined, he was fifty-seven, yet the announcement to staff stated that he would be fifty-eight on his next birthday. It was as if the message was: don't worry, he's only going to be around seven years, then he'll be retiring. A few months later, McCaughey was addressing a large group of staff and picked up the theme, mentioning that he had seven years to achieve his goals. Came a voice from the back of the room: "Six years and nine months." Still, he recalls, "nobody wanted me to fall on my face."

He was a breath of fresh air. Pretty had run a consensus-style firm where nothing too unusual happened. "It was a predictable style," says Lloyd Kirk, who was promoted to the position of senior vice-president a month before McCaughey arrived. "Drew didn't unnerve us, but he asked fundamental questions that nobody had asked before." Little wonder. Even with the improvements put in place in the recent past, McCaughey was aghast at what he found at

North American. At the time he joined, he told a friend, "Nobody knew the meaning of the word profit. Nobody realized that it took more than actuaries to run a life insurance company."

North American was founded in 1881. After six months, the first two employees added a third, an office boy, Thomas Bradshaw, who was paid $5 a month. He later became president, in 1928. Like many presidents of his day, he was a remote man. Once, he decided that he should improve communications with his wife. They would, he announced, bring to each other's attention any petty grievances they had before the small problems became large ones. Bradshaw began the process by citing a lengthy list. It was so long that when his wife's turn came, she could only say, "Thomas, I have nothing to say—you are perfect."

As the business grew, North American expanded into the U.S., but the move backfired because the offices were too distant to be managed properly. The office in Illinois, for example, had to be closed in 1933 when North American discovered that its agents there were, in fact, working for three different insurance companies, not to mention running real estate rackets and sending in phoney applications approved by fake doctors. At times, the agents even doubled as applicants themselves in order to meet quotas and earn commissions.

Until 1962 the company was on King Street in downtown Toronto. Part of the offices included a dark third-floor walkway that connected two buildings. It was known as "the Bridge of Sighs" and was a great place for practical jokes. Some were quite macabre. One time, a tailor's dummy was rigged up in a dark corner so that when someone tripped over it, the dummy would fall and spill red ink. The downtown locations have meant lucrative land deals for North American. The firm owned the Piccadilly Hotel at the east side of the offices, purchased in 1946 for $146,000. It was sold in 1969 to Olympia & York for First Canadian Place for $1.6 million. North American still has a 25-per-cent share of the property. Annual revenues are not made public, but the project cost $200 million. Olympia & York estimates that today the land alone is worth that much and that the building would cost $800 million to duplicate.

North American's current office on Adelaide Street West is its sixth headquarters. The firm has been there since 1962. The brass and glass doors on the second floor, where the executives work, are from the earlier King Street building. They will probably be carted north in 1986, when North American moves to the suburbs of Toronto. North American and Xerox Canada Realty Inc. are building a $200-million joint-venture development in North York. Phase one is a twenty-four-storey office tower with twenty-three retail stores as part of the office complex and thirty residential units in separate buildings.

Shortly after McCaughey arrived, Dick Crawford left to head Maritime Life. Rather than using an employment agency, McCaughey gathered names from his senior people. He approached the half-dozen candidates himself. One was Jacques Deschenes, vice-president and actuary of Sun Life in Wellesley Hills, Mass. McCaughey had dinner with him one Friday night, liked him immediately, and offered him the job two days later. "Within nine days of the announcement of Dick's departure, I had a notice up on the board announcing that Jacques was coming. I had just joined and it was important that I got the message out that no one was irreplaceable. Anyone who wanted to leave could do so."

He didn't have the same success with board appointments. Once, he sent along to the nominating committee the name of someone he thought would make an excellent director. Word was sent back: "No friends of the president, please." The board was more receptive to his changing strategies. McCaughey had planned originally to broaden North American by putting it into new financial services areas through acquisition and merger; however, expansion has not been as rapid as he had hoped. Although he has added some staff at the senior level, he found North American did not have the resources he needed for his grand plan. Second, he decided that North American should do one thing well—sell life insurance—rather than head out in all directions. As he puts it in his inimitable and blunt style: "One thing we don't want is a whorehouse in Venezuela." Translation: he doesn't want to own a business just because it's profitable; it must have some relationship with the core business of life insurance. Still, he admits some disappointment. "I thought I'd do more than I've done. I'm not broadening this company, I'm making it narrower. Does that disappoint the board [of directors]? No. We've taken them through the logic of it. We're not big. We'll never be number one— but we can be number one in quality."

Because McCaughey doesn't understand all the corporate

numbers and accounting mumbo-jumbo that go into a life insurance company such as North American, senior vice-president and actuary Ted Hill is his right-hand man. McCaughey calls him "the guardian, the conscience of the company. As the actuary, he is in charge of ensuring that the company will be around long enough to pay all claims." What he did understand was how to run a business and how to draw talent from people. After a dozen take-overs, he knows how to get what he wants and leave people with their honour, feeling that they've won, too. McCaughey rejected the idea of improving the bottom line by making large cuts in employment at North American. He had no appetite for hacking people out. Victor Koby, who worked with McCaughey at Molson, remains a close friend today. "People have a picture of a senior executive as a distant, terrifying individual at one end of the room. He puts you right in the living room." Adds Koby, "There's a saying: show me a man who has no enemies and I'll show you a man who hasn't succeeded. It isn't true of Drew. He's left a trail of friends." In fact, when he turned sixty in 1982, McCaughey's wife, Lorraine, organized a party for him at the Toronto Club for about sixty people. A few had been on the other side of negotiating tables. The evening became a love-in as guests rose to speak, unscheduled, in praise of McCaughey.

As McCaughey set out to expand North American, four companies were studied closely by a management team looking both at how North American's business would fit with the acquired company and at the "chemistry" of the people managing both. By January 1983, The Monarch Life Assurance Co. of Winnipeg had been spotted as a prime candidate. It was strong in individual life insurance business in Canada (the core business North American had decided it wanted to be in); its geographic strength in western Canada balanced North American's Ontario and Quebec markets. Adding Monarch to North American would increase both assets and life insurance in force by about 25 per cent and almost double the number of sales agents.

North American had no inside access to financial information at Monarch. All of the scrutiny was done with public financial statements. Although there were no apparent signs that any other company was interested in buying Monarch, McCaughey was worried that someone would get there before he did. Monarch was owned by CanWest Capital Corp., a Winnipeg-based holding company run by chairman I. H. (Izzy) Asper and vice-chairman Gerald Schwartz.

CanWest had been formed in 1977 with the financial backing of the Canada Development Corp., the Toronto-Dominion Bank, and Great-West Life. It had bought a number of companies, including Na-Churs International Ltd., a U.S. fertilizer company with $50 million in sales, Global Television, Crown Trust, the Canadian retail chain MacLeod Steadman Inc., and Monarch. CanWest had recently sold Crown Trust and might, McCaughey assumed, be ready to sell off more of its parts. McCaughey was also well aware that former CanWest executive Don Payne had recently joined Crown Life as executive vice-president. Payne, McCaughey surmised, might be recommending that Crown Life buy Monarch.

Any move on the Monarch acquisition was delayed for a few days by the Ontario government's seizure on January 7, 1983, of Crown Trust. The province, worried that the depositors and shareholders of Crown Trust were at risk because of the firm's entanglement in a complex real estate scandal, moved to expropriate Crown and other firms, seize the assets, and run the companies. The following Wednesday, January 12, North American submitted an offer to the Ontario government to manage the seized companies. While McCaughey was aware that current legislation did not normally allow such intermingling (a mutual life insurance company could only own 30 per cent of a trust company), he felt it was his duty to step forward and at least make the helpful offer to wind the companies down, dispose of assets as required, and do a management job.

By then, former federal superintendent of insurance Dick Humphrys had been called in by the Ontario government to oversee Crown Trust's future. It was Humphrys who told McCaughey that North American would not be involved. Said Humphrys, "I don't want to see the government forced to see a life company get into the trust business on an emergency basis. Thanks for the offer, but we'll look for another home for [Crown]." McCaughey turned back to Monarch, knowing that Crown Life was likely looking at Crown Trust as well. Crown Trust would have been a perfect vehicle for president Bob Bandeen's acquisition strategy—not even the name would change. Because Crown was a stock company, there were no restrictions on its owning a trust company. Bandeen could have bought Crown Trust through Crownx, the holding company that owned Crown Life, thus satisfying Humphrys's concern that a life company not be an emergency owner.

Then word reached McCaughey that Crown Life would not be

getting Crown Trust. That made him more concerned about Monarch. If Crown Life had been ready to buy *something*, went McCaughey's thinking, Crown might quickly turn its attention to another company just to satisfy the itch. Payne would likely point to Monarch. McCaughey thought he received further proof of his theory Friday, January 21. He had been at Canadian Foundation's office in the Toronto Star building on Yonge Street, near the waterfront. As he rode the elevator down, a man got on the elevator on the floor housing Extendicare Ltd., Crown Financial's nursing home operation. The man was lugging a stuffed satchel.

"Quite a load you've got there," commented McCaughey to the stranger. "Yeah," came the reply, "no rest for me this weekend." McCaughey's worst fears were confirmed. He concluded that Crown was on the acquisition warpath, probably for Monarch. He returned to his office and put out the order to senior management: "I want an offer on the table by Wednesday."

The take-over team went into overdrive. As with all such potential offers, both the intended company and the deal itself were given code names. Monarch became known as Leo because its logo was a lion. Not a very imaginative selection, perhaps, but it allowed discussion to continue and documents to be typed without revealing the target to eavesdroppers or office staff. At this stage of any take-over, the plotters become almost paranoid about leaks. They hope that no one else is looking longingly at the same target, and they don't want to tip anyone off that they themselves are, either. Another bidder only confuses things and jacks up the price. McCaughey didn't want a bidding war.

On Tuesday, January 25, the work almost done and the offering letter in its final stages of drafting, McCaughey telephoned Asper in Winnipeg to let him know that an offer was coming. "I have no desire to sell Monarch," replied Asper. "You've really upset me." Asper knew, however, that he could not reject an offer out of hand on his own. "We do have other shareholders," he said. "I'll have to take it to my board."

Asper was distraught. He put down the phone and walked into the adjoining office occupied by his president, Gerald Schwartz. While he was intrigued that someone was about to put a price on his company, he also had no interest in selling it. Schwartz did. "We had differing philosophies of what CanWest should do," recalls Schwartz. "He wanted an ever-larger CanWest. I was interested in managing the rate of return and getting money back to the share-holders. Izzy felt emotional about the subject. He was committed to helping build Winnipeg." They agreed, however, that they would await the written offer and take it to the board of directors.

There were still some final details to be set, among them the price. North American had previously decided on a bidding range for Monarch—$55 million to $65 million. The night before the offer was delivered, the take-over team gathered one last time in the boardroom beside McCaughey's office. On hand were McCaughey, three senior vice-presidents—Lloyd Kirk, Ted Hill and Tom Inglis—as well as vice-president Brian Moore. McCaughey wanted to bid $55 million. The rest urged an opening bid of $60 million. McCaughey pointed out that there appeared to be no other bidder. After further debate, McCaughey agreed to go in at $60 million. The offer was delivered Thursday.

On Monday, January 31, Asper was no more in favour of selling than he'd been before. He phoned McCaughey to let him know that a CanWest board meeting had been scheduled for later in the week. He also added: "You ruined my weekend." Asper worried that if Ottawa did not approve any deal eventually agreed to, then not only had a lot of time been wasted, but Monarch would have become "damaged goods."

The CanWest board met to consider the offer on Wednesday evening. The meeting, which began at six, lasted six hours. The Monarch investment, all agreed, had paid off handsomely. CanWest had bought Monarch in 1978 for $32 million in a leveraged buy-out, where the revenues of Monarch were used to reduce the debt CanWest took on. CanWest had put up only $6 million and financed the remaining $26 million. Monarch dividends had paid the interest and reduced the amount owing to $22 million. Asper's argument to the board was that CanWest was earning $5 million a year on its $6-million investment, an 83-per-cent return on its money. "Where are we going to earn that kind of money?" he asked.

Schwartz looked at the numbers differently. North American was offering $60 million. If that offer were pushed a bit higher, say to the mid-sixties, and the debt of $22 million paid off, CanWest would have made $40 million on its original investment of $6 million in four years. While Asper saw the earnings as $5 million a year on a $6-million investment, or an 83-per-cent return, Schwartz pointed out that if the deal went through, CanWest would have $40 million to invest. Based on that amount, the $5 million in earnings was only a 12.5-per-cent return on their money. Recalls Schwartz, "I wanted to get at the $40 million."

Among those consulted by the board was Harold Thompson, president of Monarch. He spent thirty minutes answering the board's questions. No member asked him the key question: should CanWest sell? If any board member had, he would have said no. Said Thompson later, "Nobody likes to see a company that they have been associated with for a long time appear to disappear." During his dozen years as president, Thompson had built Monarch from nineteen branch offices to thirty-seven, increased the number of agents from 120 to 415, seen the average income of those agents grow from a range of $10,000–$15,000 per year to $40,000 per year, and overseen a twelvefold growth in the company. The company was founded in 1904 and began selling insurance in 1906. It was largely rural-oriented until Thompson took over. During the next decade, Monarch's sales growth was among the top three in the country. In 1983, after the company had been selling insurance for seventy-seven years, it sold more than $1 billion in insurance, more in a single year than it had had in force after its first sixty-seven years.

When the meeting began, Asper and perhaps two other directors among the ten CanWest directors favoured hanging on to Monarch. In the end, however, only Asper voted against the offer. The hands-up vote was nine-to-one in favour of selling to North American. Asper then asked if CanWest would allow him to buy Monarch, but he put a number of conditions on the sale, including a lower purchase price than North American might negotiate. Fearing the appearance of favouritism, the board worried that it should not sell to Asper, already involved in CanWest, at a lower price. Schwartz was dispatched to do a deal with North American, at a higher price than the first bid. While some members suggested various numbers he might aim for, their main advice was simple: close the deal.

North American's offer was good until 4:30 P.M. Friday, February 4. While Asper tried unsuccessfully to find backers in Winnipeg to join him in a bid, Schwartz met with the most likely other interested buyer, Crown Life chief executive officer Robert Bandeen, in Bandeen's Toronto office Friday morning. Crown was interested, the price mentioned was not too different from North American's, but Schwartz concluded that Crown was not far enough along in its study of Monarch and would take some time to prepare an offer. He decided his best deal was with North American.

Schwartz and McCaughey met for lunch at twelve-fifteen Friday in McCaughey's boardroom, the same second-floor room where the price had been set ten days earlier. McCaughey accurately assumed he was the only bidder, but he cautioned Schwartz not to use North American's bid to flush more interested parties out of the bushes. Said McCaughey, "If you want to shop it, our deal is off the table." Only North American was in the running, so Schwartz could readily agree that there would be no auction.

Schwartz had positions of his own to lay out. McCaughey was unaware of the board vote, but did assume that Schwartz was authorized to negotiate. Still, Schwartz spent some time at the beginning of the meeting telling McCaughey at length about Monarch and describing its worth and position in glowing detail. Says McCaughey, "My reading was that he was there to do the deal and get the price up as high as he could." The two men conducted the negotiations alone.

McCaughey had expected to hear some complimentary descriptives. After all, Asper had already expressed great reluctance to sell, a stance that McCaughey assumed was meant to increase the selling price. "I was cynical," recalls McCaughey of Asper's position. "I thought he was posturing." In the end, when he heard of the board vote and the eventual split between Schwartz and Asper, with each going his own way, McCaughey realized that there had been some fundamental differences over how to proceed with CanWest.

One of the offer's features was a commitment by North American that the merged company would maintain a Winnipeg presence and employment levels. While at the time, Monarch had about 225 people in Winnipeg, McCaughey's commitment was not to keep that specific number but to ensure that the only reductions would be proportionate to cuts in Toronto. In other words, if staff were cut at North American by 10 per cent across the board in the future, such cuts would apply to Winnipeg, too. In fact, over the next two years, employment in Winnipeg grew to 260.

In addition to describing Monarch in glowing terms, Schwartz also claimed that McCaughey did not have his own board's backing to negotiate the purchase. A regular meeting of the North American board of directors was set for ten days away. Schwartz wanted the deal concluded (including Ottawa's approval) within sixty days, and he wanted that written into the offer.

More important than the timing, however, was the price. Schwartz told McCaughey, "You're not going to be the buyer at that price." By that time, the two had moved next door into McCaughey's office. McCaughey left his office, discussed price with the others, and returned to up the ante by $2 million to $62 million. They agreed to negotiate the next day, and the offer was extended to 4:30 P.M., Saturday. Schwartz left to report to a CanWest executive committee meeting in the nearby TD Centre. McCaughey showered and changed at the office and took his wife and some friends to a black-tie dance at the Royal Canadian Yacht Club. Although he didn't arrive home until two in the morning, he was back in the office at nine to prepare for Schwartz's arrival at eleven o'clock.

Schwartz had rejected the $62 million; McCaughey added another $3 million and by two-thirty, they had agreed to $68 million (a figure that included $3 million in interest, the amount the $65 million would have earned from January 1 to closing). McCaughey hoped to have the loose ends tied up quickly and the deal typed and signed, because he and his wife were expected at the house of a friend who had just bought a house thirty minutes west of Toronto on the Niagara Escarpment. The McCaugheys had been invited for dinner but were to arrive in the afternoon, while it was still light, in order to inspect the house outside and admire the view. McCaughey wouldn't make it before dark.

The problem was mechanical. A secretary had been called in and she went to work on a word-processor, getting a final document for Schwartz and McCaughey to sign. It went through five drafts over the next three hours and took far longer than the two men wanted. The operator was both nervous and new to the machine. As a result, mistakes kept creeping in. Further, Schwartz, a practising lawyer twenty years earlier, had a certain pride of authorship when it came to such drafting. He made numerous changes as the drafts were produced.

McCaughey and Schwartz spent the afternoon together as drafts were shuttled by North American's in-house lawyer, vice-president and general counsel Andy LeMesurier, back and forth between them on the second floor and the seventh, where the secretary was working. McCaughey phoned his dinner companions several times, delaying his arrival, embarrassed that he couldn't tell them the reason. Schwartz and McCaughey kept themselves fuelled with cheese, crackers, soft drinks, and beer (only Molson's—McCaughey is on the board) from the pantry attached to the executive dining room. They swapped stories about holidays in France. Schwartz talked of the future at CanWest; he told McCaughey about some of the players at Monarch, said it was time to sell. McCaughey agreed and said, "You can't marry things forever."

Bob Bandeen would later complain publicly that McCaughey had paid too much and that he'd been able to do that because he ran a mutual company. Bandeen had bid $50 million against McCaughey's $68 million. Bandeen charged that as a mutual, North American could use internal Monarch cash surpluses built up from policyholders long dead. McCaughey agrees with Bandeen—at least on price. "He's right to say we could afford to pay more than he could. I could have paid $10 million more and justified it."

McCaughey supported his claim by pointing out that a mutual company like North American is owned by the participating policyholders, so all the earnings go to one group. A stock company sells participating policies, too, but it also has shareholders. Federal regulations insist that the two areas be kept separate on the books. The shareholders, however, receive profits from non-participating policyholders as well as a small share of the profits from the participating business. If Bandeen had bought Monarch, Crown would have merged those mutual assets with the mutual element (the non-participating part) of its business. When North American brought in Monarch, all profit went to one set of owners, the participating policyholders, rather than being split.

But while he might agree with Bandeen in principle, McCaughey is silent on how high he would have gone to get Monarch. "[Schwartz] goes out not knowing how much I would have paid. There is no one in senior management who knows how much I would have paid." (The deal turned out to be far more favourable than McCaughey expected. He thought that the $65 million was about $5 million more than the net book value. What was delivered was worth $75 million rather than $60 million. McCaughey expresses bafflement himself at the swing. "I don't really understand it, either," he says.)

The letter of intent completed, ready for the approval of the North American board and the superinte dent of insurance, McCaughey and Schwartz left at five-thirty, McCaughey for his much-delayed dinner. By coincidence, Schwartz was scheduled to have dinner with Larry Tanenbaum, president and chief executive officer of KVN Construction and a board member on Canadian Foundation, the company for which McCaughey is chairman.

On February 10, McCaughey flew to Winnipeg to meet the management of Monarch. He was not overwhelmed by what he saw. President Harold Thompson assembled the six vice-presidents in the Monarch boardroom. What McCaughey found, at that meeting and in the individual conversations, was, in his words, "pretty parochial." All but one of the seven men had been born and brought up in Winnipeg, most had graduated from the University of Manitoba, and four had joined Monarch immediately after university. Four of the seven were actuaries. The president and longest-serving executive, Thompson, was once a goalie for the Winnipeg Rangers and had been on the Junior A team in 1940–41, the year it won the championship Memorial Cup.

In the midst of the Monarch negotiations, McCaughey had received a telephone call from Joe Dowling, a business broker in Philadelphia. Dowling knew that North American was interested in acquiring a U.S. firm. He had one for sale, Capitol Bankers Life Insurance Co., of Milwaukee. McCaughey was too busy with Monarch. "I've got something else on the table," McCaughey told him. "Give me a week and I'll bring a team to Milwaukee and go through it with a fine-toothed comb and let you know that day by five o'clock if we're interested."

Now that the board had approved the Monarch purchase, McCaughey was ready to look at Capitol Bankers. At seven in the morning on February 17, McCaughey headed for Milwaukee on a rented Learjet with a lawyer and five other North American officers from various departments including datasystems, actuarial, taxation, and accounting. Each man met his counterpart at Capitol Bankers during the morning. They met at lunch to report on what they had seen, split up for the afternoon again, and regrouped at the end of the day.

McCaughey spent the day with the president, Dick Beightol, and met the owner, Douglas Seaman. McCaughey had brought recently acquired senior vice-president Jacques Deschenes with him. Deschenes knew the American scene from his time at Sun Life in Wellesley Hills, Mass. Seaman had bought Capitol Bankers in 1978 for $1.8 million, looking to use it for tax-loss purposes. However, he had hired Beightol to run the place, and Beightol had immediately turned it into a growth company. As a result, Seaman had to add more money to operations every year to finance growth. By 1984, he had ploughed in an additional $9 million. He also owned a snowblower manufacturing business, where sales were listless. Rather than pump more money in to keep it growing, Seaman wanted his money out of Capitol Bankers.

The North American team met at four-thirty and compared notes about the various departments each had surveyed for the day. The distribution network complemented North American's operations in the U.S. Capitol Bankers was strong in the west and south, where North American was non-existent, and the company had, among other products, a good form of universal life policy. Assets were $25 million, liabilities $15.5 million. There were fifty-eight employees. Capitol Bankers was headquartered in Wisconsin, but it was incorporated in Minnesota, so two specialist lawyers who knew that state's tax law were on hand. Within an hour, McCaughey had decided to buy the firm.

Beightol's secretary stayed on to type up the offer for McCaughey, but with various drafts and changes the process dragged on for three hours. At one point, tired of waiting, McCaughey drew up in a matter of minutes his own offer to purchase. It was a handwritten double-spaced document that covered two pages and part of a third. One of the key elements of the offer was a clause agreeing that "arrangements shall be entered into which are satisfactory to North American for the continued employment of key management of Capitol Bankers." McCaughey wanted the management currently in place to stay on and continue running the firm after acquisition, but did not want to have to deal with outrageous salary demands from any of them as the price for their transferred loyalty. "When you're buying a company," said McCaughey, "you're buying people. You don't want the president to demand double the salary to stay." The deal was set to close March 24.

Finally, around a quarter after nine, the offer was ready. They filled in the price, put a one-week expiry on the offer, and headed home via Ottawa, where McCaughey stayed overnight. The rest went home to Toronto. The next morning, February 18, McCaughey, accompanied by Ted Hill, told Paul Cosgrove, minister of state for finance, about the proposed take-overs. Included in North American's requirements was an independent appraisal of Monarch. It was done by Rob Dowsett, a partner at William M. Mercer Ltd. and a former president of Crown Life. McCaughey also told Cosgrove about the job guarantee in Winnipeg and his plans to merge Monarch and North American. (Under Canadian insurance law, one life insurance company cannot be a subsidiary of another life insurance company; instead there must be a merger within two years. A U.S. subsidiary company, like any foreign company, can be run separately.)

McCaughey heard from Capitol Bankers owner Doug Seaman the following week. On the phone, with Seaman's lawyer listening in, the deal was accepted. Seaman had additional concerns. Sitting in the midwestern state of Wisconsin, he worried about his old firm being run from the east. "We're very proud in the west," said Seaman in his slow drawl. "One thing I'm very concerned with is that you'll move this business to the east."

McCaughey hurried to reassure Seaman that such a shift would not occur, but McCaughey had Monarch on his mind as he said, "We will continue to run Capitol Bankers from Winnipeg."

There was a moment's silence, then Seaman croaked, "Winnipeg?"

McCaughey, realizing his error, apologized. "I'm sorry. That's a Freudian slip. I've got something else on my mind. I meant Milwaukee."

In the end, the $17.2-million Capitol Bankers take-over was a success. Growth in the next year was 51 per cent; within two years, the number of employees rose to eighty-five. It also cost more to fund expansion than originally thought. At first, North American planned to invest $10 million over five years. In the first year alone, $6 million was spent to back the higher-than-expected sales levels. For McCaughey, however, the price was worth it. "It's put us on the map," he says. "In the U.S., they've heard of us."

Final signing for Monarch was in Toronto, February 22. The deal was approved by the North American policyholders (97 per cent voted in favour) at an April meeting and Ottawa gave its consent in May. Although the law allowed up to two years to complete the merger, it was done in eleven months, in time for McCaughey to announce it at the April 1984 annual meeting.

For Schwartz and the reluctant Asper, the deal was over with a minimum of fuss. "There are always casualties from a merger," says Schwartz. "There were fewer here than normal." Afterwards, of course, all such deals seem simple, even preordained. Says Schwartz modestly, "It was a plain vanilla deal." For Monarch president Harold Thompson and McCaughey, celebration was muted. A photographer was hired to take a picture of the two of them for the cover of the firm's house organ, *The North American*. The prop they were to be pictured with was a four-foot high Roman numeral VI. It was made of styrofoam, painted gold, and meant to represent that with the merger, the new North American had jumped from twelfth place in Canadian individual life insurance sales to sixth.

The photographer shot about ten frames of the two of them leaning against the VI, smiling, but looking formal and reserved. For the final frame, McCaughey decided the two of them should ham it up a bit. He suggested that they each give a "thumbs-up," the well-known signal that everything is OK and proudly so. That photograph, although it captures the inner sparkle of both men and what they accomplished, was never used. The two men felt their glee might be misinterpreted. Says Thompson, "We didn't want any of the other companies to think we were sticking it to them." The photo, however, was good enough for personal use and McCaughey gave a framed version to Thompson. An engraved brass plate on the presentation frame reads: "To mark 'V'-day, our merger victory. April 2, 1984." McCaughey's signature is also etched on the plate, and it sits in Thompson's office.

North American's first step in absorbing Monarch was to form a six-member steering committee in March 1983, chaired by Monarch president Harold Thompson. Thompson had started out as an actuarial student, but he had headed up other departments—marketing, administration, group, and datasystems—before becoming president in 1971. In May 1983, at sixty, his future was assured in the merger when he was named executive vice-president and chief operating officer. At Monarch's final annual meeting in February 1984, he was presented with a set of car keys from the agents and branch managers. Out back of the building was parked his gift—a 1949 Monarch, one of only three said to be in existence. The blue vehicle, draped in oodles of chrome, had sat on a Saskatchewan farm for years and had only 45,000 original miles on it. It had been carefully restored to mark the end of an era Thompson had begun, the agents thought, in 1949. (He didn't tell them his career had actually started in 1946.) The classic auto came complete with a new set of whitewall tires and, in the trunk, the original wide bands used to simulate whitewalls. The engine is in perfect order. Thompson has driven it to work and has had it up to 120 km/h on the perimeter highway outside Winnipeg.

Thompson's other memento of Monarch is a ring, a 1976 gift from the Monarch agents and branch managers. It is 14-karat gold with a raised lion's head, complete with flowing mane, diamond chips for eyes, and a ruby in the mouth. It is similar to the ring Monarch agents used to receive from the company for various levels of sales achievements. Thompson spent four days a week in the Toronto office in 1984, a little more than three days a week in 1985 as his responsibilities for group insurance (the department in Winnipeg) grew.

Thompson's first action as chairman of the steering committee was to set up thirty-five task forces involving seventy-five employees in various areas of the two head offices, to work out the complexities of bringing the two companies' many departments together. They worked hard at making the employees part of the solution and at eliminating the "we-they" syndrome that exists when two companies are merged. In six months, the task force members had set up subcommittees so that the total number of staff involved grew to 200. By merger date in April 1984, about 75 per cent of all head office employees were involved in some way.

The merger eliminated four senior executives and four middle managers. Included were Monarch's chief actuary Charlie Stafford and both companies' corporate secretaries. Severance arrangements cost about $750,000. A hiring freeze was put into effect in November 1983, to ensure that employees whose jobs were cut found a place elsewhere in the firm. Still, there were staff reductions at all levels. At the end of 1982, there were 1,086 head office employees in the two companies. By the end of 1984, that had shrunk—through attrition—to 1,011. By the end of 1985, the target was 940, down 11 per cent. Some departments (policy benefits, premium and commission accounting, and underwriting and policy issue) were chopped by as much as 20 per cent. Only fourteen people moved from Toronto to Winnipeg, and a similar number transferred in the other direction. The employees in Winnipeg were retrained to work in the group division, which moved there. Even during the transition, group sales in 1984 were up 24.3 per cent. Overall, sales increases were huge. The amount of life insurance sold by North American, Monarch, and Capitol Bankers in 1984 was $7 billion, up 13 per cent from 1983. Health insurance sales jumped 18 cent to $13.4 million of premiums. Total life insurance in force at the end of 1984 was $31.3 billion, an increase of 16 per cent.

Other management changes included moving senior vice-president Tom Inglis to the Edgecombe Group (North American's real estate division) as chairman, to administer $1.3 billion in real estate financing and properties worth $400 million. McCaughey had hived off both real estate and investment into separate functions away from the life insurance company. In 1982 he hired David Scott to head investments. Scott, a six-foot-four former chief executive officer of both Scotiafund Financial Services and Bolton Tremblay Funds Inc., urged that McCaughey buy Elliott & Page Ltd. as North American's investment subsidiary. Elliott & Page, an investment counselling and funds management firm, had been founded in 1949. In 1982, it was owned by Andy Sarlos, Barry Zukerman, and Jack Mackenzie, three high-profile investors who have all made and lost millions. At the time, the threesome were splitting up certain of their assets and Elliott & Page was for sale. North American paid, according to Scott, about half the $1-million asking price for the firm, which managed $850 million from twenty-five clients who included pension funds and university endowment funds; North American's $1.5 billion in investments was added to the portfolio.

During the next two years, Elliott & Page's client list rose to forty, and new products, such as a money market fund, were added. As well, Scott put $4 million into eight venture capital investments, including International Verifact, a Canadian company that built a credit card verification system for use by retailers. Instead of telephoning for authorization on purchases over $50, the retailer puts the card into the supplied terminal, receives instant verification, and freezes the amount of the purchase to be credited to the retailer's account. Since Elliott & Page became involved, the share price of the firm has risen from 80 cents to $5.50. Although the overall investment is small, Scott spends up to one-quarter of his time on the projects, picking management and watching growth, looking for a 50-per-cent annual return on the initial investment.

Elliott & Page, under Scott, is run differently than some life company investment departments, and that's exactly what McCaughey wants. "Investment professionals tend to be more independent," says Scott, "more comfortable with the kind of situation a lawyer finds himself in. People [here] are prepared to disagree. I've got a lot of guys out there," he says, waving at his colleagues' offices, "who are prepared to tell me I'm full of shit." At a larger company, like North American, the corporate culture is more rigid. "The rules tend to be fixed. There is more difficulty in getting feedback up from the bottom. There *is* an effort made at North American, but it's difficult."

There has been little improvement in two key areas at North American—the four-year retention rate for agents and the persistency rate for policies. The retention rate when Kirk arrived in 1975 was 15 per cent, meaning that of a hundred agents recruited only fifteen were still employed four years later. By 1984, following the merger, that rate had risen only marginally, to 17 per cent. Persistency, keeping policies on the books and not allowing them to lapse, had actually worsened. It fell from 86 per cent to 84 per cent.

In 1985, North American plans to hire 400 new agents (including fifty women), with at least half of them expected to be university graduates—up from 10 per cent of total hiring in 1975—in an attempt to get a higher-quality recruit. Further, poor agents will be fired. "Those agents not writing quality business," says Lloyd Kirk, "will be terminated." But quality agents require solid training, and North American's training expenditures are very low. With an annual budget of $800,000 ($600,000 on new agents), North American spends an average of only $1,500 per agent annually, compared with Mutual Life, which claims it spends $120,000 over three years to produce an agent.

Under McCaughey, life insurance is a fast-changing business. In 1984, 8,754 of the 40,378 individual life policies sold by North American (about 22 per cent) were the new, more flexible "universal" life. That grew closer to 25 per cent in 1985. Universal policies, in simplest terms, are the same policies that a few short years ago insurance companies said they couldn't or wouldn't sell. In effect, they allow policyholders to "buy term and invest the difference"— something that consumer advice columnists and industry critics have been advising buyers to do for at least twenty years. Now the insurance companies have a policy that allows that to happen. "I guess," says Kirk, "we decided to join the buy-term-and-invest-the-difference group."

The Air Canada flight to Boston is picking up speed on the Toronto runway. Drew McCaughey, the former wartime pilot, flicks on his stopwatch. "Forty seconds," he says, "that's all the pilot's got to get airborne. He can't abort after eighteen seconds—by then it's too late." The seconds tick away, speed builds, and the plane lifts off. "Thirty-five seconds," announces McCaughey, almost as triumphantly as if he were flying the craft himself. "I like," he says, "uneventful flights."

When he was at Molson's, the pilots of the firm's DH-125 corporate jet used to let him take the controls while in flight, if there were no other passengers, but his licence has since lapsed. Anyway, his new wife, Lorraine, is not keen on the dangers. He tried gliding but thought he'd soon find it boring. These days, all he can do is participate vicariously by timing the take-offs and criticizing the landings. "Been flying long?" he'll ask an airline pilot who lands too hard.

The flight to Boston is a semi-annual visit to his U.S. operations, in the suburb of Wellesley Hills. Last year, 1984, was a rough one for the U.S. division, and he wants to hear that the turnaround has begun. North American, whose logo today is a map of North America and a rainbow, began selling in the U.S. during the nineteenth century, but the real expansion began in the 1950s under president Norman Robertson because, as he put it, you have to go outside Canada for large numbers of customers. "You don't sell insurance to trees," Robertson used to say of thinly populated Canada. He was succeeded by William Anderson, a bridge life master who did mathematical calculations for the Goren Point Count bidding system.

By the 1980s, U.S. branch managers were prospering, individual agents were making up to $300,000 a year, and growth continued— but no one was paying any attention to the bottom line. Support staff, office space, and administrative costs were all paid by head office. When McCaughey took over, North American had a cumulative loss of $55 million in the U.S. since the the 1950s. U.S. senior vice-president Dick Crawford had tried to wrestle with costs in the twelve branches, but they continued to rise and prices continued to fall, as the business became more competitive.

In 1983, McCaughey moved to stem the losses by closing branches and selling through general agents. Career agents were told they would become independent; North American would no longer pay all of their expenses. The company gave six months' notice and transition subsidies, but after that, the umbilical cord to head office was cut. The savings were immediate. Distribution costs dropped from 275 per cent of first-year commissions to a more manageable 135 per cent. Staff costs were chopped as 111 people were laid off in the branches, for an annual savings of $4 million. Some top agents, however, felt badly treated, quit in a huff, or switched policies to companies they thought were more sympathetic. The result was a staggering drop in sales. From 1982 to the end of 1984, U.S business was cut in half, from a high of 7 million new premiums to 3.5 million new premiums. The number of policies in force plummeted from 61,800 to 43,400, as agents took what clients they could and switched their policies to other firms. For most of the year lapses of old policies outnumbered new policies being written. "The repositioning cost something," admits McCaughey, "but there is no question that not only were we losing money, we were running the risk of losing more money."

McCaughey plans to hang tough. "The concept will work. I'll change the people before I'll change the concept, and I've told them that. You don't put the gun on the table unless you're prepared to pull the trigger. If they ever see that you won't pull the trigger, well..." The target for 1984 was a modest $8 million in new premium business—$5 million from the old-time agents and $3 million from new producers signed on after an advertising campaign. At mid-year, the target appeared out of reach. By year-end, sales began to climb, but the total was only $4.8 million, well below the targets. The majority of sales came in the last few months of the year. McCaughey is confident that the turnaround has occurred: "These fellows have got their tails up."

Today's dog-and-pony show, as McCaughey calls it, is to bring him up to date on sales so far, prospects for 1985, and recruiting of the new agents who will sell North American's products. The group gathers around a rectangular table in a windowless room. Chairing the session is Richard Hansen, vice-president for individual marketing. With him, senior vice-president Jacques Deschenes, two regional agency vice-presidents, Michael Kaufman and Jim McMillin, actuary John Vrysen, who is charge of product development, and Bill Atherton, a vice-president who heads North American Security Life. The news is good. After only two months of 1985 sales, they are already at levels that took ten months to reach in 1984.

North American's business is changing faster in the U.S. than anywhere else. At the moment, sales there are about one-third of the company's total. The division consists of three parts: North American Life, which sells participating policies through independent general agents; North American Security Life, launched in 1985 to sell variable products; and Capitol Bankers Life, with its non-participating plans and interest-sensitive products. Each of the three is run separately. The report today is on North American Life.

McCaughey homes in on one city. "The guy in Duluth, did he ever get off the ground?" "No." "He talked a good game," says McCaughey. "He still does," comes the reply. The morning continues in that vein, with McCaughey poking and prodding in every corner of the operations and the U.S. division people responding with confidence. McCaughey commands their respect, but they are not in awe. The two regional heads list sales levels of individual agents, tell the 1985 targets, and report on recruiting. There is an endless recitation of states where North American is trying to obtain licences. McCaughey listens, but he is more interested in going after rich markets in Connecticut and Pennsylvania, and finding out why they aren't getting more business out of territories for which they already have licences. McCaughey likes what he sees, but he is feeling tentative. Much of the future success will depend on a few dozen high producers. "We've got a lot of eggs in a few baskets," he says. Assurances are given, but McCaughey keeps holding up crossed fingers, a symbol to fend off evil spirits.

At the moment, agents in some cities are doing better than others. In Los Angeles, for example, a Korean agent is selling well, mostly to his countrymen. "Has that caused any problems?" asks McCaughey. He is told: "He hardly speaks any English, but he has big dreams." McCaughey worries about frauds among ethnic groups; similar problems have surfaced with other Canadian companies selling to people in countries where the company has no office. "They not only look the same," says McCaughey, "they all have the same name." "One of three," adds McMillin. (Later, McCaughey explains. "I think when you're dealing with worlds that are not our world, you have to be careful of false death claims. That's why I don't want South American sales or the Hong Kong Chinese or the Koreans.") Next, they talk about Tennessee. In that part of the U.S., someone suggests, it helps to be a Canadian company—the folks don't want to deal with Yankees. Agent Patti Huey's clients are affluent landowners. One sale was for $20 million face value of insurance, one of the biggest the division has ever had.

With the noon sandwiches comes a discussion of incentive trips for agents. They've given up attempting to conduct business sessions during the trips because the junkets are not tax-deductible anyway, so now they are straight vacations as rewards for high sales levels. Switzerland is a likely future destination. Then John Vrysen outlines the difficulties of getting licences for some states. Rhode Island is a particular problem. "If you know the right people," he says, "you can get in." He mentions an ex-commissioner of insurance who helps applicants. McCaughey perks up: "That's the kind of guy you need." He urges Vrysen to scout for insurance consultants; like people who help companies obtain beer licences, they are valuable because they know their way around state legislatures.

Vrysen tells about the universal life products that they developed in record time—less than six months. Notes Deschenes: "Sun Life took a year and a half under a high-pressure top-priority situation." McCaughey congratulates them, but the mood doesn't last long. The variable products are meant to pay clients in interest rates that can be adjusted according to a Moody's bond index, a well-known rate that responds to current rates. North American, however, has put a cap on its rate and McCaughey is displeased.

McCaughey is also concerned about the low policy loan rate on amounts borrowed by the policyholder from North American. "That's a bum pricing decision," he snaps, urging that policyholders should be charged the going rate. Vrysen defends his action. McCaughey continues to return to the topic. "I don't want to flog it, but..." He is angry that a pricing decision of such consequence has been taken at a relatively junior level. In all, he is not pleased with Vrysen's performance, saying later that he talks too much and needs training in how to make a presentation.

The topic switches from pricing to getting the word out to agents. He is assured that all the agents understand the new universal policy because they have sold other universal products. "That's an answer, but not *the* answer. What are we doing to communicate—just send out a letter?" McCaughey is told that diskettes for the agents' computers will be sent offering illustrations. Still, McCaughey is not satisfied. Suddenly, the product that was produced in such a short time isn't that exciting after all. Says Deschenes, "This is not an innovation. This is five years late. You don't want to make too much of it. They may laugh at you."

The discussion trickles off into housekeeping matters. An investigation has begun into the courier systems North American uses.

Currently five different firms are being used; there may be some rationalization possible. "You should know that we have [the insurance for] the Purolator group in Canada," says McCaughey, "so we feel friendly towards them." Someone mentions a new photocopier; McCaughey, alert for another corporate connection, asks if it is a Xerox, pointing out that they are partners in the suburban Toronto development that will become North American's headquarters. Will we get better service, someone wonders? McCaughey says that is not the point. "I'm embarrassed if you go elsewhere. We should scratch each other's backs, all things being equal."

The presentations are finished around four o'clock and McCaughey gives them a twenty-minute talk about where the company is going. Although new premium sales goals for this division are officially $8 million for 1985, he tells them, "I'm going to be disappointed if we don't come up with $12 million this year." (The group had also showed him an even higher possible goal of $19 million, which was the total of all the targets they had discussed with individual sales agents. McCaughey says later, "They shouldn't have shown me the $19 million. That was naive.") He outlines the slow-down in growth at Capitol Bankers. "They outgrew themselves. They had to put their house in order." After 50-per-cent increases in each of 1982 and 1983, in 1984 premium income fell by 17 per cent. Such admissions don't faze McCaughey. "I like to put my faults on the table because that helps your credibility when you brag."

Later, he is equally honest about his own success to date with North American. "I'm disappointed that I couldn't expand the breadth of the business." While other companies are moving into other financial services, the only likely addition North American will make is trust services. "I'll experiment, but only on a follow-the-leader basis. The pioneers don't make any money." If he leaves a mark anywhere, he wants it to be on a group of executives who understand all aspects of the business, not just their own responsibilities. "I want them to understand the *economics* of the business. It's surprising—even people who have been there twenty-five years don't understand."

Some chief executive officers who come in from outside would regard it as a failure if they did not create a successor within the company. Not McCaughey. "You should have a chief operating officer who knows the business," he says, "but for the CEO role, the one who plans the strategy, he could come from the outside. The inside guy may have tunnel vision." He has yet to designate his heir apparent. One thing is sure, however: when McCaughey retires from North American in 1987, he has no intention of retiring from the business world. He will continue as chairman of Canadian Foundation.

In June 1985, McCaughey spoke to the Million Dollar Round Table annual meeting in San Francisco. In his speech, he recalled his first MDRT meeting in 1981 and how uncomfortable he felt at the beginning of a particular presentation involving an agent whose client had died. "I was frankly horrified that what was coming could be so crass as to combine the commercialism of selling a life policy with the tragedy of death." The fear was soon washed away by the presentation, and by the time the widow had come on stage to tell her story and was joined by her children, "there wasn't a dry eye in the house. It was quite a new experience for me. I'd never sat surrounded by 5,000 people with tears in my eyes and anguish in my heart in common with everyone around me. I don't mind telling you I was deeply moved."

He began to practise his speech in March, as do all main-platform speakers. He was called to Chicago to perform for the show's producer and have his text placed on the prompter. His coach prior to Chicago was none other than MDRT president and North American agent Ron Barbaro. Barbaro, himself a polished speaker, made some suggestions about the script. McCaughey didn't mind the guidance; he knew his performance would profit from it. "In this world," says McCaughey, "it doesn't just matter how smart you are, it's how smart you look."

And how smart you work. Each of the "new boys" in the Canadian insurance industry has a different management style. At London Life, Earl Orser added nearly twenty new executives to the ranks. Bob Bandeen attacked Crown with a meat cleaver. Except for two additional officers, McCaughey has worked with the original team. "It may be the same old gang, but they're not doing the same old jobs." He will let history judge which management method is best. "Mine is slower, but the challenge is to get people to do what they can, not what they cannot."

CHAPTER SIX

FRENCH POWER
Laurentian Group Corp.

THEY WERE an unlikely pair of soul mates: Claude Castonguay, lifelong federalist Liberal, and Jacques Parizeau, separatist Parti Québécois finance minister. But for all his economic radicalism, Parizeau did share a fondness for unfettered free enterprise in Quebec, and until he resigned in late 1984, he was Castonguay's ally, creating the most progressive and deregulated financial services environment in Canada. Castonguay, fifty-six, president and chief executive officer of Laurentian Group Corp.—Quebec's largest insurer and the Canadian company at the leading edge of one-stop shopping—owes Parizeau a certain debt as the fast growth of the past is about to accelerate. In the last ten years, Laurentian has gone from a quiet mutual company with $80 million in assets to a diversified $3.4-billion empire. In downtown Montreal in 1986, Laurentian will open Canada's first financial supermarket on the ground floor of its new $75-million 27-storey office tower. The ironic counterpoint squats across the street, the former Sun Life headquarters, empty of executive officers who fled to Toronto six years ago to escape the same separatist hordes. The soul mates have created a new giant.

But the buildings tell more than the tale of two cities. They also portray the two poles of an entire industry in crisis. As consumers clamour for more services, there are some in the industry that can't comply or are simply too sleepy to try. Sun, Canada's second-largest life insurance company, has been adrift on the stagnant pond of federal legislation that has not been fully updated since 1932. Laurentian, by contrast, is a Quebec-chartered company operating in an environment that is hurtling towards full deregulation. As a result of corporate strategy and changed legislation, Laurentian is the only financial services company in the country with affiliations in all four financial pillars. (Jacques Parizeau was fond of describing them as "a pillar and three posts," reflecting the comparative immensity of the chartered banks.) The corporate holdings include insurance—The Imperial Life Assurance Co. of Canada, The Provident Assurance Co., and The Personal Insurance Co. of Canada; banking and mortgage services—Montreal City and District Savings Bank and Crédit Foncier; and securities—Geoffrion, Leclerc Inc. Castonguay and his mentor and chairman Jean-Marie Poitras have also created U.S. operations through Loyal American Life Insurance Co. of Mobile, Ala., as well as operations in the Bahamas and Great Britain.

Castonguay revels in his leadership position. "We are growing at a faster pace than many others. Also, we are preparing for the future. There are frustrations," says Castonguay. "It is somewhat difficult on account of all the constraints, but as they are removed we will be ready and we will be in front. We will sustain [past] growth while others who are not adjusting, I'm afraid, will not be able to maintain the pace."

As Laurentian's total staff has expanded from 400 employees to more than 4,000 in all its operations during the last decade, growth through acquisition has also proved to be profitable. Annual income has risen from $25 million to more than $1 billion. Laurentian expects to double both its assets and its profits in the next five years. The initial driving force was Jean-Marie Poitras, sixty-seven, a former insurance sales agent who ran Laurentian as president and CEO until 1982, when he turned the running of the company over to Castonguay and continued as chairman. Poitras put an acquisition strategy in place beginning in 1965 that started slowly, then became a $150-million ten-year acquisition binge when Castonguay rejoined Laurentian in 1976 (he had worked there as a young actuary in the 1950s) after serving in the cabinet of Quebec Liberal leader Robert Bourassa. The two became a team: Poitras, the classic up-from-the-streets entrepreneur with native cunning, and Castonguay, the university-trained organizational man with connections. The backgrounds were different, but the direction was the same. "In business," says Poitras, "you grow, or you disappear. You have to be large in order to have the best people and reduce costs. The insurance industry trend in the U.S. and the U.K. has been for life and casualty to come closer together [organizationally]. We wanted not to follow, but to lead. As changes came, we wanted to be ready."

Nowhere have the changes come as quickly as they have in Quebec. Only now, with the federal government's 1985 discussion paper and proposed changes to allow more financial holding companies, will firms in other jurisdictions be able to do what Laurentian has. While federal legislation awaits further action, provincial legislation has put the Quebec-chartered mutual insurance companies on the same footing as federally chartered stock companies. There are thirty-three Quebec-registered insurance companies—fifteen are life insurance companies, the rest are property and casualty. The two largest are Industrial (which owns federally chartered North-West Life of Vancouver) and Laurentian.

While the Quebec legislation is new, the idea has been around since 1969, when Parizeau wrote a report as chairman of a Quebec government study committee on financial institutions. The report set out nearly all that he later accomplished as finance minister in changing financial services legislation. To date, however, while Parizeau's action has given homebrewed firms a head start, it has not achieved his other goal of more foreign-owned firms settling in Quebec. Typical is The Prudential Insurance Co. of America, the world's largest insurance company and one of the huge foreign firms Parizeau hoped to attract. Prudential has its corporate hands full with the recent addition of property and casualty insurance to its life insurance products in Ontario. The new lines were added in Quebec in 1985. "A lot of companies are just going to wait and see how things develop," says a Prudential spokesperson. "Insurance companies don't move very fast, you know."

To date, however, the advantage goes to Laurentian. Says Marcellin Tremblay, francophone vice-president of the industry's Association canadienne des compagnies d'assurances de personnes inc., "Laurentian is going in all directions and much faster than we thought they might." For Laurentian, the strategy seems almost simple in retrospect. "The goals and objectives are set for three years at a time and revised every year," says Claude Bruneau, chairman, president, and chief executive officer of Imperial Life, one of Laurentian's companies. "Jean-Marie [Poitras] was very much at the helm during his time. Claude maintained the same sense of goals and objectives but incorporated his own culture. Jean-Marie was more impulsive, Claude is more the mathematician, the actuary." Both were among the first in the life insurance industry to realize that real growth was only possible if life insurance became a part of something larger. The routes to survival and to success were the same.

The Laurentian Mutual Insurance Co. was chartered in Quebec in 1938 to sell life insurance in Quebec, Ontario, and New Brunswick. Founding president J. A. Tardif is still on the board of directors. It began as a stock company, owned by shareholders, but in 1959 it became a mutual company, owned by policyholders. Through the 1960s, under chairman Jean-Marie Poitras, the company acquired other small life and general (property and casualty) insurance companies, and by the end of the decade, the Laurentian Group controlled assets of $67 million.

Poitras himself moved up in Laurentian by the sales route. Born in Macamic, Que., he was the son of a civil engineer and land surveyor. His father was approached by the local bank manager, who lacked facility in English, to help contact the insurance companies in Montreal to set up insurance contracts for local businesses. Poitras, who had been educated in English at Queen's University in Kingston, Ont., would be the go-between.

When Jean-Marie was seven, the family moved to Quebec City. What had been a part-time occupation for his father developed into a full-time insurance agency. His father's health was poor and Jean-Marie, by then twenty and the oldest of nine children, joined his father's business. Jean-Marie Poitras's connection with Laurentian came early, and the father predicted the future. When shares in the firm were first offered for sale, his father said, "I'm too old for that. My son should buy them. He will grow with the company." The young Poitras bought 100 shares for $2,500. Two years later, the older Poitras was dead and Jean-Marie was able to carry on in the business as his father had planned. While his formal education had been interrupted by work, he did continue learning even as he supported his brothers, sisters, and mother. He took painting lessons from world-renowned Quebec artist Jean-Paul Lemieux, learned Italian, and did engineering studies—all on the side.

His connection with Laurentian, in addition to his stock purchase, deepened when Laurentian's first life insurance sales office moved in on the floor above Poitras's agency in Mountain Hill in Quebec City. He began to do more and more business with Laurentian and by

1962, he was the company's top salesman. The company decided it should begin selling property and casualty insurance as well, but there was disunity among top management. The rancour was so bad, in fact, that the founder, Tardif, had not spoken to the general manager, Jean-Paul Guimont, for two years. The rift had been exploited by staff, who played one off against the other. The politics of the place became more important than the business. Finally, after a lengthy board meeting, Guimont was no longer general manager.

As Tardif looked around for a successor in 1963, he decided there could be no better man than his top salesman, Jean-Marie Poitras. His brother, Guy, had previously joined him in the business, and the agency had grown to employ forty persons. Laurentian had moved its head office across the river from Lévis to its present site on the highest spot in Quebec City, Diamond Peak, close to the Citadel and the Legislature on Grande-Allée. Poitras had followed and occupied offices on the ground floor. Tardif asked Poitras to be president; Poitras turned him down at first. Tardif persisted, suggesting that he move upstairs to the Laurentian executive offices and install an agency telephone line so that he could serve as an adviser to Tardif and sell insurance at the same time. Nine months later, in September 1965, Poitras was named president and chief executive officer. The company had a little more than $30 million in assets.

Tardif had made a good choice. After the factionalism that had existed, Poitras had the vision to build. "He is of another generation of entrepreneur," says Castonguay. "He relied more on his flare, on his ability as a deal-maker." Poitras's first step was to put Laurentian into the property and casualty business, by buying into the business rather than beginning a new company. "There is a limit to growth from within. It was a single decision at the time," he recalls, but the strategy of acquisition became a pattern for expansion that would last twenty years and beyond.

The first target was a Montreal-based company, La Paix Compagnie d'Assurances Générales du Canada. It had a federal charter and was the Canadian arm of the financial group La Paix S.A. of Paris. The company had been losing money, because it was new and because its foreign ownership meant that it could not ride the nationalist trend of the day and appeal to Quebeckers. Laurentian had little money for investment, so Poitras negotiated a deal to buy a 30-per-cent interest with an option for another 40 per cent anytime in the next ten years. With the growth of Quebec ownership and management, the company prospered, although nationalism was a rising tide about which Poitras had some fears. "The line between nationalism and racism is very close. I worry about that." Laurentian's connection with the French company continued and it became a financial backer for successive deals, as did the National Bank, in a joint acquisition strategy that Poitras had come to favour. That way, Laurentian shared risks with corporations that offered both continuity and support that no individual could guarantee. (La Paix later became Le Groupe Victoire.)

Poitras applied the same team thinking to the acquisition studies. Rather than just relying on Laurentian management, he hired legal, accounting, and actuarial assistance on a consulting basis. The accountant, Marius Laliberté of Coopers & Lybrand, had been doing Poitras's work since he owned his own insurance agency. The lawyer, Gaëtan Drolet, is now vice-president and general counsel at Laurentian. The actuarial consultant was Claude Castonguay.

In 1969 Poitras bought two more Quebec City-based companies, Quebec Automobile Club Insurance Co. and Universal Protection. He negotiated the deal in the days leading up to a federal budget. He had arrived at a price of $4.5 million, but that price would stick only until the budget speech began in Ottawa at 8:00 P.M. There had been rumours that a capital gains tax would be invoked. After eight, the deal would be off and negotiations would begin anew the following day, possibly under a new tax regime. The talks went right down to the wire. "There I was at eight o'clock," recalls Poitras, "looking in the stock room for a company cheque. I had to phone the company secretary to tell me where to find one." The deal was struck on time. As it turned out, the deadline did not matter; there was no capital gains tax imposed.

Real growth at Laurentian began in the mid-1970s. Poitras bought The Provident from Montreal entrepreneur Jean-Louis Lévesque in a deal worth $13 million with backing from La Paix and the National Bank. Poitras then looked for a new target, outside Quebec. He settled on Imperial Life, owned by Power Corp. Paul Desmarais's conglomerate was coming under close government scrutiny, leading to the Royal Commission on Corporate Concentration. Poitras suspected that Desmarais, who also owned Great-West Life, might be ready to sell Imperial and concentrate his efforts on one insurance company. Further, Imperial had been losing money, but Poitras suspected that management might respond to new owners.

The Imperial purchase was a huge step to contemplate. Laurentian had grown to $150 million in assets, but Imperial, at $700 million in assets, was almost five times bigger. Poitras knew he needed additional management help to run Laurentian if the purchase succeeded. This time, when he consulted his team, he had an additional question for Castonguay. Castonguay had quit politics in 1973 and returned to his actuarial consulting business. "Give me your reaction," Poitras asked, just as he had done with other deals. Then, the new question: "I won't buy this company without having good men. If I make this deal, may I approach you?"

Born in Quebec City, Castonguay was educated at Laval and the University of Manitoba. From 1951 to 1956, he had been an associate actuary at Industrial Life, then an actuary with Laurentian Mutual from 1956 to 1958 and the Provident from 1958 to 1962. The actuarial profession was then, as it is now, a mysterious and little-understood calling, and the image of actuaries as an uninteresting bunch is not unknown to Castonguay. He once took his wife, Mimi, to a meeting of an actuarial society. Afterwards, she said quietly to him, "If you don't mind, I won't go back." The solid nature of an actuary was, however, of some consolation to Mimi's mother when Castonguay first dated her daughter. Mimi was the daughter of Gaspard Fauteux, a former speaker of the House of Commons and a lieutenant-governor of Quebec. Said Mimi's mother, "At least with Claude, Mimi is running no risk of going through what I have as a politician's wife."

In 1962, he formed his own actuarial firm, Castonguay, Pouliot, Guerard & Associates Inc. As time passed, however, he shed actuarial work like a heavy cloak that kept him from moving quickly. "I like action. I like progress. I like to see things happening. I would not have been very happy if I had continued to do actuarial work." He turned more and more to social policy. "We live in a wealthy country from many points of view," says Castonguay. "We have to make sure that people can share in this wealth and receive proper services. Legislation and social programs have to be updated for these things to happen. That was my initial attraction to social policy." He served as chairman of a Quebec royal commission on health and social welfare from 1966 to 1970. Then, in spite of his mother-in-law's prediction, he turned to active politics. Robert Bourassa had just been elected leader of the Quebec Liberal Party. Former leader Jean Lesage had retired and Castonguay was living in Lesage's riding of Louis-Hébert. Both put pressure on Castonguay. He had only four days to make up his mind. He decided to run, agreeing to serve for one term, and won. During that term, he was in the Bourassa cabinet as minister of health and minister of family and social welfare, then minister of social affairs.

As a result of his time in politics, Castonguay became one of a rare breed among Canadian businessmen, those who have made a contribution to public policy. Further, he must be the only Canadian businessman with a name that is literally a household word. As chairman of the health and social welfare commission and a cabinet minister for three years, Castonguay created the Quebec Pension Plan and gave the province its medical insurance scheme. Even today, the plastic identification card each Quebecker carries to the doctor's office is known affectionately as "la Castonguette." After he resigned from the Bourassa government and returned to pension consulting, he was a member of the steering committee of the Federal-Provincial Joint Review on the Social Security System from 1973 to 1975 and served on the federal government's Anti-Inflation Board in 1974–75. By that time, actuarial work held little appeal. "I cannot say I was excited about going back to the evaluation of pensions." It was just then that Poitras, with Imperial on his mind, came to ask Castonguay to study Imperial and think about joining. Castonguay said yes to both questions.

Paul Desmarais was a tougher sale. He controlled 53 per cent of Imperial. Poitras met with him for an hour in November 1976, but they could not agree on a price for Desmarais's shares. Poitras offered $9 million, Desmarais asked $15 million. When no deal was forthcoming on Imperial, Desmarais, looking to sell him *something*, offered to sell Poitras his newspaper, *La Presse*. Poitras declined. They agreed to think about the Imperial price negotiations and meet again in a month or so. In February, at the second one-hour meeting, they agreed to a price of $24 million, including what would be paid to Desmarais and to the minority shareholders.

They further agreed to wait until after the annual meeting in the spring before ownership actually changed hands. That way, Laurentian would have a full year of running Imperial before having to face shareholders. Poitras went to Barbados, but his vacation was interrupted by a telephone call from a staff member who read him a brief story that had appeared in a Toronto newspaper. It said that Imperial was to be purchased by an "obscure, separatist company" from Quebec. While Poitras didn't think Laurentian fit either of the descriptives, he knew he had to close the deal sooner than the planned spring deadline—before a small story became a political firestorm between Ontario and Quebec. Says Poitras, "A deal is finished only when you have the shares in your hand." He cut short the holiday and had the closing date moved from April to February. Poitras had his Ontario beach-head.

In the mid-1970s, Laurentian began to buy shares in Montreal City and District Savings Bank. Poitras added Raymond Garneau— like Castonguay, a former politician—to help him run it. Garneau, minister of finance in Quebec from 1970 to 1976, became a Laurentian vice-president in 1979 and chairman and chief executive officer in 1981 of both Montreal City and District and Crédit Foncier, which City and District had bought in 1979. (In 1984, he returned to politics as a member of the Liberal opposition in Ottawa.) By 1981 the Montreal City and District holding had grown to more than 40 per cent. Laurentian now has about 31 per cent of the company, which has $5 billion in assets, more than a fivefold increase since the purchase of Crédit Foncier.

With Imperial already operating in the U.S., Laurentian expanded its American interests further with the purchase of Loyal American Life Insurance Co., of Mobile, Ala. In 1981, Laurentian bought The Canadian Provident-General and its subsidiaries, The Personal Insurance Co. and Paragon Insurance Co. It also bought Canadian Provident-Life Insurance Co. of Montreal and merged it with Laurentian Mutual. A merger of Northern Life and Imperial did not work out and Northern was put up for sale.

In 1983 Laurentian bought 20 per cent of Southland Capital Investors Inc. of Florida, to use as a vehicle for further expansion. That same year, Laurentian reached out to Britain through an Imperial Life subsidiary that offers portfolio management and is able to accept deposits through an affiliated company. In 1984 Laurentian added Canagex, a Montreal-based investment consulting firm that manages $1.1 billion in assets from pension funds, insurance companies, and other funds. Laurentian also took a 10-per-cent position in Le Groupe Pallas, a Luxembourg investment house. Other shareholders include Power Corp. and European interests.

Poitras retired in 1982 as president and chief executive officer, turning power over to Castonguay. "I have been in insurance all my life," says Poitras. "I'm not interested in following, but I'm not afraid of having strong men around me. Men are more important than finances. I have tried to be honest, but I can be tough. Business is not a social organization. The CEO has to find his successor and be strong enough to leave his place."

The more analytical and systematic of the two, Castonguay has carried on in the acquisitor's mould. He does, however, have an artistic side that is all but hidden from public view. The only indication of it is a small canvas, a landscape, hanging in his Quebec City office along with another painting called *Orchard* by British artist Roger DeGrey, which replaced *Ariane* by Jean-Paul Lemieux when Castonguay had the Lemieux moved to the executive dining room. Castonguay is *un peintre du dimanche*—a Sunday or amateur painter. "It is restful inasmuch as it captures your attention," says Castonguay of his hobby. "If you paint and you try to do a good job, it requires a lot of concentration. It's another kind of fatigue from what you do normally. If you paint for a few hours, it keeps your mind away from everything else.

"The reward you get can be exciting. While I have played golf and I have seen people play golf, as a rule when they're finished their game they complain about their bad shots and they come out of the golf course frustrated, because they always go there thinking that they will play a little better than they have played before—and it seldom happens. With painting, there is not that sense of frustration you find in some other kinds of relaxation. You're left with something concrete."

To achieve anything lasting in business, however, corporate shuffling must be constant. Currently, Laurentian Mutual Insurance Co. is the parent of Laurentian Group, which will probably go public in 1986. Minority interests in certain subsidiaries held by Le Groupe Victoire are being switched into Laurentian Group; National Bank will invest $5 million, and pension funds will also be investors. Laurentian will create a downstream holding company, so called because it appears on the organization chart below Laurentian Mutual. A similar company, Laurentian Capital Corp., has already been created in the U.S. Both holding companies will be stock companies, with shares, and will provide new money-raising capacity in both countries. Laurentian, as a result, will be able to raise money for acquisition by the exchange or sale of shares in the new company.

With Poitras as the architect with the vision to build Laurentian and Castonguay as the general contractor, Laurentian's past growth is even more impressive because much of it occurred well *before* Bill 75, a piece of legislation passed in 1984 that gives Quebec-chartered insurance companies more freedom to market a whole range of products, more than in any other jurisdiction. Laurentian is poised for expansion that may be unparalleled in Canadian insurance. Possible new areas now include guaranteed investment certificates, travellers' cheques, credit or debit cards, deposit instruments, life and health insurance, annuity contracts currently issued by competitors, property and casualty insurance contracts, equity-type investment products, as well as some government and corporate securities. With the finance minister's prior approval, and without any additional legislation, another flotilla of businesses can be added: deposit-taking, underwriting, stock, commodity, and bullion trading, real estate brokerage, foreign exchange, acting as transfer agents and registrar, as well as handling fiduciary and trustee services.

It's not so much deregulation that Parizeau created, it's open season. Asked to address the annual meeting of the Canadian Life and Health Insurance Association in May 1984, Parizeau told the group: "We're breaking down the barriers." As for any head start Quebec companies now have over federally chartered companies, "I consider the advantages given with some glee."

Now there's just one more thing that's holding Castonguay back. It's not the law, for although Castonguay wants further removal of the rules so that his companies are not, for example, overseen by so many different bodies, he has great freedom. It's not the consumer, who is clamouring for accessible, integrated services. It's the stodgy nature of the industry itself, specifically Laurentian's sales agents. They fear change and they worry that technology or self-serve financial centres will replace them. "It's difficult," admits Castonguay, "to go faster than they're prepared to go."

Ten years out of government, he has this new political problem to solve. He must create a new culture within Laurentian. He is again out on the hustings, flitting about in his corporate jet, the only such craft at the command of a life insurance executive in Canada, putting a program into place that he is sure the consumer wants. "We pay attention to maintaining a positive climate in the company. There is no tension among the top officers. One of my main concerns is to maintain that." Much of the effort to keep the management team happy involves performance-oriented monetary incentives for the senior executives, already well paid. Castonguay himself earns a salary of $250,000 a year. In 1984 directors' fees paid by other Laurentian companies, plus his performance bonus, boosted his annual income to $375,000. The other officers receive similar treatment. At Imperial, for example, the various vice-presidents earn in the $85,000–$135,000 range. Performance bonuses can boost that by 30 per cent. At the chief executive officer level, salaries range from $165,000 to $200,000. Bonuses can add 50 per cent to salary, so that in a good year Imperial CEO Claude Bruneau could earn $300,000.

Castonguay goes outside the office to sell his message as well. In a speech to the Canadian Club of Montreal in October 1984, he said, "Bill 75 will not turn anyone overnight into a financial Provigo [a major Quebec supermarket chain]." His main audience for that line was not in the room, however; it was back at the office where he has banished the term "financial supermarket" from his vocabulary forever. The phrase implies self-serve shopping by consumers who would then pay no commission to sales agents. "When an expression creates a negative reaction with your own sales force, what do you do? Do you keep repeating it and see your people unhappy? Or do you try to reassure them? We're trying to avoid a one-word expression that would disturb them. We're talking about the integration of financial services, we're talking about making financial services accessible, we're talking about one-stop shopping, we're talking about all these things which all mean the same thing, I agree, but we're trying to avoid the expression that worries them." He will go so far as to use "one-stop shopping" (in French, *guichet unique*), because that at least suggests that the appropriate Laurentian agents—drawn from the various companies involved in specific services—will be on hand to sell stocks, insurance, or certificates of deposit—and to earn their commissions.

The terminology problem is the only other enemy blip on his radar screen as Castonguay's antennae feel out the future. Although Industrial Life is the largest Quebec-based mutual company, with $1.3 billion in assets (Laurentian Mutual is second at $595 million), the overall Laurentian Group with its tentacles everywhere and its $3.4 billion in assets has more synergy. Laurentian's expansionary strategy has been dictated by the market itself. For life insurance sales, Castonguay notes, "Canada is not a huge market. There is an ample supply of services. There is a large number of large companies." In addition, the market has been shrinking and banks have overpowered the insurance companies in registered retirement savings sales and mortgage business. Tax changes in the 1981 federal budget ended a huge insurance company market in income averaging annuity contracts (IAACs); the economy has been growing slowly; group insurance benefits over a certain level have become taxable benefits in the hands of employees. In all, life insurance companies have been fishing in smaller and smaller pools. There is no place to go but to buy into other financial services.

It has taken some time, but others in Quebec are following the lead set by Jean-Marie Poitras twenty years ago. Alliance Compagnie mutuelle d'Assurance-vie recently increased its holdings in Trust Général du Canada to 20 per cent; Mutuelle d'Assurance-Vie Les Coopérants has bought a 10-per-cent interest in the brokerage firm Molson Rousseau Ltd. That process has now been further advanced by Bill 75, although Castonguay downplays its effect. "It's not Bill 75 that's so much ahead of its time, it's the fact that the legislation in Ottawa and in the provinces has not kept pace. Bill 75 puts us on the same basis as the [federally chartered] capital stock companies. It won't do any miracles, but at least it will put us on an even basis with them." Not everyone agrees. Mutual Life chairman John Panabaker has noted an important difference: because the ultimate owner of Laurentian Group is a mutual insurance company, the parent company cannot be bought by anyone, friendly or hostile. "Parizeau," Panabaker says, "has not made Laurentian vulnerable to a take-over by Trilon."

Outside Quebec, many in the industry assume that because Bill 75 helps Laurentian (along with the other Quebec companies), Castonguay must have guided Parizeau's hand as he wrote the bill. Castonguay denies he did more than write two letters to Parizeau urging that the legislation be amended. "Parizeau is his own man," says Castonguay. Although Castonguay admits he likes what Parizeau has done to the industry, he claims he wanted Parizeau to go further, not towards more products or services, but away from government rules, to lessen the role of overseers and reduce corporate reporting requirements. "It is difficult for one province to move too far ahead of the others," says Castonguay, "so he was limited."

However the changes came about, the life industry outside Quebec generally resented Parizeau's unilateral moves. Said Mutual's Panabaker, "Mr. Parizeau is an apostle of integrated financial services. He sees the present situation as an opportunity to put his ideas into practice and give Quebec life insurance companies a head start over the rest of us. From his viewpoint, independent action is all gain at no cost. He believes that integration is inevitable. What happens elsewhere is of little concern to him." In fact, prior to his resignation in 1984, Parizeau was freeing up financial services in general. Earlier the securities industry was given more freedoms, in steps that were laid out sixteen years ago when he headed the provincial committee on financial institutions. That body's report, issued in 1969, stated: "The ultimate aim is to simplify the legal structure applying to financial institutions, allowing them to engage in a wide variety of transactions and activities and to retain the greatest flexibility in the means they use for obtaining, investing or lending funds, but to keep them subject to supple, yet constant, meticulous and—need it be said—competent supervision." The committee also said that it presumed "the emergence of institutions offering the whole range of financial services needed by consumer and saver—what might be called 'departmental' financial institutions, using the analogy of department stores."

In 1984, as Parizeau introduced Bill 75 at a news conference, he sounded triumphant: "For the average guy, it means he will be able to go into a financial institution and put money into a savings account, set up a trust for his son's college education and buy life insurance and buy fire and theft insurance for his house—in one visit. By putting a large part of their total assets in financial subsidiaries, there is almost no limit to what insurance companies will be able to do."

Some in the industry, however, worry that Quebec officials do not even realize what they have created. London Life's Earl Orser, for example, points to Bill 75's investment provisions. A life insurance company can invest up to 15 per cent of its assets in any one financial subsidiary; a total of 50 per cent of assets can be invested in equity-type investments, such as shares in all subsidiaries (financial or non-financial), including downstream holding companies, income-producing real estate, and common shares held by the life company. Orser worries that if Quebec life companies approach 50 per cent of assets in equity-type investments, they will have too few liquid funds. "That [provision] almost facilitates pyramiding," he says, fearing the collapse of a shaky corporate structure. "It may be harmless, but I wonder if the authorities in Quebec understand."

For his part, Castonguay notes that Laurentian's equity investments are currently at 22 per cent of assets and are unlikely to go much higher. Castonguay also says he won't take advantage of the law outside Quebec. "As far as our activities are concerned in Ontario, [Bill 75] won't change much," he says. He has been obeying the spirit of Ontario law. When Laurentian bought into the brokerage firm Geoffrion, Leclerc in 1983, it bought 9.9 per cent of the firm, thus staying under the 10-per-cent ceiling insisted upon by the Toronto Stock Exchange and the Ontario Securities Commission since Geoffrion, Leclerc, although headquartered in Montreal, does business in Toronto. "Bill 75 won't have much of an impact unless [the other provinces] follow," he insists. The importance, for Castonguay, is more basic. "Finally, insurance legislation, in one jurisdiction in Canada, has been updated."

It's not just the Quebec consumer who stands to benefit from the Castonguay strategy. There are internal and organizational advantages also. One datasystems centre in Montreal serves operations of Laurentian Mutual, the Provident, and the Personal. Another in Toronto covers Ontario operations, thus reducing equipment duplication. Most of Laurentian's investments are handled through Canagex. The pooling means more clout in the marketplace and the combined operations can attract a larger and more experienced management.

There will be more acquisitions, but there's that one other role remaining for Castonguay. As the man who sold medicare and pensions, his final sales pitch is to convince his employees to adopt his high-speed strategy. For now, the timid cross-over experiments, with products of one department sold by another, continue. For the past two years, forty of the 300 Imperial Life agents have been selling property and casualty insurance, too. They were among the first life insurance agents to begin selling general insurance. Some Laurentian life agents will soon be adding mutual funds to their quiver of products, and Castonguay thinks he may soon order a Geoffrion, Leclerc rep to move into Laurentian offices to sell securities.

As experiments succeed, he is convinced, employees will quickly copy their colleagues. More movement towards deregulation, however, will help. Right now, for example, if an agent in one area refers business to an agent in another, Quebec law does not allow the resulting commission to be split. It is a rule that, understandably, forestalls many referrals. In general, Castonguay feels that professionals should be able to acquire more than one licence and deal with combinations of life and general insurance, mutual funds, and brokerage services. Still, as he surveys the competition and sees what giant holding companies like Trilon, Crownx, and the others are doing, he knows he is in the first rank. "Nobody has found the magic approach or the magic formula." And he knows, too, that his one-stop experiments are just beginnings. "We're not going all out. We realize that if we try to go faster than people are used to or ready to go, we will just spend energy unnecessarily."

However quickly one-stop occurs, Poitras and Castonguay have already created something else: a company where French Canadians can prosper. "A lot of young people in Quebec have not felt that they were getting a fair deal in the business world. We have demonstrated in a few organizations, such as [engineering consultant] Lavalin and [food wholesaler and retailer] Provigo, that we can succeed. We have shown that if we want to expand outside Quebec, we can.

"It was important to show that French-speaking people and English-speaking people could work together. With the referendum now in the past, it may look as if it could have been taken for granted." Castonguay pauses to reflect on his own contribution. "It shows we can do as well in Quebec as others can elsewhere. I have my pride, like anybody else. The challenge has been to build something that lasts. When I look back, I find that I have had an interesting career. I have built some bridges."

CHAPTER SEVEN

ACTS OF GOD

*Global Catastrophes and the
Collapse of Pitts Insurance Co. Ltd.*

THE TELEVISION NEWS announcer gives the headlines in quick flashes: a gas well is burning out of control off the east coast; a torando has levelled buildings in southern Ontario; a leaking toxic dump threatens a municipal water supply in British Columbia. The videotape footage that follows shows man and nature at their destructive worst. What's rarely shown, however, is the story behind the scenes, the insurance adjusters and their crews called in to clean up the mess and put things right just like the sweepers who follow the elephants in a circus parade.

August 16, 1984, was just such a day at the Syncrude plant in Fort McMurray, Alta. Among the first people at the plant after the $300-million fire the previous night was the prevention engineer from Marsh & McLennan Ltd., the world's largest insurance broker. As he surveyed the scene, he knew full well that the direct damage caused by the fire would be only part of the eventual cost. Production was halted; Syncrude was neither meeting its commitments nor making a profit. In addition to covering the direct damage, insurance companies would also have to pay for business interruption. One of the cokers was repaired a month later, but the plant limped along at half-capacity until late December before the other coker started working. Total lost production was more than 8 million barrels of oil. At year-end, as he renegotiated Syncrude's coverage, insurance administrator George Wilkinson lamented: "We had the loss when the [insurance] market was getting very tight. We'll have a considerably higher deductible and considerably higher premium."

Syncrude is by no means alone, either in suffering the loss or in facing higher premiums on renewal. Around the world, property and casualty claims have been soaring. The disasters have been diverse: multimillion-dollar medical malpractice suits in the U.S.; fierce storms in Europe; the 1984 Petroleos Mexicana oil-tank explosion just north of Mexico City, costing US$100 million; more than $100 million for the *Ocean Ranger* rig, lost off the coast of Newfoundland in 1982; $125 million in damage in a 1981 Calgary hailstorm; more than US$180 million paid for two errant satellites launched into wrong orbits; US$306 million for passenger liability on the Korean Air Lines 747 shot down by the Soviets; US$440 million paid out by Lloyd's of London for computer technology insured against obsolescence; more than US$600 million in shipping losses in the Persian Gulf since 1983 because of the Iran–Iraq war; US$10 billion–$30 billion for asbestosis claims against asbestos manufacturers; and a $15-billion class action suit against Union Carbide after the toxic gas leak in Bhopal, India, in 1984. When famed counsel Melvin Belli flew to India to take on the case, insurance firms around the world shuddered in unison. A settlement of that magnitude could not just bankrupt Union Carbide, it could strain the international insurance system to the limit—and beyond.

Canadian buyers of business insurance have been feeling the effects of such international pressures as contracts come up for renewal. Insurance is not a home-turf industry. The Canadian property and casualty insurance industry, two-thirds of which is foreign-owned, relies heavily on world markets in reinsurance—insurance for the insurance companies. When coverage amounts get too large for insurance companies in Canada—or anywhere—they turn to the reinsurance market to spread their risk. In the past half-dozen years, that has been easy. There has been an abundance of reinsurers, an estimated 400 firms doing $50 billion in business annually, almost all of them operating out of London. Of that $50 billion, $28 billion was handled by professional reinsurers, with the rest taken by an estimated 2,000 firms known as captives.

Recently, however, the supply of reinsurance has been shrinking. Captives, originally set up by, say, a manufacturer to handle the manufacturer's own insurance, were expanded to take on other risks as well, doing business from various tax havens such as Bermuda, the Bahamas, and Guernsey. Now, with heavy losses around the world, captives are closing up shop and London-based reinsurers are withdrawing from the markets. Typical is Gulf Oil's Bermuda captive, Insco Ltd., which stopped underwriting risks in 1984. Many Lloyd's insurance syndicates are up to their premium limits and are taking on no new business at all. Fewer companies taking on business in London means higher prices around the world and in Canada.

At home, Canadian property and casualty insurance companies have been suffering as well. The 300 general insurance companies doing business in Canada have had underwriting losses every year from 1979 through 1984, paying out more in claims than they collected in premiums in the same period. The only way they have stayed profitable is through income from investing their more than $14 billion in assets. During the ten years 1974–1983, underwriting losses were $3 billion, investment gains $6 billion, for a net profit of $3 billion. Interest rates, however, are lower now than they were three years ago, and that revenue has begun to fall. In 1984, the industry had its worst year ever, losing $917 million. Only investment income of $1.3 billion kept the industry profitable. In a competitive and fragmented market where no one dominates and where the largest company, The Co-operators Group Ltd., of Guelph, Ont., had a mere 5.7 per cent of the total market of $8.3 billion in annual premiums in 1984, the cry has gone up for rate increases to put the industry on a more profitable footing. Without such increases, say some in the industry, companies will fold.

There are those who predict more difficulties. Says Ted Belton, president of the Insurers' Advisory Organization of Canada (IAO), an industry-funded group that inspects buildings and suggests rates, "There will be a tightening of the marketplace in '85. We will see a mild correction; there will be some companies that won't make it. For those companies it will be an orderly withdrawal and not a collapse." A shake-out of stragglers is necessary, says Paul O'Donoghue, chief executive officer of Marsh & McLennan: "To get some order back in the market, we almost need some big losses. People who were flying blind were landing on their feet." Says Wayne Scott, senior vice-president of Co-operators General Insurance Co., a subsidiary of Co-operators Group, "There has been an over-supply. Insurers are hurting badly and some are pulling out." The property and casualty business is poised at the abyss. Will it fall in or scramble safely to the other side? "It's that bogeyman," says Jack Lyndon, president of the Insurance Bureau of Canada. "We're in a very spooky period."

The last time the industry went through such a crunch, in 1981–82, three high-profile insurance companies went out of business, Pitts Insurance Co. of London, Ont., and Strathcona General Insurance Co. of Ottawa in 1981; and Cardinal Insurance Co. of Toronto, in 1982. Pitts is still dragging through the courts. Policyholders who had claims against the company will be lucky to get 70 cents for every dollar owed. They were the first federally chartered property and casualty companies to go bankrupt in fifty years. While each company had a slightly different problem, there were some common elements. They all passed too much of their business on to reinsurers, who either backed out or hiked rates, leaving the primary companies with insufficient funds to pay claims. Poor management, costly administration, and high-risk policies didn't help.

Pitts and Cardinal were typical. Both had experienced dramatic growth in the years immediately prior to their failure. They were involved in high-risk business: Pitts in non-standard automobile and motorcycle policies and insurance for fishing lodges with no security in the off season; Cardinal in long-haul trucking, commercial fishing, and municipal liability. Pitts, Cardinal, and Strathcona all suffered reinsurance problems. Strathcona, for example, was retaining only about 5 per cent of its insurance and ceding all the rest to reinsurers. It wasn't really acting as an insurance company; it was more like a broker, taking commissions and passing coverage on to another company. Cardinal collapsed when one of the firm's major reinsurers said that a contract was not valid. The firm had $14 million in outstanding claims from policyholders—of that, the reinsurer was responsible for $6.5 million. There are two actions against the reinsurers that are still before the courts. If the actions are successful, the claims could be close to fully paid, but another two or three years could pass. The pay-out, now at 20 cents on the dollar, might go as high as 40 cents on every dollar owed, or even higher if the reinsurers are found liable.

Time was when the industry was more predictable. Good times followed bad, three years of each in a cycle. Companies would make money, others would rush in, thinking it was a profitable business, over-supply would be created and rates would fall. Profits would then narrow and as losses occurred, companies would collapse or withdraw until supply was short and profits—and the cycle—returned. The six-year cycle began after the Second World War and continued until the early 1970s. Then there were four bad years, followed by three good years, 1976 through 1978. That was the end of predictability. There have been underwriting losses for the past seven years, and no one really knows where the cycle will go from here.

The market problems have been compounded by new types of claims. Product liability pay-outs, for example, non-existent in the past, have become commonplace. A. H. Robins Co., the U.S. manufacturer of intrauterine contraceptive devices, and its insurer had settled 8,300 claims for US$315 million by the end of 1984 with a further 3,800 claims to be settled. The claims began after the company took its Dalkon Shield off the market ten years earlier amid reports of injuries to users. In April 1985, Robins announced that it had set up a US$615-million fund for further claims, only a handful of them in Canada. Such unpredictable and widespread suits give the insurance industry the cold sweats. "Underwriters are getting nervous," says O'Donoghue, of Marsh & McLennan. "They're afraid they'll wake up one morning and discover that somebody has embezzled the world."

There are those, however, who see the ongoing concern and the accompanying clamour for rate increases as just so much hype. According to Bill Andrus, a property and casualty actuarial consultant with Wyatt Co., of Toronto, the only people making noise about rate increases are those with a vested interest in charging higher premiums. "I have a client who'd like to buy a company," says Andrus. "If things were so terrible, you'd think there'd be more companies for sale." He looked for months and found very few. In response, IAO president Belton urges patience: "If he waits for a little while, he may have lots of customers. There is going to be some kind of shake-out in '85 because the results are deteriorating so rapidly."

Andrus is not convinced. He points to the level of pay-outs by property and casualty companies. For every $100 of premium a company receives for auto injury liability, for example, Andrus says that only $5.40 has been paid out in claims after one year, $40 after three years. The companies may eventually pay out more in claims than they collect in premiums, but because claims, settlements, and court cases take time (this is known as "long tail" in the business), they retain that original premium income and can earn interest all that time through their investments. "The insurance industry is quite successful in getting all the attention focussed on the underwriting results," says Andrus. "I see a lot of hype." Andrus is also technical author for Colander Publications, which produces the annual *Insurance T.R.A.C. Report*, a listing of insurance companies that shows which ones are near the brink of bankruptcy. None is currently in that much trouble, he says.

Part of the reason is that companies have been paying more attention to solvency, something that was overlooked during the last crunch in 1981–82. Also, like most other Canadian industries, the general insurance industry has been automating, cutting costs, and making productivity gains during the last three to four years, largely at the expense of jobs. Overall, lower employment in the industry has brought internal savings. From a high in 1981 of 48,000, all the companies now employ about 46,000. Royal Insurance Co. of Canada is typical. Until 1983, when it was overtaken by Co-operators, Royal sold more general insurance than any other company in Canada. Royal had as much as 10 per cent of the Canadian market in 1978 and expected to have $1 billion in premium income by 1983. Actual premium income that year was $390 million—an indication of how the demand for insurance flattened and how competitive the industry became. In response to lower sales and stiffer competition, Royal staff was reduced to 2,100 from a high of 3,400 in 1979. As the company trimmed back, arrangements were terminated with one-quarter of the independent agents selling Royal products.

Profitability is better now, but the gains are slow. The level of rate increases put in place in 1985 is unlikely to improve things much, says Royal CEO Jean Robitaille. He hasn't put rates up as much as he'd like to—and not all the reasons are business decisions. Personal auto insurance is a good example. "The industry needs a 15- to 20-per-cent rate increase," said Robitaille early in 1985. "It won't happen. This is an election year in Ontario and nobody wants to embarrass a Conservative government. Increases would give the NDP an election issue and force the Conservatives to do something they wouldn't otherwise do." Something like bringing in a provincially run auto insurance scheme, anathema to the free-enterprisers in the insurance business.

As a result, personal auto rates increased by no more than 7 per cent—not enough to cover recent auto underwriting losses in Ontario. "All our projections are going in the wrong direction," says Teunis Haalboom, chief executive officer of The Co-operators. Even the weather has been against the companies. October 1984, for example, was the worst October in five years. Winter weather always means higher claims. "A snowstorm in Toronto can cost us $1 million," says Haalboom. But if one company tries for, say, a 10-percent rate increase on its own in order to raise revenue, clients shop around. "If the rest [of the companies] haven't changed, people will move," says Haalboom. "That's very costly. But at some point, you have no choice."

Rate structures for commercial business have been equally competitive. Wayne Scott of The Co-operators cites one example in which a business was paying an annual premium of $132,000. The Co-operators, working with broker Reed Stenhouse Ltd., put in a bid of $126,000. A competing broker, Marsh & McLennan, found another insurance company that would underwrite the business at $98,000. "There's no logic there," says Scott. "Our cost on reinsurance for some of the stuff approached the [actual] price the competition offered." If the competition was paying the same reinsurance costs as The Co-operators, there would be no profit in that contract, Scott says.

Overall, claims have been higher, and premium increases have not kept up. In 1984, for example, claims increased 16 per cent while premiums went up only 3.4 per cent, only slightly less than the increase in inflation. One reason for higher pay-outs has been changes in the law. In Ontario, revisions to the Family Law Reform Act six years ago allowed people who are not directly involved in a car accident to sue for damages. For example, the grandson of a woman injured in a car accident can sue the person at fault and recover damages for loss of affection. Loss of affection in cases involving injury as well as death has not spread to jurisdictions outside Ontario. Manitoba is the only other province where people can sue for loss of affection, but in the event of death only. Robitaille, who also serves as chairman of the industry group, the Insurance Bureau of Canada, hopes to contain the changes within Ontario. "If we lobby correctly," he says, "it may not happen in other provinces."

Another reason for higher settlements is that courts can now add what's known as pre-judgment interest to pay-outs; the judgment is increased by the amount of interest that would have accrued at usual bank rates between the time of the accident and the time of the award. There are other wrinkles that are causing the insurance companies headaches. If, for example, a youth from Ontario is standing on a street corner in Buffalo, N.Y., and is struck and injured by an uninsured driver of a stolen car, the parents can claim and collect damages from their own car insurance company even though the child was not insured as a driver in their policy.

The industry worries about such incidents because no one can predict how many will occur—or the size of court settlements when they do. Rate-setting, already a nightmare of possibilities and pessimism, takes on even more shadowy overtones. Meanwhile, because people sue more readily in the U.S. than in Canada, U.S. rates on commercial insurance coverage for Canadian companies doing business in the U.S. are double 1984 levels. In specific areas, where there have been heavy claims, rates are skyrocketing. In the U.S., commercial rates have jumped as much as 300 per cent, with average increases in the range of 30 to 40 per cent. No insurance is available at any price against claims for asbestosis, for example; asbestos manufacturer Johns-Manville was hit with so many lawsuits that by 1982 insurance simply became unavailable. One Canadian aircraft manufacturer has seen its annual premium go to more than $9 million from $2.5 million. Coverage on brokers' blanket bonds for the "three Ds"—dishonesty, disappearance, and destruction—cost financial institutions about one-third more in 1985, even if the firms have had no losses. For firms with recent claims, the rates have doubled.

In some cases, premiums are soaring simply because fewer companies are offering the business. There are only three firms in Canada writing environmental impairment (pollution) coverage; 1985 rates are 70 per cent higher than 1984 rates. The number of insurers taking on high-risk petroleum companies has recently shrunk to five from fifteen. Because of industry losses, petroleum firms that have had losses have seen rates triple and quadruple, with higher deductibles. In addition to the Syncrude fire, there was the 1984–85 $200-million oil well blow-out at Mobil Oil Corp. on Sable Island, N.S.; a $38-million fire at an Alberta Gas Trunk Line Co. Ltd. (now Nova Corp.) compressor station in 1980; and an estimated $100-million compressor house fire in 1982 at the Suncor Inc. plant in Fort McMurray. On the Suncor loss, 160 insurers in eleven countries were involved in the settlement. Says Suncor's corporate risk manager, Pamela Dixon, "It taxed the world-wide insurance market to the limit."

Yet for all the losses and the talk of needing higher rates, the industry has been remarkably healthy. Looking at rates of return—net income after tax as a percentage of net worth—the general insurance industry compares very favourably with other Canadian-based industries. From 1978 to 1983, the general insurance industry had an average rate of return of 11.7 per cent, exactly the same as other industries. There is, however, so much unused capacity for more business in the Canadian general insurance industry that profits may deteriorate. One way to measure that capacity is to compare premiums to capital and surplus. For every dollar of capital and surplus measured by the particular accounting system that the industry uses, companies can write two to three dollars in premiums. At the end of September 1984, for example, premiums paid totalled $7.6 billion, and capital and surplus was $5.4 billion—a ratio of only $1.42 of premiums to $1.00 of surplus and capital. "Rates should go up," says Stan Griffin, director of research at the Insurance Bureau of Canada, "but there is a pretty hefty chunk of unused capacity [keeping rates down]."

Corporate insurance managers, or risk managers, as they are known, can play on this capacity. Bill Andrus cites a client whose annual premium for third-party liability coverage (injuries to employees, customers, passers-by, and the like) had been $500,000 a year. When the client recently put the coverage out for competitive bids at the time of renewal, most of the bids were in the $300,000–$600,000 range—although one was an out-of-whack $1.4 million. The client, a company that had few claims, settled on a bid of $360,000, thus *saving* $140,000 over the previous premium at a time when many are screaming that rates are going up. Andrus urges risk managers to ask for several bids. As a buyer, he says, know claims history, don't insure expected losses (that's like insuring certainty), ask the insurer what profit levels it seeks on underwriting (5 per cent is reasonable), and make the insurance company stick to those margins. "Companies that have blown the insurance company away [with claims] will feel a substantial rate increase," says Andrus. "Those that haven't, shouldn't."

From the insurance companies' viewpoint, the long-term answer, of course, is fewer firms in the business. Royal's Robitaille would like the fragmented Canadian industry to be more like the genteel British system. The ten largest property and casualty companies in Canada write only 30 per cent of the business. In Britain, the top six write 70 per cent. That means a more orderly market and profits all round. Still, for all the talk of a coming crunch, Robitaille is sanguine. "In the long run," admits Robitaille, "we get what we need. It may be a year behind. In Britain, rates go up regularly. With fewer players [in Canada], the competitive heat will disappear."

As yet, however, the temperature remains high. Continuing bad results, stiff competition, any economic downturn, and continuing slack rules on reinsurance could mean a return to 1981–82, when companies wobbled and collapsed. In such situations, the public suffers. If a bank or a trust company goes under, the Canada Deposit Insurance Corporation steps in to guarantee losses up to $60,000 of deposits for each individual. The insurance industry has no such back-stop. If an insurance company goes bankrupt and there are insufficient funds to pay all debts and claims outstanding, creditors get less than they are owed. (The life insurance business is more stable. No death benefit has ever gone unpaid because a company went out of business.)

In the case of Strathcona, all policyholders were paid in full. During the time the company was under the superintendent's control, $35 million in claims were paid. In August 1983, Strathcona was merged with another company that took over the rest of the $5 million in claims to be settled. While there is no guarantee fund, the industry does pay wind-up costs, so that what assets do exist go only to policyholders, not to lawyers and accountants. In the case of Pitts, Strathcona, and Cardinal, the industry was assessed $10 million in administrative costs.

While Strathcona claimants, mostly commercial firms, were satisfied in two years, Pitts policyholders, for the most part ordinary consumers with automobile and home-owner protection, were not so lucky. No one rallied to pay off those claims. In fact, of the 80,000 policyholders, some 4,000 had $23 million in claims when the company went under in 1981. Their claims payments are still trickling out four years later. First payments, 30 cents for every dollar owing, were not made until March 1983. By 1985, 70 cents had been paid on the way to a likely eventual payment of 89 cents. Pitts also nearly ruined the man brought in to save it, John Ingle.

Pitts Insurance Co. Ltd. began its corporate life on a borrowed reputation. It was named after two eighteenth-century English statesmen named Pitt, presumably to give the company, founded in

1956, an air of respectability and instant tradition. After a few quiet years, Pitts was in trouble by 1978, well before the 1981 collapse. Under financial tests set by Section 103 of the Canadian and British Insurance Companies Act and overseen by the federal superintendent of insurance, Pitts's reserves had become insufficient in 1978. Under Section 103, a company must have assets that exceed liabilities by a margin of at least 15 per cent of unearned premium reserves and outstanding claims. The problem was corrected by the owner, Robert Trollope.

In 1980, the reserves shortage recurred. Pitts was more than $600,000 short. The company blamed the installation of a computer system for temporarily fouling up its books. According to Bill Andrus, the situation was desperate. Pitts had receivables (money owed to it) of $10.3 million on assets of $17.5 million, a ratio of 57 per cent. At the time, the industry average was 14 per cent. Still, the company appeared to be a going concern. Gross premium income was $26 million in 1980 from business coming in through about 800 agents.

For its part, the insurance department's federal examiners had begun watching Pitts monthly, rather than through the perfunctory annual visit. In early 1981, Pitts was late in filing its 1980 audited statement. The superintendent gave Pitts more time and began looking for someone to buy the company and inject necesary funds. The monthly inspections became weekly ones and by spring, the filing was complete.

Then problems arose with Pitts's share of an $8-million policy. Executive vice-president Don Smith wasn't happy with what he saw as a "substantial exposure in excess of ability to repay," changed it, then told owner Robert Trollope he had done so. Trollope fired him. (In an ironic turn, Smith was later hired by the superintendent to help with the wind-up of Pitts.) While the handling of the policy showed a "rather cavalier approach to management," that was not the reason why Pitts eventually foundered, says Smith. In July, First Atlantic Assurance Co. of Bermuda stopped sending money to Pitts to cover amounts it owed. When the reinsurer balks, the primary company runs short of money. In this case, there was a twist. First Atlantic and Pitts were both owned by the same man, Robert Trollope.

Robert Woodland Trollope, seventy, is a native of Toronto. Early in his career, he held a variety of sales jobs; for four years, he was a cough-drop manufacturer. In the mid-1950s, he bought North American Automobile Association Ltd. and built several associated companies, including Pitts Life Insurance Co. (Not associated with the failed Pitts and unaffected by the furore, it later became Westbury Life Insurance Co.) For the next twenty-five years he was a typically conservative businessman in London, Ont., a city filled with clean, white-collar jobs and insurance company head offices, including those of London Life and Northern Life. Trollope has ridden to the hounds in Britain; locally he has been master of the hunt with the rest of the horsy set. He lives in a manor called Darwood on eighteen acres near Hyde Park, west of London. In 1980, his personal worth was declared at $7 million. Clearly, the insurance business and real estate deals had been profitable ventures for him.

At least part of the trouble at Pitts came about because it shared out an unusually high proportion of its risks with reinsurance firms, including Trollope's own First Atlantic. First Atlantic is one of more than 1,200 insurance companies on Bermuda, a speck in the Atlantic where there is a minimum of regulation and even less tax. Pitts was reinsuring three-quarters of its total business, much of it outside Canada, with companies beyond the jurisdiction of the federal superintendent. At one point, for example, First Atlantic reinsured some 90 per cent of Pitts coverage on high-risk drivers.

Reinsurance is common among Canadian companies. It is even sound business practice to share out the risk over certain levels. That way, when a large number of claims—or a single catastrophe such as a major storm—occurs, the insurance company has back-up funds available. The reinsurer, however, must be sound and able to pay when claims are made. When Pitts finally did go under, the liquidator found a deficit of $8 million. About $4.5 million of that related to money owing to Pitts from reinsurance companies. And of that $4.5 million, $500,000 was owed to Pitts by Trollope's First Atlantic. While Trollope has confirmed that Pitts used reinsurers, he claims it did not weaken the firm. In an interview with Robert McKeown of CBC-TV's *the fifth estate*, Trollope said: "We did invest in a reinsurance company. We did cede business through that...[but] there is no evidence that the First Atlantic...makes any money on Pitts Insurance Co."

Reinsurance wasn't Pitts's only problem. At a time when all insurance companies were struggling with premiums that were too low and claims that were too high, Pitts was taking on high-risk policies that other companies wouldn't touch. The substandard risks included low-rent rooming-houses in Quebec with transient populations. In many cases, the property being insured wasn't even visited to assess the risk before the policy was issued. On this group of business, claims outran premium income two-to-one.

There were internal system problems as well. At one point, in 1980, the company secretary wrote a memo saying that the claims department was withholding payment of $1 million in claims because the policies had not even been received by head office from the brokers who had placed them. As far as Trollope is concerned, however, none of this background contributed to the Pitts collapse. For him the single reason is that the buyer, John Ingle, did not invest the money he had agreed to put into Pitts.

The white knight who tried to ride to the rescue of Pitts was John Ingle, forty-one, an engineer and an MBA. He is a millionaire with a 5,500-square-foot home with an indoor swimming pool in Mississauga, Ont. He had made his money in real estate investments and had been looking to buy a small insurance company since 1968. He had made about ten offers on small firms. Ingle's father is an insurance broker, so the son grew up knowing something of that world. Among the other companies he had looked at was Strathcona—before its troubles. Ingle replied to a newspaper ad placed by Trollope, but talks between Ingle and Trollope broke off in July 1981. At the time, the 1980 financial statement was months late; it was not signed by the auditor, Thorne Riddell, until July 10. Trollope, Ingle was told, was not in good health, and the firm needed hands-on management.

Discussions began again in August and continued through the month. Little financial information seemed to be available. The superintendent's office had the company under tight rein and was renewing the company's licence on a monthly basis, something that Ingle says he was unaware of at the time. A meeting took place August 27 between Ingle and his lawyer and five officials of the superintendent's office. Recollections of the discussion differ. Ingle says his investment was to be $1.5 million: a $500,000 deposit and a further $1 million after the deal was successfully closed. According to department official Lawrence Savage, Ingle said he had a net worth of $3 million, and Savage got the feeling all the funds from his various business ventures would be available. Ingle felt he had been assured by the superintendent's office that Pitts was sound. "They boasted to me that they knew more about the company than management." (The department later denied giving Ingle such assurances.) Ingle's money would improve Pitts's liquidity, satisfy the federal reserve requirements, and allow new policies to be written. He knew the firm was not healthy, but he had turned around companies before and felt confident he could do so again.

At the same time, there was another bidder, insurance entrepreneur Alan Symons, but Ingle was assured that there was no deal with anyone else, so Ingle signed a deal only to have Symons sue. Ingle says he was assured by the superintendent that the Symons bid and lawsuit was not a problem. "We'll quash the writ even if we have to put a candle to Symons's charter," Ingle recalls being told. He became president of Pitts September 21 and put the $500,000 in trust, awaiting resolution of three problems: the Symons lawsuit, confirmation that $1.5 million was all that was needed, and approval by the Department of Insurance. "I thought," says Ingle, "I knew what I was doing."

He spent the first few days being squired about London by Trollope. Early on, however, he realized he had made a serious error. Figures handed to him for the month of July showed operating losses of $500,000 in that one month alone. Pitts employees suggested to him that the computer, which often made errors, must have made another. A weekend's work confirmed not only that the computer was correct, but that the losses were far worse than he had been led to believe. Out of every dollar of business retained at risk, 78 cents went to administration costs and paying agents. That left a miserable 22 cents to pay claims from policyholders—and claims were 8 per cent higher than premium revenue. For every dollar coming in, Pitts should have been paying out $1.08—but there was only 22 cents to do it. Pitts was running on empty. It had been paying too much to put business on the books, laying off too much of that business to reinsurers, and getting too little back from the reinsurance arrangements. For every dollar coming in through premiums, taking expenses and all costs into account, Pitts was losing two dollars.

This problem was compounded by others. Ingle had sent employee Durham Stephens out to collect receivables, money the books said was owing to Pitts. As far as Ingle could tell, receivables were around $4 million, a sum that would go a long way towards putting the company's cash flow aright. Stephens collected $200,000 in a week and a half and reported to Ingle that there was little more out there. "They don't exist," he said of the receivables. "It's a shell game. The key to this business is who's got the pea." If estimates of the company's health had been partly based on money said to be owed the company, this was, according to Ingle, another indication that Pitts was ailing.

Ingle found other problems as well. Insurance contracts were found in the back of the main office, contracts made out in Pitts's name, but with premiums actually passed on to another company, Northern Union. There were thirty to forty policies, each with a value of $100,000. He could only presume that they were written in Pitts's name because they covered parts of the country for which Northern Union was not licensed. The contracts were not entered into Pitts's books.

In addition, Ingle says he found that claims payable by Pitts in the spring were held back to swell the coffers. When they were paid and the cheques were drawn on Pitts in July, the losses began to show. He wanted out, arguing that accepting premiums from clients was fraudulent when there was little likelihood that claims on those policies would ever be paid. Within days, he figured that Pitts was in the hole at least $6 million—including $1 million in unprocessed claims he says he found in a locked cupboard. He sat down and did a quick calculation. As best he could figure it, Pitts had lost $16 million during the previous four years.

On October 3, after two weeks at Pitts, Ingle phoned the superintendent's office to alert them to what he had found. He asked them to freeze the assets of First Atlantic and invited inspectors to come to look at the books of Pitts. No one showed up for two weeks, until October 16. That day, on Ingle's instructions, Pitts stopped writing insurance. The same day five federal examiners met Ingle in London at Ingle's request. There were harsh words as Savage tried to get Ingle to put money into the firm. Ingle refused, saying, "I'm no martyr." He had not yet transferred the $500,000 to Trollope. He told the department that he wanted the department's assurances in writing of Pitts's soundness before the $500,000 and the further $1 million to come were transferred to Trollope.

The following Monday, October 19, Ingle met with twenty reinsurers for lunch at the Ontario Club in Toronto, trying to patch together an industry-based rescue operation. He had requested a meeting with Pierre Bussières, then minister of state for finance. It was all for naught. That morning, the superintendent had frozen the assets of Pitts, cancelled the firm's licence, and told a branch of the Toronto-Dominion Bank to freeze the account in which Ingle was holding the $500,000. Less than a month after Ingle had moved in, the superintendent took control of Pitts. It was officially wound up November 6, 1981, and the superintendent was appointed to liquidate the firm.

In a sworn statement filed with the Supreme Court of Ontario, Ingle says that Pitts was insolvent at the end of 1980, fully nine months before he took over. He further claims that the amount necessary to make Pitts solvent was not the $1.5 million the superintendent talked about, but $6.5 million. It was his view that Pitts had a negative worth of $5 million–$6 million when he took it over. Later he could only lament that he wished he had screamed while the firm was still open so the books could have been shown to others. Ingle was particularly upset with the Department of Insurance. "They tried to bring me in to soften the blow." Ingle sued everyone involved: the TD bank, Trollope, the superintendent, and five officials in the superintendent's office, claiming damages as a result of what he alleged to be misrepresentation and negligence. Once he sued, the superintendent launched a counter-suit to keep the $1.5 million for the creditors.

Trollope denies that Pitts was in financial trouble before Ingle arrived. Trollope was quoted by Gordon Sanderson and Cheryl Hamilton in the London *Free Press* as saying: "I made no warranty or guarantee on the condition of the company." Still, it did not help that, according to the superintendent's office, First Atlantic owed Pitts's claimants $800,000, although Trollope said, in the same interview, "First Atlantic is not admitting that liability."

After the failure, the superintendent stoutly defended his action. The whole massaging operation of working with the company for months, waiting for audited statements, and talking to prospective buyers was portrayed as part of the style of the office, a style that had worked well for decades. Richard Humphrys had been superintendent since 1964. (He retired in 1982 and was replaced by Robert Hammond.) In December 1981, before the House of Commons Standing Committee on Finance, Trade and Economic Affairs, Humphrys explained the philosophy at work as he tried to keep Pitts going: "Should we have acted sooner? It is always a question of judgment of when you act. I believe the worst solution to these problems is liquidation. If we can get additional capital, if we can get another company to take it over, I believe it is worth considerable effort to do that. Usually we solve the problems in that way."

As for the system itself, Humphrys maintained that it was sound. In 1979, Pitts was making marginal profits and was close to the minimum requirements of capital and surplus. "In the spring of 1980," said Humphrys, "we took firm action with the owners and said we needed a great improvement in the accounting records, we needed additional funds to give a safer margin, and we extracted firm commitments from the owners to rectify the situation. We had every reason to think, in the early months of 1980, although the margins were thinner [and] the claims were rising, the company was still solvent."

By fall of 1981, however, when Ingle pulled out, the situation, in the eyes of the superintendent's office, seemed to have changed. The federal examiners found that the expenses had been high and that the last quarter of 1980—a year with an audited statement already approved by the department—had, according to Humphrys, "produced an enormous swing in the incidence and size of claims—part of the bad experience coming in the property and casualty industry." While the other companies survived, Pitts went under. "All these things coming together were just more than the margins the company could stand, so we had to close the company."

There is a question as to how accurate the superintendent's soundings of the company were. In October, for example, the same month as Ingle lost control of Pitts, there was a signed statement by an officer in the superintendent's department saying that Pitts had $500,000 in assets free and clear after all debts were paid. The court-appointed liquidator (again, the department) found a different situation when it looked at Pitts over the next few weeks and discovered Pitts had a "huge deficit" when it collapsed.

There was a shortfall in the First Atlantic account, too. As in all reinsurance cases, the superintendent requires the reinsurer to maintain a Canadian trust account that matches liabilities in Canada. When First Atlantic did not send its July cheque, Trollope told the superintendent that it would be covered by a bank loan. It wasn't. By October 1981, First Atlantic's Canadian trust account contained $4.5 million; it owed Pitts $5.3 million, thus creating the $800,000 shortfall. In 1984, the amount owing was about $500,000; First

Atlantic's account with the Bank of Bermuda contained $5,168.17. When auditors Thorne Riddell had finished the audit in July 1981, they said Pitts had a shortfall on reserves of $643,382 from the asset position required by the Canadian and British Insurance Companies Act. According to a sworn statement filed by departmental official Lawrence Savage, the deficit had grown to $2.6 million by September 30, nine days after Ingle took over the firm.

Humphrys maintained that closer examination would not have turned up trouble any sooner. "I believe even had we twenty examiners into the company, instead of two or three, I am not sure we would have arrived at a different solution." As for Trollope, the liquidation did not hurt him. Trollope himself feels no responsibility to the policyholders. "I was an investor," he told *the fifth estate*. "How could you be personally responsible?" For him, the policyholders' interests had been guarded by the federal watch-dogs. "We had auditors coming out of our heads."

Ingle is not so sure. "Be careful of the government. If you hear that saying 'I'm from the government and I'm here to help you,' be cautious. I wasn't fooled by Bob Trollope. Bob Trollope in this transaction received no money from me. However, I did trust Her Majesty's Government and I did trust Her Majesty's civil service, and I was fooled."

In one bizarre turn, the battle between Ingle and Trollope focussed on the whereabouts of five prints of hunting scenes that Trollope said Ingle stole from the Pitts office. Trollope had Ingle charged with theft, and the case ended up in a London court. Ingle admitted to the court that he had taken the prints home when the company collapsed, but only because he thought they would disappear. During the trial, Ingle was able to put on the record his views of what happened when he took over Pitts from Trollope.

Trollope took the stand twice to refute charges Ingle made about him, including one that he had used company funds to pay for his daughter's wedding. Trollope claimed he had done nothing dishonest, but conceded that the company was between $1 million and $2 million short at the time of the sale. At one point Ingle's lawyer, David Humphrey, asked: "Did he [Ingle] call you a crook and say he was holding the pictures as security?" "No," Trollope replied. "He used another expression. He said, 'I've been hosed.'"

Trollope conceded the sale was "quite controversial" but under the terms of the sale, "I warranted nothing about the financial position of the company." He told the court that he was quite attached to the prints. He had purchased four of them in England; the fifth depicted the first hunt at the London Hunt Club, where he still rides to the hounds. Ingle told the court that the prints were of "trivial value" compared with other things in the company. "If I'd really wanted to take something, I would have looked around." Judge Walter Bell dismissed the case, saying that the Crown attorney had not proved any criminal intent on Ingle's part.

From 1981, when he first sued, Ingle hung tough for the next three years. "Mr. Ingle and his sister [former York mayor Gayle Christie] can be very forceful people," says superintendent Hammond. "The minister could never understand why we were having difficulty dealing with them until he met them." The stalemate suddenly ended two days after the September 1984 federal election, which saw a new government swept into power. Ingle received a telephone call from the superintendent's office saying they wanted to meet with him with a view to settling the dispute. They even offered to come to Toronto.

"My caustic, cynical comment is that they may feel that the Tories will take a different attitude towards things and [they] may have their eyes on their jobs," Ingle says. Whatever the motivation, Ingle was eager to meet them and work out a settlement. "From my standpoint, the war is expensive. It doesn't matter who is right and wrong." As the negotiations dragged on, his demand for an open hearing became a simple request for full access to the books. Ingle agreed to drop the suits in provincial court (which included his action against Trollope) but insisted he would carry on in federal court against Humphrys and the superintendent's staff. Under the terms of the offer from the superintendent's office, Ingle was to receive half of his $500,000 back, plus interest, a sum close to $300,000. He still feels he was led astray by the regulators. Because of the continued threat of court action, the regulators have made no official comment throughout.

Ingle estimates his loss on the Pitts fiasco at about $700,000, assuming the return of the $300,000, meaning he lost $200,000 of his initial $500,000. In addition, when the firm went under, the bank asked for $500,000 he had borrowed. The loan was secured by a $1.3-million mortgage that he held on a property. He had to sell the mortgage at a discount to pay back the bank, with a loss of $275,000. In addition there were $200,000 in legal fees as well as lost interest he could have earned on his investment. "Those," Ingle sighs, "are the penalties of business."

In response to the industry's difficulties and to protect individual policyholders, superintendent Hammond put forward several proposals in 1982 to prevent another Pitts, Strathcona, or Cardinal. They include raising the minimum capital and surplus requirement for a new property and casualty company from $1.5 million to $5 million; requiring that companies not cede more than 50 per cent of their reinsurance to unregistered reinsurance companies that are not supervised by the Department of Insurance; shortening from ninety days to forty-five days the period during which premiums due from agents, but unpaid, can be counted as an asset for solvency purposes; and establishing a guarantee fund for policyholders. In case of loss or damage to property, such a fund would cover claims under $200,000 or the first $200,000 of larger claims; for third-party liability claims, the guarantee would be limited to $1 million or the first $1 million of larger claims.

The industry has long been against a guarantee fund. It does approve, however, of the steps to make a firm more solvent and more likely to last. No matter. None of the three-year-old proposals has yet become law. The wheels of government grind as slowly as do pay-outs to Pitts claimants. To date, 70 cents on the dollar has been paid to the 4,000 claimants of Pitts—and it has taken four years. John Ingle has yet to find a company that he can buy. He's still looking to own one. "One, hopefully," he says, "that's solvent." For its own sake, the public should hope so, too.

CHAPTER EIGHT

LOOKING OUT FOR NUMBER ONE

Manufacturers Life Insurance Co.

EDWIN SYDNEY JACKSON is bouncing around in his executive suite, showing how he received his artillery training during the Second World War. Here he is, the president of The Manufacturers Life Insurance Co., leaping from the silk-covered couch in his luxurious office onto his Persian rug to reconstruct the rituals of four decades ago. He describes in fond detail the landscape model they used with its various targets and mock-up artillery piece standing nearby. The operator of the gun was required to make various settings as the instructor barked out the make-believe co-ordinates. Underneath the model, a man in a scooter zipped along to a point beneath the spot where the shot would have struck so he could send up a puff of smoke. The realism! Why, if only they could have figured a way to spill some tomato juice on the spot, they might have done that, too.

Jackson, sixty-three, is playing all the roles and relishing the retelling. His beak of a nose swings this way and that as he describes and sights the targets. First he is the commander, calling out the shots; next, the gunner setting the range; then he folds up his six-foot-three frame to show how the third man scrunched himself under the model, dragged on his cigarette, and waited for the "hit" so he could send the plume of cigarette smoke up through a tube. Jackson describes everything, even the foul taste in his mouth from the cigarette, the last that ever touched his lips. Not a fragment of the wartime memory is amiss.

161

After the basic instruction, he was sent to Fort Benning, Ga., for officer training. There were assault courses, a lot of belly-crawling, and various tests of his capacity to direct soldiers and devise strategy. He passed muster but the human needs of the war kept changing. Artillery lieutenants were no longer wanted; infantrymen were. When that training was complete, he was too late again. The Pacific theatre was heating up; it required further special courses. Each time he finished a program and was ready for the front, he'd be ordered back for different training. "I was," he guffaws, "a secret threat." Then he pauses and adds, his eyes serious behind his glasses with the recollection of the embarrassment he felt with each new assignment: "It was the most frustrating time I've ever spent. It got so I was afraid to go home."

Since becoming president of Manufacturers in 1972, Jackson has faced similar frustrations. He wanted ManuLife to be the biggest in the life insurance firmament, measured by assets, yet every time he got close, victory eluded him. In 1978, he almost achieved his goal, but a deal that would have joined ManuLife and the Canadian operations of Standard Life Assurance of Edinburgh, Scotland, fell apart after months of squabbling. In 1985 the trooper who was always ready but never fought won at last. ManuLife policyholders approved the $157.5-million purchase of The Dominion Life Assurance Co. from its U.S. parent, The Lincoln National Life Insurance Co. of Fort Wayne, Ind. The combined assets of the two firms—Manufacturers and Dominion—vaulted Manufacturers into first place among the 170 life insurance companies in Canada. ManuLife's total assets of $13.5 billion topped Sun Life's $13 billion and knocked Sun from the first-place position it had held in the Canadian industry since 1908.

As president, Jackson has done more than just push ManuLife up the asset ladder. He has pulled the firm into the twentieth century. From an autocratic and benevolent old codger of a place when he joined, he has remade it into a lively and decentralized company. Today it offers savings and insurance products in Canada, the U.S. and Puerto Rico, the United Kingdom, Asia, the West Indies, Israel, and Cyprus—a total of thirteen countries.

"In the 1960s and '70s," says Paul McCrossan, MP for York-Scarborough and a former insurance consultant, "a lack of brand loyalty began to show up, particularly in the cities." Firms such as Mutual of Canada did well because they focussed on small towns and rural areas where loyalties were stronger. For the rest, the market-place was a jumble of claims as consumers shopped around on the basis of price. "Manufacturers decided to go into money management, the investment side, money markets and annuities. They built an outstanding investment department—and stayed out of the [unprofitable] health insurance market."

Jackson has been unable to achieve one goal, the demutualization of ManuLife. Like several large insurance firms in the late 1950s and early 1960s, Manufacturers was mutualized when legislation permitted the process in order to prevent foreign take-overs. Unlike some mutual company presidents, Jackson sees nothing mystical about mutuality. "If there is such a religion, we haven't caught it. I think mutuality is an obsolescent concept. We mutualized because there was no other way to protect ourselves against foreign ownership." Mutual companies do not have to fear suddenly being taken over by an unwelcome corporate buyer. "You're not always concerned about the price of your stock every day and whether or not somebody is taking a run at it. You can take the long view without the short-term flak. A lot of people are distracted by the thought: 'Are the Bronfmans going to take us over tomorrow?' "

Still, there are disadvantages. One is that not everyone pays attention to the bottom line; there isn't the same control on profit and loss. "Some of the young people at ManuLife are not as interested in profits as they should be."

Jackson paints a scenario where more and more policies would become linked to stocks or short-term guaranteed investment certificates. Rates for the policyholders would be better and from the company's standpoint, there would be no need for long-term actuarial calculations to ensure pay-out. Participating—or "par"—policies, where premiums are set high, then reduced by dividends, would become unnecessary. The surpluses created by the overpayment of premiums by par policyholders, however, become a problem for the mutual companies. The surplus is made up of the funds created because of the way life insurance companies price their products. "You pay premiums for forty years and nobody other than God can tell you what's going to happen to mortality," says Jackson. "We're going to price pretty conservatively. I don't know whether to charge you $42 or $60, so I'll charge you $70 and give you any excess back. That's the mutual concept." What's not paid back to policyholders before they die becomes the surplus.

"If there were a million policyholders all with identical par policies and the surplus is a million dollars, then an equal amount for each policyholder would be one dollar. Well, that's kind of ridiculous," Jackson says. "We've been in business 100 years, so why should this generation of policyholders get that million dollars that's been built up over the years? How that evolves in the future will be quite a fascinating thing. We really need far more discussion among lawyers, actuaries, and interested academics."

What happens, however, as more and more insurance clients hold non-par policies? "You might end up after 150 years with five par policyholders with a claim on millions of dollars of surplus." To date, no one has a solution to the dilemma; most mutual company executives won't even admit that it's a problem. Jackson admits it, and he has a solution, although it is one that he recognizes is not without flaws. Jackson sees his solution to the dilemma in the same way democracy has been described—it may be bad, but all the rest are worse.

"I say what the non-par policyholder is entitled to is just what he's guaranteed. The par policyholder is entitled to the part of the earnings of the company while he was a policyholder. In a sense, his participating policy is like a unit-linked policy. What is left over is a trust held by management and the board of directors for the benefit of the entity; that is, the present and the future policyholders. In other words, it's the capital which allows you to carry on doing business.

"And then my lawyer friends say: 'Who's the ultimate owner or beneficiary of the trust?' [Chief actuary] Robin Leckie wrote a paper on this for the Society of Actuaries, saying in that theoretical situation, since we don't know who the owners will be, the money would go to the government. Robin made that statement to the Society of Actuaries, which is 90-per-cent American, and, God, he damned near got run out of the meeting. It was just the very thought that everything would go to the government." Says Jackson, "It causes great debates. What I am saying makes sense, but they say, 'You're smoking pot if you think that [idea] will ever sell.'"

If ManuLife, for example, were ever to demutualize (as some in the U.S. are now doing) and become owned by shareholders, what would happen to the surplus built up over the years? Who does it belong to? Those who paid it are dead. Those who are current policyholders didn't pay it. Jackson hasn't convinced the world he's right, but in a business where too many executives are passionless, Jackson's views are refreshing, right or wrong. Forty years after that first artillery lesson, the old gunner is still firing, trying to hit the targets that others fight to protect.

Jackson was born in Regina, graduated from the University of Manitoba, and joined ManuLife in 1948, one of the many men of his generation who received their first actuarial training under the university's Dr. Lloyd Warren. At twenty-six, Jackson was among the youngest at Manufacturers, because there had been very little hiring since the Depression. The next generation up the ranks was much older than he was, so promotions were speedy. By 1956, he was chief actuary; he became executive vice-president and a director in 1970 and president and chief executive officer in 1972.

With the position at the top have come a few perks, including a Buick Park Avenue, but for a long while, no chauffeur. Only recently did the board of directors force Jackson to accept a driver, but he rarely uses his services. Some evenings, when he and his wife, Nancy, go out, he will hire a limo because she suffers from arthritis and a driver frees Jackson up to help her. ManuLife pays for part of his membership in the Toronto Club and the Rosedale Golf Club. He golfs, curls, and skis, usually in Colorado or Vermont, and owns a condominium in Palm Beach. His salary is among the highest in the industry. Jackson will reveal only that it is "in the $200,000–$500,000 range."

ManuLife top brass have always been paid handsomely. The company was founded in 1887 in Toronto. Sir John A. Macdonald, Canada's first prime minister, was president until he died in 1891. The first managing director, J. B. Carlile, received a salary of $5,000 a year at a time when the average wage for a worker was $6 a week. In 1909, the new head office at King and Yonge Streets in Toronto cost $506,000. A contemporary newspaper commented: "Larger prices per [square] foot have been recorded, but no larger total amount has changed hands for a single property." In 1925, head office was officially moved from the downtown Toronto financial district north to Bloor Street. The reason, it was said at the time, was to "provide ample light and air, space for growth and adequate parking." Others, notably Crown and Confederation, followed, thus creating an insurance row.

The original building with its wrought-iron fence, manicured lawn, and imposing Doric portico has been expanded three times.

The addition begun in 1950 had as its consultant Charles S. Leopold of Philadelphia. It was Leopold who did the air conditioning and heating design for the Pentagon, the New York Stock Exchange, and Madison Square Garden. The attention to architecture and surroundings goes so far that ManuLife has its own greenhouse and gardener. The cafeteria is subsidized for staff. A full-course meal with dessert costs $1.50. The best entrée is Monday's roast beef. The best deal is the salad. With care the small bowl, for 35 cents, can be piled so high that once the diner has reached the table, the amount taken fills a small plate that would have cost 80 cents. The law department on the tenth floor of the North Tower pays for coffee and juice. It has become a favourite for employees from other floors who visit and partake.

The most recent building addition, officially opened in 1983, continues the ostentatious tradition. The $40-million thirteen-storey reflective gold glass North Tower is joined to the limestone building on Bloor by a copper-roofed rotunda, designed by Clifford Lawrie Bolton Ritchie Architects. Inside are marble floors, brass-clad columns, and delicate brass railings circling a second-storey catwalk. Peering down on passers-by is a bust of Sir John. On a nearby wall hangs a Krieghoff painting done on a cast-iron table-top. It weighs 600 pounds and had to be hung using a fork-lift truck.

In the centre of the rotunda is a double-tiered fountain that caused no end of problems when it was installed. A saucer-shaped brass base was meant to catch the spray of water, then allow the water to fall cleanly off the edge, all the way around the perimeter of the base. The base would not remain level, however, thus spilling all the water out one side rather than smoothly around the full perimeter. Says construction manager Kent Harvey: "It was like trying to fill a twelve-foot-wide champagne glass." That was corrected by bolstering the base so it couldn't tip. The next problem occurred as the water fell onto the travertine marble below. In some places, there were travertine blocks in the catch-basin that caused the water to trickle to the floor before it had a chance to gather. Deep slots had to be cut in the marble blocks so the water would be directed into the catch-basin for recirculation.

Above the fountain hangs an ornate sunburst chandelier designed by the architects. The cupola of the rotunda features stained glass by artist David Morgan. Even the elevators, by Mitsubishi, are unique. They are panelled with cherrywood and the manufacturer's name is nowhere in sight, at ManuLife's request. On the second basement level of the North Tower is the largest corporate fitness facility in Canada: 15,000 square feet of space including a banked track, group exercise rooms, dance bars, saunas, and showers for the 2,000 employees at head office. The eleventh and twelfth floors of the North Tower are joined by a winding staircase and contain the executive offices, dining rooms, and boardroom. They rank with the most luxurious suites in the country. Jackson's office is on the eleventh floor. His desk and credenza are built of Carpathian burled elm, the walls are covered in silk, and the floor has a Persian carpet. He has his own four-piece bathroom *en suite*, personal storage closets, and a built-in bar.

On the twelfth floor, there are walk-out terraces, a boardroom, an executive lounge with fireplace, and three dining rooms seating four, eight, and sixteen—all served from a single kitchen nearby. Company officers are encouraged to eat in a large dining room (it seats forty) to discuss business. All corridors and mouldings are custom cherrywood. The walls of the executive offices and lounge area are covered in Jack Lenor Larsen silk. The ivory wool broadloom was bordered and sculpted by five women working on their hands and knees with tiny scissors for two weeks. The furniture in the dining rooms ranges from modern designer to Chippendale. A 100-year-old Persian rug in the lounge cost $20,000.

The oval boardroom measures forty by twenty-five feet and contains a custom-designed table built right on the site. The two dozen chairs are covered in grey suede, and each place has a grey leather Nienkamper desk pad. The acoustics are such that a whisper can be heard from one end of the room to the other. The cherrywood was chosen from veneer flitches one-sixteenth of an inch thick, two feet wide, and eight to ten feet long. The wood from 100 trees was examined to find just the right panels. A single tree supplied all the veneer for the boardroom. Construction of the room and the table took three months.

As the surroundings have changed, so has the company's atmosphere. ManuLife has gone through a culture shock, moving from a warm family feeling to a more heartless place. When executive vice-president Tom Di Giacomo was working at Manufacturers as a summer student in the investment department in the early 1960s, chairman George L. Holmes called him into his office to talk about a particular deal. As Di Giacomo started to explain, Holmes interrupted. "Just hold on," he said. "You know more about what you're talking about than I know what I'm talking about, so take your time. We're on the same team."

As the financial world became more competitive, however, Manu-Life changed along with the rest. The boss became more aloof and removed from day-to-day operations; conversations between lowly clerks and the executive were rare. "There was a large degree of loss of family as the company got bigger," says Di Giacomo. As society became more open in the 1970s, however, Manufacturers tried to respond by having an open-concept office design. There were no offices—only six-foot dividers separated the president from the underlings. The system worked for a while, then change was necessary again. "Noise levels were high," recalls Di Giacomo. The idea, as with all office design concepts, lost its glamour after a while. "The place was getting tatty."

With the move into additional new quarters in 1983, ManuLife ended both the tatty look and the open concept. Middle and upper management moved into private offices. Jackson knows that the move will alter how the company works. Under the old system, "You got a good sense of what was going on. People got used to being accessible. It had served a very useful purpose. [Now] people want confidentiality. I have a fear that we'll lose that open communication. As we get to be bigger, we've got to change our ways. We've got to get more formal rather than be a group of vice-presidents all being together over a cup of tea, having a quick conference and making decisions."

Under the new office system, flat wiring is hidden under the carpets so that people, phones, and any of the 1,100 computer terminals can be moved easily. The wiring system is the largest such installation in North America. Such design considerations, the health facilities, and general ambience mean that Manufacturers is consistently seen in the corporate world as a good place to work. When *Canadian Business* magazine selected Canada's six best working environments in 1984, ManuLife was one of them.

Growth, however, has not been easy. There is only limited potential for growth in any company. The only way to make a quantum leap in sales or assets is to acquire another firm. In 1978 Manufacturers tried and failed to buy the Montreal-based Canadian operations of Standard Life Assurance Co. of Edinburgh, Scotland. The deal would have made ManuLife the largest life insurance company in Canada, based on premium income, at the time. For Standard, as for Sun Life, Quebec was becoming a tough place to have an anglo head office. The ManuLife offer was an escape hatch and would have added a sales force of 200 to ManuLife's Montreal operations.

The first announcement of the proposed purchase was made in July. Not all the Standard policyholders were pleased about the prospect, and a committee of disgruntled policyholders was formed to fight the take-over. Because Standard is a mutual company, there was a lengthy debate between the two firms about how to take account of the surplus amounts on Standard's balance sheet. Standard was said to have a $200-million surplus. Would that be removed from the Canadian operations to be distributed among British policyholders, because it belonged to Standard policyholders? Or would it go to ManuLife as part of the spoils of the take-over? In the end, Standard disagreed with Jackson's intentions to transfer the surplus to ManuLife and use it for expansion. The deal fell apart in November. Jackson could only retreat, with his plan to become Canada's largest life insurance company in disarray.

Expansion has been a historic problem. When ManuLife was formed in 1887, Canada was just too small a market. The solution then was to follow the British Empire connections to Hong Kong, Ceylon (now Sri Lanka), and the Philippines. The first foreign policy was sold in Bermuda in 1893; in 1897 ManuLife was doing business in Shanghai; in 1898 it opened agencies in Japan and Hong Kong; and it went into the U.S. in 1903 and the U.K. by 1925. At the turn of the century an agent would climb on a boat and spend months visiting countries from Ceylon through the Philippines to Japan. Tales of the fanaticism of the Pacific Rim employees are legendary. One ManuLife branch administrator in Manila hid policy records and a quarter of a million dollars of the company funds in her home during the Japanese occupation from 1942 to 1945. After hostilities had ceased, she dug up the money, discovered who had died, and paid the appropriate beneficiaries.

In the United Kingdom, ManuLife helped pioneer the agency system common in North America. For years, ManuLife was among the few companies in the U.K. with a direct-selling sales force. Today more and more companies are switching to this form of selling. In 1984, 60 per cent of ManuLife's premiums came from the

U.S., 28 per cent from Canada, 7 per cent from the U.K., and 2 per cent from Hong Kong. (About 35 per cent of all the life insurance sold in Hong Kong is sold by Manufacturers.)

In 1984 Syd Jackson, the man who trained for every role in the war and tried none of them, had another chance to make ManuLife number one: Dominion Life was placed on the auction block for any and all bidders.

John Acheson, sixty-three, has been Dominion's president since 1970. He started with the Royal Bank in 1939, then went to war as a member of the bomber command. His Halifax aircraft was shot down by a night fighter. Acheson was the crew's only survivor. He spent two and a half years in a prisoner-of-war camp in Europe. After the war, he studied to become an actuary at the University of Manitoba; he joined Dominion in Waterloo in 1951. As president, he presided over asset growth from $356,000 in 1971 to $1.5 billion in 1984; premium and investment income grew from $64 million to $401 million.

Early in 1984, Dominion's U.S. owner, Lincoln National Corp., decided to sell after a consulting firm had studied the Canadian operations and handed in a bleak report. "We Canadians malign our country unnecessarily," says Acheson. "We're great talkers-down of our own country. They listened to a bunch of Canadians sing the blues." Acheson was in England in April attending a board meeting of another company in which Lincoln National has an investment when David Silletto, executive vice-president of Lincoln National Corp., the holding company that owned Lincoln National Life and, in turn, Dominion, invited him to breakfast April 30 at his London hotel. Silletto told Acheson that Lincoln was going to sell Dominion. Says Acheson, "It was a shock."

The decision marked the end of an era. Lincoln National had purchased a 51-per-cent controlling interest in Dominion in 1957 from three Canadian families. The offer was extended to other shareholders and Lincoln National obtained 94 per cent of Dominion for about $7 million. A stock purchase program later introduced for employees reduced Lincoln National's holdings to 89 per cent as employees bought stock through payroll deductions. Dominion, based in Waterloo, Ont., was one of the Canadian firms whose takeover by foreign owners led to federal legislation allowing mutualization.

Lincoln's reasons to sell in 1984 were tied to its changed view that

Canada was no longer a good place to have an investment. Lincoln was fed up with Canadian investment rules. If Dominion invested in oil and gas development, for example, because of its foreign owner-ship it did not receive the same level of petroleum incentive grants under the National Energy Program rules as did a Canadian-owned life insurance company. Further, U.S. tax law had changed, Silletto told Acheson, making it more advantageous to repatriate the assets. They agreed on four goals for the sale. First, Dominion should remain in hands of unquestioned integrity; second, the new owner should preferably be Canadian; third, a significant presence should be maintained in Waterloo; fourth, Dominion should, if possible, remain a separate company, not be merged and lost in another balance sheet.

At first Acheson was not bothered by Lincoln's plan to put Dominion up for public auction. As time passed, however, he realized it was a horrendously slow process. Usually deals are negotiated between two parties, perhaps using another bidder for leverage, but Lincoln was interested in the highest price so it decided to adopt the auction technique that was becoming quite common in Britain. Lincoln hired New York merchant banker Salomon Broth-ers Inc. to handle the deal. The process would wander along for six months.

Word began to spread in June that Dominion was for sale. Tom Di Giacomo received a telephone call in early June from Salomon Brothers. "Would you be interested in buying a Canadian life insurance company?" he was asked. Di Giacomo was told the asset size of the company and when Di Giacomo pushed, the particular company was also identified—Dominion, the eleventh-largest firm in Canada. There was no additional financial information available yet beyond what was public. Di Giacomo was non-committal. "We'll think about it and get back to you," he said, and agreed to keep the auction secret.

The secret didn't last. The next day, the sale was announced in all the newspapers. Equally speedy was the joke that spread in the industry. Confederation would buy Dominion, according to the story and the new, merged company would be called Condom Life. There was even a new slogan proposed: "Condom—when you want to be safe."

After Di Giacomo read Lincoln National's announcement, he phoned Salomon Brothers and said drily: "Well, I guess it's not the secret they want it to be." The Salomon team in charge of the sale was also surprised by the public announcement and didn't know how much time was available for bidders to consider their offers. Di Giacomo called a meeting of ManuLife executives to discuss the prospect. Attending were Di Giacomo, Jackson, senior vice-president and chief actuary Robin Leckie, senior vice-president Joe Davin, senior vice-president John Clarke, investment vice-president for Canadian equities Jalynn Bennett, and others from the legal and actuarial departments as well as from the Canadian division.

The man heading ManuLife's team, Tom Di Giacomo, forty-three, had scrabbled his way up from the bottom. His first job, as a summer student in 1963, was in the mail room. He was very nearly fired when he scared a female co-worker with a rubber spider. After a dressing-down, "I became meek and mild for a week." During the next five summers, he worked in the investment division while he obtained his degree in commerce from the University of Toronto and his MBA from the University of Chicago. He joined Manufacturers just as the industry was changing, dress codes were relaxing, and a young man could progress quickly. By the time he was thirty-one, he was a vice-president for finance. A generation earlier, such an appointment would not have come until he had reached fifty. Today he is everyone's choice as heir apparent to president Syd Jackson, who must retire in two years.

Di Giacomo's take-over team quickly concluded that it didn't cost anything to take a look at Dominion. As the group began to study the type of business Dominion had, they realized that Dominion would strengthen ManuLife's group life and health insurance totals. Dominion also had a few products ManuLife did not have—specifically a universal life policy. (Universal life policies were begun in Canada by Dominion Life in 1981. They combine renewable term policies with savings keyed to current interest rates. They allow premiums to be stopped or started, increased or decreased; coverage of other family members can be included; growth in the value of the policy is tied to current interest rates.) About 80 per cent of Dominion's new individual business was in this area. Of all the companies operating in Canada, Dominion had had the most success with universal life. Few other companies bothered with the product, simply because most Canadians didn't seem to want it. In the U.S. universal life accounts for one-third of all new insurance; in Canada it accounts for less than 5 per cent.

Another figure was constantly below the surface during all the discussions—total asset size. The prospect of being number one in assets was an incentive, although all might deny it. Certainly the industry view was that Manufacturers had such ambitions. Said Mutual Life chairman John Panabaker, "Syd would like to take over the Sun as number one. Also he feels that there are too many firms in the business and that there should be rationalization. I guess he's doing his part."

Jackson would admit to thinking there are too many life companies in Canada. "I wouldn't like to see fewer than ten big ones—anything from a couple of billion dollars up. Smaller companies will have to find a niche, become a part of a group, or merge." ManuLife's move on Dominion would move ManuLife from fifth position to fourth in individual insurance, increase the group business, bring in new products, and allow such areas as computer services to become more efficient by serving a larger need. ManuLife's business in Canada had not grown at the same pace as it had in the U.S. This purchase would put a lot of Canadian business on the books immediately, because more than 85 per cent of Dominion's 370,000 policyholders were Canadian. The ManuLife committee soon realized that each company had offices in thirteen Canadian cities that could be consolidated, thus saving money. If the combined operations could be run at lower cost, they would be achieving synergy, where the whole is greater than the sum of its parts.

While ManuLife was deciding it was interested, Panabaker's Mutual was coming to the opposite conclusion. Mutual already had a universal life policy, so gaining Dominion's was no advantage. There was a mix of sales agents and brokers at Dominion. That would have meant changing the overall Mutual system, where only Mutual agents sold Mutual products, and those agents sold no other company's products. Finally, there were disadvantages to combining the operations of two employers in the same city. "To merge our companies would have spilled a lot of blood," says Panabaker, "and I didn't have the stomach for that."

If Panabaker wasn't interested, others were. Sixty people or organizations showed an interest in June and July. The time dragged on, and employees and agents of Dominion became targets for competitors trying to hire them away amid the uncertainty. "The wolves were at our heels looking for career agents," says Acheson. Job placement agencies were constantly on the phone, trying to pry employees loose. Acheson himself had a job offer. He turned it down. "When you're just hung out to dry for a few months, it's very unnerving."

Finally, at the end of July, the prospectus was mailed out to about forty of the sixty who had shown an interest, the other twenty being excluded as cranks or firms unlikely to be able to afford Dominion. The thick booklet outlined Dominion's organization, structure, market value of assets, market share in various areas, plans for the future, and management comments. For its part, Lincoln National wanted three pieces of information from potential bidders: price, method of payment, and intention with regard to employment and operations in Waterloo.

By the end-of-August deadline, about twenty of the forty interested parties had entered bids. From that group, six finalists were chosen. The six included ManuLife, Imperial, Aetna, Crown, Confederation, and a west coast man, who has never been identified, acting on behalf of a number of pension funds. Each was picked on the basis of the first bid and stated plans for jobs in Waterloo. ManuLife, for example, had entered a bid in the $145 million–$150 million range; Crown's range was wide, $100 million to $150 million; Confederation bid about $100 million. (The bid figures were for all of the 1 million shares outstanding, not just the 89 per cent owned by Lincoln National. Most of the 11 per cent not owned by Lincoln National were owned by current and former employees or directors. Within weeks of the initial announcement, the listed share price value had jumped by 50 per cent. The final price would go even higher.) Each of the six would be allowed closer scrutiny of Dominion's books and time with management to poke and pry into the company.

The bid amount wasn't the only criterion for selection to the final round. One bidder among the twenty was excluded: First City Financial's Sam Belzberg. "They have a history of buying and selling," says Acheson. "The last thing I needed was someone to buy it and sell it again. I just wasn't comfortable." The Belzbergs, however, had taken a shine to Lincoln National's operations. If Dominion wasn't available to them, a stake in Lincoln National would have to do, so the Belzbergs bought shares of the parent company. The exact number was never revealed, but it must have been less than 5 per cent, because a purchase of more than that would have required a filing with the U.S. Securities and Exchange Commission. No such filing, known as a 13-D, was made. The Belzbergs probably did well on their investment. At the time, Lincoln National was selling for about $32. Within six months, it was more than $10 per share higher.

In September, teams from the six final bidders visited Dominion. Each spent about two days with Dominion executives, going through the books and asking endless questions. Di Giacomo and his crack team nearly didn't arrive at Dominion to investigate the firm. He was behind the wheel of the car as the group left the Valhalla Inn in downtown Kitchener, Ont. With him were senior vice-president and chief actuary Robin Leckie and senior vice-president Joe Davin. Dominion was ten minutes away in Waterloo. Davin and Leckie were acting as navigators. Ten minutes passed, then fifteen, then twenty. Dominion was not yet in sight. The three big shots, in from Toronto with their natty suits, briefcases, and big dreams, were lost. "We can mastermind how we can buy a company," said Di Giacomo, "but we haven't been able to mastermind how to find it." They finally did what all lost travellers do. They stopped at a gas station and got directions. In the end, the ten-minute run took half an hour.

Acheson and his senior officers spent most of September dealing with similar investigating teams from the six interested bidders. "At the end of the first week," recalls Acheson, "I was exhausted. It was like they were walking into a home with people still living there." Di Giacomo sympathized with Dominion's situation. "When you've been told you're for sale in May and you're still for sale in September, the organization gets pretty nervous." Acheson was under particular emotional strain. He told Di Giacomo, "When you're a subsidiary, you're not in charge of your own destiny." Di Giacomo knew that Acheson felt the ownership change very deeply. "He had told Lincoln National that Dominion was on a turn-around," Di Giacomo recalls. "His voice cracked. He had a tear in his eye. He was very tired."

The executive committee of the ManuLife board had been kept up to date; now it reviewed Di Giacomo's report and gave him the go-ahead to make a final offer. Two days later, a five-member management committee, including Jackson and Leckie, met to pick the price, within a range approved by the board. Di Giacomo told the group: "Let's all write down on a piece of paper what we think the price should be." Di Giacomo collected the papers and read them out, identifying his bid of $157.5 million as he read it. One was lower than his suggested price; three were higher. The group went with Di Giacomo's number. "I guess they trusted my instincts," he says. The full board met in Boston on October 18 and approved the bid. Di Giacomo flew to New York that day and showed up at Salomon Brothers offices the next morning, the day bids were due. "This is the longest damn process I've ever been through," he complained.

Only three of the six in the final round made an offer. After studying Dominion's books, Aetna, Confederation, and Crown decided, for various reasons, not to bid. Imperial was second-highest, at $152 million. Manufacturers had to wait until the following week to hear the outcome. Jackson, Di Giacomo, Leckie, and Davin were scheduled to go to IBM World Trade Corp. headquarters in White Plains, N. Y., for two days of discussion to see how IBM's control of its decentralized management might be applied to ManuLife. While there, Di Giacomo received a call from Lincoln National's Silletto. "I'm happy to inform you that you are the winner," he said. Di Giacomo rejoined his colleagues who were lunching with IBM staff. He couldn't talk about the deal because it wasn't yet official, so he telegraphed the news to Jackson by giving him a thumbs-up signal. In response, Jackson nodded and allowed himself a slight smile.

The deal was struck November 16, subject to approval by at least three-quarters of the 780,000 ManuLife policyholders in 138 countries before a special meeting called for February. (Only 19 per cent of the policyholders voted; 98 per cent of those who voted approved.) Staff at ManuLife were not immediately receptive. Di Giacomo knew the reason: "Uncertainty and change bother everybody." Two meetings were held November 24 to calm down the troops. Both Jackson and John Clarke spoke to the 250 employees who gathered at each meeting and answered their questions. Canadian operations, the employees were told, would be combined in Waterloo. At the time, Dominion had 550 employees at its head office, ManuLife had 500 in its Canadian division. The merged division, to operate effectively and achieve the desired cost base, could not be larger than 750 or 800. That meant that about 300 employees would be without jobs.

Assurances were given that few would be found redundant. Employees were reminded that about 9 per cent of the staff departed voluntarily each year. That meant that out of the 1,050 employee total in the combined Canadian operations, about 180 could be expected to leave during the two years leading up to amalgamation of the division. That left 120 people to be taken care of. To reduce that number even further, a hiring freeze had been put into effect in other departments. As jobs came open there through attrition, applicants from the operations being trimmed would be given priority. While ManuLife's Canadian division moves to Waterloo over a two-year period, Dominion's investment department is moving to Toronto.

As those two departments merge, ManuLife's final plan for Dominion awaits legislative changes in Ottawa. Under current rules, ManuLife cannot own another insurance company; the two firms have to be fully merged in two years, although that can be extended by the minister of finance. "We are assuming that we can hold a life insurance subsidiary in Canada. Even if it takes ten years to get around to it—perish the thought—they *have* to extend the law," says Jackson hopefully.

For ManuLife there are advantages to keeping Dominion separate. One possibility would be for Dominion to become licensed in New York state so ManuLife could do business there. In the U.S., insurance companies are licensed on a state-by-state basis. New York's laws are particularly onerous, and once a company is licensed there, New York law is deemed to apply to that company's operations in all states. The particular problem for most companies occurs in the regulations applied by New York to a firm's expenses. The stringent rules impose limitations on commission paid to agents, about half to three-quarters of the usual level. Dominion's universal life policy, however, currently has a 50-per-cent commission level, which falls within the New York limits, so the product is no less desirable from the sales agent's point of view.

For their part, Dominion employees were elated by the take-over. Their jobs were assured, and only a few in the investment department would have to move to Toronto. Someone even had buttons printed, blue with white lettering. The buttons, handed out around Dominion's office, read "We're number 1"—in reference to the combined assets of ManuLife and Dominion. Jackson claims he doesn't care. A vice-president had once said to Jackson: "My ambition is to be the biggest in Canada." "That's not mine," Jackson had replied. "My ambition is to be the best." And yet in the days following the deal's announcement, he was at several industry functions and came away disappointed that not one of his peers congratulated him on the purchase.

If Syd Jackson cannot get his kicks outside ManuLife, then he'll just have to get them inside. Few other life insurance executives have wrestled a company into the modern era as smoothly as he has. The changes began when he was still executive vice-president and heir apparent to the president. The most significant physical change was the attempt at moving the firm to an open-office concept, which worked as long at Manufacturers as it worked anywhere. The number of levels in the company was cut to yield a shorter chain of command, meaning better communications. More attention was paid to competence. Previously, because there had been so many positions on the ladder, promotions were almost automatic. A technical clerk would be promoted to supervisor and if successful there would be named a manager even though he might not have had any management skills. "A lot of these people were technical specialists but crappy managers," said Jackson. "A lot of them were promoted out of their competence. There was a lot of stress in the organization."

He tackled communications by starting a weekly staff magazine that encouraged an exchange of employee views. A column called ManuLine was begun. In it, employees could remain anonymous, make comments, and receive answers. Job descriptions and job evaluations were prepared and followed. "The first two years weren't happy years for me," says Jackson. "It was such a radical change. People weren't used to it." No wonder: in little more than a decade, the firm had gone from the benevolent and autocratic ways of the 1950s to the wide open spaces of the 1970s. As the family feeling disappeared, Jackson tried to introduce a sense that everyone was part of a series of small businesses within the larger whole.

In 1970, then president Alf Seedhouse set up a task force to study corporate reorganization. Jackson co-chaired the group, which spent eighteen months studying the organization along with consultants from Hay Associates. The decision was taken to decentralize. It was a major move for a company that had required head office approval for such far-off items as salary increases for branch managers in the U.K. ManuLife also hired consultants to help examine the North American market. It was, says Jackson, "our first approach to strategic planning on a non-intuitive basis. . . a 'top-down' planning phase for the company as a whole, but concentrating on North America. This really was our first attempt at any formalized type of market-driven strategic planning."

Management realized that the firm could no longer hope to sell the same products in Detroit as it did in Hong Kong. Only by organizing on a geographic basis—away from vertical product lines where individual insurance, say, covered the world—could each division decide what was best for its area. As a result, Jackson created five distinct divisions—Canada, the U.S., the U.K., Pacific Asia, and a collection of areas under an international division. Under this decentralization, each division was responsible for its own planning and the strategy required to reach its markets.

The changes he began to put in place broadened his own management skills and made him the obvious successor as president. In 1972, when chairman George Holmes made him president, he told Jackson, "You're now president. You're not an actuary any longer." He even urged Jackson not to use the letters F.S.A. after his name, which designated him a Fellow of the Society of Actuaries.

Not everyone was happy with the changes Jackson made. For some, the future had arrived too fast. There were three or four early retirements as people who no longer fit fled, and, recalls John Clarke, senior vice-president, some of those departing "made a terrible fuss about it. If you picked up a paper it looked as if we were hurling people on the lawn." The Jackson style remains demanding. "Syd's a good thought-provoker," says Di Giacomo. "He makes sure that you've thought it through. He leaves it up to people to decide how to do things. He pays attention to the general direction."

What Jackson has created is no longer just a life insurance company. Annuities are a huge business—in 1984, annuities on the books totalled $6.3 billion. In 1982, major changes were made in the marketing approach in the U.S. when Manufacturers suddenly realized that its average policy size—measured by premium—was fully two and a half times larger than that of its closest peer company. "Not only had they achieved their goal of reaching America's top income-earners," says Jackson, "they had actually overshot that goal and found themselves specializing in products for the *crème de la crème* of America's ultra-affluent. The [U.S.] division found itself precariously balanced on an extremely narrow market base, and completely vulnerable to changing tax regulations." Now ManuLife is actively seeking sales among small-business owners, salary savers, and what it calls the "mid-affluent market," through new products such as variable life policies that are linked to common stock investments for their growth.

In Canada, the recent directions haven't been quite so easy to plan. The regulatory environment is difficult to predict and growth here hasn't been as spectacular as in other markets. In a speech to the Life Office Management Association in Fort Lauderdale, Fla., in 1984, Jackson outlined the problem with the Canadian environment. "There are a great many unknowns," he said, "and in that kind of environment your strategies tend to become defensive. For example, as a defensive strategy—but also as a good investment—we recently bought a 25-per-cent interest in Canada's second-largest trust company." Manulife has since increased its holding to 30 per cent, the maximum allowed a mutual by law.

That purchase in Canada Trustco Mortgage Co. highlighted one of the unresolved controversies in ManuLife's ownership. Many in the industry regard Manufacturers as a non-Canadian company because the majority of its policyholders are non-resident. The purchase of Dominion Life did not add sufficient Canadian policyholders to tip the balance. Further, about 52 per cent of ManuLife's assets are in the U.S. and more than 60 per cent are outside Canada. Manufacturers does, however, have a letter from former minister of state for finance Roy MacLaren stating that it is a Canadian company. Under the Canadian and British Insurance Companies Act, Manufacturers is Canadian because its head office is in Canada and a majority of the directors are Canadian residents. Further, under the rules of the now-defunct Foreign Investment Review Agency and National Energy Program, ManuLife always passed the test to be classified as Canadian.

Canada Trustco president and chief executive officer Merv Lahn remains unconvinced. He has publicly chastised ManuLife for what he sees as its non-Canadian status because the majority of policyholders are non-resident. Under federal legislation governing Canada Trustco, non-resident shareholders owning more than 10 per cent of a loan company cannot vote their shares. Lahn also dislikes the fact that ManuLife is a mutual company. "Perhaps his mutual policyholders should be given stock," Lahn has said of Jackson. "Then he'd be back in the real world of capitalism." Although

Manufacturers owns nearly one-third of Canada Trust Co., Lahn has kept the firm's representation to one board member, Syd Jackson. The stand-off is an embarrassment for ManuLife, admits Di Giacomo. "We feel like orphans, our employees don't like it, and the whole thing is silly," he says. Jackson is confident that legislation will change to allow ManuLife to own other financial services. "Unless you want the banks to take over the whole damn world, you have to break down the walls. I think there's better than a 50-per-cent chance we'll be allowed to own a trust company." Meanwhile, the stock, which cost about $100 million, produces about $6 million a year in dividends for Manufacturers.

Some other investments have been equally problematic. In 1983 ManuLife opened a $100-million thirty-six-storey office building in Edmonton. Two years later it is only half leased. Another two years will likely pass before it is full. A $3-million initial investment for 15 per cent of a pay-television company, First Choice, is not yet profitable. Real estate holdings total about $1 billion and include office towers in most major Canadian cities as well as Chicago, Dallas, and Los Angeles.

Under Jackson, the firm, long called ManuLife, became known officially as Manufacturers in the U.S. in 1984 and in some corporate areas in Canada in 1985. Along with the name change came a corporate logo redesign by Lister Butler Inc., of New York, which also did logos for Exxon and Citibank. The M became three vertical lines, the basic design a box in green, silver-grey, or blue, depending on the aspect of the company depicted. The design will be brought into Canada, ending the wide use of the stylized man who appeared in the orange logotype between "Manu" and "Life." The figure had two legs but only one arm, and so became known fondly around the place as ManuMax, the one-armed bandit.

Among his other changes to the corporate culture, Jackson has done more than most male executives to encourage female officers. Investment vice-president for Canadian equities is Jalynn Bennett, forty-two, one of the first female vice-presidents in an organization where only 12 per cent of the senior officers are women. "It's not an impressive number," admits Jackson, "but it's a dramatic change." He recalls, for comparison, the advertisements that ManuLife ran twenty years ago to sell life insurance. A young child is standing with her mother at a bus stop. The mother, recently widowed, is off to work because her husband died without leaving her any insurance money. "Mommy," the child is saying, "why do you have to go to work?" "If we ran that ad in the paper today," says Jackson, "we'd be crucified."

Bennett manages ManuLife's $300-million Canadian stock portfolio and another $60 million in stocks for pension fund clients. She is one of four VPs who report to Don Parkinson, vice-president for Canadian investments, and among the first females to join that male bastion the Society of Financial Analysts. Her function is to invest in the stock market, to know when to take positions in stock and to know when to get out. "We're held accountable for sins of omission as well as sins of commission," she says. The company, with its $12.4-billion investment portfolio, is among the largest institutional non-U.S. players on Wall Street. Although ManuLife's size can't affect U.S. markets, she must move carefully in the Canadian market because if ManuLife starts to take a position in a stock, others will follow. The greater demand will cause the price to rise, thus making ManuLife's purchase more costly. When a buy is under way, says Bennett, "We'll stay in the reeds and quietly take it in." As important as the low-profile approach is the courage not to act. "It's not when to say yes that matters," goes her motto, "it's when to say no."

As women enter the executive suite, Jackson has other changes in mind—particularly at the distribution level. In the past, ManuLife has relied on its career agents to sell its products. That is coming to an end. "There will always be a place for the agents, but there will be a place for other ways, too. There will be more and more segregation of markets. Most of the experiments will fail, but some will work and be tremendous successes. The trick is to know which ones they are." Changes in the distribution system will occur before advertising direct to consumers is stepped up. "If we did $10 million of advertising, I don't suppose it would increase sales by $1 million."

The outcome of these decisions will be in the hands of his successor, Tom Di Giacomo. In signalling that he is the heir apparent, Jackson is letting the world know what he knows already—ManuLife is no longer just a life insurance company. Di Giacomo's financial background is proof that the world of the actuary—even an actuary with a broad base like Jackson's—is too confined for tomorrow's financial services. Di Giacomo will also have to deal with the company's expense problem—another good reason to have a man in place who knows how to punch the bottom line into shape. "We think we've got something of an expense problem," admits John

Clarke. "It costs a great deal to deliver our product." The ratio of expense to revenue across the company runs about 110 to 112 per cent. For every dollar that comes in, $1.12 is spent. Investment income keeps the firm profitable. Getting business up and costs down won't be easy. "It's a real ball-breaker," says Clarke. He reflects on the surroundings; no savings to be made there. "There are no gold taps in the washrooms." In fact, he notes, the new dining and meeting rooms are actually saving ManuLife money. Before they existed, the company spent $1 million a year in entertainment costs outside the office. Now that they have such spiffy quarters, everyone is being urged to entertain clients in house.

That old gunner, Syd Jackson, has to leave a few targets behind for the fresh troops who are moving up to the front.

CHAPTER NINE

UP AND DOWN ON THE NORTHERN FLYER

Northern Life Assurance Co. of Canada

J. A.(BOB) CARTER is sitting over dinner at Chiaro's in Toronto's opulent King Edward Hotel, considering his prospects as an insurance company owner. On this October 1984 night, there are so many plans, so much to do. Yet the past keeps getting in the way of the future and his hopes for The Northern Life Assurance Co. of Canada, of London, Ont. For Carter, forty-three, business survival and corporate credibility have not been easy. In 1983 in Vancouver, he was charged with rape, buggery, gross indecency, and indecent assault. "I was mad that anybody would think I'd ever do that," Carter says. Rather than keep quiet and await a court appearance over the incident, alleged to have occurred in 1980, he went public. "I was in the middle of a messy take-over," he recalls. "Normally, a person would keep a low profile. Not me."

The charge was thrown out after a preliminary hearing in 1983. The Crown attorney appealed, and in 1984 the British Columbia Supreme Court said the charge should be relaid. "You can't blame the police for what happened [in 1980]," Carter says. "Those were wild days in Vancouver." During the period, he spent some time in jail, an eye-opener for a former narcotics officer. "I've put people in jail on drug charges. It sure looks different from the other side." Although he says he's spent $250,000 in legal fees, the money doesn't matter. "That's not the loss. It's in the deals you weren't offered. I defied people to take shots at me."

For his part, he says he has no memory of the 1980 event in question. Even hypnosis and a polygraph test have produced no recollections of the night. "I was a raving alcoholic. It was a hooker

184 *Risky Business*

who got laid and was told by somebody she could make [more] money at it." He pauses and then asks, "I wonder what I could have done if I hadn't got drunk that one night." He now claims to be a new man, remade through a diet that dropped his weight by thirty-five pounds in fifty days. Today he carries 220 pounds on a six-foot-three frame. He has donated $150,000 to a public school alcohol education program and is trying to control his drinking. "I haven't taken the pledge," he says. "I can't think of not having another drink ever again."

The incident has not hurt him, he says; in fact, it has taught him something about himself and others. "Some people who I thought were superficial friends didn't run away when the shit hit the fan. That changed me. I'm not the guy I was eight months ago." In the intervening months, he said, he has turned his attention to Northern. Among other actions, he has ordered a study, for example, on living benefits for policyholders in order to move insurance policies away from simply offering payments at death. He has looked at housing for senior citizens and an energy-related registered retirement savings plan—all manner of ideas are spilling out as the food on his plate grows cold.

His plans for Northern call for expansion, perhaps by purchasing another life insurance company, then a trust company. He is not, however, setting out to create a one-stop financial supermarket. "We'll be more of a financial boutique." Certainly this night, his life seems well in hand. He and his wife (they have two pre-school-age children) plan to build a new home on the west coast. Carter has promised her that he will make a couple of million dollars in side deals, money that will be put towards building their dream house. After taking only three vacations in twenty-eight years, he has agreed to enjoy a little more of life with his new family.

The trappings of success surround Carter. A ski cabin at Whistler outside Vancouver, a Rolls-Royce to drive to work, a Jeep for weekends, and an E-type 12-cylinder Jaguar for the highway. He is generous with what he has. When one-legged runner Steve Fonyo needed to get to Vancouver for a check-up, Carter sent his corporate jet. Fonyo's support vehicle for the run was supplied by Carter. Carter seems to understand what went wrong for him in the past. "The end result of successfulness is probably the most hollow, oversold thing in the world. It's the *getting there* that's good. A couple of times I thought I was *there*, three times. That's when I got into trouble with drink. I could still get into trouble with drink now."

He acknowledges that success has brought loneliness. "There was no peer group." Yet even when a peer group was offered, he rebelled. He was to be invited to join the Young Presidents' Organization. YPO is a prestigious international society with 4,500 business members in fifty countries. To join, a prospective member must have become, before age forty, president of a company with at least fifty employees and annual gross sales of US$4 million. There are only 350 active Canadian members who meet in regional chapters to hold off-the-record discussions about business problems. For most, membership in YPO is a plum to be savoured. Not for Bob Carter. "The night I was going to be asked to join, I was loaded and told them what I thought." The invitation was never extended. He hopes that Northern, and his plans for it, will change all that.

Other owners with other plans have preceded him at Northern. He is the fifth to own the company over the past ten years. Long-time chief executive officer George Bowie, sixty-two, is prepared for the most recent new owner, including his notoriety. The morals charges, admits Bowie, caused some people "a little bit of concern. It was thrown up at a few people around Northern, but it is not a topic of conversation. He's a good fellow. He's up front. He has Northern for a long-term investment," says Bowie. "He sees oil and gas as a depleting resource—which it is. Northern may be the cornerstone of a financial services business."

They make an odd couple, Carter, the cowboy, and Bowie, the establishment man. Bowie's quiet ways befit both the business and the city he's in. His sandy-grey hair is thinning on top, his carriage is erect, his manner always proper. He is the sort of man who looks like he is presiding over something important, even on the first tee. He is conservatism incarnate. In 1984, Bowie was president of the London Club, a downtown lunch club and a symbol of the city's corporate community. He has also served as president of the London Art Gallery Association, co-chairman of the construction management committee for the new London Art Gallery, a member of the board of governors of the University of Western Ontario, and a member of the board at St. Joseph's Hospital.

His company has become, from an ownership standpoint, a roller-coaster that might be called the Northern Flyer. Bowie and the other 300 employees have been hanging on for dear life as the firm has been hauled up the mountain of one owner's dreams only to be abandoned to career wildly down the other side. Throughout, morale has been low and growth stunted; products have been slow to emerge and strategies impossible to plan and put in place. "A lot of our efforts were directed at stabilizing the sales force," says Bowie. "Each owner had a new idea and some worked better than others." In fact, Northern's ownership changes are unparalleled in the modern-day history of financial institutions.

Only in the quiet inner sanctum of the London Club has there been a continuity in Bowie's life. There, the rabble and the women are both kept from the portals. The 400 members, who pay initiation dues of $3,000, regularly vote down the proposition that women guests be admitted to sit at table. Among the club's treasures is an A. J. Casson painting valued at $100,000.

George Leslie Bowie has spent his business career in London. By the time he was thirty-three, he was in charge of production control at General Motors Diesel in London, one of four men who reported to the general manager. He was responsible for all movement in the plant except for labour on the assembly line. His success brought him to the attention of one of London's venerable families, the Iveys, who owned between 85 and 90 per cent of Northern through the family firm, Allpak Products Ltd.

In fact, London businessmen had owned Northern since a group of them met at a London hotel, the Tecumseh House, in 1894 and decided to apply for a charter. The company began business three years later. On the prestigious first board of directors was a clutch of southern Ontario businessmen, mayors, and members of Parliament, as well as the commissioner of the Dominion Police and Lord Strathcona, the man who drove the last spike in 1885 to complete the CPR's transcontinental rail line. In 1925 ownership was gained by a group of London businessmen under C. R. Somerville, and in 1931 Richard G. Ivey was elected president. Assets had grown to $8 million.

By 1937 ownership was concentrated in Allpak, with R. G. Ivey as principal shareholder. His son, Richard M. Ivey, became chairman in 1969, succeeding Dr. G. Edward Hall, who had previously been president and vice-chancellor of the University of Western Ontario. It was Ivey who brought Bowie in as an agency assistant in 1963. Northern grew steadily through the century and by 1968 had thirty-seven offices across Canada, four offices in Michigan, and assets of $81 million. Bowie worked his way up through various posts, and when president and managing director Edward A. Palk had a policy disagreement with the board and resigned in 1973, Bowie succeeded him, first as vice-president and general manager, then as president and chief executive officer in 1974.

That year, Ivey sold Northern for $10.5 million and the firm climbed on the ownership roller-coaster. At the time, Northern was, as it remains today, one of the smaller companies in the Canadian system. In 1974, assets were about $125 million and business in force was $1.2 billion. The first purchaser was the Prenor Group Ltd., of Montreal, headed by Lorne C. Webster. Prenor, a holding company, managed investment funds and was active in real estate. At first there was reasonable stability. Prenor owned Northern for five years and left Bowie alone to run it. He corrected expense problems, launched some new products, and generally tried to organize the company under modern management methods. Northern had been doing business in Michigan since 1937. Bowie decided to close down there and concentrate on the dozen or so Canadian cities where Northern had branches and agencies.

Prenor watched Northern grow to $165 million in assets and $2 billion in insurance in force, then announced in 1980 that it would be sold to the Laurentian Group Corp., of Quebec City, to raise funds. For Bowie, although it was the second sale in five years, the reasons made sense. Laurentian, under Jean-Marie Poitras and Claude Castonguay, was expanding outside Quebec in its bid to create a financial services empire. It already owned Imperial Life Assurance Co. of Canada and in 1980 added Loyal American Life Assurance Co., of Mobile, Ala. Northern was pleased to be part of that plan. "Castonguay was innovative and ahead of his time," recalls Bowie.

The Northern sale closed in March 1981. Castonguay was negotiating the merger of Northern and Imperial with the superintendent of insurance, but after months of talks, Castonguay and the superintendent couldn't agree on certain of the financial aspects of the merger and Northern was once more for sale. Robert Bégin, president and chief executive officer of Industrial Life Insurance Co. of Quebec City, had been interested in Northern, so he was phoned, told Northern was for sale, and given a few days to put in a bid.

At the time, Bégin was negotiating the purchase of North West Life Assurance Co. Ltd., of Vancouver. He set that aside, bought Northern, then returned to the North West deal, completing it the following month. He had time neither to think about Northern nor to tell Bowie his plans for the newly acquired company. The other ownership shuffles might all have been explicable within Northern, but this switch was a disappointment. The enthusiasm for Castonguay and his expansionary plans had been real. Now Northern had become an unwanted orphan being carted from door to door in a hamper. The recession had hit, business was flat, and morale was sinking. Recruitment of new agents became difficult. Says Bowie, "We were just trying to keep our heads above water."

From the time that Bégin bought Northern (the deal closed in June 1982), Bowie told him that Northern would leave Quebec to Industrial, concentrate on Ontario, and maintain Northern's national marketing network. That would allow Northern's western agents to serve current clients and maintain market share, adding new clients only as industry-wide business grew. "I was still promoting that plan early in 1983," says Bowie, "because no one had said it wasn't a good idea." Over the months, the two firms held four strategy sessions in both Quebec City and London. Bégin attended all except one, but never declared any strongly held personal views. Says Bowie, "That would have been the perfect opportunity for him to appear and say, 'This is what we're going to do, now get on with it.'"

Finally, after almost a year of dithering, Bégin announced his plan in April 1983. North West would do business west of the Manitoba–Ontario border; Northern would be restricted to Ontario. While the majority of Northern's new business was in Ontario (70 per cent, compared with 15 per cent in Quebec and 15 per cent in the west), the plan flew in the face of Northern's history of selling nationally. And what about long-time clients, Bowie wondered. Of business in force, 54 per cent was in Ontario, 25 per cent in Quebec, and 21 per cent in the west. How would Northern look after all of them if it was to focus on Ontario?

Bégin was insistent: he wanted Northern to shrink back to operating just in Ontario, and he wanted the switch to be done within twelve months. Bowie pleaded for more time and suggested a three-to-five-year wind-up. He worried that under the divided country system, new business in Ontario would not come along fast enough to replace the business Northern was giving up in other provinces. Bowie didn't know, for example, what would become of Northern branches in Vancouver, Edmonton, and Winnipeg or of agents in places like Saskatoon, where $25 million in business was done in 1983.

Bégin was also proposing that while the companies should operate in different provinces, Northern and North West should have a common portfolio of products. Bowie disagreed. "The markets were different. They were blue-collar. We were middle-income and upper-middle-income." Worse, Bowie felt that he was not an equal partner in planning the overall strategy. In the end, it was only Bégin who called the shots—and Bégin could have prevented the wasted months by announcing his view earlier. Says Bowie, "What was alarming was that he had known [his plan] all along."

In October 1983, the Northern board of directors met in London. Bowie took the opportunity to present a final set of five options for Northern's future in the hope of changing Bégin's mind. Bowie had worked the possibilities out with Ron Brown, then Northern chairman and a lawyer with the Toronto law firm of Blake, Cassels & Graydon. The first option was to allow all three companies—Northern, North West, and Industrial—to go out and compete in all markets against each other. The options then proceeded to the fifth and most outlandish: sell Northern to another company.

Bowie tabled the options in a memorandum at an advisory committee meeting scheduled for 9:45 A.M., fifteen minutes before the board meeting. In attendance were Brown, Bowie, Bégin, and Industrial chairman André Charron. Bégin and Charron were irate that Bowie would even think of proposing that Industrial sell Northern. Bowie further indicated that he had a possible purchaser in mind. (He didn't reveal the name at the time, but it was Traders Group, a Toronto-based company controlled by brothers Fred and Jim McCutcheon, who were operators in finance, land development, trust, and insurance.) Charron was so upset at the sale proposal that he took Bowie's memorandum, crumpled it up into a ball, and threw it across the table at him.

The board meeting that followed was a frosty affair, but Bowie did appear to have bought both time and a part in the planning. The board decided that Bégin and Bowie would develop a plan by which the companies would divide the country, sell common products, and blend their administrative systems. The plan was to be presented at the December board meeting, scheduled to be held in the Blake, Cassels boardroom in Toronto. When Bowie did not hear from

Bégin after several weeks, he phoned Bégin only to be told: "I'm still upset. I haven't been able to think about the plan." Bowie went ahead with a plan on his own and placed it on the agenda for the December meeting. That particular agenda item was never discussed.

After the meeting, they all trooped over to the National Club on nearby Bay Street for lunch. They split up at tables for four and Bowie joined Brown, Charron, and Bégin. As lunch ended, Bégin asked Bowie, "What are your plans for the afternoon?" Replied Bowie, "I'm taking the 3:30 train back to London." Bégin asked him to return to the Blake, Cassels boardroom instead, and he agreed. When the four were seated, Bégin said, "We're prepared to sell Northern." Bowie said, "Fine. Let's consider only legitimate prospects. Let's keep Northern's best interests in mind."

It was agreed that prospective purchasers had to submit a letter of intent, dated before the end of January, so that all proposals could go before the board of Industrial Life, then be taken to the Northern annual meeting in February. Bowie saw the McCutcheons between Christmas and New Year's, but the time available was too limited for them and they declined to make a bid. There were several other possibilities, but the purchaser finally approved was Kelvin Energy Ltd., of Calgary, and Northern was sold in a deal that closed in April 1984 for $32.5 million. Kelvin was 48-per-cent owned by Bob Carter. The Northern Flyer had taken a new and very high-profile turn.

Bob Carter arrived on the life insurance scene with as little advance notice as he had given when he hit the oil patch. He had exploded onto the business pages in 1979 when he purchased the Canadian properties of Hamilton Brothers Petroleum, of Denver, for $532 million. Until that publicity, few had ever heard of him. He was born in Montreal, finished Grade Eight, then travelled the country working at just about every job that existed, from bar-room bouncer to financial columnist for the Vancouver *Times*.

After working for five years for a U.S. anti-drug squad, his first business venture was into pay-television, but it was too early for consumer acceptance and he lost everything. He bummed around for a while, and one day he was flying from Saskatoon to Vancouver.

As luck would have it, the economy section was oversold and he was bumped up to first class. There he met Clyde Kissinger, head of Denver's Kissinger Oil & Gas.

That meeting, according to Carter, changed his life. Kissinger liked Carter immediately and during the two-hour flight explained all there was to know about the oil business. Kissinger's philosophy was simple: it was hard to raise money for oil exploration, everyone was trying to do that. Instead, since the oil reserves were all for sale, the wise investor would buy them—there was no risk. It fit with a philosophy Carter had already developed: "The less risk you take, the more money you'll have at the end of the day." Through early deals with Kissinger and others for oil reserves, Carter was a millionaire before the Hamilton deal in 1979.

Carter kept his own money at risk to a minimum when he bought Northern. The purchase price of $32.5 million included $4 million in cash, a $2-million bank loan, and $2 million in shares. Northern and its owners, Industrial, put up the rest as follows: $13.5 million in three loans due at various times, at interest rates ranging from 8 to 13.5 per cent; a $5.5-million dividend payable by Northern, and $5.5 million from the sale by Kelvin to Northern of a block of oil and gas properties. All insurance companies under federal charter are strictly controlled by federal regulation, with specific limits to investments in such areas as stock and real estate. Conflict rules prohibit a company from lending money to or investing in any person or company that has more than a 10-per-cent interest in the company. Nothing says, however, that the company cannot buy real estate from or sell real estate to a shareholder with more than a 10-per-cent interest.

While the $5.5-million sale by Kelvin was a long way from 10 per cent (Northern assets in June 1984 were approximately $210 million), Carter had an independent engineering appraisal done so that there would be no question about value. Carter says the valuation report found that the assets had been evaluated fully 22 per cent too low—proving that Carter was not trying to sell something to Northern for more than it was worth. In fact, he claims, the board wanted to buy into all the wells in question. He allowed them to buy only a 60-per-cent share and claims that the wells pay a 20-per-cent return on money invested before tax—and Northern, like many life insurance companies, pays no income tax, a situation of which Carter approves. "If you tried to design a tax system today for life insurance companies," he says with some relish, "you couldn't design a better system than exists."

Carter hired two firms—Peat, Marwick, Mitchell Ltd. and Tellinghast, Nelson & Warren Inc.—to do independent studies of Northern and advise him on reorganizational steps to take. Carter was told that Northern's overhead costs were too high; he decided to cut 20 per cent of the staff and asked Bowie to come up with a plan to achieve the reductions. In June, Bowie flew to Vancouver to tell him his plan, which had been worked out with the vice-presidents. "It was too heavily weighted to cutting out clerical and lower-level staff," says Carter. "He told me he had no heart for the downsizing. He couldn't get rid of a lot of people he'd hired." Bowie offered to resign in a year, allowing Carter time and help with the transition as a new boss was put in place. They worked out an early retirement scheme that would allow Bowie to leave in December 1987 rather than October 1988, when he would have gone if he were to stay to sixty-five. It was agreed that Bowie would remain as president and chief executive officer until a replacement president was found, then he would step aside into the less onerous duties of vice-chairman until retirement.

As a first step towards seeing if a successor existed inside the company, Carter told Jim Oatman, Northern's actuary and vice-president for insurance operations, that he would be promoted to executive vice-president. Oatman said he would not take the job without the support of Maurie Breen, vice-president of marketing. Carter, Oatman, and Breen met July 10 in Toronto in Carter's room in the King Edward Hotel. It was agreed that both Oatman and Breen would be executive vice-presidents. In Carter's mind, Oatman had the edge over Breen as heir apparent and Bowie would ease into the vice-chairman's role whenever Oatman appeared ready to take over as president. Oatman and Breen were asked by Carter to rework Bowie's proposal.

A few days later, on July 15, Carter had lunch with Breen and Oatman and their wives in London. The wives went home and the three men met in Carter's room in the Holiday Inn to discuss the downsizing plan. Oatman and Breen were proposing that Bowie stay as president and chief executive officer; Oatman and Breen would be senior vice-presidents. Carter told Oatman and Breen that he wanted Bowie out immediately. Carter asked the two to go away and return with a reworked organization chart and new president.

They returned that evening with a plan that saw Breen as president until March 30, 1988. Oatman would be named an executive vice-president immediately. "I'll stay three years, then Jim [Oatman] will become president," Breen said. Oatman agreed, according to Carter, saying: "Maurie can teach me a lot."

For his part, Carter says he was flabbergasted that Oatman, in his mind the heir apparent, would stand aside for someone else. While he didn't like the proposal, he didn't know how to change the situation. Working with people, Carter is the first to admit, is not his long suit. "If you don't like an oil well, you shut it off. People aren't my strength." Now he had a lame-duck president and a succession that was being planned from below. "I was between a rock and a hard place. They knew that and it made me mad that they knew that. When they have you by the balls, your heart and mind will follow." Carter says he "acquiesced" to the joint proposal.

Carter then called director Michael Carten to come to the room and showed him the joint proposal without explaining that he'd asked for it. Board chairman John Evans, of Blake, Cassels (he had replaced Ron Brown), was telephoned and told about the Breen-Oatman plan—again without being told why the plan even existed. Recalls Breen, "It looked as if we were doing a knife job on Bowie. Our loyalties were to our president. We did this simply because the owner told us to."

The Oatman-Breen plan was to be presented next day, at a meeting of the advisory committee of the board of directors. The two felt a bit vulnerable, however, after hearing the negative reaction of Carten and Evans. They presented their downsizing ideas but made no mention of the plans to replace Bowie as president. Carter passed Oatman a note saying, "You've just snatched defeat from the jaws of victory." Oatman wasn't able to ask Carter what he meant until later. Carter told him that he had convinced fellow directors Carten and Evans that the Oatman-Breen plan was a good one— then failed to tell the proposers.

During the afternoon continuation of the meeting, the Oatman-Breen plan was resuscitated, with Bowie's departure included. There was heated discussion and Bowie was excused from the session; some of the board members agreed, says Oatman, that a lame-duck president wouldn't work. There was no unanimity for the Oatman-Breen idea immediately, however, because the board members wanted time to consider it.

The board committee met again the next morning for an hour and a half. Oatman and Breen were invited, and Breen was asked if he would accept the presidency. He agreed, but only if Oatman concurred and if satisfactory pension and termination arrangements could be made. Breen was fifty-seven and he wanted to make sure he had some security in place if things didn't work out. At his age, another job would be difficult to find. It was proposed that Oatman be made an executive vice-president. At thirty-seven, pension arrangements weren't as important for him. As discussions continued over the next couple of days, Oatman recalls, he and Breen remained wary of working under Carter. "What happens if he wants to terminate us?" was a question that ran through Oatman's mind. They both wanted contractual promises in place if they were fired. Oatman's arrangement was straightforward. He was promised fifteen months' termination pay, plus an additional month per year with the company, up to eighteen years. For Breen, the termination pay was about two years' salary, or $200,000. It was finally agreed that the firm of William Mercer Ltd. would be hired as consultants to work out the deal.

According to Carter, Mercer advised that the deal was too expensive. Carter and Evans discussed it, then misunderstood who was to tell Oatman and Breen that the proposal was not going forward. Evans thought Carter would relay the news, Carter thought Evans was going to make the call. Carter, by now back home in Vancouver, went off boating for the weekend of July 28. Oatman and Breen, meanwhile, were feeling a bit vulnerable both about their positions and about their future capacity to get things done in the company. By the first of the next week, Carter realized there was confusion and phoned Oatman and Breen to come to Vancouver in advance of the Thursday board meeting. On the plane, says Oatman, he and Breen agreed that they weren't going to accept the positions and wrote out a memo for Carter detailing their views.

The board was to meet Thursday, August 2, after which there was to be a party to introduce the two to the Vancouver business community and announce George Bowie's retirement. According to Carter, the pension deal was struck at slightly lower levels than Breen had requested; then Oatman, Breen, and Carter talked of the cuts to come at Northern. It was agreed that four vice-presidents would get the sack. Carter thought everything was on again.

Until Thursday, the day of the board meeting. At ten o'clock,

Breen and Oatman met Evans and Carter in Carter's Vancouver office. Carter recalls that Breen was nervous. The conversation touched on several topics, but it was clear Breen had something on his mind. "Let's save everybody a lot of time," Breen said. "I've decided not to accept the presidency." Without missing a beat, Carter said, "Fine." He turned to Oatman and asked, "You'll be executive VP?" Replied Oatman, "We came as a package and we'll stay as a package." "Good," said Carter. "Thank you very much. Goodbye." Oatman and Breen said they would not help with the staff reductions. Carter repeated, by way of conclusion: "Thank you very much." They shook hands all around and the two left. Breen returned to ask if they were still expected at the board meeting. "Yes," said Carter, "to present the [downsizing] report."

The board, however, was not amused at the turn of events. The members refused to hear their presentation, and the report was reviewed at the board meeting without either Breen or Oatman present. The two sat outside the meeting for an hour. Finally they were brought into an ante-room with Carter and Evans and shown an organizational chart. They had their original jobs back. The position of president was blank.

The party set for that evening went ahead as planned for the sixty invited guests at the Wedgewood Hotel, owned by Eleni Skalbania. London-based executives and their wives had been flown out for the occasion. Breen sat at a table with Carter and Bowie. Recalls Oatman, "It was all very awkward." Since there was now no replacement for George Bowie, his retirement was not announced as originally intended. His retirement gift, a set of golf clubs, was presented without comment and without apparent reason. Word of Carter's acceptance of the withdrawal of Breen and Oatman had obviously spread. For whatever reason, perhaps because they thought their husbands might stand a better chance at promotion, Carter says that several wives of London-based executives told him, "You've done the right thing." Finally, Carter's wife, Sheila, asked him, "What did you do right? You didn't think you'd fit in." "I'm not sure I fit in yet," replied Carter.

The party over, Carter retired to a suite upstairs to work on the downsizing plan with several people, including Kathy Bullock of Thorne Stevenson & Kellogg, a consulting firm hired to help. About one-thirty in the morning, Carter's secretary phoned Breen and Oatman and asked them to come to Carter's suite. Oatman felt they should get legal advice and phoned a lawyer in Toronto. He advised them to go to Carter's suite, with their wives as witnesses. As they all stood in the suite, Carter said, "Maurie, nice and simple. You're fired." Turning to Oatman, he had a different message. "These are troubled times, but they will pass. Your best career decision is to stay with Northern." Carter made no specific promise, but Oatman recalls Carter saying, "At some point, you'll be president of a company and I would like to talk to you." Oatman, still reeling from the events, demurred, saying he'd like some time to think, and everyone left.

Over the August long weekend, Carter arrived at Northern's London offices; he put security staff in place and set about changing office door locks and access codes on the computer. Material in Breen's office was emptied into a truck. The downsizing had begun. "I had to go ahead with the downsizing," says Carter. "Northern was bleeding." The previous year there had been an operating loss of $45,000, with assets of $206 million. Forty employees, including four vice-presidents, were dismissed from the total staff complement of 300. "It cost me a million-plus [in severance] that day," says Carter, "but we save $2.5 million a year." The cowboy had arrived.

Carter argues that he was not trying to buy respectability when he purchased Northern. "You don't buy respectability, it can't be done. If I could give one piece of advice to young businessmen it would be this: don't ever waste your money trying to buy acceptance. That's a better word than respectability. What was it that Sam Goldwyn said? Asked how many showed up, he said, 'A thousand people.' 'How did you get so many there?' 'Give 'em what they want and they'll come.'" The deal was done because insurance, he argues, is the best investment during non-inflationary times. There is also a permanence to the business. "Insurance," he says, "is here forever."

So, he thought, was he. As he sat over dinner that October evening in 1984, he knew that the 1980 morals charges could surface again. He wanted them to be laid again so that he could plea-bargain with the Crown attorney and put the charges behind him forever. The future, the plans for Northern, everything Carter wanted—all seemed so possible. His goal for personal net worth, a goal that he often changes because "one has to grow," was $100 million that October night. He claimed to be one-fifth of the way there. The target was a way to keep score. "I don't know of anything that's more fun than business, trying to come up with a concept that will last. And you can always add up your bank balance at the end of the month to see if you're winning or losing." Northern, he felt, was a way to add to that net worth and a way to create a corporate monument. "Being rich," he said, "is the ability to make mistakes and survive."

Eight days later Carter was charged with gross indecency committed during a session with two teen-aged prostitutes earlier in the year. He pleaded guilty in November and was fined $3,000. Evidence showed that a fourteen-year-old girl tied up a seventeen-year-old female with a leather harness provided by Carter. Carter then hit the seventeen-year-old two or three times with a whip, and had the younger girl perform oral sex on him while she whipped the seventeen-year-old. The fourteen-year-old was then asked to put on the harness, but refused. Carter paid each of them $1,000. After being fined, Carter announced he would resign his directorships, including Northern, Kelvin, and the Vancouver Whitecaps of the North American Soccer League, a team in which he has invested $2.2 million. He began receiving offers to buy Northern.

In January 1985, a new owner was announced, the Inland Financial Co. Ltd., parent of Sovereign Life Assurance and itself a subsidiary of the Cascade Group of Calgary. Inland, a diversified company active in development, insurance, investment services, petroleum exploration, and leisure activities, paid $31.5 million.

George Bowie retired in January 1985. John Walsh, president of Sovereign, was named president of Northern. Oatman left Northern in March. Throughout, Bowie has remained sanguine about his career. There is no hint of recrimination in his words or ways. "I can't recount any policyholder or widows we've saved from the poorhouse, but I do feel proud of the way I have run the company through difficult times. I know the people at Northern. I think I have done a pretty good job in the environment we've been through. It was just trying to survive."

At the close of that October evening, as Bob Carter smoked a Davidoff cigar—one of four he had bought from the waiter for $76—he cast his life story into cryptic headlines. "It's Horatio Alger. Boy makes it. Boy blows it." Boy can make it again, it was suggested. He put up a cautionary hand: "Maybe. I can sit in here and be called *Mister* Carter, but it's how the superintendent of insurance looks across the room at you [that counts]. It's a five-year plan."

Boy blows it again.

CHAPTER TEN

WOMB TO TOMB
Trilon Financial Corp. and
London Life Insurance Co.

I T WAS no usual corporate confab with soporific speeches and mind-numbing numbers. The 350 shareholders and other Bay Street types who gathered in April at the annual meeting of Brascan Ltd. in Toronto weren't there to catch a glimpse of the elusive owners, billionaire brothers Peter and Edward Bronfman. Nor did they care to applaud or query management. It was the booty that brought them out, a shopping bag laden with goodies and a buffet lunch of products from the dozens of firms in the Brascan empire. The carry-away loot included a digital clock, a screwdriver with changeable heads, a pewter duckling, a pen, a key tag, various coupons on dairy products and other consumer goods, even a white spruce seedling ready for planting. "Some years the more elderly shareholders have had trouble lugging away the bag," said Wendy Cecil-Stuart, Brascan's vice-president for business development. "So we lightened up the load." That means fewer packages of pasta and more coupons, but the same broad range. After all, the diversity is what attracts both free-enterprisers to the company and free-loaders to the meeting.

The Bronfman hand is everywhere in Canada. Measured by assets, only Paul Desmarais's Power Corp. is a larger family empire. From their personal holding company, Edper Investments Ltd., the Bronfmans control investments in three major holding companies that in turn have significant stakes in a dozen major Canadian companies with assets of about $100 billion, including Canada's largest forestry, mining, and trust companies. Brascan's involvement in the natural resources sector is through Brascade Resources Inc., with its 46-per-

199

cent interest in Noranda Inc. and 63-per-cent share of Westmin Resources Ltd., which in turn owns 28 per cent of Lacana Mining Corp. The group's activities include oil and gas exploration and production, newsprint and other forest products, gold and aluminum. The consumer products division holds a 37-per-cent interest in John Labatt Ltd. (beer, wine, cheese, and the specialty television channel The Sports Network) and 25 per cent of Scott Paper Co. (operations in twenty-one countries, producing sanitary paper products and printing and publishing papers). In addition, Great Lakes Group Inc., a merchant bank, competes with the brokers by raising investment capital. Other high-profile companies at least partially owned by the Bronfmans include pay-TV network First Choice-Superchannel, MacMillan Bloedel Ltd., Kerr-Addison Mines, and Continental Bank; as well there are investments in household names such as Catelli spaghetti, Habitant pea soup, and the Montreal Forum. In addition, Brascan has investments in Brazil, ranging from cattle ranches to a luxury hotel.

For all the reach, however, the area that has attracted the most attention is the financial services arm, Trilon Financial Corp.; it is the country's largest financial holding company, with $55.2 billion in assets under administration and 18,000 employees in its various companies. Brascan owns 39 per cent of Trilon, and the Reichmanns, another powerful Canadian family, own 13 per cent through Olympia & York Holdings Ltd. Other participants are the Toronto-Dominion Bank and the Jefferys of London, Ont., the founding family of London Life Insurance Co. of Canada. In turn, Trilon holds 50 per cent of Royal Trustco Ltd. (trust services), 98 per cent of London Life (life insurance), 100 per cent of Wellington Insurance Co. (property and casualty insurance; formerly Fireman's Fund Insurance Co. of Canada), 51 per cent of Royal LePage Ltd. (real estate brokerage), and 51 per cent of CVL Inc. (vehicle leasing and fleet management).

"Trilon has had a significant impact on financial services," says Susan Cohen, an analyst with the brokerage firm F. H. Deacon Hodgson, in Montreal. "It is recognized that this is the way to go." Barbara McDougall, minister of state for finance, seems to agree. The proposals in her department's 1985 discussion paper use Trilon as a role model for other financial holding companies. Yet, to date, Trilon has not been a runaway sales success. For example, Royal Trustco and London Life have more than 4 million customers between them, with each firm serving quite a different market. London Life deals mainly with younger, middle-income people, while Royal Trustco's clients are older and more affluent. The combination seems sound, yet in a six-week 1984 pilot project, thirty London Life agents sold only four Royal Trust RHOSPs. "Hardly worth starting up the car," was the way one agent described a RHOSP prospect. (RHOSPs were ended by the May 1985 federal budget.)

"It's not a great success," admits Earl Orser, chief executive officer of London Life. Mel Hawkrigg, chief executive officer of Trilon, agrees: "We really have not been able to effectively market the cross-referrals." Another product did better, however; Royal Trust sold its clients $25 million worth of London Life annuities in the first four months they were available. Claims Hawkrigg, "The bankers are paranoid. People are very conscious of us. The supermarket concept has caught the imagination of a lot of people." It certainly caught the attention of the rest of the insurance business. When the Canadian Life and Health Insurance Association booked keynote speakers for its 1984 annual meeting, Robin Korthals, president of the Toronto-Dominion Bank, spoke at dinner; Hawkrigg was the keynote speaker at noon.

Trilon's ambition is to create life-cycle financial services so that the needs of a client can be looked after from womb to tomb under one corporate umbrella. At best, a person buying a house through one of Royal LePage's 9,000 sales representatives is visited by one of Wellington's 1,000-member agency force, then by one of London's 2,500-person sales force, then by a will and estate services officer with Royal Trust. The competition, not surprisingly, remains dubious. Says Robert Bandeen, chief executive officer of Crownx Inc., another financial holding company, "It'll be twenty years before they get the synergy they want there, trying to put together those two corporate cultures."

The effort began in 1979 when the Bronfmans bought Brascan after a bloody take-over battle that first brought them into the public eye. In one swoop, they bought one-third of all Brascan shares, worth $175 million, through the American Stock Exchange; they gained control, with a total outlay of $340 million, a few weeks later. Brascan was a cash-rich Brazilian power utility, and the Bronfmans dismissed chairman J. H. (Jake) Moore, who had just engineered the withdrawal of nearly $500 million from Brazil following the sale to the Brazilian government of its Light Services de Electricidade S. A.

Until then, the two had been in the shadow of their cousins, Edgar and Charles, who had inherited the Seagram fortune from their father, Sam Bronfman, brother to Peter and Edward's father, Allan. The "other Bronfmans," as they became known, had a $20-million legacy that began to grow slowly through investments in the 1960s and 1970s through Carena Bancorp Holdings Ltd.'s holdings in Continental Bank of Canada and Trizec Corp., a real estate company.

Peter is the more outgoing of the two brothers. At fifty-six, he is chairman of Edper and a fitness fanatic who jogs an hour a day. Married twice, he has three children and is now divorced. Edward, fifty-eight, is deputy chairman and faced the glare of publicity in 1983; he found himself on the front pages after his girlfriend, a flight attendant, accidentally plunged to her death from the third storey of his $3,000-a-month townhouse in Toronto's downtown Yorkville.

The man driving Brascan's corporate strategy is president and chief executive officer Trevor Eyton. Eyton, fifty-one, formerly a practising corporate lawyer, has described the Bronfmans thus: "They are not only my employers, they are also my partners and my very close friends." Total staff is small for the empire it surveys: only twenty-six people, including support staff. Eyton's sidekick is executive vice-president Jack Cockwell, a South African-born chartered accountant. Another key man is Trilon chief executive officer Mel Hawkrigg, fifty-five, the 1952 quarterback for the Hamilton Tiger-Cats and former president of Fuller Brush Co. Hawkrigg's chief operating officer, Gordon Cunningham, forty-one, came from a Toronto law firm, Tory, Tory, DesLauriers & Binnington. Trilon chairman Allen Lambert, seventy-three, is a former chairman of the Toronto-Dominion Bank. At Royal Trust, chief executive officer Michael Cornelissen came from another Brascan company, Trizec Corp. Two other officers, chairman Hartland MacDougall and executive vice-president William Harker, were both recruited from the Bank of Montreal in 1984. The Bronfmans are passive investors who have gained the loyalty of Eyton, Cockwell, and the rest with corporations to run and loans to buy stock in the various companies. Eyton, for example, owes the company $3.3 million loaned to him to purchase 125,000 shares. With a share value in the $30 range, his holdings have a net worth of $450,000. Executive vice-president

Jack Cockwell has 85,000 shares and loans of $2.2 million for a net value of $350,000.

The Brascan style is to align its various parts with others in the business community. For example, the grab earlier this year of 48 per cent of Union Enterprises by Unicorp Ltd. was carried out after a Brascan company agreed to part with its 16-per-cent interest and other associated companies purchased Unicorp preferred shares, thus aiding the take-over financing. When a private-sector group was organized to provide financial backing for Toronto's proposed domed stadium, Eyton was chairman. Two Edper companies, Trilon and Labatt's, are among the twelve corporate partners.

Trilon also carries on merchant banking functions, putting deals together for corporate clients. It lends money to corporations, deals in foreign exchange, bond trading and financial futures, and does management consulting. With so many functions under one roof, concentration of power is clearly an issue. Last year, when Royal Trust and A. E. LePage Ltd. merged their real estate divisions into Royal LePage, the federal combines investigation branch studied the links among the Bronfman interests in Royal Trust, the largest trust company in the country, and LePage, Canada's largest real estate firm. Even so, the combines branch did not stop the merger.

More worrisome for Brascan are low copper prices that have depressed Noranda profits. Brascan, according to Dominion Securities Pitfield Ltd. vice-president Michael Graham, has "been through the wringer. They're suffering from a disease called Noranda, and Noranda's suffering from a disease called copper." No such trouble exists at Trilon; even Hawkrigg expresses surprise: "Trilon went faster than any of us dreamed." Last year, Trilon's profits nearly doubled, to $75 million, from 1983 levels of $38 million. Says analyst Cohen, "It has been an example of a shining success in the financial services area. Who's going to argue with success?"

Much of the success is due to the efforts of Earl Orser, who holds titles at both London Life and Trilon, where he is deputy chairman. He is a blunt and aggressive manager, one of the outsiders who has shaken up not just the conservative city of London, Ont., but London Life and the entire industry. He is not a man to stand on niceties. When the London Life board of directors met in Halifax in July 1984, Orser met the local media. The news conference, with about half a dozen journalists in attendance, began quietly enough with London Life chairman Allen Lambert and Orser commenting on financial results. Orser, one of fifteen members on the committee created by the federal government to examine financial services in Canada, was asked about the group's report. It had met for six months, then taken the summer off, and now the country was in the midst of an election campaign. He was diplomatic about progress. "It has been quietly put to bed for the summer," he said, "while the bureaucrats put together a policy paper and the politicians prepare for an election." He assumed the committee would reconvene in October, no matter who formed a government. "This is not likely to be a partisan matter," he said. "The work that's been done will be useful for a future government." (The committee's final meeting was in December, leading to the McDougall discussion paper in April 1985.)

The news conference had been under way for about twenty minutes when Lyndon Watkins, a local free-lance journalist, straggled in. Orser happened to be talking about investment opportunities in Atlantic Canada. Watkins, unable to contain himself, launched an attack on the carpet-bagger from Upper Canada: "All we hear about these days from the big investing companies is what a great opportunity is being offered in Nova Scotia because of the offshore energy potential. Where were you when we needed you years ago?" He had picked the wrong time and the wrong man. Without a moment's hesitation, Orser shot back: "Where were you when the press conference started? I told your colleagues we've been here since 1898." *Zap.*

Where most Canadian business executives might have walked a more careful line, been a little more deferential, Earl Herbert Orser, fifty-seven, is cowed by no one and is not reluctant to show it. Where some executives run for cover and rarely hold a news conference, Orser regularly meets the media. And, on occasion, he will be properly combative, even feisty. They are essential characteristics for a man who, in the last half-dozen years, has taken London Life, a 111-year-old *grande dame* of a company, and reincarnated it as a lively débutante.

Orser is a stocky five-foot-ten and weighs 175 pounds. His grey, kinky hair looks like a puffed-up Brillo pad. Usually his face is flushed pink and often it glows with perspiration as if he'd just stepped from a sauna. He regularly twitches his head from side to side as if his collar were a tad too tight. His puckish eyebrows bounce up and down like butter on a hot skillet. A smile tugs down the corners of his mouth in a way that suggests he might have been a bit of an imp as a lad. When he's not smiling or talking, he works away on a lozenge planted in his cheek. Even when he is watching or listening, he seems barely able to contain himself. On a chair, he wriggles; at a podium, he tap-dances; in a hallway, he hurtles. Just the sort of jump-start jockey needed to invigorate a near-comatose company in a conservative town.

Earl Orser, a distant cousin of Canadian figure-skating champion Brian Orser, was born in Toronto in 1928. He and his wife have four daughters, all of whom were married during a flurried eighteen-month period in 1983–84. He graduated from the University of Toronto in 1950 with a bachelor of commerce degree. He joined the accounting firm of Clarkson, Gordon & Co., earned his CA in 1953, and became a partner in 1958. Over the next fifteen years, he was successively treasurer, then vice-president for finance of Anthes Imperial Ltd.; senior vice-president, Molson Industries Ltd.; vice-president for finance, Air Canada. In 1973, he joined the T. Eaton Co. Ltd., rising to president and chief executive officer in 1975. Among other tasks there, Orser successfully closed the catalogue business for the Eaton family; but he rubbed the family the wrong way and departed.

Larry Clarke, chairman and chief executive officer of Spar Aerospace, makers of the Canadarm, asked Orser to join Spar's board of directors shortly after. "The Eatons had asked him to clean up quite a mess. He did that, but he stepped on quite a few corns. I guess the corns hurt more than the mess." Clarke didn't care that at the time Orser had no job, no corporate connection. He was looking for Orser's individual expertise. "He has a very catholic background," says Clarke. "He added a practical financial element from the operating side. Because he is so probing in his questions, people who are presenting their story must have all the facts. He doesn't permit any flim-flam." Orser has remained on the Spar board ever since.

At the time, Orser asked Canadian Pacific chairman Ian Sinclair for career advice. "What you should do," urged Sinclair, "is get a job running a financial institution. There are more opportunities to improve the management of financial institutions in Canada than any of us know about." Shortly after, Orser was approached to take on an advisory role at London Life. "A lot could be done, he felt, to bring out the real worth of the place," recalls Clarke. And so Orser arrived in 1977 as a consultant, with a free hand to study London Life and make recommendations for change to the board of directors. Says Clarke, "It was a pretty sleepy place. It was a gold brick that needed processing." Says Trilon's Hawkrigg, "He brought a lot of discipline to that company that wasn't there before. It was a good company, it just needed professionalism. In business, you're always judged by the companies you create and the company you keep. Earl's done well with both."

London Life is Canada's sixth-largest insurance company measured by assets ($5.7 billion), but using two other yardsticks, it is the country's largest. London Life has more sales agents and more individual policyholders than any other life insurance company. Some 1.3 million individual Canadians have 1.9 million London Life policies worth $49 billion. In addition, another 600,000 employees in 11,700 businesses have London Life group coverage. About one in six Canadian households does business with London Life. In terms of market share, that kind of penetration places it safely in the number one spot. London Life has about 12 per cent of the total premium income of the 170 companies doing business in Canada—more than one and a half times its nearest competitor in the individual insurance business. Forty-six per cent of the insurance it sells is traditional permanent insurance that pays dividends and death benefits and has a growing cash value.

There are 5,020 employees, including 1,500 at head office and 2,200 sales agents (expected to grow to 3,000 by 1990) at 165 branches across Canada. (It does not operate in the United States.) London Life has $5.3 billion in invested assets, with about half that amount safely ensconced in mortgages. More than 137,000 Canadian families live in homes or apartments financed through London Life. These days, more risky and imaginative investments are also being made. In 1983, London Life purchased a $10-million interest in 725 producing Alberta gas wells held by Coseka Resources Ltd. London Life also bought and leased back forty-five trolley-buses in Vancouver and did a purchase and lease-back deal with Royal Trustco for potash mining equipment in Saskatchewan. A similar deal with the British Columbia Railway means that London Life owns 153 coal cars worth $8 million. The firm also owns industrial malls in Nova Scotia and Ontario, seventeen industrial buildings in Richmond, B.C., office buildings in Montreal, Regina, and Vancouver, as well as a 60-per-cent interest in the fourteen-acre College

Street Centre in Toronto. With a planned value of $700 million when completed in 1990, this office-hotel-apartment complex is the largest mixed-use real estate project in Canada.

London Life was formed in London, Ont., in 1874 by a group of local businessmen. In those cautious early days, only certain lives were insured. Hotel- and tavern-keepers, railway workers, and Great Lakes sailors were sure to be rejected. Founding president was John Jeffery, and over the years, the Jeffery family emerged as the major shareholders. Alex Jeffery was appointed solicitor for London Life in 1934 and named to the board of directors in 1946. He was first vice-president in 1958, president in 1971, deputy chairman in 1980, and chairman in 1982. He was also a Liberal member of Parliament from 1949 to 1953.

Alex and his brother, Joe, known to everyone as Captain Joe, presided over London Life for twenty years. In 1974, however, both Alex and the number three man, executive vice-president Mel Price, suffered heart attacks. Long-time employee G.D.S. (Bill) Rudd became acting general manager. In 1975 he became chief operating officer. Price returned and went on the executive committee of the board, but he wasn't as active as he had been. Alex was president, but Rudd looked to be heir apparent.

In 1977 Lonvest Corp. was created to hold the shares of the major stakeholders in London Life, the Toronto-Dominion Bank, Brascan, and the Jefferys. The pooling gave them 40 per cent of the outstanding shares. An offer to the general public increased the holding to 65 per cent. (In 1982, when Trilon was created, Lonvest traded all its London Life shares for Trilon. Trilon made a further public offering and ended up with 98 per cent of London Life.) Late in 1977, Jake Moore, chairman and CEO of Brascan, who was also chairman of the executive committee at London Life, approached Orser—with the support of TD chief executive officer Richard Thomson—to evaluate the company.

Orser signed on, promising a report in six months, and reached out to some professionals he had used in the past. They included the chartered accounting firms of Touche Ross from New York and Clarkson Gordon from Toronto, Richard Johnston, a founder of the personnel consulting firm of Hickling Johnston, as well as actuary Ken Clark from Millman & Robertson Inc. The result was a sixty-page report to the board. "I suggested that the management attitudes, the management orientation, style, and process could use some change. The most important thing I said was that this company should have a marketing orientation. It had a technical and a conservative investment orientation, and it ought to have a marketing orientation—that's what selling financial services is all about." As for the sales organization, Orser concluded, it was a little bit adrift. The sales performance standards "weren't particularly demanding." The group insurance division wasn't profitable. "I had the impression," says Orser, "that there wasn't even the requirement to make a significant amount of money."

After he delivered the report, Orser took off for a Vermont vacation. Board member J. Allyn Taylor, former chairman of Canada Trust, telephoned to say that they wanted him to return to London for further discussion. The directors had concluded they wanted Orser to show management how to achieve what he'd recommended. The short-term contract became a full-time job. When Mel Price retired in 1978, Orser received his title of executive vice-president and chief operating officer—and a three-year contract. Not everyone approved. "There were various levels of enthusiasm about the whole thing," admits Orser. Certainly, Bill Rudd had lost his status as heir. Laments Rudd, "He took, in effect, the job I would have had."

George D'Alton Stafford Rudd was called Bill because, as his father joked when he was born on November 30, 1929: "He came at the end of the month with the rest of the bills." Rudd joined London Life in 1951 and rose to be next in line for the presidency—until Orser arrived and got the coveted title of executive vice-president. Says Rudd, "In theory, at the end of the three-year period, a decision would be made whether I continued my interrupted career, or whether Orser was hired permanently." The decision didn't require three years, nor did an ownership change affect Orser's rise.

In 1979, under Jake Moore, Brascan made a $1.3-billion bid for F. W. Woolworth Co., the five-and-dime chain that had grown in 100 years from one Utica, N.Y., store to more than 5,600 outlets around the world. Within weeks, Brascan was itself a target as Edper Equities Ltd., the holding company of Peter and Edward Bronfman, bought first a third of Brascan, and then control of the firm. The Bronfmans, through Brascan, now owned 24 per cent of London Life. Although Jake Moore left the boards of Labatt's and Brascan, he stayed on the board of London Life. His connection with the firm was historic. After all, the firm of his grandfather, John M. Moore, had been architects for the building.

Rudd took this as a sign that he might still have a chance. By then, he was senior vice-president, and in the summer of 1980 London Life sent him to Harvard University for the advanced management program. It wasn't enough. On July 21, 1980, Orser became president, and in March 1981, he added the CEO's title as well. Concluded Rudd: "There was no future for me in the company." He left early in 1982 and set up a pension consulting firm in London. "They were trying to change the culture from a family-run stock company—run like a mutual company—to just another financial corporation in the arms of a large conglomerate. I've had some unhappy people cry on my shoulder. It's a culture change. Joe Jeffery ate in the cafeteria with the rest of us."

Rudd also realizes, however, that the change was needed and accepts not only what Orser did, but the fact that there was no place for him in the new London Life. Rudd, the Progressive Conservative who ran against Ontario Liberal leader David Peterson in the 1985 Ontario election, is philosophic about the change that left him behind. He quotes Tennyson: "The old order changeth, yielding place to new, / and God fulfils Himself in many ways, / Lest one good custom should corrupt the world." Orser's first phase had taken three years; Rudd's was the only senior defection. About the time Rudd was leaving, Orser felt there had been enough change that he could tell the company house organ, *Focus*, for its January 1982 issue: "We're not hearing [the phrase] 'sleeping giant' anymore."

London Life epitomizes the city whose name it carries: conservative, quiet, and authoritative. Head office belches little smoke, produces nothing visible, and utters not a sound. Just the sort of industry for the straight-backed spinster of a city that London has been for decades. In the 1920s, London Life was a scatter of four offices around the city. Plans were announced to build a single four-storey edifice opposite Victoria Park, just north of the downtown core. City council passed a by-law to block what some saw as an unsightly venture. Hamilton and Toronto quickly made it known that London Life was most welcome and the London council relented, fearing the job loss.

Construction began and the building was opened in 1926. It was done in neo-classical design using Queenston limestone with Indiana limestone columns. Bronze adorned the window frames and doors. After the Second World War, when more space was needed, the original building was twinned with a repeat of the first structure. Insurance firms in those days were swamped in paper, forms, applications, records, and clerks to keep track of everything. By 1951, a further seven-storey addition was required, and another four-storey structure was built in 1965. For a time, it looked as if everyone in London would one day work there to handle the paper-flow. In the late 1960s, an office tower was considered. Fortunately, by then computers had halted the need for exponential spatial and employee growth.

By the time Orser arrived, the number of head office employees had actually shrunk from a high of 2,100 to 1,700. He ordered an inventory of employee space needs in the fourteen and a half acres in the four buildings that make up head office. The consulting architects discovered that more efficient space usage actually freed up 88,000 square feet, about 14 per cent of the total. That unneeded amount, the equivalent of an eight-storey office building, could be rented out to tenants. Renovations to head office began in 1979, took three years, and cost $16 million; they included restoration work, mechanical updating, and new furniture. The part of the original 1926 building now for rent was designated the Victoria Park Executive Centre. It features marble floors, fine woods, and bronze as well as an intricately sculpted and gilded ceiling.

The centre and the London Life executive offices also boast what must be the most carefully controlled access of any insurance executive in the country. The executive offices are ranged off the main reception area, in a hallway behind shatter-proof glass doors that are locked and can only be opened by sliding an identification card into a slot, then placing one's hand flat on the mechanism. A light flashes within and the machine measures the width between the fingers, a distance unique to each individual. The device matches the information it receives from the hand against information recorded on a magnetic strip on the card. Thus only the approved user can use his own card. Perhaps there is a reason for all this security beyond the usual protection of the executive from unknown no-goods bent on extortion. When the system was being discussed and after Orser had approved installation, he commented, "Besides, it'll stop people from bugging you in your office."

By contrast, the rest of the building is done in an open planning concept with fabric panels for privacy. Where each person works is called not a desk or an office or even a work station. Instead each employee works at what London Life euphemistically calls a control centre. Each has a very specific amount of space depending upon his or her position in the hierarchy. Clerks work in a space measuring 70 by 75 inches, supervisors stretch out in 140 by 150 inches and managers have 280 by 300 inches. Orser's own perquisites include a chauffeur-driven Cadillac for business trips and a condominium apartment maintained in Toronto by the firm. His personal auto is a Lincoln Town Car.

The company is not stingy with benefits. While the days of the subsidized 25-cent hot meal in the cafeteria are gone, food is still cheap. For example, a full-course meal costs $2.50. Half the cost of physical fitness club memberships is paid, up to a maximum of $100. Mortgages are available at a 15-per-cent discount from prevailing rates, with no administrative fee and assistance on legal fees. About 1,500 employees participate at an annual cost to London Life in excess of $1.3 million. There are 800 free parking spaces at head office. In all, the various health, pension, vacation, and Christmas bonus plans cost the company more than $21 million in 1984.

When Orser arrived, he found that the cosy and warm surroundings of the London Life womb had made the firm complacent and parochial. Every one of the ten officers and senior executives not only had been brought up in London, but had attended the local university, the University of Western Ontario. For years the company had been run as if it were different from other businesses; Orser concluded that it was not. His time at Molson's, Eaton's, and Air Canada had told him that London Life was just as much in the consumer products business as his previous employers—yet it was not being run that way. "Like most of our competitors, our operations seemed to cruise along with no particular sense of urgency. We had a lot of management committees, decisions took a long time to be made, and the management structure was the product of tradition rather than a reflection of modern management organization and techniques long since used in other kinds of businesses."

One of the few areas requiring no updating was the company's computer system, which ranks with the best in the country. London Life has an IBM 3084, the largest IBM makes, worth $12 million; it is connected to 1,500 terminals in head office and 130 offices across

Canada. The system is huge; its capacity is 32 million instructions per second. The software used has been developed over a twenty-year period; 5 million lines of programs have been developed, worth an estimated $60 million. Without the computer, the firm estimates it would need three times its current staff to handle the 160,000 transactions a day and the 1.1 million cheques a year.

Not everything worked as well. For example, Orser found some executives, below the rank of vice-president, overpaid for what they did. While he didn't fire anyone or cut salaries, some people received increases over a five-year period at lower rates than others. He also set out to recruit fresh talent. His catch included Norm Epp as vice-president for finance, like Orser a U of T Commerce grad and a CA, and a twenty-four-year veteran of manufacturing and retailing; John Andrachuk from Systems Dimensions Inc. as director of corporate planning; I. P. Brady from Massey-Ferguson's European operations as director of information services; D. A. Bratton from Price Water-house as director of human resources, and Tom Allan from Central Trust Co. as vice-president for investments.

Orser also raided other insurance companies to snag specific people he liked. They included Robert Lackey, vice-president for corporate development, from Beneficial Standard Life Insurance Co. of Los Angeles; and Charles Kimball, vice-president for group insurance, from Excelsior Life. By 1984 eighteen of the top fifty executives—nearly 40 per cent—were new under Orser. In the key operating committee, however, half are career London Life employ-ees and half have arrived in the last six years. All forty senior officers are paid over $50,000 a year, vice-presidents receive about $100,000, and Orser himself earns $200,000.

In addition to finding his own company sleepy, Orser found the whole insurance industry to be an inbred and outdated bunch. He was astounded at the number of organizations in the business, all patronized by the various companies, where they traded what would be regarded in other industries as confidential information. "If someone came up with a good idea," he says, "the first thing they'd do would be to phone someone in another company and see what they thought of it." While he has changed the thinking at London, he finds the industry reluctant to adapt. "There is still a 'Fortress Insurance' mentality, the idea that we can somehow band together to protect our turf. Of course, that's impossible."

London's fortress mentality was altered by a combination of long-range planning and incentive arrangements for staff. Orser's first priority was information. Systems were established so that each month senior management receives forty pages of numbers. Says VP Epp, "Now we can make decisions based on knowledge and fact rather than letting things drift or going by the seat of our pants." Senior officers spend all or part of ten days a year setting financial and marketing goals, using reams of computer-generated information. Orser also took the unusual step of putting into place an incentive compensation program. While most insurance companies are still wrestling with executive performance ratings or basing bonuses on a few measurements, Orser installed a system for every senior officer that measures dozens of elements related to personal and corporate performance. Depending on the rating, bonuses can go as high as 40 per cent of annual salary. In 1983, for example, at the senior level they added an average of 25 per cent to base pay.

Nine members of the London Life executive have a Trilon stock purchase plan that allows them to borrow the money to buy stock. Interest on the loan is covered by dividends. Orser, for example, had a loan of $499,982 outstanding in 1984, the maximum allowed by the plan. Orser's stock investment has done well. He, Lambert, and Hawkrigg have made about $1 million among them, on paper, on Trilon stock. As a London Life sales agent said at the 1985 Trilon meeting, "I wish there was a way that we as salesmen could get in on a money-for-jam deal like that." In fact, in 1983, all employees were able to buy Trilon shares through a less lucrative one-shot offering using a London Life share loan plan. More than 60 per cent signed up, more than doubling the number of Trilon shareholders to 4,000. (There are now 5,200.)

Orser added productivity bonuses for all staff in 1985 and became so involved in details that he ordered that mail deliveries to the various offices be cut from fourteen times a day to four to save money. Orser did not, however, touch the core: individual life insurance sales. He concluded that London's Life agents should continue to have exclusive rights to London's life insurance products. Of the 2,239 sales agents, 539 are in the general sales division (GSD) and 1,700 are in the district sales division (DSD). Each DSD agent has a specific geographic area in which to sell. While most agents in the industry find prospects through referrals and phone solicitation—as do DSD agents—some of the DSD agent's time is also spent out knocking on doors, doing cold calls, looking for prospects in the local neighbourhoods and subdivisions. The process gave rise to one of Orser's favourite descriptions of his firm and its approach: "We make house calls." Selling to blue-collar households, DSD has been incredibly successful. During one five-week campaign in 1984, DSD sold some $447 million worth of insurance to 24,000 policyholders.

While Orser could see, in those first months of scrutiny, that a wider portfolio of financial services (although not property or casualty insurance) was possible in the future, he decided that each agent must first have an updated and competitive portfolio of life products. He could also see that new strength was needed in marketing. "It seemed to me that everyone was responsible for product development, which was a slow and ponderous process, and our product line was becoming uncompetitive. We were a solid company but we would have to make some changes if we were to be successful in the future." Market share had been falling because premiums charged on term products were not competitive and the by-then-popular new money products, combining term and investment, were not even available from London Life.

In 1979, he wrenched the term insurance premiums into line with those in the rest of the industry; in 1980, he saw that an accumulation annuity was introduced to reflect the high interest rates consumers were demanding. The battle to get accumulation annuities launched was not easy. The actuaries and some other senior executives did not like people regularly putting savings into annuities with interest rates that constantly had to respond to market pressures. "There was an element who were going to study the thing to death," says Orser. Finally he got fed up and said: "We're going into the annuity business now. They said: 'Well, we can't promise you that we'll make any money.' And I had to say, 'Well, look, I don't give a damn whether we make any money, we're just going to go into the business so that you guys can learn how to manufacture and market this product.'" (Annuity sales reached $209 million in 1984, a profitable part of the business.)

By 1981, he was already able to see changes and reflect publicly on the reasons why they had to be made. He told the *Globe and Mail* that while he was fully aware that London Life was "a very powerful company" when he had joined, he also knew that "maybe it's lost a bit of momentum." The answer was deceptively simple. "What we had to do was wind things up a little and that means developing some new standards of performance in the management area. Bringing some modern and aggressive technique to the company." He shook off easy labels. "I don't think 'being tough' is the way to say it." He was diplomatic towards those who had gone before. "Sometimes in the past in other companies, very difficult decisions had to be made and implemented simply [to] survive. That wasn't the case here."

Orser continued to add new products and in 1984, individual disability income insurance policies were also made available. Rather than develop one for London Life, Orser chose to "network" and sell a product already available. In this case, the policy came from Paul Revere Life Insurance Co. He also pushed through a new permanent life product that provides additional coverage paid for by policy dividends. Coverage that once cost $17 per thousand was reduced to $4.50 per thousand, about the same as once-cheaper term insurance.

In addition to encouraging product development, Orser set out to press his own brand of personal leadership onto the field force. He devoted thirty working days annually to visiting sales agents in the field offices. Seen by many to be the interloper from outside who was going to change their comfortable ways, Orser was not universally loved. On one visit to a field office, an agent greeted him by saying, "Mr. Orser, we all know you're a monster." During the twenty-one months from January 1979 to October 1980, he visited 97 offices—more than half of London's total—and spoke personally to 3,000 agents, main-streeting and passing the message that there was a new aggressive stance and the products to back it. By the fall of 1984, he had visited every office.

He stills spends up to twenty days a year on the road, touring the offices a second time in a well-established pattern. The sales reps gather, often in a nearby hotel meeting room, stand around with coffee, and chat to Orser and at least one other senior executive. There are brief speeches and then an hour of questions from the sales staff. Topics range from complaints about slow commission payments through benefits to new product ideas. Orser is scrupulous in his replies. In Hamilton, Ont., one questioner asked about combining various applications to save time and paperwork. Senior vice-president for individual marketing Dale Creighton responded, "They're looking at that now." Orser, who was beside Creighton, looked slightly askance and asked, "Are they?" "Yes," confirmed

Creighton. "Like honest?" Orser pressed. "Oh yeah," Creighton said. He wanted to be absolutely sure that Creighton wasn't just stringing the field a line.

When he is around head office, he rarely misses a chance to massage an ego, even if he doesn't know the employee. "I have a philosophy," he once confided to a colleague. "I say hello to everyone within two blocks of London Life. Nine times out of ten, they work for London Life. They know me, even if I don't know them. And if they don't know me and don't work for London Life, I'll never see them again so it doesn't matter." Still, for all his attempts at diplomacy and his reverence for the past and the traditions of London, Orser aroused suspicion and fear in the community. With 1,500 employees in head office, London Life is the city's fifth-largest employer. Only the university, hospitals, and government employ more. Orser was throwing people out the windows, went the stories; Orser was running things from Toronto; London Life was going to move to Toronto. Any number of tales roamed about the tree-lined streets.

Orser recognized the problem. "Some people who'd known the company for many years got very worried," he told the *Globe and Mail*, "and wrung their hands and talked about all the changes that were happening and all the rest of it—Londoners in particular—and I'd say to them: 'Well, have you talked to any of the people who have left?'" The reply, according to Orser, was always no. "The reason is there are none. I'm not that tough a guy. I have a pretty demanding standard of management requirements, and I don't apologize to anybody for that." He rejected the gun-slinger image that was growing around his shake-'em-up style. "If that means precipitous, ill-considered moves, no. I don't think there's room in this industry for that. This industry is one of trust and confidence and full disclosure. My background is chartered accounting, so I have to believe in good disclosure."

The disclosure includes explanations of financial results by executives to staff at quarterly head office meetings. At one 1984 meeting, for example, Norm Epp, vice-president for finance, walked several hundred employees through the results of the recent three-month period. He reported that dividends paid to individual policyholders were 17 per cent higher than the previous year, but net income (profit) was lower, a decline seized upon by the local newspaper, the London *Free Press*, when the results were announced a few days earlier. "The London *Free Press* felt that this decline deserved head-line status," Epp complained to the meeting.

He explained what he termed "the facts behind the headlines." Said Epp, "Policyowner net income was above budget but below last year, and that's what gets to the *Free Press*. The variance from last year is due to a higher level of policyowner dividends and increased acquisition costs related to the sales results of our permanent insur-ance products—all good news. On a year-to-date basis, policyowner income was below budget by $1.4 million and below last year by $5.7 million. But, if we were to consider the total return to the policyholder [dividends and net income], we are comfortably ahead of last year.

"What the *Free Press* really should focus on is the shareholder net income, or earnings per share." Epp noted that figure was up 26 per cent over last year. "Once again, good news." Then another sally at the paper: "I guess good news does not produce favourable results for the *Free Press*!" And a final wry shot. "The editor at the *Free Press* took early retirement recently, but," he said, pausing for effect, "it has nothing to do with London Life." Indeed, London Life has a rate of growth that's the envy of the financial services industry, he notes. "Have you seen the banks' results lately?" At London Life, return on equity is a healthy 17 per cent, administrative productivity is up 11 per cent, field sales productivity is up 9.8 per cent. "If we can do it [in the next six months as well] it's going to be the best we've done for the last five years."

Such sessions, begun by Orser, are more than communications vehicles offering ammunition for over-the-back-fence chats. The gathering is group therapy, the corporate equivalent of a hot tub at a Big Sur spa. They come here from all levels of the hierarchy to vent their spleens and be part of a joint attack on the outside world. In the financial press they find a common foe and receive official ammuni-tion for the holy war against ignorance. They come for the bestowal of rewards for their daily toil and to feel their egos being massaged among their peers. Here they can submerge any secret personal shortcomings and strut professional success.

It was at another quarterly meeting in 1983 that Earl Orser announced a personal decision, perhaps as big as the one he had made in coming to London Life. He had been acting unofficially as chief executive officer of Trilon, but the task was too big to continue along with his London Life responsibilities as well. "I had the fun of launching Trilon," says Orser. "Then we got down to discussing who was going to do what." Mel Hawkrigg was picked to be CEO.

Hawkrigg was born in Toronto and in high school was the Canadian juvenile broad-jump champion. He attended McMaster University in Hamilton, Ont., was on the track team, played centre on the hockey team and guard on the basketball team. He was also a football star and one year held the scoring record, seventy points in six games, including thirty-five points in a 50–6 rout over Windsor. In 1952 he was quarterback and halfback for the Hamilton Tiger-Cats the year they met Toronto in the finals, losing out in a three-game series. He went on to become a chartered accountant with Clarkson, Gordon, joined Fuller Brush in 1959, rising to be president, then was vice-chairman for the central Ontario region at Canada Trustco from 1972 to 1981. He then joined Brascan Financial Services as an executive vice-president, became senior VP at Brascan, then was picked to be Trilon's president and chief executive officer in 1983.

"I joined Brascan to get Trilon up and running," says Hawkrigg. "London Life had already done a lot of work, so Earl and his people were allowed to launch it. It all came from the philosophy of putting together a unique blend of financial services." When Hawkrigg became CEO, Orser was named deputy chairman of Trilon in addition to his continuing role as CEO of London Life. Orser claims, however, that he could have had the CEO's job if he'd really wanted it. "I think if I felt really strongly about that, that probably could have been done." Orser says he stayed at London Life because Trilon was a holding company. "I like being an operating executive."

After the switch, Orser became more involved outside London Life in industry committees; and in 1984, his participation on the federal committee on financial services was a sign that conditions at London Life were sufficiently improved for him to leave more of the daily running of the place to others. The committee had representatives from each of the four financial pillars—banks, trust companies, the securities firms, and insurance. The other insurance company executives were John Panabaker, chairman of Mutual Life, and Jean Robitaille, chief executive officer of Royal Insurance. Of the fifteen members offering advice about future legislation, Orser was among the most aggressive. Wearing his hat as deputy chairman of Trilon, Orser was unique among the participants because he represented more than one pillar—insurance and trust services at once. "He was neither fish nor fowl," says Larry Clarke, of Spar Aerospace, who was chosen as a representative of the corporate consumer of financial services. "And it wasn't even clear what kind of herring he was. In the group, he was the most capable of original thought, the least hidebound."

Among insurance company executives, Orser is also one of the most successful. From 1979 to 1984, London Life's earnings per share grew at a compound rate of 22.9 per cent. There are, however, improvements yet to make. He rarely visits an office without asking the manager if women are being recruited to sell insurance. To date, about 10 per cent of DSD agents and 16 per cent of GSD agents are female. "Some offices I visit have no women representatives," says Orser. "This is something I find difficult to accept." The situation is worse among management. While 76 per cent of the head office staff is female, only 17 of the 620 management personnel (including 10 of the 165 sales office managers) are women—less than 3 per cent. Orser's target is to increase the level to 10 per cent by 1987, and there are currently 135 women in pre-management supervisory jobs.

The other main project is to stock the Trilon supermarket with more products. To achieve that, three interconnected Trilon committees, called joint opportunity committees (marketing, investment, and systems), have been set up to see what other products and services can be interchanged. "The priority has been to put the companies together and make sure they operate effectively," says Hawkrigg. "Now we have to develop programs. We do not intend to be all things to all people. We will be boutique-y in selected markets." At London Life, new products are being developed in what's called a "wind tunnel"—a marketing and technology laboratory where ideas for tomorrow are developed and tested. One area currently under study is personal computer use by sales agents. Orser continually presses for results. "Most everybody works on the basis that you have to have the system or the technology perfect before you implement, otherwise you'll get into all kinds of trouble. Part of the implication of 'wind tunnel' is that there's a lot more improvisation in what's happening there. If they see a problem, they fix it and they go on to the next thing. Systems people have to change their style in order to work like that. Usually they're told that everything has to be documented three times over. Now we're saying: 'Go fast. We'll take snapshots at the end and see how it looks.'"

Bumping up against tomorrow, however, are some problems from today. One that Orser has yet to fix is the rate of life insurance policy terminations. An amount of old business equal to more than half the new business premiums written each year goes off the books because of terminations. The firm's administrative costs for establishing these policies are wasted, and sales agents lose remuneration that is paid in later years. Terminations also cause the agent's persistency rate to drop, thus affecting various incentive and payment plans.

The other phenomenon is a direct result of Orser's success. The rest of the industry, apparently, is not so sleepy any more. Competition is increasing as companies battle for business. The area where this is most noticeable is in replacement policies, or "twisting," whereby one company's sales agent convinces a client to cash in a policy from another company in favour of a new one from the agent's own company. This accounts for many terminations. "There is simply too much targetting by one company on the customers of another," Orser complained in a 1984 speech to the senior marketing officers section of the Canadian Life and Health Insurance Association. "Many of the new policies are not doing the same job as the older ones. The customer is ripped off and the game is to generate a new commission at the expense of the customer. That's dangerous stuff."

It was an odd reversal, really, that speech in Montreal's Four Seasons Hotel. After all, Orser had come into the business complaining about the number of industry organizations that existed and the lack of competition. Here he was, seven years later, at just such an industry meeting, complaining that there was too much competition. The outsider had finally joined the club.

CHAPTER ELEVEN

THE OTHER SIDE OF THE DOOR

A Day in the Life of an Insurance Agent

H E WORKS from a back-room bullpen, one of eight sales agents occupying separate cubicles. Hard by, two tiny offices contain telephones for private pitches. A female agent has recently joined the staff and the previously male bastion has had to adopt some manners. A hand-lettered sign hung on the supply cupboard door reads like a manifesto and an apology. "There is now a woman in the back room. The 4-letter word costs 25¢ in the jar."

The bullpen is Ed Maindonald's office, but it isn't where he works. As a London Life sales agent, he spends 80 per cent of his time going door to door. In a world of financial services where the talk is of one-stop shopping, video terminal selection, and computer-programmed sales, Maindonald's role is almost a throw-back to a bygone era. But it works. Last year, London Life sold $5.2 billion in policies door to door. For all the change that London Life chief executive officer Earl Orser has caused since joining the firm in 1978, the agent's methods were left untouched.

Maindonald is fifty-eight, six feet tall with a crop of sandy hair gone mainly grey. At 235 pounds, his weight is a constant struggle. He likes to eat; three games a week of racquetball let him work off some of the excess. "I exercise," he says, "but I eat a good shot." He wears his belt slung below a pear-shaped belly; his bandy legs are slightly smaller than his size dictates. He is not a graceful man, but he sports a cheerful disposition. "I'm a bull in a china shop," he admits. His fingers, like a bunch of stubby carrots, are working the

221

phone, trying to confirm an appointment for later that day. Most of all, he just wants to get the hell out of that office, out of Barrie. The city's population is 45,000, far too big a place for a just-folks guy like Ed Maindonald. South of Barrie is his home, a converted cottage on Lake Simcoe. And his territory. There, he is king of the roads. Here, he is a bear on a chain doing paperwork.

Office tedium is not the reason he came back into sales after being a manager. He was the top London Life salesman in Canada in 1956, then he was a manager in Scarborough, a Toronto suburb, from 1957 to 1967; he became a regional manager in Sault Ste. Marie in 1967, then Hamilton in 1969. There he took over one of the four regional offices with its thirty agents and propelled it from last place to first in the area. For a time it was fun, but along about 1978, when he'd been teaching and cajoling others to sell for twenty-two years, he'd had enough. "I was getting close to fifty and I was bringing the job home, stewing about it and just not wanting to do it any longer." Still, there was some prestige to the role. "I liked being *somebody*, with my big office and a secretary." He thought about being a rep again, but wondered: "Am I going to be happy? I'd been telling people how to sell for twenty-two years, but I didn't know if I could sell again."

He talked it over with his superiors at London Life head office. "You need more help," they told him. "Think about it for three or four months." He did, but his mind was made up. They offered to move him from Hamilton to be manager in another region. He turned that down. The reasons were both personal and professional. At the top, the business was changing faster than he was.

"I didn't feel I had full control over the agency. [Sales] objectives started to jump. Levels of bureaucracy were created; they came in and told me my job. There was human rights [legislation]. Is he black or green? You couldn't fire anybody." The internal rules changed, too. "I have no complaint about London Life. It's changed a lot. It was a family business, but you can't survive that way any more. Earl Orser has come in. He's a super guy, he's moved the company and that was needed. But an old guy like myself, I didn't want to be a manager any more. I wanted to get back and run my own show."

His intention had always been to retire to his Lake Simcoe cottage. What he decided was to move there early and keep working, selling insurance again. Head office agreed. As luck would have it, the rep who had been working the area near Maindonald's cottage retired.

So in 1979, he left his managerial role with its perks and its pains, he sold the house in Hamilton, and he and his wife, Mary, renovated the cottage and moved in year-round. He went back on the road. For London Life, the reversion was not unusual. Points out Maindonald's new manager, Ron Cowan, "No one is ever frowned upon for doing what they want. It's not like going from bank manager to teller."

Maindonald didn't need to worry that he had lost his ability to sell. In his first year, he sold $2 million in insurance. As a manager, he'd been earning $40,000 a year. As a salesman, he earns $60,000. He gets six weeks of holidays a year with pay because his policies are rarely cancelled by clients. For a company, cancellations are expensive. They urge reps to keep an eye on wavering policyholders by paying for vacations if the persistency rate is high. As a result, Maindonald receives $300 to $400 a week when he's on holiday—even though he's not earning any new commissions—because his persistency rate is 96.2 per cent. (The region's average is 88.8 per cent.) That means that 96.2 per cent of the people to whom he sells policies are still paying their premiums in the second year. It is a key measurement for both the company and the individual. For each new policy, the company has head office administrative costs, including the sales agent's commission. If a policyholder cancels too soon, the company loses money. The $60,000, therefore, also includes some commission and bonuses for keeping policies in force. More important than the income, however, is the fact that he's having fun again. "I can make that with a lot less headaches. I see Ron [Cowan] with a problem at five o'clock and I say, 'Gee, that's too bad. You'd better stay late and work it out. I'm going home and have a swim.' I never fail to rub it in."

Maindonald is one of 1,700 reps in London Life's district sales division (DSD). DSD has 200 managers and 62 regional managers. Every rep gets a territory with about 5,000 or 6,000 people in it. About two-thirds of the population is regarded as the agent's target market—that is, households where the head of the house earns up to $25,000 annually. While the reps can sell outside their areas, they are encouraged to stay within the boundaries with cash bonuses in the $3,000–$4,000 range if 70 per cent of their sales are within their district. Maindonald's region stretches from Tottenham in the south, 150 miles north to Parry Sound; from Georgian Bay in the west, 60 miles east to Sutton and Beaverton. There are fifteen communities in the region and thirty-one reps under regional manager Ron Cowan, who is stationed in Barrie. Under Cowan are four staff managers who hire, train, and oversee the reps. Each has been in sales for a minimum of three years before joining management. Their average age is thirty-four. Under them, in nearby Orillia, are eight reps who are in the office daily and ten "detached" reps who work out of their homes and come into the office once a week. In Barrie, there are fifteen reps in the office and six "detached."

For the most part, the reps in Barrie lack insurance experience. Eighteen of them, more than half the total, have been with London Life less than two years. Of the thirty-one, three are women. The average age is thirty-four. Most have had previous sales experience, and their average income prior to joining London Life was $23,000. When they joined, they spent six weeks being trained by the manager, then two weeks at a sales school in London learning what's known as "sales tracks," or memorized sales pitches to use on clients. London Life rarely hires from other life insurance companies; usually an agent who wants to switch companies has had personal or performance problems that London Life does not want to inherit. The company prides itself on its four-year retention rate: at London Life, thirty-two out of every hundred reps in the DSD remain, about twice the industry average. DSD reps are expected to maintain a high profile in their area, making sixty contacts a week with potential clients (this is known as prospecting) and closing two sales. Their average income after a year at London Life is $35,000.

London Life also has a general sales division (GSD). There, 539 representatives go after the white-collar and professional market, people earning more than $25,000. The two divisions, totalling about 2,000 sales agents, form the largest single field force for any Canadian life insurance company. No other agent or broker can sell London Life policies. By 1990, London Life plans to have 3,000 agents. GSD reps tend to be university graduates; they are not held to fixed areas, have less supervision than DSD agents, and earn more money. The average annual income of a GSD agent is about $50,000 after a year. London Life recruits GSD agents on forty-seven campuses every year. Contact is made with over 3,000 people; about 1,100 of them are interviewed on campus. Regional managers then interview 600 of them, and about 250 are brought to London for further interviews. About 65 are hired. In 1984, another 125 were hired directly by field managers from a variety of backgrounds. In DSD, there are 151 women, or 9.8 per cent of the total; in GSD, there are 88 women, or 16.3 per cent of the total.

One of the first things prospective GSD agents must do is try to drum up prospects by phone and watch the manager pitch policies. The hopeful agents get the commission if there is a sale, but more importantly they can decide if the process is one they want as a career. If an applicant can quell the initial phone whim-whams, beat the nervousness, and rise above the rejections, he or she is hired and given training. GSD recruits get more training than DSD reps. Recent university grads, for example, spend three weeks in the field, then seven weeks at head office, three months more in the field, then another three weeks at a refresher course in London. Each agent represents an investment by London Life of $40,000 in training during the first two years.

The average DSD sale is a policy giving $17,900 of whole life protection, with an annual premium of $320. About 30 per cent of sales are to existing London Life customers. The typical DSD customer is twenty-six to thirty-five years old, a blue-collar worker earning $20,000 to $25,000 a year. Three-quarters are married. Nine times out of ten, the sale is made in the home; 60 per cent of sales are in the evening.

Ed Maindonald is one of the more experienced reps in the Barrie office. He is also one of the top producers. In 1983, he sold $2.9 million of insurance. The first-place salesman sold over $3 million. A good, average rep might sell $1.6 million. The Barrie region itself is the sixth most productive in the country, and eight of its agents sold more than $2 million each in insurance in 1984.

As members of a DSD group, agents do not have the individual freedom that might be expected to come with high performance. They are given cost-effective cubicles, not offices, so they feel "pushed" to go out and sell. GSD agents, on the other hand, have individual offices because they make many of their sales to clients brought into their offices. Most of the upscale GSD clients have their own offices and feel more comfortable knowing their life insurance agent has one, too. While DSD agents are encouraged to hit the road and sell around kitchen tables, the office keeps a close eye on them. They are constantly monitored and motivated by management. "There is pressure in keeping people productive," says Cowan. "In any commission business, if things aren't right, productivity falls off. If you're not out working, standards fall. Nine times out of ten, they're sitting at home, worrying about it and not doing anything." The answer to such a slump is to put the individual on an action plan, in effect a forced march to produce sales. Effort is checked daily. Cowan has worked with an agent as long as five months before finally giving up and firing him.

Ed Maindonald has always been peddling something door to door. He was born in Toronto and left school after Grade Twelve to sell baked goods door to door for Canada Bread. Then he bought two trucks and went into the ice business. He enjoyed the independence, but it was the early 1950s and refrigerators were becoming common. He realized that the ice age was ending. He was thinking about life insurance sales, Sun Life in particular, when his wife arranged for a friend, a London Life salesman, to visit.

Maindonald got into the business the same way many have, encouraged to join by an acquaintance or friend who has already succeeded. At twenty-five years of age, in 1953, he began a new career. He took his first train ride to London for training, was put on a draw of $66 a week for thirteen weeks, and never looked back. In his first year, he made $6,000 ($10,000 in the second), working in Scarborough when the eastern Toronto suburb was exploding with new residents.

This day, more than thirty years later, his work began even before he left the house, as often happens. An early-morning call came from a widow asking if he'd pick up a water sample at her house and take it to the township office for testing. "When her husband died, I told her, 'If there's anything I can do, just give me a call.' She's never forgotten." In fact, the trip serves a double purpose. One of his clients works at the township office and her monthly policy premium payment is due. He picked up the cheque on the same stop.

Ten years ago, there were more such non-productive stops because the agent picked up the monthly premiums from most policyholders. Each sales agent would spend four hours a day collecting from clients. Today, only about 5 per cent require a regular visit. Most pay London Life directly, by automatic bank chequing (ABC) systems. While the new method does free up time, there is a negative result, according to Maindonald. "In the old days, even if you didn't feel like it, you were out making contact, talking insurance. When we switched over to ABC, I had an awful lot of agents going down the tubes because they suddenly had nothing to do."

The first few hours of the two days a week he starts at the office are taken up in completing applications for insurance successfully sold to clients, dealing with phone calls, and opening mail from head office. Ed's secretary, Kim Ridpath, bustles in and out with paperwork. First, several death benefit cheques from head office. "Jeez," says Maindonald, inspecting the cheques, "a lot of people are dying lately." Laughs Ridpath: "You're not going to have a district left." He checks the name on one of the benefit payments in one of the four grey binders containing information on all his clients. "Oh, yeah," says Maindonald, "he was born in 1903. He's had a good run." The cheque goes in the briefcase to be delivered personally to his widow.

He has also received three policies issued by head office along with computer-printed ledger sheets showing growing cash values. Maindonald puts the sheets and the policy together, pulls out a rubber stamp and pad, and carefully stamps his name across the front of the policy. "I like to go in and deliver the policy," he says, tossing it in his briefcase. A pink slip from head office shows that another client's automatic bank payment for $47.86 has bounced. It will automatically be run through again by head office five days later in case the account just happened to be low on funds the first time. If it bounces again, London Life will inform the policyholder and the agent. As a last resort, the company uses dividend build-up to pay the premium and keep the policy in force. When the cash value in the policy is used up, the policy lapses. For Maindonald, a pink slip is bad news. If the premium goes unpaid and the policy lapses after two years in force, the amount of the agent's insurance credit is deducted from his current net production. Also, any commission still to come (he gets a share of premium payments for three years) ends as well. "I don't want that lapse. I don't like those words, 'potential lapse.'" He'll follow up with the policyholder to make sure the premium is paid.

There is some joshing going on in the office about who's on top. In 1984 Maindonald was third in the office with $3.6 million: first place went to René Pohl with $4.1 million. Maindonald laughs, turns his head, and pretends to spit when he says Pohl's name. Behind the jocularity, however, the jousting is serious. After his manager leaves, Maindonald's joking manner disappears. He dons a serious look and says quietly, "If I was twenty years younger, I guess I would sell a million dollars more than I do." But those were other days and he is looking forward to retirement, perhaps in two years. "I don't think I'll go beyond sixty," he says. "The changes in the business in the last ten or fifteen years would curl your hair." He led the office in 1982, was second in 1983, third in 1984. But even with the flush of youth gone, the flagon of competitive spirit remains full. "I didn't come up here to be first or second, but it's pretty hard to lose that drive."

During his previous sales incarnation, Maindonald was second among all London Life agents in Canada for two successive years, 1954 and 1955. First in the country was Sigmund Reiser, a Winnipeg agent. Maindonald's manager, Russ Freeman, was to visit head office and asked Maindonald if there was anything he wanted. Replied Maindonald, "You get Sigmund Reiser fired or promoted out of the field. I can't beat him." Before Freeman returned to the office, he wired Maindonald: "Mission accomplished. Sigmund promoted to head office. Anything else, my friend?" The next year, 1956, Maindonald sold $850,000 worth of policies and stood first in Canada.

It's hard to tell whether Maindonald's drive to succeed comes deep from within or is enforced from without. It is probably a combination. Certainly, the sales campaigns, rewards, and ego feeds run by head office are endless. In 1956 he was named "Man of the Year" by London Life. His picture and biography were in the company publication. This month, almost thirty years later, he is in the middle of another campaign, a six-week affair called "Breakthrough." Along with the five-week spring campaign, it is one of two periods each year when every region and each individual is given a sales quota and a contest with prizes. Maindonald's quota is $650,000 — almost as much as he sold during a full year thirty years ago. (He sold $900,000 in the six weeks, well more than his target, his best Breakthrough result ever.) London Life has more contests under way than a corner store has lottery tickets. In addition to the annual spring and fall campaigns, there is a longer-term contest that offers a Florida trip in March. London Life pays air fare for the agent and spouse plus four days' hotel accommodation at Clearwater's Sheraton Sand Key Resort. Maindonald needs $2.65 million in sales by the end of January to be a winner. "I'm on track for that," he says. (He went.) In addition there is a merit corps for annual standings and local office give-aways.

Prizes for Breakthrough include such items as portable telephones, golf clubs, television converters, and home work-benches. "I like to win stuff," says Maindonald. "For years as a manager I gave it away." After the summer holiday lull, Breakthrough is meant to get production rolling again. Like a lot of agents, Maindonald has saved a few sales he had just prior to the period to be sent in to head office during the six weeks.

Finally, the day's paperwork finished, he flees the office before lunch, grabs the parking tickets (before the office moved to a new building with a parking lot, he averaged two a week) from the windshield of his Mercury Grand Prix, and heads for his first call. His first stop is to place a policy bought a few weeks earlier by a twenty-one-year-old woman who works as an office receptionist. She is busy on the phones, so he doesn't take much time explaining the fine print. "Everything came through OK," he says. "There were no problems." He points to the face amount, $30,000, and flips through the pages quickly as she stares at them. "I won't bore you with all the details. If you have any questions, just call me." She smiles, nods agreement, and returns to the phones.

There are more clients on a nearby downtown street. Although this is not in his district, he can sell here and he has. He strides along the sidewalk like a politician, knowing the landmarks and pointing out the conquests. "I bought my VCR in there three years ago," he says, pointing to a shop. "Then I sold the owner, his son, and his grandson." A stop at the jewellery store to pick up two gift-wrapped silver-plate spoons; he gives away about fifty a year to clients who've recently had babies. They cost $8, and he spends another $4 to have the name engraved.

One store is a group insurance client. The sale was months in coming, and it took a tragedy to spur the final deal. Maindonald had several conversations with the owner, who seemed to be leaning towards a full London Life package including life insurance, health, disability, and dental for his ten employees. Maindonald even met with the employees for an hour before the store opened one morning to answer their questions. But the owner was reluctant to sign the deal, saying he wanted to think about it some more and talk at the end of the month. Before the month was out, an employee drowned while fishing. A policy in place would have meant a $42,000 death benefit to the man's widow. Without the policy, she was forced to sell her home. It took some days before the body was found. During that time, the owner asked if the policy could be put in so the deceased would be covered. Maindonald told him that he thought the company might be a bit reluctant under the circumstances. He made the sale, but it was three weeks too late for the widow. "If only he'd signed when I told him to," says Maindonald, shaking his head, "but he wouldn't." Now a full employee benefit package is in place.

He heads south from Barrie and stops at a roadside coffee shop. Away from the city and the office, the freedom he suddenly feels is obvious; it's as if he'd hoisted a revolutionary flag. "This is my country," he says, waving an arm towards his district. Lions, Big Brothers, the boys who hang out at the marina, he belongs to a lot of groups. "Anybody you see, I probably know." And, he might mention, any one of them is a possible sale—or might lead him to a sale. As he walks to the coffee shop, he says wistfully, "I haven't got any clients here, but I'm working on it."

Over lunch, he talks about his weekly schedule. Except for the two mornings a week when he is in the office, doing paperwork, he is out selling, often four nights a week and a few hours every weekend. The evenings are best to catch couples together, but he has to feel *right*. "I tell ya, it's tough to come home from work at four-thirty and get revved up to go again at six. But if I don't feel up for a sale, I might as well turn around and go home." He usually works about forty hours a week, more when a campaign is on. While most appointments are set in advance, he does make about twenty cold calls a month, hitting maybe four or five doors in a row. His weekly gas bills run to $100. The telephone is cheaper and faster. Twenty calls might turn up three appointments and perhaps one sale. Word of mouth, neighbourhood gossip, baby announcements—the leads are as numerous as the population in his district, his mouth is planted on the phone looking for more.

The next stop, another policy delivery, catches a thirty-three-year-old housewife cleaning out her basement. The family is moving in two days. The place is bedlam. Still, there is time for coffee at the kitchen table, the first of half a dozen he will sit around today. Maindonald explains the policy her husband took out a few days ago and gives her a portfolio in which to keep it and the family's other insurance policies. She pulls two other London Life portfolios out of a kitchen drawer and searches for an old policy. She shows it to Maindonald and says, "I took that out when I was nineteen." Interjects Maindonald, "That was just a couple of years ago." She laughs and continues. "What should I do with it?" He takes it from her, gives it a cursory look and says, "That's a good policy, you can hang on to that. It provides a $2,500 death benefit." " I've changed the beneficiary on it," she says. "When I took it out I made my grandfather the beneficiary. I just started work and I wanted them to have enough money to bury me if I died." Concludes Maindonald, "That'll be paid up when you're thirty-nine, then it'll stay in force."

He switches the subject to the $100,000 term policy she recently bought. He wants her to change that to whole life. He explains that the term policy will need to be renewed in a few years, at a higher premium. Whole life premiums stay flat. Also, if he sells her another policy now, he's got another notch in his belt during Breakthrough. She's not quite ready. "My husband got that so he can hire someone to look after the kids." Ed chimes in, "And I know just the woman he's got in mind." More laughter. "I wish he'd get her around here now to help with this move," she says. They gossip a bit about another woman's second marriage and agree to talk in two or three months about her term insurance. "Give me a call when you get settled in and know your exact address so I can update my records," he calls back to her as they part on the porch. At the road he looks back and says, "There's nothing like someone who knows a lot of people and is prepared to talk about them." That's where the prospects come from.

In all his years of selling, from the time he peddled bread full-time as a teenager, through the four years in the home-delivery ice business, and now in life insurance, Maindonald has been propositioned only once. He was eighteen when a bread customer gave him the come-on. He fled and never returned. The classic lonely housewife has not surfaced again in his selling life. "I've heard other insurance guys talk about it. They'd say, 'I went around to such-and-such a place today to pick up a premium, and oh boy, was she asking for it.' I'd say, 'Can I get transferred into that district?' Nothing like that ever happens to me."

Next stop is a woman recently widowed. Her husband was killed in a highway accident four months earlier. She was left with two children and monthly mortgage payments of $700. Usually London Life requires a death certificate before the benefit is paid, but in this case the police investigation dragged on and no certificate was issued. Finally, in frustration, Maindonald sent photos of the crash scene to head office as proof of the accident. London Life bent the rules and immediately paid $40,000; the final $10,000 followed when the death certificate was filed. The widow used the death benefit to pay off part of the mortgage on her house. In that way, the monthly payment for principal, interest, and taxes was reduced to

$243 a month. The new figure was low enough so that with a part-time job, she was able to keep the house.

The husband also had a Prudential policy. It was paid off much more slowly. In fact, when she phoned Prudential to talk about the death benefit, the Prudential agent said he wouldn't come around during the evening, even though she had just started the job to earn the income she needed to stay afloat. "I don't work after four-thirty," he told her. Maindonald has kept a copy of the letter she sent to London Life. "Prudential may have a piece of the rock," she wrote, "but London Life cares about life." She became one of Maindonald's biggest fans. She even carries his calling cards to pass out and sings his praises to her friends.

Today, with the kids at school, she is painting a ceiling. She tells Maindonald that she is not going to press charges against the other driver. "I've gone through the hate stage of my grief. I've spoken to the other driver; he doesn't remember a thing. Maybe he's trying to block it, I don't know." Maindonald is as much social worker as life insurance salesman, as he hears about her recent operation and the hostility her young son feels towards any man who offers help. She tells Maindonald that at first she vowed never to remarry. She wouldn't even date. Now she's having second thoughts. "I'm reconsidering that." The neighbours offered assistance with the painting. "I told them I needed someone to scrub my back. No one has done it for four months. And you know," she says, feigning surprise, "no one came over to do it."

Around the corner, he makes a collection. Here the payment used to include policies for the four children, too, and ran to $30 a month. With the kids grown and gone, the amount is so low that Maindonald now calls just twice a year for the six-month payment of $26. They talk about the imminent marriage of a mutual acquaintance, the jobs the woman's children have, and the life insurance policies they don't have. "They're on their own now," she says. "I don't know what they've got." No sales there. "Anybody moving into the area?" Maindonald asks. Yes, two houses away. Maindonald makes a note of the house number and prepares to leave. "Merry Christmas," he says, "since I won't see you until the new year." "And thanks for your calendar," she calls down the driveway. A good prospect uncovered. He'll call there once the new family is settled.

A cold call proves less productive. Maindonald knocks on the door of a house where former clients, a young couple, lived. They moved to a larger house; he hasn't met the new occupant. A chihuahua barks behind the door and finally an ancient crone arrives. Her button-front dress has more buttons undone than fastened. Her slip blows in the breeze as she holds the storm door open. Maindonald pretends not to notice her attire, introduces himself, and tells her that he just wanted to say hello. She looks baffled. He tells her that the previous occupants have had their baby. She says she didn't know them. He gives her a calling card and tries to help her get the yapping dog back inside the house. "An older woman," he says after the door closes, "living alone like that, is not likely to want any insurance." He won't call again. He shows no embarrassment at the encounter, no recrimination in the rejection. "I've been in the business too long for that. Oh, it troubled me in the beginning, but you get over it." He knows, however, that such turn-downs can be tough on some agents, particularly in the first two years in the business. "It's got to suit you and you've got to like it—or it'll kill you."

The next two doors bring no response at all. He leaves a brochure and his calling card tucked between the door and the sash, high up at eye level. At the fourth call, a young woman in her late twenties invites him in. They sit in a living room only half filled with furniture. The soaps are playing on the television. The house is plain, the floors linoleum, but it has been scrubbed clean since the previous owner left six months earlier. Maindonald can't get over the improvement and says so. "Six loads to the dump," she laughs, "and the garbage at the road."

They talk about her husband's work and his group insurance on the job. Asks Maindonald, "Does he have any insurance personally?" "No," she answers, "but he wants some. Your timing is good." Maindonald arranges to return the following evening at seven to talk to them both. As a cold call, they don't come much better, but Maindonald allows himself little pleasure. Back at the car, he kicks himself. "I should've been in there two months ago. Somebody else could've got to them first." Often, as in this case, it is the wife who is won over first. When Maindonald returns, sometimes the husband isn't in agreement. No one has ever laid hands on him, but a few irate men have ordered him off the property on a return visit. Maindonald never argues. (In the case of this cold call, he came back the next night and sold a $60,000 whole life policy that gives the insured $240,000 at sixty-five, providing a $2,000-a-month annuity. The premium is $90 a month. Maindonald earned $540 commission on the sale, plus $162 in the second year and $108 in the third year if the policy stays in force.)

The next house call has been pre-arranged. It was, however, no easy appointment. It took Maindonald weeks to find them. The family had moved from another area; the previous London Life agent had alerted the Barrie office and Maindonald was assigned to be their local rep. The only address available, however, was a post office box number. Letters went unanswered. Telephone attempts to reach the policyholder were fruitless; the number was unlisted. Finally, a query in a local restaurant turned up a waitress who knew the location of the newly arrived couple's house. Maindonald visited and found that the wife thought her husband, a thirty-two-year-old policeman, might want to add to his insurance to cover the new mortgage.

Maindonald has prepared a variety of alternatives in advance of the return visit. Term insurance worth $50,000 (protection but no cash values) for twenty years would cost $20 a month, $240 a year. Maindonald has also requested a printed ledger from head office to show that an option called Econolife (a mix of term, whole life, and growing cash value) could be purchased for a similar amount. For an annual premium of $298, the client would receive $10,000 whole life and $27,000 term, a total of $37,000 in protection. The bonus with Econolife is that the policy is fully paid for in thirteen years. Later, the cash value buys a retirement annuity.

In terms of Maindonald's gain from the sale, in cash or in credits towards prizes, there is little to choose between the two policies. His commission does differ slightly. The term policy pays him $180 over three years, Econolife $223 over three years. In the totals for merit corps, they are about equal. If the sale were in term insurance, Maindonald's total credit would be 40 per cent of the $50,000, or $20,000. On the Econolife, the $10,000 plus $27,000 term, he receives credit for the full $10,000 plus 40 per cent of the $27,000, or $20,800.

The sales duel begins at the kitchen table. The husband is not as keen as his wife. Maindonald wishes the wife would join them as his ally. Instead, she worries about disruption and tries to keep a pre-schooler quiet by watching cartoons with him in the recreation room downstairs. The policeman points out that he has $75,000 in group coverage. In addition, he notes, he increased his personal coverage to $40,000 just a few years ago. Maindonald inspects the policy that was purchased and points out that the policyholder's memory is wrong. The coverage was increased in 1978 from $10,000 to $25,000, not $40,000. The husband takes another tack. He says that he's paying too much per month for all his insurance, including policies on his wife and two children. "Jeez," he says, "I must be paying over $100 now." Maindonald takes a moment to total the monthly premiums; he points out that they come to $82. The husband is beginning to soften, even his posture seems less tense. He is beginning to relax. "Well," he says, "if I can stay under $100, that'd be OK."

There is a rhythm to the conversation. It hardly seems as if Maindonald is selling him at all, yet hurdles have been cleared, arguments have been stilled, and the man is ready to buy. Maindonald asks about the size of the mortgage; it is $31,000. He thinks about the two proposals he prepared. The Econolife option ($37,000 in coverage) cost $298, or about $25 a month. On top of $82, the total would be $107. Too much. Instead of Econolife, Maindonald talks about the term insurance policy. He doesn't, however, settle for just $31,000 in coverage. He knows that $20 a month will buy $50,000, so $17 a month will buy a little less. He mentions the figure that he has in mind, $45,000, but the client doesn't really hear. He is concentrating only on the total monthly payment.

Maindonald senses that it is time to close the sale. He pulls an eight-page application form from his briefcase and fills in the client's name. From across the table, the buyer offers address information. His participation in the process at this point means that the deal is done. After Maindonald has inspected the birth certificate and asked various family health questions, he asks, as the forms require: "Have you used marijuana within the past two years?" "No, never," replies the cop. Maindonald ticks off the appropriate box. "Have you used non-prescribed narcotics, barbiturates, amphetamines, hallucinogens, LSD or similar agents within the past five years?" "No," comes the reply, then the policeman laughs: "This is just like joining the police department all over again." Maindonald is enjoying himself. "I've always wanted to do this to a policeman." The forms are signed, a cheque for the first month's premium is collected, and the deal is done.

Later, Maindonald admits that he probably sold the policeman a larger policy than the client originally wanted—or realized he was buying. "I mentioned it would be close to fifty [thousand dollars of coverage]. He may not have heard that, but I'll go over it with him when I go back, and he'll be happy he has it. He's got two young kids there; he needs the coverage."

Nearby is a grocery store in a small village. For Maindonald, this is what's known as a centre of influence. People ask here where to get boat engines repaired, who's got a cottage to rent, who sells insurance. For their part, the store employees get to know whose family is growing, who has a new job or a new house. Maindonald has already sold the store-owner a personal policy and a group policy for his staff. Most of the dozen or so employees have since become individual clients as well.

All, that is, but the young man pushing a cartful of flattened cardboard boxes outside the store. "I don't need any insurance," he calls out as soon as he spots Maindonald heading towards the store. "That's OK," says Maindonald, "I haven't got any left." It is a favourite riposte, one that Maindonald has rolled dozens of times in his career. It is part of his style in order to ease the tension people often feel when first approached. "There's a wall there," says Maindonald. "As soon as you've broken that, they'll listen to what you're saying."

Inside the store, Maindonald talks briefly to another employee who has been approached by a Sun Life salesman to convert an old policy. He passed the details on to Maindonald for his advice. The employee is busy at the moment restocking shelves, so Maindonald agrees to return later in the week. Maindonald passes the time of day with the women working at the check-out counter. Then, on to a nearby bank branch, another centre of influence. He has his account here, and has sold most of the staff.

There is also a quick stop at his home. The lawn runs from the cottage to a steel retaining wall at the water's edge. A kingfisher flashes past, intent upon quarry in the water beyond. The lake is quiet today, only a few lazy waves all the way out to the two islands visible on the horizon. Maindonald takes a longing look at his boat, an eighteen-foot runabout with a 175-horsepower inboard/outboard motor just begging to be taken for a spin. No time for that today, although some summer days he does grab a few hours off between calls to come home. The tidy three-bedroom cottage is chock-full of his career. Plates he has won hang on a wall, stories announcing his 1956 award are close to hand in a coffee-table drawer, small appliance prizes are easily pointed out.

The final visit of the day is outside the district, to a young couple who moved but asked that Maindonald continue to be their rep. The wife has called, interested in insurance on herself. Both members of the couple work, and both cashed in their previous policies two years earlier to get at the cash values that had built up so they could invest the money in the new house. At the time, Maindonald had tried to talk them out of cancelling, urging them to borrow on the policies and keep them in place, but they had refused. The man replaced his policy with a term insurance plan with $70,000 coverage, but it needs to be renewed every ten years and premiums go up every time. Maindonald is not happy with the coverage they have and he hopes to set them in a new direction.

He grabs a quick dinner on the run and arrives at their home, an hour away, early in the evening. There is small talk about the two children, their jobs, and the new neighbourhood. The husband is friendly enough, but he really does not want to talk much about insurance. The wife, who runs the bank accounts and the household budget, wants her husband to have some money from an insurance policy on her if she dies, to be able to hire help with the children.

As they all sit around the kitchen table, the whole discussion is too much for the husband. He sits fiddling with one of the place-mats, sips on a beer and moans: "I hate insurance." They discuss the cancellation two years ago; Maindonald reminds them that the term coverage will have to be updated at a higher premium when it comes due in eight years. The husband is not really interested in leaving his wife too well off for some other man. "If I croak tomorrow," he says, "I don't want some guy coming in here and drinking my beer."

Maindonald concentrates his sales talk on the wife, pointing out what he sees as the pitfalls of term insurance: the need to renew it and the fact that it doesn't build any funds for retirement. "You've got to change your way of thinking," he says. "Term is like fire insurance, you get protection and nothing to show for the premiums. That's gone money." Maindonald tears a piece of lined paper from a pad and draws a large L that acts as the axis of a simple graph. The vertical axis is money, the horizontal axis, time. The couple watches intently as he draws a line that begins high on the vertical line, then drops as it crosses the graph until it hits the horizontal line, worth nothing in the end. That's term insurance. Then he draws a wavy line, representing savings going up and down during that same lifetime, money set aside for a purpose and then spent. Again, it ends at zero in the end. Finally, he draws a straight line that begins at zero where the two lines forming the L meet and continues upwards at a 45-degree angle forever. That, he says triumphantly, is an insurance plan with death benefit and cash value building for retirement.

Such an option would be Econolife. At her present age, twenty-seven, he points out, the wife can buy $15,000 whole life and $48,000 term, for a total of $63,000 coverage immediately. The monthly premium is $22. That's enough to cover the $60,000 mortgage if she dies. At age forty, she can stop paying the premium and continue having the $63,000 coverage, or she can continue paying, keep the coverage, and have a retirement fund that will be worth about twice what she invested.

The husband is beginning to show some interest, and he talks about changing his own policy. Maindonald, however, continues to focus on the wife until he is sure that he has sold her, overlooking the kibitzing that goes on as he fills out the wife's application. Her answer about her weight brings a guffaw from the husband. On marijuana, he interjects: "We grow it in the basement." As the questions continue, the husband is seized with a coughing fit. "Sign me up quickly," he says. Throughout, the wife pays no attention to her husband's shenanigans. After being in the house about forty minutes, Maindonald has completed the paperwork on the wife's policy and turns to the husband.

He knows that the current premium is $25 for the husband's $70,000 term policy. The wife has just bought a combination of whole life and term totalling $63,000 in death benefits for $22. Before arriving at the house, he had discussed converting the husband to Econolife, but thought it was "too early." He was, however, ready for anything: "I'll just go by the seat of my pants," he had said. Now with one half of the couple sold and the other showing interest, he senses another sale possibility.

Maindonald wants to discover what new level of monthly premium the husband might feel comfortable spending, so he begins by saying: "You earn what, $80 a day? I like to look at it this way: I haven't got $80, I've got $78. I'm going to put that $2 away for me. Can you afford to spend $1 a day? I guess if you could have put insurance on your house [for $1 a day] when you bought it, you would have."

Maindonald compares the value of the term insurance the man now has to what else is available. He points out that the rates will go higher when the policy comes up for renewal at the end of the ten-year term. He wants the husband to get into an insurance policy where the rates are fixed and there are savings building for retirement. Says Maindonald, "When I was young, I thought I'd have a pile of money when I was fifty-five. Well, now I'm that old and I don't have a pile of money. I've got other things, but I don't have a pile of money. I do have some money." From a life insurance policy, of course, and he's glad he had it.

He admits that the particular option he's pushing tonight, Econo-life, didn't exist when he sold the term two years earlier. But he also points out that he was against selling them term at the time. The husband agrees to buy. The evening has been a good one for Maindonald. The two policies will add about $34,200 in credits towards his merit corps totals. His commission for the evening's work (and a follow-up visit to place the policies) is calculated this way: in the first year, the wife pays $264 in premium; Maindonald receives half, or $132 in commission over the next twelve months. In the second year, the commission rate falls to 15 per cent, 10 per cent in the third year, so an additional $66 is paid by London Life to Maindonald during the following two years. On the husband's policy, the premium increases from $21 a month to $40 a month. His commission on that policy is measured on the $19 difference. His total commission, spread over three years, from the evening's sale: $369.

After the sale, he heads home to spend some time in his office in the back of the garage. He checks the paper for baby announcements, looking for names of young parents who may suddenly feel new responsibilities. He makes a list of other prospects he has heard about. If there is time, and there usually is, he makes a few phone calls, looking for appointments next week, discovering other doors. And it takes him a bit of time to wind down after he's been out selling. To have a good interview with a prospective client, he has to be up, be flexible, be ready for any question. After that, he can't just come home and go to bed. He might have a drink, but most likely he'll just watch television for a couple of hours to try to get himself calmed down enough for a night's sleep. And another round of kitchen tables tomorrow.

It is, all in all, a homely business. A lot of hours are spent around kitchen tables listening to people talk about their lives. He doesn't like living rooms very much. The chairs are too far apart. The kitchen is best. There, people are more comfortable and relaxed. The coffee things are handy. This is the domain of the woman of the house, and she very often makes the insurance decision. At the table, numbers can be shown, simple graphs sketched—and papers can easily be slid across the surface for a signature to close the deal.

For many of those folks in their kitchens, Ed Maindonald is more than just a salesman, he is someone they trust: a combination itinerant pedlar, social worker, town crier, and financial counsellor. "You get to know people real well. It gets so that people just can't buy from anyone else. There's a world of knowledge in how people live," he says, "what they live in, their values and their priorities. Some people don't care about tomorrow; some people have everything all laid out." He pauses for a moment and reflects on his own tomorrow and the doors he faces. "You never know whether you're going to get a sale or a fight," he says. "You never know what's on the other side of that door."

CHAPTER TWELVE

REACH FOR THE TOP
Royal Insurance Co.

J EAN ROBITAILLE was playing the particularly tough Crag Burn golf course in East Aurora, N.Y., near Buffalo, one day in 1984. The weather was terrible, fifty degrees and raining. Robitaille, who is president and chief executive officer of Royal Insurance Co. of Canada, was with his son, André, twenty-nine, a former Quebec junior golf champion, and two insurance broker friends, George Moore, of Moore-McLean Corporate Insurance Ltd. of Toronto, and Ken Mead, president of Guy Carpenter & Co. (Canada) Ltd., a reinsurance broker. The competition was as stiff as the winds that were playing havoc with the ball. Robitaille was doing well, one under par after four holes, but the wind caught his first shot from the fifth tee, and the ball fell short of the green and rolled back down towards the edge of an oily-looking pond.

The ball looked to be unplayable, yet teeing off again would cost him a penalty stroke. "Go for it," counselled André, urging his father to play the ball from where it lay. Robitaille took off his shoes and socks, rolled up his pants, and marched towards the ball, his iron in hand. But the closer he got, the muckier the ground became. As he planted his feet near the ball to prepare for his swing, he began to sink. The ooze was engulfing his feet so quickly that he couldn't reposition himself, yet he wasn't even facing the hole forty feet away, he was aimed to the right. To compound the problem, he was behind a six-foot embankment and couldn't see the green. There was only one hope: swing anyway. Robitaille choked down on the club, gripping it farther down the shaft than normal, and swung at the ball as the muck crept up around his ankles. The ball took off in a perfect arc and landed on the green. He two-putted, salvaging a one-over-par four on the hole, scraped off the mud, and went on to shoot a seventy-eight on the day—an excellent six-over-par round. Says André, "He doesn't quit, he never settles for second."

Since 1983, however, Robitaille has had to settle for second place among the just over 300 property and casualty insurance companies in Canada. Judged by premium income, The Co-operators Group of Guelph, Ont., is first. In 1984 The Co-operators had $441 million in premium income from auto, home, and commercial liability policies, compared with $397 million for the Royal. The competition among all the companies has caused price wars, particularly on personal auto insurance rates, where premium increases have barely kept pace with inflation for the past two years. "There has been a fight for market share," says Robitaille, fifty-eight, "so there have been depressed rates." In 1982, when Royal tried to increase some rates, the independent agents who sell policies to consumers simply moved their clients away from the Royal to other companies. It's an industry dilemma: keep rates low and lose money, or raise rates, lose clients, and lose money. Notes Teunis Haalboom, chief executive officer of The Co-operators, "One of the problems of being big is that you can lose a lot of your business if you move [rates] and others don't. But you can lose a lot of money if you don't move." The Royal moved once and lost; The Co-operators won't go out on the same limb.

The whole property and casualty industry has been losing money on its policies. In 1984, underwriting losses amounted to $917 million. Only by earning $1.3 billion on investments have firms made any profit at all. The battle between the two companies for the hearts and pocket-books of consumers means that Royal regularly reviews its marketing methods, looking for ways to improve. Royal deals through brokers who earn commissions on policies they sell; The Co-operators has direct sales, usually done over the counter by salaried staff. About 14 per cent of all general insurance sales in Canada are done direct (through The Co-operators, Allstate, State Farm, and others). Direct sales are cheaper and may be a route that Royal will follow in the future. "The ideal company will be dealing direct in urban areas," says Robitaille. "But outside? No. What do I know about Timmins? But The Co-operators goes to Timmins and hires someone who knows Timmins." Achieving the ideal is difficult, however. "Every year we ask ourselves: should we go direct?

But we can't find a way of doing that without affecting our current clientele, the individual agents."

Yet for all his desire to battle at the top and be number one, Robitaille knows the risks in an industry where there has been no underwriting profit for seven years. Once before, during the 1970s, the Royal stretched to become an out-of-reach number one by setting out to double its market share to 10 per cent. The strategy succeeded, but at great cost. Expenses rose, and when the market turned sour, Royal was left paying out more in claims than it took in in premiums. Since 1979, when Royal had 3,720 employees, Robitaille has had the singularly unenjoyable task of chopping staff, cutting costs, and reducing expenses. By the end of 1983, staff had fallen to 2,333, with 540 people disappearing—a 19-per-cent drop—that year alone. At the end of 1983, all remaining staff were paid a bonus equivalent to one week's salary, "in recognition," in the euphemistic words of the annual report, "of the extraordinary effort required by staff across Canada to implement this major reorganization in a relatively short period of time." The bonus cost Royal close to $1 million. In 1984 a further 12 per cent of staff were cut and employment was down to 2,058, a level fully 40 per cent below 1979 numbers.

The cuts have substantially altered the Royal's corporate culture. Says Royal executive vice-president Roy Elms, "During the growth period, people got used to the idea of a promotion every six months. Now we're grappling with the situation of getting people to reduce their career expectations. Instead of a promotion every six months, people have to get used to promotions every two, three, or four years. It's easy to turn people on when you're booming. Now you have to persuade people that despite the down-turn there are still solid prospects. We've gone through most of the trauma of involuntary termination. We think that we can likely manage any remaining downsizing through attrition.

"Prior to this period," says Elms, "Royal was perceived as a benevolent family. No one got fired. It was probably overdone. Now, if you have poor performance, you tackle it head-on. That's healthy for everybody. The culture has changed. Involuntary leave-taking doesn't come as much of a shock any more. Commercial realities, nationally and internationally, dictate that you can only have people who are working hard." To buttress morale and try to respond to staff nervousness, quality circles are being established in

Royal offices. Volunteer groups of six to eight people meet, usually once a week (the discussion leader is selected by management), to talk about topics of mutual concern. Four times a year, the group meets with its supervisor and management for similar, informal conversations. When the plan is fully implemented, 10 per cent of all staff will be involved. "One has to be patient with these sorts of things," says Elms, "but there is a positive involvement that helps with morale, which undoubtedly fell during the downsizing. It's almost impossible for any organization to be on a performance high. Quite a number of the firms featured in *In Search of Excellence* have fallen flat on their fanny. I take great comfort from that."

Robitaille has ridden the fall in staff all the way down and watched the firm change beneath him. "There's not the same degree of comfort that was always there." The firings and career disruptions don't bother him. "I've been an SOB from way back," says Robitaille, who joined in 1951 as a trainee. "After I'd been with the company two years, I fired a dodo and had the entire building mad. I was responsible for the first early retirement in the company—an assistant branch manager in 1968. A lot of people criticized keeping anyone around in a paternalistic sense and putting them on a shelf and making alcoholics out of them. People don't like that. I used to hear that all the time when I was a junior. I don't think that has changed. The first few times [I fired someone] I lost sleep over it, but I soon realized that most people agreed that was the right thing to do. I used to look around and say if someone had been kicked out, he might have made something of himself."

The tough talk does not, however, mean that he is totally hard of heart. When he worked for Royal in Quebec City he headed a fund-raising campaign for the Quebec Retarded Children's Association. He was not a distant bagman. He visited the retarded children's centre so often that some called him "Dad" and one asked him to be godfather at a first communion. "That opened my eyes to the miseries of some people, to their needs and doing something for them that's understood." He and his wife, Lucie, have four children ranging in age from thirty-one to twenty-five. All live in Toronto and every Sunday they can, they show up at their parents' with spouses and friends in tow for dinner prepared by Jean. He buys everything Saturday at the market and spends four hours or more cooking dinner the following day. Robitaille is such a softie that he even admits to crying at the movies and the opera. The tough guy at the office is more of a chocolate cream soldier in real life.

Robitaille is five-foot-seven and built like a fire plug. Fluently bilingual, he has an easy, if wheezy, laugh and a bag of quips for every conversation. He is the first native Canadian to be named president and chief executive officer of the Royal, a subsidiary of a British company. Notes his daughter, Louise, "It's not often a French Canadian makes it as far as he has." He earns about $175,000 a year. For a time, his perks included a chauffeur, but Robitaille found that the driver just got in the way. After the children were grown and gone from home, he and his wife moved to a downtown townhouse. Some mornings he likes to walk the fifteen minutes to work. The driver would follow in the Cadillac in case it rained. Robitaille decided he'd rather drive himself and walk when he chose. The Cadillac and the driver were replaced by a company-supplied BMW and then a Jaguar Sovereign.

Robitaille was born and raised in Mile End, the polyglot part of Montreal popularized in Mordecai Richler's books. The racial epithets were hurled about regularly, he recalls: "There was a lot of 'kikes' and 'micks' and 'pepsis.'" He grew up as a street fighter, mostly against the Irish, but the tough side was balanced by a sensitive father who owned a few small houses that he rented out during the Depression. "He used to come home with empty pockets, weeping at the misery he'd seen." When he was nine, his parents separated; at fifteen he finished high school and went to work as an office boy at a woollen mill, then toiled in a patent attorney's office. At nineteen, he began attending evening classes at Sir George Williams University; he obtained his bachelor of arts degree after attending classes two nights a week for six years.

At twenty-three, he joined Equifax Services Ltd., investigating insurance applicants' claims and benefits. "That's shitty work," Robitaille says, "snooping into people's lives." He also found claimants weren't always truthful, particularly on disability claims. "You find that there's a lot of larceny in people." At Equifax, Robitaille had his first contact with the general insurance business. Life insurance sales never had any appeal. "It just seemed like a con game." After two years at Equifax, he joined Royal in Montreal in 1951 as a trainee. Among his first tasks was to mark city maps with the locations of Royal's commercial risks in order to check the company's total potential loss if fire swept a whole block.

Within four years, he was named a branch manager and assigned to open an office for Royal in Quebec City. He was the first Royal management trainee to be promoted directly from the program into management. In the nineteen years he was in Quebec City, he built the branch into the second-largest of twelve in the country. Staff reached 200 and annual premium levels were $30 million, almost as much as at the long-established Montreal office. In 1974, he was named vice-president for marketing and development at Toronto head office. His meteoric rise continued; in 1976 he was named a senior vice-president and in May 1978, executive vice-president. The next year he was made president and chief executive officer when Alan Horsford, president since 1974, was named general manager of the Royal Group at head office in London, England. (In 1983 Horsford was named deputy chief general manager and in 1985 he was promoted to the top role, chief general manager, thus becoming Robitaille's boss again.)

Royal Group operates in Britain, Canada, the U.S., the Netherlands, and Australia and writes about $3.9 billion a year in premiums (exclusive of life), about 10 per cent of that in Canada. The U.K. insurance industry has been a world leader for centuries. British insurers are responsible for writing 11 per cent of the world's insurance, although Britain's share of the world's gross national product is only 4 per cent. In Canada, Royal's roots go back to 1833, when it operated as the British America Assurance Co. in York, later Toronto. Royal's other international arms began writing business in South America in 1846, Australia in 1848, and the U.S. in 1851. Today, Royal operates in more than eighty countries through ninety-five subsidiary companies and twenty associated companies and has 21,000 staff in 500 offices. The company writes almost all classes of general insurance in both commercial and personal lines, including property, auto, liability, marine, aviation, and engineering. Forty-two per cent of the world-wide business is done in the U.S., 28 per cent in Britain, and 10 per cent in Canada. In Canada, Royal's business is fairly evenly split between personal and commercial, with slightly more than half of the total in Ontario.

Alan Horsford, who now runs Royal world-wide, put both Royal and the industry on the map in the 1970s by riding the populist consumer awareness wave. When Horsford arrived from Britain to take over Canadian operations in 1974, "he burst on the scene like a bombshell," says one Royal executive. "He was outspoken and dynamic, and he identified with the consumer." In 1976, Royal began an ombudsman program called Royal-Aide to help clients with personal lines policies when there was a dispute with the company. The policyholder could appoint an "aide" of his choice to adjudicate. The only limitation Royal insisted upon was that the arbitrator could not already be involved in the loss adjustment. Royal listed some possible arbitration candidates, but did not limit the choice to the following: contractor, home furnishings merchant, repair garage representative, jeweller, furrier, doctor, lawyer, mayor, reeve, town clerk, bank manager. The report had to be filed within fifteen days of the conclusion of the arbitration, and it was binding on the policyholder and the company. In an industry where the company had always maintained the last word in settlements, the move was revolutionary.

In 1977 Royal took another step towards modernization when it led the industry into plain-speaking policies. Homeshield, the householder's insurance policy, had its previous legalese replaced with simpler wording. Using a test called the Flesch Scale of Readability, the Royal set out to make its forms as easy to understand as *Reader's Digest*. "Liability" became "legal responsibility." "We" and "you" replaced "insurer" and "insuree." In 1979, Autoshield policies were defogged as well, but to this day, no provincial superintendent has given them the requisite approval. In announcing the first plain-language policy, Horsford pointed out that he thought the industry had been doing a good job, but admitted that not all customers agreed. "We have two problems that face us," he said. "First, we have to respond to the increasing attention that is called for by the movement we all call consumerism. But secondly, because of the public's attitude towards our business, we have to go that extra step compared with other businesses."

For Horsford, that extra step included giving the whole industry a higher public profile. He wanted the policyholder to know the insuring company, not just the independent agent. Says William Campbell, who joined Royal in 1975 as director of corporate planning, "He got insurance established outside itself as an industry." In the early 1970s, as society became more mobile and more demanding of companies, many insurance companies had responded badly. Service was poor, public relations was non-existent, and the heat for more government involvement was coming from the political left, particularly from New Democratic Party proposals in various provinces for government-run auto insurance. Horsford took it upon himself to respond on behalf of the industry. "Had he not been a president, he would have made a socialist MP in Britain," says Campbell, himself born in Scotland. "He was a free-enterpriser, but a social activist."

Horsford was also unafraid to state controversial views. During his presidency, the government of Ontario authorized a study of the insurance industry, including property and casualty. The author, Douglas Carruthers, suggested some revisions without consulting the industry itself. Rather than grumble behind closed doors, Horsford noised his views in speeches, calling the suggestions "a matter of surprise and concern to executives in the property and casualty industry... As far as we are aware, Mr. Carruthers had no contact whatsoever either with our trade association, the Insurance Bureau of Canada, or with any of the major companies in the market in the course of his research." Horsford continued to berate the regulators: "There may well be an adequate explanation for this approach but I must confess that I find it extremely difficult to fathom."

Just as government had paid little heed, neither did the public recognize the efforts of the property and casualty business, complained Horsford. "I can think of no other business which is so regularly accused of not wanting to do the job for which it was created. In our case, I am afraid, we were hung with this albatross a long time ago, and like the ancient mariner, find it hard to get rid of. We pay out $100,000 in automobile losses every hour of every day of every week throughout the year. I think that figure speaks for itself."

The outspoken themes continued right to Horsford's final speech as president in 1979. "It is absolutely vital that the public comes to see the insurance companies not as remote bureaucratic and overpowering institutions, but as open and approachable bodies, staffed by good and conscientious people," he said. "We must press on with our efforts to demystify the business by providing clear and easy-to-read contracts, straightforward, readily understood pricing structures, and quick, efficient, and sympathetic service when losses occur. The lack of public acceptance of what the companies do is an industry weakness."

Robitaille argues that the industry has advanced little in the years since Horsford made those comments. "Nobody knows anything about this business in this country. Nobody knows bugger-all. People think we're on the gravy train and there are no problems. There's an awful lot of property and casualty insurance chief execu-

tive officers who are asleep at the switch and they love it that way."
When the federal advisory committee on financial services was
appointed in 1984, property and casualty insurance was at first
unrepresented. The industry complained and Robitaille was a
belated addition to the committee. Robitaille is not convinced that
the group was of any value. "It was a cacophony in there. [Deputy
minister of finance] Mickey Cohen said he found it helpful. I don't
know; if I was one of them, I would find it bewildering."

One of the main, ongoing vehicles for reaching the public and the
politicians is the Insurance Bureau of Canada (IBC). The IBC is the
major organization of property and casualty insurance companies
doing business in Canada. Statistics are gathered, industry committees discuss topics of mutual interest, and there are public education
programs. The IBC, claims its full-time president Jack Lyndon, is
not a lobby group. "Unlike our U.S. counterparts, we have no
political clout." Among his other talents, Lyndon is a pianist of note.
During his time as a deputy minister with the Alberta government,
he had a piano in his office. He claims he had nowhere else to store
the piano at the time; still, the sounds of music after hours gave him
an unusual profile among his fellow civil servants. In addition to
Lyndon, the IBC has a staff of 135. Every two years a different chief
executive officer from the industry acts as chairman and chief
spokesman for the IBC and the 100 members. Chairman for 1984–
86 is Jean Robitaille. If the policy planning committee meeting he
chaired in February 1985 is any indication, the IBC and the industry
have a distance to go yet to capture the minds, let alone the hearts, of
either the politicians or the public.

The meeting starts at noon and includes Robitaille, Lyndon, Barry
Wilson, general manager and chief agent for St. Paul Property &
Liability Insurance Co., and IBC staff members John Cranford,
Nigel Dunn, Alex Kennedy, and Bob Monte. As the group gathers
around a boardroom table in the IBC offices, they munch on
sandwiches and trade gossip about the recent cabinet shuffle in
Ontario under Premier Frank Miller. "I see you got your wish,"
chortles Robitaille. "Gordon Walker as minister [in charge of insur-
ance]." (Walker, a right-wing Conservative, is a noted hands-off
legislator, favouring self-regulation rather than government intervention.) "That fellow who used to be Robert Elgie's parliamentary

secretary is solicitor-general," adds Kennedy. "I'm not much impressed." There is a discussion of possible freedom-of-information legislation and how it might apply to insurance companies. Opening up files is not a welcome thought for insurance companies. Policyholders give information expecting it to be kept confidential by the company. Says Lyndon, "The old claim files are a problem."

Nigel Dunn, manager of public affairs, reports on media coverage of the release of an IBC position paper on impaired driving. "A Canadian Press story got wide coverage," he says, "but only in one Toronto paper. The best television coverage was on [Hamilton's] Channel 11." The IBC has agreed that police should have the right to impound a vehicle after a driver has been convicted of drunk driving and is found driving while his licence is under suspension. The IBC, however, insists that the driver have an appeal process. "We've got 40,000 to 50,000 people driving around Ontario, or even Metro [Toronto], if you accept some figures, on suspended licences," laments Dunn. The system is not working after a driver is convicted, nor do spot checks catch anywhere near all the drinking drivers. "The odds are that you can make 2,000 drunk-driving trips without getting stopped in a spot check." The group discusses how the industry's concerns can be brought to the attention of government. Dunn points out that people don't want to hear about going through the windshield in an accident if they don't wear seat-belts. "The public says ho-hum. That's why our appeal on drunk driving is to the guy's friends."

If the public can be roused against drunk driving, argues the IBC, perhaps the politicians will put in stiffer laws, thus reducing accidents and insurance claims. "What's Gordon Walker's background? He's a lawyer?" asks Robitaille. "He's an ultra-right young Turk," says Lyndon. "He's seen in the bureaucracy as someone more interested in..." "Image?" Robitaille suggests. "Yeah," replies Lyndon, "he's a Genghis Khan." Someone points out now that Walker has returned to the post of minister of consumer and commercial relations, and that when he had served there under Premier William Davis the IBC never got to see him. (Walker was defeated in the May 1985 election.) "Can we get to him more easily through Elgie?" asks Robitaille. "No, that wouldn't work, the left–right thing," says Lyndon, referring to the fact that Elgie and Walker represent different wings of the party. A more likely connection might be through London, where Walker's riding is located. "We might be able to use the London South connection through Ernie Jackson at Reed Stenhouse." (Jackson, senior vice-president of the insurance brokers, was a long-time confidant of Ontario premier John Robarts.)

Getting the ear of politicians is a problem for this group. As executives in a regulated industry, they want the legislators at least to understand their views, even if they don't follow the industry's recommendations. Without such access, the IBC would just be talking to itself and to other members of the converted in the industry. "As least with Bob [Elgie], we could get to see him," says Robitaille. Lyndon recalls that when Walker was minister previously, he did public battle with Henry Knowles, head of the Ontario Securities Commission. "[Walker] has a way of leading with both feet," says Lyndon. "If he gets into financial services issues, he might get his ass in a wringer. We'll just have to work harder." Adds Monte, "He seems to make his mind up quickly without taking much advice."

As with all industry associations, one of IBC's problems is the difficulty of achieving consensus on issues so that a united view can be presented. For example, one of the unresolved debates in the industry is how to set up an arbitration system that would allow disputes to be reconciled more efficiently and cheaply outside the courts. Many in the industry like the idea of such a system but don't want to pay for it. "Raising money for that is like raising money for Stalin," says Robitaille. "The antipathy is in the industry," notes Monte. "Every time it's raised by [president of the Mercantile and General Reinsurance Co. of Canada] Don Batten the temperature in the room drops by ten degrees. Why is that?" "I don't know," replies Robitaille, "why don't you ask the claims guys?"

After forty-five minutes of such general discussions, the group proceeds to the main business of this meeting, the ranking of various industry-related public issues in order of their importance. By such rankings, they argue, the IBC will know how to divide its time among the issues in the future. Robitaille removes his suit coat and stokes a pipe. A chart, begun at an earlier meeting, is produced and hung on an easel. On the paper is a large square divided into nine sections. The three squares from left to right are called A, B, and C. They show the time period. The choices are immediate, near, and monitoring. From top to bottom, the three boxes are numbered 1, 2, and 3 to show levels of importance. Thus an important and current topic, such as Ontario auto insurance rates, is given top priority, 1A. Studies of demographics are less urgent and need only to be monitored, so they are put into the box in the lower right-hand corner, marked 3C.

Robitaille begins by asking for a definition of how the issues are ranked. "When do you reach a crisis state?" Replies Lyndon, "The closer you get to an election." With that loose criterion, they spend the next thirty minutes putting issues into various boxes. Crime gets a high ranking. "We're into custom theft," notes Lyndon. "That's right," says Dunn. "Two-door or four-door Mercedes?" The environment is ranked too low for Robitaille's liking. "My vote would be to move up environment. It's going to come and get us." Dunn, using a felt-tip pen, responds to the consensus on each issue by entering it in the agreed-upon box. As the boxes begin to fill up, Robitaille finally says, "You go down the list here and you wonder if maybe there's just too many issues." Says Barry Wilson, "We have to realize that because we put an issue in a certain box, the world may not agree." Concludes John Cranford, "But we've done something."

The final topic to be rated is propane-fuelled vehicles. Some apartment and office buildings are not allowing propane vehicles to park inside. Robitaille suggests it be ranked 2B; others say 3B. There is a brief impasse until Robitaille says to Wilson, "Break the log-jam, Barry." He picks 3B. Laughs Robitaille: "The chairman loses another." Wilson inquires, "Are you asking that question on your applications?" "I ask people about their dreams," quips Robitaille, then adds, "I don't know." Kennedy recalls how the propane regulations were put in place, citing a particular bureaucrat. "He drove everyone crazy. You know how it works on these [legislative] committees, half the members are writing letters to their constituents, and the other half are doing the crossword from the *Globe*. So here was [name deleted] lecturing the members on not listening. There was dead silence, followed by calls for his removal." "And you silently applauded," interjects Robitaille. "I certainly did," continues Kennedy. "He was sent on a sabbatical and is still on it."

The meeting ends with a discussion of a possible threat that haunts insurers whenever they gather: a megadisaster that will wipe out all the companies. During Samuel de Champlain's time, an earthquake struck the island of Montreal. They wonder what would happen if an earthquake of similar intensity hit the same area today. The main damage would not be from buildings collapsing because, in recent decades, office towers have been built on bedrock. The most expensive damage would come from the fires after fire walls shifted and water mains ruptured, allowing flames to spread easily. The U.S. property and casualty industry has estimated that it would lose US$39.5 billion if the 1906 San Francisco earthquake were duplicated. "Let's get some more data," says Robitaille.

There are, after all, only two responses possible in bureaucracy. The first is to set up a committee. The second is to study something further. Since this problem is already before a committee, it can only be put onto the "more study" shelf. That's where it will likely still be sitting when an earthquake knocks it off.

A corporate earthquake struck Royal in the 1970s when the firm set out to increase its market share, and it has been struggling ever since. Around 1974, with 5 per cent of the market in Canada, the Royal decided to grow quickly. If first place followed, so be it, went the thinking. In some northern Canadian communities, for example, property and casualty insurance was difficult to obtain. Horsford ordered Royal to step in where others would not. "It was a time when the superintendent's office phoned every day and said, 'God, we've got a group of people in Timmins or Cold Lake who can't get insurance.' We'd take them on," says Robitaille.

In addition to this stated "public service" element and a desire to take a commanding lead in the market, there was also a fear that more government-run programs would be created if the private sector did not show itself capable of fulfilling all the public's needs. Government-run auto insurance businesses were in place in British Columbia, Saskatchewan, and Manitoba; the industry wanted to halt further growth. At the same time, Royal was not going to give the product away. Most commercial policies were then in place for three years; premiums were set for the life of the policy. As inflation grew in the late 1970s, three-year pricing meant that companies were losing money during the last part of the policy period. The industry, with Horsford in the lead, did away with such policies and put one-year terms in place so that premiums could be adjusted regularly.

From 1974 to 1975, for example, Royal's growth was 54 per cent. In the next year, growth was a further 41 percent. As market share rose, employment ballooned from 2,746 in 1975 to 3,720 in 1979. A new $14-million head office was opened in 1980 in Toronto to house the growth. "Horsford managed at a time when operations were carried out on a socially responsible basis," says Robitaille. "We thought that we could adopt a commanding position in an undisciplined market. Those were good times. Assets grew rapidly; we went from 5 to 10 per cent [market share] in two years."

The game ended in 1981, when the industry had its worst year ever. "We had a terrible year, too, and we decided that playing to be number one didn't do you any good. We decided the hell with that game. The good [company] performers are pickers and choosers, the people who play particular markets, not like us, who try to serve everybody. They pick and choose products, and they pick and choose towns and cities where they will take business." Royal also had a problem with inexperienced staff. As business had expanded, Royal had hired hundreds with insufficient training. "A lot of green people were handling a complex product as it came in and as claims developed," says Robitaille. "The quality of our book of business changed dramatically."

Robitaille took over as president and chief executive officer in 1979, just as all the bad business decisions were about to meet the bad times. Horsford had promised he would appoint a Canadian replacement. Robitaille was Canadian-born; his competitor, Roy Elms, became a Canadian citizen in 1979 but was born in the U.K. Elms had joined Royal in England fresh out of grammar school. He was transferred to Canada in 1959, named assistant branch manager in Winnipeg in 1968; he became underwriting manager for Canada in 1971, then senior vice-president in 1974 and executive vice-president in 1978. Robitaille got the nod for the top job, but not without a fight. Horsford took his time to pick his successor. "I was in a horse race with Elms for two or three years," says Robitaille. "[Horsford] can be emphatic about what he says, but he can be hesitant about what he does."

In 1979 Bill Campbell, executive vice-president under Robitaille, urged him to cut staff, but Robitaille, Campbell claims, did not even respond to the suggestions. "He just wanted to bring in consultants." After an eight-month study in 1981 by Booz, Allen, Hamilton, an international firm of management consultants, reorganization began, although Robitaille claims that the consultants didn't offer ideas, just data and analysis.

Royal had been a centrally run company, so Robitaille decided to decentralize and put the decisions into the field, where information was more readily available. In 1982 he split the firm into three autonomous divisions: personal, commercial, and special lines. He created seven commercial branches, five others that handled personal lines of insurance, and two special branches for accounts in fields such as petrochemicals, resources, and engineering industries. "There was a lot of trauma," recalls Robitaille. "Some wouldn't take transfers. Morale was very bad." The concern was not just with Royal employees. Independent agents who dealt with Royal were cut back by 20 per cent, to 2,200. Those remaining were unhappy to see a local office closing and feared service would suffer. "There was a lot of anxiety," Robitaille admits. It was at about that time that someone in the industry outside Royal met Horsford and said of Robitaille: "You left him such a mess." "Yes," replied Horsford, "but he's cleaning up better than I could."

Part of the clean-up included price increases of 10 to 15 per cent in 1982, in an attempt to regain profitability. Many agents were feeling less loyal to Royal then they had in the past, and they simply took the business of clients they had insured with Royal to any one of the dozen other companies with which they dealt. "We provided opportunity for competition by putting in price increases," says Elms. "Those people who had lost market share began coming after us." Business fell in 1982 by 19.8 per cent. By 1983 The Co-operators had replaced the Royal as number one in premium volume. The Royal, with 5 per cent of the market, was number two. The explanation was simple. "They've overtaken us," says senior vice-president Roy Elms, "because our market share has slipped back. We grew very fast. We weren't masters of our own fortune. Politically, we felt it was the right thing to do. There was a vacuum. We were concerned governments might fill it, so we grew very fast."

"The cultural change we're trying to achieve is to move from a centralized management philosophy, with the attendant layers of people looking over each other's shoulders, to a decentralized structure without the layers," says Robitaille. "You're trying to tell the guy at the top he doesn't have a lot of people to double-check what he's doing. At the bottom, people can't turn to someone to help. That's tough at both ends. Auditing is easier. Management reports can be produced at will now without having to fly across the country and spend two days comforting Joe." The costs of downsizing were huge. In 1983–84, total costs were $12.3 million for severance pay, excess space, and moving costs. In 1985, Royal will spend close to a further $2 million on space it leased but no longer needs. The mood is still wary about price hikes, even if increases would help profitability. As he set 1985 pricing, Elms was not interested in getting too far in front: "We tried to send the signals once before and it cost us dearly. There is a market leader as long as there are followers. We tried to be a leader before and we were hung out to dry."

As Robitaille chopped staff, executives were not immune. Some were given early retirement, others fired as the number in the executive suite was reduced from twenty-one to thirteen. For all his self-described toughness, Robitaille himself suffered a despondent period when he was forcing fellow executives to leave. He even went so far as to calculate what kind of termination package he might be able to negotiate for himself. The mood and the moment passed, however, and he flung himself back into the job.

One of those fired was Bill Campbell. Robitaille simply froze him out of discussions and decisions for six weeks in the summer of 1982. At the end of August, Robitaille fired Campbell from his $90,000-a-year job. He received eighteen months' severance pay. "I don't think Robitaille is a president," says Campbell, now an independent insurance broker in Agincourt, in Toronto's east end. "That's why we had a parting of the ways." Campbell's office was next to Robitaille's. "I went three weeks without seeing him. He was fishing and playing golf. My big conundrum is that Royal has such a classy board of directors—but it never asks questions." Campbell further claims that Royal is essentially run from the U.K. Senior executives from Britain visit eight or nine times a year. "You're never more than five weeks away from a visit. The board is a puppet board."

Robitaille disagrees. "It's a close relationship and a hands-off relationship at the same time." Yet there are those constant meetings. In addition to visits by British executives to Canada, Robitaille travels to London four times a year to report to his parent company board of directors. A written report is sent ahead and he gives a brief oral explanation, then answers questions, for anywhere from fifteen minutes to an hour. He says that he and Horsford often have to work out their differences prior to meetings so they don't do battle during the sessions. "We disagree a lot," says Robitaille. "It's a difficult situation. I never have to change what I plan—but agreement isn't always whole-hearted. I'm not given orders. We might discuss things and not agree—and then it's up to me. The guys from the

U.K. hardly ever say bugger-all at the board. Horsford is a lot quieter now than when he was president. He'll contribute titbits, but he doesn't say as much as some of the others at the board."

Now that staff cuts are accomplished, Royal is moving slowly to increase its market while automating the independent agents. A 1983 survey showed that 27 per cent owned or rented an in-house computer system, 29 per cent subscribed to a computer service bureau, and 44 per cent maintained a manual system. After surveying a number of hardware and software systems, Royal joined with IBM Canada Ltd. in 1984 to market a system known as the Agency Manager, consisting of an IBM XT personal computer and printer plus a package of advanced software. Research on the hardware and software over three years cost $250,000. The XT with software costs $13,000 and can handle up to 10,000 customers in an office with approximately $2.5 million in premiums. A version with more storage, the AT, costs $20,000 and handles 25,000 clients. The software alone costs $5,000 to $6,000 for an agent who already has a computer. The package includes software that does accounting, general ledger, customer file update and retrieval, word processing and mass mailing, management reports, and more than 100 marketing and sales aids. The computer system will even spit out regular lists of birthdays so the agents can mail cards to their clients.

At first, Royal used the system as a business builder. The company retains ownership of the equipment and leases the system to an agent free—if the agent produces $100,000 in new business for Royal over two years. At the end of the two years, the agent can buy the system for $500. In the first eight months the system was available, beginning in 1984, 430 agents, or 25 per cent of the total, signed on. Now, with the market among its own agents saturated, Royal is selling the system to any agent who is interested.

While Robitaille has undone some of the problems that Horsford caused while he increased market share, he has followed his mentor's advice and taken the industry's views public. He gives at least half a dozen speeches a year. Among his favourite themes is the view that neither government nor government-appointed bodies can really do much for long-term economic growth. "We have got to develop more aggressive and imaginative economic strategies in our pursuit of progress," he says. "And while we're talking about imaginative economic strategies, I'm afraid that I don't include the Macdonald royal commission as one of them. Personally, I get a picture of Mr.

Macdonald and his men wandering hopefully across Canada with tape recorders and notepads as if somehow, somewhere, they will uncover a golden nugget of knowledge that is going to solve the country's economic problems.

"I stopped believing in miracles a long time ago—especially miracles promised by politicians. Even if we can believe that some useful ideas can be gleaned during this long, slow exercise, putting any of the Macdonald commission policies into practice will take years. I don't think we can wait that long. I don't feel we should be expected to wait that long. In fact, I'm not sure a lot of us will *live* that long!"

Another favourite topic is the increase in crime and the number of highway deaths. They are social problems that cost the Royal and the rest of the industry money. He notes that 6,000 people die in highway accidents across Canada annually. "The cost of car accidents in terms of medical bills, car repairs, and loss of productivity is estimated to be 2 per cent of our total national gross product—that's $2.5 billion every year—and the cost is still going up. We in Canada have become complacent about crime. We are complacent about the high cost of arson, and we are just as complacent about the true effectiveness of our judicial system." He says that one-third of all suspicious fires in Canada are deliberately set—and 150 people die annually because of arson. Convictions are obtained in only one of every 200 known cases of arson. He is so straight-talking that he even recommends that some people don't need one of the products Royal sells—specifically, collision insurance. "We don't insure our own cars against collision," he says. "A corporation or a rich individual doesn't need collision insurance. It's cheaper to replace a totally wrecked car every once in a while than to pay annual premiums."

For all Robitaille's effort and the cost-cutting steps he has taken, bottom-line performance remains poor. One problem area for the Royal is expenses. In 1983, expenses per dollar of premium were 42 per cent. They fell to 40 per cent in 1984, but remained much higher than the industry figure of 34 per cent. The operating ratio—the percentage measurement that compares premiums taken in with claims paid—also remains a problem. For a company to make money in this area, claims need to be lower than premiums. Along with most others in the industry, however, Royal has been losing money in this area. In 1982, the operating ratio was 109.2 per cent (meaning that for every $100 of written premium earned, $109.20 was paid out in claims and expenses.) The operating loss was $40.6 million. In 1983, the operating ratio was 110.5; actual losses were $40.3 million. In 1984, the operating ratio worsened to 123.5; actual losses were $93.2 million.

Meanwhile, Royal struggles along, with investment income barely offsetting the underwriting losses. The market value of the investment portfolio in 1984 was $768.6 million. Underwriting losses of $40.3 million in 1983 were offset by investment income of $53.7 million for a $13.4-million profit. In 1984 the $93.2-million underwriting loss and $51.9-million investment income meant a loss of $41.3 million.

Robitaille has little time left to complete a successful turnaround. He retires in 1989 at sixty-two. In 1985, Robitaille hopes to increase Royal's share of the market from 5.1 per cent to 5.5 per cent. Every day Robitaille tells himself and others: "If '85 isn't any better than '84, the board might want to see some changes made."

Robitaille continues to exhort his fellow CEOs to speak out and become involved in making consumers respect the industry, perhaps with the fond hope that success outside the firm will outweigh any failures inside. "There's an opportunity to kick ass, but whether ass moves or not is another thing," he says. "I can't be overly optimistic. I hope I can convince some of them to get out of our little world and participate in the economic and political life of this country. I suspect a lot of them don't do any operational or strategic planning. They don't do enough what-ifs."

He will never again go for number one at any cost—at least not that he will admit. He did, however, once advise his daughter, Louise, how to be discreet about goals. "The best thing if you decide to quit smoking or go on a diet is never to tell anyone," he said. "Then, if you go back, no one will ever know. It's better just to keep it to yourself." Public risk-taking is only acceptable on the golf course.

CHAPTER THIRTEEN

THE ABATTOIR

Crown Life Insurance Co.

I N THE classic war movie *Twelve O'Clock High*, the 918th Bomb Group based in England is manned by a hapless bunch. Their commander treats his flyers like brothers, identifying with them on their dangerous daylight missions over occupied Europe and Germany. He is, however, no leader. Bombing runs are sloppy, the crews are indifferent and lack cohesion.

Enter Gregory Peck as General Frank Savage, sent in to replace Keith Davenport, played by Gary Merrill. In order to whip the depressed group into shape, Peck uses merciless discipline to rebuild their fighting spirit. As he succeeds, he becomes torn between his growing friendship with the men and the trauma of sending them to face death. Finally, Peck breaks down under the same pressures that overcame his predecessor. He cannot board the B-17 bomber to lead a crucial mission and has to be helped from the field.

As he awaits the return of the mission, Peck sits comatose. His friends gather and try to explain his breakdown. They regard the immobilized Peck and exchange this dialogue:

Davenport: It's screwy. I would never think it could happen to him.

Stovall: I did. I watched him sweep his feelings under the carpet long enough. It had to spill out some day.

Davenport: But I never saw him more full of fight than at briefing.

Doctor: Did you ever see a light bulb burn out? How bright the filament is just before it burns out. I think they call it maximum effort!

The 1950 film, with its message of how tough it is at the top when you're turning a group of people around, is shown every June at

Bishop's University in Lennoxville, Que. The audience is made up of select members of the management of Crown Life Insurance Co. and its affiliated companies attending an intensive four-week course called the General Management Development Program. The course was ordered by none other than Crown's real-life Gregory Peck, Robert Bandeen. It was he who was brought in from the outside in June 1982 to do the turnaround as chairman, president, and chief executive officer of Crown Life Insurance Co.

Prior to Bandeen's arrival, Crown, the eighth-largest life insurance company in Canada (measured by assets), had been chugging along well enough. The Burns family of Ontario and the Jodreys of Nova Scotia, the two families who had controlling interest, wanted to expand out of insurance into other financial services. No one, they decided, was on hand to take the company into tomorrow, so they imported Bandeen. Upon his arrival, he declared war through wholesale firings, early retirements, and a tough-guy top-down direction. The course at Bishop's is just one of the sweeping management changes Bandeen ordered as he fixed his attention on creating a financial services empire. Those picked to attend the course are themselves the tough core of Crown. They have to be able to survive and thrive on the eighty hours of reading even before classes begin. They live in residence on campus, solve management problems, and soak up theory from lecturers from the University of Western Ontario, Harvard, Duke, and elsewhere. The movie, which has played before 100 or so staff from Canada, the U.S., the U.K., and the Netherlands in the three years since the course began in 1983, is key to their understanding of Bandeen's role at Crown and their part in the real-life turnaround.

Bandeen had shown his management mettle before, as president of Canadian National. At the Crown corporation, one of Canada's largest employers, he had slashed staff by 11,000 to 75,000 after he was named to that post in 1974. He reorganized CN into six profit centres and by 1976, it was making money, the world's only profitable nationalized railway. At Crown, the owners hoped he would do a performance-boosting encore. "The life insurance industry is changing very rapidly," says Michael Burns, chairman of Crownx Inc., the holding company that owns Crown Life. "Life insurance," acknowledges Burns, "has gone from being a major component of the savings dollar to being a minor component of the savings dollar. The country is working towards a financial supermarket type of environment of which life insurance is only one component." That change, concluded Burns, required a new man at the top to replace president Robert C. Dowsett, a loyal Crown employee since 1950 and president since 1971. "Dowsett was always available to step aside if he felt it was for the good of the company," says Burns. "We had to turn around what we had there and get it profitable. The Crown needed an infusion of new blood."

Robert Angus Bandeen, fifty-five, not only was new blood, he also quickly spilled the blood of others. In his first eighteen months Crown Life staff was reduced by 695 people, a 26-per-cent reduction, to 1,955 employees. Sales and service offices across Canada were cut by one-third to sixty-five. In the U.S., where 62 per cent of Crown's $76.5 billion of life insurance in force has been sold, thirteen administrative offices were centralized into three; in the overall company, divisions were reorganized into nine profit centres, and Bandeen went on a shopping spree to expand Crown into other financial services.

Bandeen has blue eyes and skin that is almost baby pink. His laugh comes easily and his voice is a deep baritone. He is a loner in a business where the other life insurance executives share knowledge and swim in each other's bathwater via a myriad of industry committees. Bandeen rarely attends building openings or other official occasions where his peers gather. While he did participate in one industry committee set up by the Canadian Life and Health Insurance Association, he has done little else. He was approached by Jan Mair, president of the Prudential Insurance Co., to become a CLHIA director on the same day as it was announced that he had picked up an extra title, president of Crownx, the financial services holding company. "I guess," said Mair, barely waiting for Bandeen's negative response, "you've got an excuse."

Bandeen doesn't care about the industry's ranks, but he does crave the public's respect. To achieve that he has set out to raise Crown's profile with consumers, the eventual buyers of the firm's products in both the major markets. "We don't have much of an image in Canada," says Bandeen, "or the U.S., for that matter. We're working on it." One method was to switch Crown's marketing strategy. For decades, Crown's main promotional efforts had been directed towards the agents, the people who sold to the public. Under Bandeen, the focus has become the consumer in order to create a demand for Crown products. "In many cases, we have been designing for agents, not the client. We've been wholesalers, not retailers. The past attitude had been that we didn't need to advertise on national TV to reach these people."

Bandeen set out to change all that. Crown became official insurers of the 1984 Canadian Olympic team, and network television advertising was created to run in 1984 on broadcasts from both the winter Olympics in Sarajevo, Yugoslavia, and the summer Olympics in Los Angeles, featuring Canadian athletes such as figure skaters Paul Martini and Barbara Underhill. The Crown Life Pro-Am, a benefit golf tournament sanctioned by the Royal Canadian Golf Association, went national in 1983. About 19,000 golfers participated across Canada, raising some $525,000 for charity and amateur golf. In addition, Crown held a sculpture competition won by Canadian artist Kosso Eloul. He created a four-piece stainless steel work called *Meeting Place.* While Crown saw the work as something for the community, something to draw attention to itself, it was typical of the new Bandeen regime that when the piece was installed outside Toronto home office in 1984, one eye was on the artistic effort, the other was on the bottom line. Because it was on public view, Crown claimed that the cost of the sculpture should be tax-deductible. The issue remains unsettled.

Crown Life is part of a financial services empire called Crownx Inc., a three-legged conglomerate put together by Michael Burns of King, Ont., and David Hennigar of Bedford, N.S., representing the Jodreys. The legs are a 94-per-cent holding in Crown Life, the major business unit in the Crown Financial group, which also includes Coronet Trust and a 40-per-cent share in Beutel Goodman, a money management firm; the Extendicare Group, with 1984 sales of $422 million through its ownership of 164 nursing homes with 21,597 beds in North America (until 1983, Extendicare Inc. was the name of the holding company); and the Crowntek Group (information technology products and services). "That's the high-risk and high-growth part of the company," says Bandeen, who carries various titles including chairman and chief executive officer of Crown Life, president of Crownx, and chairman and chief executive officer of Crown Financial Services. Now that minister of state for finance Barbara McDougall is talking about allowing holding companies such as Crownx to own banks, Crownx will likely create one. In April 1985, Michael Burns told a Crownx shareholders' meeting: "It is possible that when you enter our lobby for next year's annual meeting, you will see, on our ground floor, a bank, a trust company, a life insurance office, and a brokerage office—all under one roof."

Crown Life has over 5 million clients and 260 sales and service offices in Canada, the U.S., the U.K., the Caribbean, and Hong Kong. In 1984 Crown had assets of $4.85 billion and $67 billion worth of life insurance in force. The main focus of growth will be the U.S., where Crown has 1 per cent of the market; in Canada it has about 3 per cent. Privatization of U.S. hospitals means that Crownx, through Extendicare, can buy assets. As well, insurance regulations are less onerous in the U.S. than in Canada. "There are no inhibitions. The state regulations are quite mild compared to Canada," says Bandeen. "The breakdown of barriers between financial services is almost complete."

The strategy is clear, but Bandeen's tactics can be too direct for a firm where change has previously been slow and loyalties were once solid. Most at Crown agree that Bandeen has the right idea but wince at his methods. Having identified the U.S. as a major target, for example, Bandeen then went public with his thinking. "As far as I'm concerned, we only have a limited amount of executive talent," he told Jacquie McNish for a 1983 article in the *Financial Times*. "Let's put it in a country [the U.S.] where you don't have to worry about the regulations." This was the tough guy Michael Burns heard from one Saturday in January 1982. Bandeen telephoned Burns at home to tell him that he was about to announce his departure from CN. He wanted to inform Burns because he had been a Crown Life director since 1979 representing the holdings of CN's pension fund in Crown. He told Burns that he was resigning the Crown directorship, but Burns refused to accept the resignation. Within a month Burns went farther, telling him there might be an executive position for him at Crown.

Bandeen was also being wooed to replace Dome Petroleum chairman Jack Gallagher. The chartered banks, owed billions by Dome, were seeking a tough financial officer to go into Dome, sell assets, and work out the debt problems. Bandeen talked to Bank of Montreal chairman William Mulholland and Royal Bank chairman Rowland Frazee about the job, but no job offer was made. Bandeen picked Crown instead, and in May, he was presented to the Crown Life board of directors as chairman, president, and chief executive officer. Dowsett was shunted aside to the position of vice-chairman.

"It was time for a new chief executive," admits Dowsett. "You find yourself using the same medicine." When Bandeen moved into Dowsett's office, Dowsett moved into a tiny room near the elevators on the executive floor. The room, a kind of living museum with an ornate desk and photographs of directors from the turn of the century, had been set up to show what the chairman's office looked like eighty years ago. The entrance is on a side corridor but the office has a window on the main hall wall that allows passers-by waiting for the elevators to peer in and admire the past. Around the building, the room is known fondly as "the hot dog stand." When Dowsett worked in there, he could pull the drapes on the window for privacy. The arrangement didn't last. Says Dowsett, "I wasn't happy in the building with someone in the chair where I had been calling the shots." He left a few months after Bandeen's arrival and joined William M. Mercer Ltd. in Toronto, an international consulting firm that designs pensions and employee-benefit plans as well as handling executive compensation.

Crown was such a sleepy place that when the six-foot-two, 230-pound Bandeen began showing up for work in his chauffeur-driven Jaguar at the previously unheard-of hour of seven o'clock, the startled parking lot attendant passed the word around the building as if it were news that every policyholder had the plague and was about to pass away, collect the death benefit, and bankrupt the company. Born in Rodney, Ont., Bandeen attended the University of Western Ontario and took his doctorate in economics at Duke University in Durham, N.C. Bandeen is no soft-hands egghead, however, and likes to poke fun at both his degree and its reputation by citing a story told by Stephen Leacock, who, as Bandeen enjoys pointing out, had a doctorate and was an economist "until he discovered that he could support himself with his writing." Leacock said the degree meant "that the recipient of instruction is examined for the last time in his life, and is pronounced completely full. After this, no new ideas can be imparted to him." At one point, at least, Bandeen seemed to be living by Leacock's design. During 1982–83, he was the only member of his family not in school. His wife, Mona, was taking her master of business administration degree at the University of Toronto, and their four sons were variously enrolled in Upper Canada College, Dartmouth, Duke, and McGill.

Nothing in formal education or business experience had prepared him for what he found when he arrived, not just at Crown but in the industry. "The insurance industry was in a cocoon. They competed fiercely among themselves, but they didn't compete with the outside world. This creates a funny atmosphere. You can go on applying traditional concepts of management for years after the rest of the industries change if all the people you're competing against are applying the same standards and looking to one another for comparison. You don't suffer because you're not running out and hiring MBAs, because nobody else is. In the U.S., this was all breaking down, the traditional insurance companies there were under pressure. Either they were being bought by outside firms, or they were out buying." In Canada, there was no such change in sight. "When I was on the board, we'd look at salaries. They'd have the industry comparisons, but nothing else. I'd ask how our salaries compared to banking and they'd say they didn't know." (Bandeen earns about $400,000 a year, about $150,000 less than the chairman of a major Canadian bank.)

Before he could look outside and battle the industry, however, there was a job to do within. He joined in June 1982 and had been there precisely eighteen days when the results for the first five months of the year were handed to him. Earnings were plummeting and no one seemed to be concerned. "They weren't at alert stations by a long shot nor did they even think there was any need to be. They don't do much marketing—it's *sales*," he says with a sneer. "Life insurance companies," he concluded, "are in the dark ages."

In the early months of his tenure, everyone held his breath. He took no obvious action right away; he just seemed to be marking time. There were many who tried to reassure him that everything was all right, that any problems would simply correct themselves. "People kept telling me, 'Crown is a high-cost company,' and they seemed proud of it," recalls Bandeen. "I couldn't figure it out." Perhaps their view simply proved Michael Burns's point that only an outsider could carry out the required surgery. Says Bandeen, "Rob [Dowsett] was president for eleven years. There wasn't a thing in the company that wasn't his. It's difficult to stand up and say, 'Everything I said was OK ten years ago is going to be thrown out.' It's simpler for a brash person to arrive on the scene."

Bandeen's first changes were more symbolic than meaningful. Dowsett's desk had been positioned in such a way that he could see and be seen down the executive hallway. When Bandeen moved in the travertine-topped desk he'd used at CN, it was placed near a window, far from the door. The new placement indicated that more independent and entrepreneurial action was expected all down the line: the boss wasn't always going to be watching. Nor, for that matter, did he want to be watched. He also brought along a brass bell from a retired CN steam locomotive. It is mounted in his office and it, too, symbolizes Bandeen's new ways. In the sanctum sanctorum of the general insurance business, Lloyd's of London, there is a bell known as the Lutine bell that is rung once for a disaster that will cost members money, twice for good news on missing ships. Bandeen cares not a whit for such insurance traditions and will ring his bell whenever he likes or whenever a visitor asks.

In October 1982, there was no warning bell as dozens of employees were fired at all levels. Two high-level executives who were dumped were Mike Hutchison, vice-president and director of marketing and agencies, and VP Jack Roberts. Bandeen called them in separately one morning and was blunt. "I'm reorganizing. You don't fit. You can quit or be fired. Eric Barton of Thorne Stevenson is in the next room to help you find other employment. Sign this." Bandeen then handed each a letter in which, among other accords, the employee agreed not to sue Crown for wrongful dismissal. Roberts chose to quit. Hutchison told Bandeen, "I have a fetish for the truth. You can fire me." The choice didn't affect severance pay. Each received about two years' pay for more than twenty years' service. Hutchison, ironically, was late for his own dismissal. As treasurer of Hillcrest Christian Church, he had gone to the church that Monday morning. When he arrived for work around eleven, he found a message telling him he had an appointment with Bandeen at nine. He was two hours late for his own beheading. Hutchison later became a vice-president at Continental Insurance in Toronto; Roberts became president and chief executive officer of Canadian General Life Assurance Co. of Hamilton, Ont.

The succeeding weeks brought more cuts from the scythe. The firings were repeated down the ranks as various supervisors trimmed their departments. Scores of long-term employees were unceremoniously dumped from their positions. In many cases, people were fired without their managers being consulted. Recalls one manager, "[Senior vice-president] Bob Boeckner called me up to the seventh floor and said, 'There's no room for Mr. So-and-so under you. Are you going to tell him or am I?'" The person to be fired would be taken to the personnel department, told, asked to sign a release, given severance pay, and turned over to a "dehirer"—all in a matter of minutes.

While many within Crown agreed that Bandeen had to take drastic action, there was wide resentment at the high-handed methods. "There *was* mismanagement," one manager admits. "The company was flat. But the individual managers should have been put on budgets, told to weed out people and to salvage those who were worth salvaging. What Bandeen did, most people agreed with. It was how he did it." Deep as those first few cuts were, they weren't enough for Bandeen. In December 1982, as employees were being dumped out days before Christmas, someone devised a button for distribution at Crown. It read: "I survived '82 and I'm looking forward to '83." When Bandeen received his button, he consulted his calendar and announced ominously: "There are still twenty-one days to go."

The technique of firing a few high-profile executives and massive numbers of staff had become a common one after the recession had affected profit at many companies. "[Management guru Peter] Drucker says after six months, blow away a couple of [senior] people and make the company your own," says Hutchison. "Bandeen did it in five. The mandate is to fix the bottom line and to do that, you blow people away. The rest of the crowd comes around to do your bidding to achieve your ambitions or you'll be blown away if you don't perform. I don't advocate it, but it was the right thing to do."

Bandeen has asked himself about the effect and the ethics of the firings, because he knows they have changed Crown from a bit of a backwater to a paranoid palace. "Have I got the milk of human kindness?" he asks. "Well, I go back to my first division at CN—development planning." The department was divided in four and 120 people left. "Many were bitter at the company but they were underutilized. I fired some of them, and it was the best thing that could happen to them. You see this in the banks and other organizations. They've got vice-chairmen, deputy chairmen, senior vice-presidents—all kinds of people on the shelf. That doesn't do those people any good. Are you filled with the milk of human kindness if you keep them? Are you a tough guy if you fire them? I don't know."

As he reduced Crown's population over two years, heading towards the eventual 26-per-cent cut, there were some immediate savings—costs in thirty-one operating units fell by $5 million—but it wasn't enough. Even with such drastic action, the 1982 earnings were less than two-thirds of the 1981 totals. That's why the cuts kept coming through 1983. At one point, for example, two Crown employees met at a Washington convention. The second person arrived two days after the first and was able to list seven more co-workers gone since the first had left Toronto. Morale slumped.

People were dumped because their jobs were eliminated by reorganization, their supervisors no longer wanted them—or they were incompetent, according to Al Morson, a long-time Crown employee who was elevated to president by Bandeen in 1984. "There were people whom management had been protecting. [Supervisors] felt free when they were asked, 'Who do you want?' There were people left over. The reason people didn't work out was often that they weren't in the right hole."

Many of those who were fired were resentful of the treatment and the change in character of Crown. They were particularly appalled that they got the heave-ho so close to Christmas. In the past, the personnel department had been careful not to fire any staffer too close to the holiday season. Says John Stanley, one of those fired, "At least at CN, [Bandeen] had unions to deal with. At Crown it was a turkey shoot. People were loyal, worked for long hours for years. Bandeen ended all that. They can't count on employee loyalty any longer."

One employee who took early retirement threatened Bandeen's life. His picture was circulated among security staff. Rumours spread that Bandeen had hired a bodyguard. He hadn't. When he took over at CN as president, he had in fact inherited an armed CN driver, but Bandeen didn't feel similar precautions would do any good at Crown because Bandeen assumed the would-be assassin could not be stopped if he really wanted to carry out his threat. "He knew the building. What could we do?" That nothing came of the threat didn't surprise Bandeen. "I didn't really believe him anyway."

The level of resentment and fear that followed the cuts surprised Bandeen, but it did not stop him from pressing on amid the raging gossip. "I thought that CN was bad, but I've never seen anything like the moccasin trail at Crown. Rumours can go from the seventh [the executive floor] to the mail boys in the sub-basement in fifteen minutes. It seemed to be part of the gossipy nature of the business. My view is that we'll keep on reducing staff until there's no more time available to gossip." Bandeen even speculated on one mischievous technique. "You know how you kill weeds by overfeeding them? Well, I thought if I put out three rumours a day, those on the moccasin trail might have so many rumours to pass on they might explode." Overfeeding, however, was a technique that he knew was unlikely to succeed. "Communications are a problem," he admits. "Anything we don't want communicated spreads like wildfire. Anything we want to say doesn't get around."

While the main cut-backs were finished by the end of 1983, there were still changes going on in 1984. It was decided, for example, to move the division looking after U.S. group insurance business from Toronto into a converted former torpedo factory in Alexandria, Va. While Crown wanted to move all management personnel, U.S. immigration rules and personal refusals meant that only twenty-five of the 115 in the division could be transferred. Of the rest, fifty had been transferred within Crown, and a year later about forty were still not placed, twenty-five of them still at Crown; the company claims that by the end of 1985, all will have other positions. Even though by early 1985, controlled hiring had begun again and staff numbers had moved from the low point of 1,955 to 2,025, employees were still feeling shaky more than three years after Bandeen arrived. "In some areas, there is still uncertainty," admits Morson. "New management always creates uncertainty. But it is reduced because people are getting used to it. The reason we had morale problems was that people watched others leave and wondered who would be next. The world they worked in before will never return. You used to pick an insurance company and work there for the rest of your life. Now, as long as you do your job well and are turned on, you'll stay."

In addition to staff cut-backs, Bandeen also instituted a program called overhead value analysis, which forced operating departments to detail how they could strip budgets back by 50 per cent. The thirteen money-losing U.S. group health insurance offices were consolidated into three. He established nine profit centres to hold regional offices and those responsible for product lines more accountable. It was an idea first put to him by London Life's Earl Orser. "The biggest thing," Orser had advised Bandeen when he joined Crown, "is to get profitability by product line." "I didn't believe him," recalls Bandeen. He soon became a convert. "I've had a hard time convincing Crown that's important." He switched ad agencies and set out to quadruple the budget and raise the company's profile. He also shook hands with 1,400 home office employees at a series of "meet the boss" sessions in his first few months. It was as if he wanted each of them to feel just how tough he was.

For Bandeen, it was all a necessary, even familiar, operation. At CN, where he had worked his way up from the research department to become president at forty-three, he slashed employee numbers and made CN profitable. Of course, he had some help from government. CN's debt, which had been hanging over the company for decades, was cleared away by legislation—no small help in reducing interest payments and improving profit. Further, CN did not have quite the same family atmosphere as Crown—CN was, after all, more than thirty times larger. In the insurance industry, where many companies continue to treat employees as family, Crown became known as the Abattoir.

Robert Bandeen is ranging over his 280-acre farm in the Eastern Townships two hours south of Montreal. He bought the farm in 1972 when he was living in Montreal, then kept it when he moved to Toronto ten years later. The land was first settled in 1830. The current frame house, built in 1870, has undergone a few changes in the century or so since. The pine trim and spruce floors are original; the four bathrooms and the tennis court are not. When he bought it, the owners had a man who lived in and looked after the place. "You'll be keeping Tom, of course," they said to Bandeen. He did.

Hereford cattle dot the landscape. Unlike most of the Herefords in this area, Bandeen's have horns; the others are polled—the horns have been removed. Explains Bandeen, "French Canadians don't like any animal with horns." He has a trout pond and a garden with raspberries, strawberries, peas, cabbage, potatoes, and other seasonal vegetables. The produce supplies the Bandeens' Toronto table all winter. At the back of the house is a deck where he sits and quenches his thirst with a concoction of lemon and grape juices after yard work or tennis.

The grassy area around the house has been expanded several times as he plants more grass and moves the rail fences farther away from the house. Each spring, Bandeen gets out his shovel and plants up to thirty trees near the house—maples, white and Austrian pines, apple, and oak. One year he tried a Russian olive but it didn't survive the following winter. He has become so famous in the area for his tree-planting—there are dozens spotted around the house including spruce, pines, and cedar—that when a local artist was commissioned to make some textile hangings for the stairwell wall of the house, the farm scene included a tiny Bandeen out planting trees, a deer nibbling at one of them.

The house has an alarm system connected to the provincial police that consists of three sirens as well as panic buttons spotted around the house to set off the sirens in case an intruder is suddenly discovered. At first the phone was an inconvenient eight-party line. When Bandeen was travelling and phoned his wife, another woman on the same line would pick up the phone to listen in before she could answer. An exasperated Bandeen would say: "Madame ———, please don't pick up the phone. I'm calling from San Francisco and I want to speak to my wife. Let her answer." He'd hang up and try again; again the eavesdropper would pick up the line first, looking for entertainment. Bell Canada told Bandeen that it would be three years before he could have a private line installed. He phoned Bell president Robert Scrivener directly. The private line was quickly installed.

Highland Farm is Bandeen's refuge, the place he visits to escape the world, do a little physical labour, and wash away the corporate pressures. Here, as at home, he's up at five-thirty and at work by seven-fifteen. In Toronto, he often plays an early-morning squash game to get the heart started. Every Wednesday, if they're both in town, Bandeen plays William Bradford, deputy chairman of the Bank of Montreal, at a downtown Toronto health club, the Cambridge Club. At Highland Farm, there is tennis and also early-morning walks on his wooded land across the road, where he can see deer by the dozens.

Bandeen knows all the locals. There's Lawrence the illiterate gardener, the nearby junk-dealer who can always produce necessary machinery parts, the general store where credit is allowed, and the mechanic who can fix the ancient Land Rover that bounds around the property. Bandeen's house is a trove of local history. Along with the pioneer implements and pine furniture tucked in various nooks and crannies, he has unearthed militia gear, red uniform jackets, guns, and various mustering papers dating from 1899. The farmhouse was to be among the last bastions against the Fenian raids across the border from the U.S. Today it is a place to escape corporate combat.

Highland Farm will likely be his retirement home. Bandeen has never really liked Toronto, never felt at home, even though when he moved to Toronto in 1982, he and his wife were able to buy the same house on Cluny Drive in Rosedale that they had owned when he worked in Toronto for CN before becoming president in Montreal. Montreal remains his favourite city. In Toronto, he says, "everything works—but it's boring. Anglo Toronto hasn't learned how to enjoy. They put all their effort into organizing the event." As a mental exercise before his first management dinner, Bandeen tried to guess the menu—roast beef, peas, mashed potatoes, and apple pie. He was right. "If you served that in Montreal, they'd all throw buns at you. What about nouvelle cuisine? They'd never heard of it."

On this June weekend, a thirty-by-seventy-foot tent has been erected near the house at Highland Farm. The three dozen members of the management course at Bishop's, where Bandeen is chancellor, plus five senior Crownx and Crown executives are coming for a barbecue. As everyone stands around in the early evening with a pre-dinner drink, Michael Burns's wife, Sue, shows off her farm background by walking over to the fence, letting out a few bovine bellows, and convincing some Herefords to lumber closer. As the sun sets, the guests light into lobsters, steaks, bread, salad, strawberries, and wine, all served buffet-style under the awnings.

At the end of the evening, after the "students" have departed by bus for Bishop's, Bandeen sits in his living room with the remaining senior colleagues, telling stories about others and about himself. After a few drinks and with his upper management team gathered around him, Bob Bandeen has shed the woes of the office as easily as a pair of work boots left at the kitchen door. He sits, looking for all the world like a rotund Chinese laughing god, his belly shaking with laughter, acting more like a gossip than the guru who will save Crown.

Crown Life was founded in 1900. The first president was Charles Tupper, a father of Confederation who briefly served as prime minister in 1896. Politicians have graced the place off and on ever since. Robert Laird Borden was president from 1928 to 1937, and former Ontario premier George Howard Ferguson was president from 1937 to 1946. Liberal biggies on the board of directors have included C. D. Howe, Robert Winters, Lester Pearson, and John Turner.

The real leadership, however, came from elsewhere. Herbert Roy

Stephenson, for example, was chief executive officer of Crown from 1919 to 1953, and a director for fully twenty years after that—more than fifty years of continuity, typical of management in the Canadian life insurance business in the first half of the century. According to Crown lore, it was Stephenson who kept the firm alive. The first shareholders, so the story goes, were little more than promoters who managed to con a few politicians into lending their names and their reputations to Crown to give it a solid public image. The first batch of shareholders made their money and cleared out, leaving a struggling company in the hands of a second group. Wisely, as later became apparent, they hired Stephenson, a man in his early twenties who had started in the insurance business with Manufacturers as a young actuary. Again according to lore, it was Stephenson who put Crown on its feet. It was said the company was bankrupt from 1910 to 1925, but Stephenson never told anyone.

At a time when most companies were selling insurance that required high premiums from policyholders, then paid them high dividends, Stephenson took another route. He cut both the premium levels and the dividends to offer low-cost insurance to the masses. He also took Crown into countries all over the world, including India and Hong Kong. Those were great days of false fronts and phoney bravado. E.J.S. Brown, head of agencies in the 1930s, would travel west to Vancouver to visit agents and boost sales. He'd take the train, sleeping in an upper berth until he neared Vancouver. For the last few hours he would hire a private railway car, have it filled with flowers and his family photographs, and receive the agents upon arrival as if he and Crown were wealth incarnate.

Ownership became a family matter. Herbert Burns was on the board from 1927 to 1960, followed by Charles Burns, who founded an investment firm in the 1930s (now Burns Fry). In 1946, the Burns family bought into Crown along with George McCullagh, publisher of the *Globe and Mail*, and Bill Wright, an eccentric bachelor prospector who discovered gold and founded Wright-Hargreaves Mines Ltd. After McCullagh died in 1952, Burns convinced a Nova Scotia friend, Roy Jodrey of Midas Basin Pulp and Power Co. Ltd., one among the wealthiest families in Atlantic Canada, to buy the McCullagh holdings. Wright had died in 1951, but his estate was left tied up in such a fashion that his Crown holdings could not be sold right away. In 1975 Wright's share was finally split up, largely among a group of pension funds. The Jodreys and the Burnses continued to increase their holdings until they reached approximately 35 per cent between them by 1980. Charles Burns, president since 1959, took over as chairman in 1964 and ceded authority in 1979 to his son, Michael, who became chairman.

While the Burns and Jodrey families owned Crown, they left the running of the firm largely to management. After the Second World War, the president was a marketing man, Arthur C. Williams. E.J.S. Brown had been urging that Crown expand around the world; Williams wanted to concentrate on the U.S. Williams won the battle and Crown entered nearly all of the U.S. states before Williams stepped down in 1971 as president. Williams's view of the family feeling at Crown was typical of the paternalism that marked Crown and many other institutions of the era. His favoured description of Crown and its business was: "Doing work you like with people you like for people you like." He was followed by actuary Rob Dowsett, who had joined Crown in 1950. Dowsett oversaw the next spurt of growth so that by 1972, for example, Crown was writing more new business than any other Canadian life insurance company. He also continued the family feeling at Crown's offices on Bloor Street in Toronto. He would often be found beyond the executive suite, talking to employees on other floors.

Increasingly, however, the life insurance business did not provide the investment scope or the profit that the Burns and Jodrey families thought was possible. For his part, Michael Burns, according to Dowsett, wasn't "a working chairman." Burns didn't have an office at Crown and spent perhaps two days a month there. "He let me run the insurance business, but he called the shots on Datacrown [later Crowntek]." Neither he nor his father had been operating officers, but the father had been different. "Charles," says Dowsett, "was an inspirational leader. He would appear at board meetings and set goals through his personality. Michael was running his cattle-breeding farm."

By 1980 there was trouble on the bottom line. Group health insurance in the U.S. was losing money and Datacrown Inc., once the belle of the computer datacentre world, looked as if it would lose out to the microcomputers that were beginning to appear in every office. Burns tried to respond to the times by turning to Harold Livergant, founder and chairman of Extendicare Ltd., then the fourth-largest operator of nursing homes in North America. A deal was negotiated over a six-month period that, through an exchange of shares, meant that the Burns and Jodrey families put their Crown Life holdings into Extendicare in exchange for 6 million shares of Extendicare. Extendicare then made a follow-up offer for other Crown Life shares, to own 92 per cent of Crown. With Extendicare as a holding company, there was greater opportunity for diversification. Burns became chairman of Extendicare, which was then positioned to move into other financial services areas. Once the Extendicare deal was complete, Burns's interest was sparked. He moved into the Extendicare offices and began to devote his full effort to the business.

Meanwhile Crown Life's troubles were most obvious in the U.S. division. U.S. sales had always been important, but as the 1970s passed, the contribution of U.S. sales to the total premium income was slipping. It rose from 56 per cent of total premium revenue in 1977 to 58.7 per cent in 1979, then fell until it reached 54 per cent in 1981, a figure that included pension, group, and individual insurance sales. The man in charge of individual sales in the U.S. was a swashbuckling former vaudeville performer named Clarke Lloyd, senior agency vice-president for the U.S.

Clarke Lloyd had an unbroken record of success and a unique personal style. He earned $80,000 a year and spent more than that on entertainment—mostly on the people who handled Crown products in the U.S. At the time, Crown sales were through general agents, as many as 131 under Lloyd at one point, in 110 cities. (The number is now ninety agents, in ninety cities.) The general agents were, in effect, wholesalers for the products that Crown manufactured. They, in turn, worked through a number of brokers who then "retailed" the policies to the general public or made group insurance sales to companies. Since there was little consumer advertising to create public demand, Crown's strategy was to keep the general agents and brokers happy with incentives, trips, commissions, and bonuses so that they would push Crown products, not the other firms' policies that they were also licensed to sell. For example, the Crown general agent in Fresno, Calif., Rudy Facciani, sells a lot of insurance for Crown through a number of his brokers who are with New York Life. This system kept Crown's expenses low—no training costs, office space, or administrative tab to pick up.

Clarke Lloyd was the man who exploited and expanded the U.S. system. Born in 1925, he had grown up in Toronto. Beginning at fourteen, he split his time between school and the stage in various vaudeville houses, first as a boy singer and later as what was known as a "baggy-pants comic," rolling his snappy patter and jokes during the show, which would include a movie, strippers, animal acts, and other entertainers. During the Second World War, Lloyd was a song-and-dance man in the army entertainment shows that toured Europe, and in 1947 he joined Crown's field services department, where the advertising was done. Crown's growth during the next two decades was in the U.S. through general agents. As sales grew, Crown's methods were criticized in the industry because Crown contributed nothing to the expenses of the broker. Office, financing, and other support services were paid by another company for whom the agent sold. "We became, according to our competitors, the whores of the business," says Lloyd, who joined the U.S. agency division in 1966. "We were considered parasites."

Crown's general agents, however, did very well. Many became millionaires. It was they who decided how the commission arrangements would work. On most policies, for example, an amount equivalent to the first year's premium paid by the insured is paid out, over three years, by Crown. On some products the commission could go to 200 per cent of first-year premiums. The standard commission, however, was 70 per cent of the premium in the first year, 20 per cent in the second, 10 per cent in the third, and 3 per cent every year thereafter for life. (Today some of the products with first-year commission in excess of 100 per cent have been cut to 100 per cent in order to keep products competitive.) In the U.S., the general agents decide on their own how much of that premium is passed on to the broker who sells the policy and how much they will retain for themselves on the way through. Some of it goes for office expenses, overhead, and incentives to the brokers. Fresno's Facciani, for example, may tell the New York Life brokers he deals with that if they sell a certain amount of Crown insurance over the next year, he'll send them and their spouses to Singapore for a holiday. In addition, Crown offers a major trip every three years.

It was Lloyd's job to keep the general agents happy, assist in recruiting new brokers, and promote Crown's products. Entertaining the general agents, supporting their effort, and massaging their huge egos were key aspects of the strategy. Clarke Lloyd was a master at all three. At six feet, in his fifties, with greying wavy hair and glasses, he was at the height of his power in the 1970s. He did nothing in half-measure. He worked hard and played hard. Associates admired his drive and staying power. "I'm surprised," says one who knows him, "that he made it as long as he did." His blustering, full-hearted manner fit in well with the American way of doing business.

At Crown he was a whirling dervish, one of those people who is always in motion. As a former vaudeville performer, Lloyd never lost the knack of telling a story, of keeping his table entertained, of kidding president Dowsett, for example, that the only thing he'd ever done at Crown was invent, years earlier, the twenty-year endowment policy. He was also a big spender. Crown will admit for the record that his annual travel and entertainment expenses ran to $100,000. His associates say that his annual expenses may well have run to $200,000 a year. "He didn't throw money away," says Mike Hutchison, to whom Lloyd reported, "but he was a believer in and a participant in conspicuous consumption." Lloyd doesn't know what he spent. All he knows is that it worked. "I built the U.S. operations," he says. "How I did it may be questionable. I may have spent, as you say, $400,000 a year on booze and meals," and here he winked and laughed, "but whatever it was on and however I did it, it was successful."

Agents or prospective brokers were flown into Toronto, met at the airport in huge limousines, and taken to ostentatious dinners where the steaks and the wines were the best, the tips grand. Lloyd was known to maître d's everywhere. Typical was Creighton's in Toronto's Westbury Hotel, where his favourite bottles of wine would already be decanted and breathing when he arrived. Another favourite haunt was Winston's, corporate Toronto's cafeteria. There, owner John Arena would serve Lloyd and his agent guests personally. Arena would also intervene if some of the less sophisticated general agents didn't measure up to standards. On one occasion, for example, the waiter overlooked the gaucherie when an agent ordered a Coke with his dinner, but he did visibly flinch when the agent requested ketchup for his filet mignon. Arena brought the ketchup himself. Lloyd also favoured his club, the Royal Canadian Yacht Club, and, of course, there was always the Crownx "lunchroom," The Greenery, in the Hotel Plaza II next door to Crown, a hotel that Crownx owns. In a year, he might royally entertain half the hundred-odd agents, either in Toronto or elsewhere as he spent more than one-third of his time on the road.

In the office, Lloyd fought hard against the cautious actuaries, battling against their reluctance to develop new products. The three agency vice-presidents who worked with him—Art Thomas, Dave Williams, and Peter Hobbs—had little to do because the agents dealt directly with Lloyd. They knew he was the one who made all their dreams come true. "He was one of the most imaginative marketing guys I've ever met," says Hutchison, "and almost unmanageable. You just had to give him enough head to achieve things and pull on his ankle once in a while." Says Al Morson, now president of Crown Life, "He was a very creative guy, a lot of mental energy, a great salesman, a good recruiter and good at getting things done. When he had a good idea, he badgered people. He was able to get things done by the force of his own personality."

Lloyd's style was to appoint an agent for a city and work hard for a while getting that agent established. He would lavish attention on those agents who were the largest producers, while urging others who weren't doing as well to do better. "Some of the older generation of agents couldn't run up the hill any more," says Hutchison. "Clarke would jab them." Also, Lloyd played favourites. "He developed so much power," says Morson, "that a lack of trust developed between him and some of the general agents." Because most of those long-term service agents knew Dowsett and chairman Michael Burns from conventions and other Crown gatherings, they would complain about what they felt was unfair treatment. Some agents who may have been doing well felt someone else was getting Lloyd's favours and they weren't. In the late 1970s, those who were being jabbed by Lloyd and those who felt forgotten began to complain to Hutchison, to Dowsett, to Burns, trying to find a sympathetic ear. Hutchison supported Lloyd, but increasingly, Burns responded to the complaints from the agents, many of whom he knew personally. "Michael was receptive to end plays," says Hutchison. "He'd phone Rob and say Clarke was being mean to someone."

One of the complainers was agent Robert E. Lee. He had agencies in Los Angeles, San Bernardino, San Diego, San Francisco, and Sacramento in California; and in Honolulu, Houston, Seattle, and Anchorage. Even Crown's business in Hong Kong went through Robert E. Lee, Crown's biggest general agent. Lloyd and Lee had been great friends for a long time; Lloyd had been very attentive to Lee's needs. About 1978, however, Lloyd's relationship with Lee began to wane as Lloyd moved a new agent, Kerry Craig, into Chicago. Lloyd had plucked Craig from another area in Crown, brought him into the agency department, pushed him up the ladder as a protégé, then positioned him in Chicago as a general agent. During the next few years, with Lloyd's full backing and support, Craig's power grew to the point where with partners, he controlled ten agencies.

Lloyd's strategy was simple. He thought Lee had become too powerful, and he wanted to create another powerful agent to offset Lee's clout. One huge sale that went through Craig was some of the individual insurance business for all the McDonald's franchises in the U.S. The particular policy, known as retired lives reserve (RLR), allowed the individual franchise-holder (or manager) to purchase life insurance at special rates because of the number of participants. The premiums were tax-deductible as a business expense, but unlike many group plans, the insurance was paid up by the time the employee retired at sixty-five, and continued in force. Thus, what eventually became personal life insurance had been paid for by the company. Tax rules changed in the U.S. in 1984, rendering the deal less enticing, but at the time, it was Lloyd's attempt to mass-market insurance.

Mass-marketing techniques, however, were not employed. While RLR was available to all general agents, McDonald's sales were available only through Chicago because Craig's office had placed it with extensive help from head office, giving rise to charges of favouritism. To assist Craig, Lloyd dispatched his assistant, John Stanley, to Chicago to help out for three months. The contract, worth millions, lost Crown $3 million to $5 million, according to one estimate. Lloyd denies any money was lost by Crown. He notes that it was a lucrative deal for Crown because sales reached face values in excess of $100 million—and all expenses were paid by general agents, not Crown.

As Craig's power grew, the other general agents began to resent the attention Lloyd was lavishing on Craig. "They were all egocentric," recalls Lloyd. "Wherever you went you were favouring someone. That was a historic bitch. Whenever anybody became successful, it was because, supposedly, I had engineered it. In Lee's case, his concern was real and valid. I told him I was going to build an offsetting agency. He was too powerful."

Not all of the general agents agreed with Lloyd's strategy. They gathered twice a year for regular meetings and presentations from home office. At the 1980 meeting in Phoenix, the complaints hit a crescendo. Many of them owed their positions, their agencies, their very careers to Lloyd, but now they began to turn against him. Dowsett, who was in Phoenix, was hammered in a room during a meeting called particularly to complain about Lloyd. "It was," says Hutchison, "a palace revolt." Lloyd's style had been condoned by home office because it produced results. That support in Toronto began to wane. "How much of a leash do you give him?" asked Morson, summarizing the dilemma. "The results were pretty good, but there was this distrust."

There were other problems. An agency in Newark, N.J., run by Craig was disbanded, and as is often the situation in the U.S., where litigation is common, there were lawsuits between agents and Crown. In Pittsburgh, a legal battle over another Craig agency has been raging since Malley-Duff and Associates Inc., a former general agent, was fired by Lloyd and eventually replaced by Craig in 1978. Charges of wrongful dismissal, anti-trust charges, and actions under the Racketeer-Influenced and Corrupt Organizations Act and the Civil Rights Act have been going through the courts ever since. On the anti-trust matter, a judge ruled there was inadequate evidence. On the civil law conspiracy count, a jury awarded against the company in the amount of $900,000. The jury's finding was reversed on appeal and a new trial is awaited.

Some of this was yet to come in 1981, but Lloyd was on the way out of Crown nonetheless. It took some months after the Phoenix meeting, but Lloyd was eventually moved out of the U.S. agency area. It was announced that he would develop a New York subsidiary and work on international business, but the salad days were over. At a Crown convention in Vienna in May 1981, few would even speak to Lloyd. He had been ostracized. Within six months he was gone, given the final push by Burns and Dowsett, his departure eased with a six-figure severance pay settlement. "I don't think I'm paranoid," Lloyd told an associate at the time. "I think they really *were* out to get me." Gone, too, was Lloyd's assistant, John Stanley, seen as Lloyd's man on the scene. His three and a half years of service were rewarded with six weeks' pay. Lloyd worked with Craig for a year in Chicago and is now a general agent there for Confederation Life. Stanley works for the government of Ontario.

The affair had repercussions on Dowsett. "If you were Michael, you would say Rob was not doing a good job because he had allowed this palace revolt among U.S. agents and was losing money in the

[U.S.] group life and health business," says Hutchison. "And Rob and Michael really never did get along. [Rob] agonized over what he could have done to prevent what happened to others and to *his* Crown Life. It wasn't [just] what he had built himself, but what his predecessors and peers had built." There was probably little he could have done and, in the end, Dowsett was shuffled off to the position of vice-chairman. Bandeen was brought in with a free hand to fashion a new Crown.

Bandeen's interest, it soon became apparent, was not in the core area of the company—life insurance. Crown was to be the cash cow that provided funds to expand into other areas of financial services operations. Says Don Payne, former executive vice-president for investment operations, "Bandeen wants the insurance end to be profitable, but just running insurance he'd get bored. He wants to create a major North American financial services company." Adds Crown president Morson, "Bob has never developed a deep under-standing of the insurance business. What he brought in were man-agement principles. He leaves Crown Life to me." A similar view is held in the industry. Says Mutual Life of Canada chairman John Panabaker, "[Bandeen] pays more attention to Crownx than to Crown Life. That's where the fun is." Bandeen even scoffs at the way life insurance accounting is done. If a company has a good year, for example, costs on the balance sheet are heavy because commis-sions and the administrative load must be included. As a result, profit is reduced. If there were no sales, there would be no costs and profits would be high. Bandeen has a plan that he has often repeated, a way of going out in style: "The year before I retire, we'll stop selling insurance. We'll have a spectacular year."

Bandeen's attitude towards insurance is entirely practical. Even when he considers the corporate response to lawsuits from unhappy policyholders or beneficiaries, his views are direct and disarming. On U.S. court cases, for example, Bandeen claims that black-dominated juries are more sympathetic to an individual battling an insurance company than are white-dominated juries and will award higher amounts than a negotiated settlement. "You always check the jury in a court case," he says. "Is it black or is it white? If it's black, you settle. Fast."

Bandeen takes an equally pragmatic view of Crown Life as an organization. In addition to cutting expenses by firing staff, he reorganized the structure. In the past the levels of bureaucracy had been too numerous. From the top of the organization down to the lowliest clerk, there were twenty-three titles. Bandeen cut that to nine to improve communications. Also, there were people in Crown who were supervisors—but in a department or area that might include only one other person. That was changed, too, so that supervisors would usually have ten staff reporting to them. In the past, the organization had been centred on products. That was changed to a geographic structure so that employees could focus on specific markets. Operations were divided, by region, into nine profit centres. "It was like starting all over again," says Morson. "There is a lot more accountability now because we are looking at nine different profit centres, not just one bottom line. There is less focus on growth and more on the bottom line."

After the initial reorganization, Bandeen's plan was to buy his way into expansion through Crownx and Crown Financial Services. In 1984 Crownx purchased North Canadian Trust Co., a federally licensed trust company. The company was renamed Coronet and its head offices were moved from Edmonton to Toronto. Several of the early acquisitive lunges missed. When A. E. LePage Ltd. was looking for a new partner, discussions were held with Crownx, but LePage decided to merge with the real estate arm of Royal Trustco Ltd. instead. Crown also lost out when Monarch Life was purchased by North American. Bandeen thought Monarch was worth no more than $50 million and was furious when North American paid $68 million. Bandeen charged that North American, as a mutual company, had excess cash he didn't have because of the different way the accounting is done at stock companies like Crown. Bandeen can become quite abusive about the mutuals, calling them "socialist" and "messianic." Because mutual companies are actually owned by the policyholders, Bandeen says their management and boards of directors are not as performance-oriented as those of stock companies, so they don't have to worry as much about the bottom line.

For their part, the mutuals charge that stock companies such as Crown have more organizational freedom. Under current legislation, for example, stock companies can establish upstream holding companies (companies that appear on the organization chart above the life insurance company), which in turn control the life insurance companies. The upstream companies—such as Trilon, which controls London Life—are not restricted in their ownership positions in other companies. Thus they can purchase trust companies, other insurance businesses—or any other financial institution without fear of regulation. Products can be networked among the brother organizations, datasystems can be shared, customer lists exchanged.

The mutuals want what the industry calls "a level playing field." They want to be able to organize downstream holding companies to achieve the same kind of synergy as Trilon provides. As a brief was being prepared by the CLHIA for presentation to the government in 1983, internal bickering developed at the CLHIA between the mutuals and the stock companies. Bandeen led the fight against the mutuals and at one point felt confident enough of his position to say: "We've got them by the balls."

The first time Bandeen was quoted as saying that was in a story of mine in *Toronto Life* magazine. It caused quite a stir in the industry, and Bandeen has stayed away from most industry association meetings since. Mutual's Panabaker was chairman of the association at the time. He regretted the loss of Bandeen. "They miss him," he said.

Bandeen, his comments, and his actions at Crown became a focus of attention. At Confederation Life, chairman Jack Rhind devoted part of his 1984 annual meeting speech before policyholders and staff to Bandeen's comments. Rhind's performance was brilliant, his delivery worthy of a stand-up comedian. He enjoyed every minute of it. And Rhind knew whereof he spoke; he was, after all, the chairman of the CLHIA committee preparing the brief about which Bandeen was talking. "The committee," he told about 300 at the meeting in February 1984, "worked out some recommendations which provided a reasonably level playing field for the stock and mutual companies. You can imagine my reaction when I read the following in an article on Mr. Bandeen in *Toronto Life*, entitled 'Crown's Prince.'

"Before I read this I warn the more fastidious among you that this contains an expression that I would not normally use at an annual meeting. In referring to the Association Committee discussions and the mutual companies he said, 'We've got them by the—.'" At this point he stopped, his eyes twinkling with merriment, a smile playing across his face like a flat stone hopscotching across water. The audience hooted with delight. As the laughter died down, he dead-panned: "I cannot bring myself to say this word at an annual meeting of Confederation Life. The Fathers of Confederation would rise from their graves." More laughter.

But Rhind wasn't finished. He waved a newspaper clipping and said it was a recent column by *Globe and Mail* social reporter Zena Cherry, in which Bandeen was wrongly named as head of Confederation. "Not only does Mr. Bandeen feel he holds us in an uncomfortable fashion," said Rhind, "but he appears to have taken over my job."

Before delivering the speech, Rhind had sent a copy of it to his president, Pat Burns. At first Burns, who took over as chief executive officer when Rhind retired in 1985 (he stayed on as chairman), couldn't believe what he was reading. He thought it must have been a joke. "This is a special copy," Burns said hopefully to Rhind. "You've written this just for me." But Rhind delivered it—much to the delight of his audience. It was a mark of the impact Bandeen had had on the industry less than two years after joining it.

Bandeen's brash style at times even flummoxes his partners. A Dutch insurance firm, Aegon N.V., owns 26.5 per cent of Crownx. Aegon's decision-making style is much more structured than Bandeen's impetuous methods. Once, after he heard about a U.S. company that might be for sale, he thought he'd ask Aegon to see if it was interested in putting up any money with him. He phoned and asked directly, " 'Are you still buying insurance companies?' They were terrified," he said, laughing at the recollection.

While the association with the Dutch firm, begun in 1982, has been successful, not all the Crown deals have been. Datacrown, for example, has been a problem of long standing. The computer services firm, begun by Crown in 1971, was the largest computer service company in Canada in 1978, then began to struggle. Datacrown owned huge computer service bureaus, running information through them on contract for other companies. Trying to keep up with changing technology was a costly business. As microcomputers became more popular, fewer and fewer firms needed Datacrown. In 1983, Datacrown jettisoned its facility in Ottawa, one of three operated by the company. It was sold to Canada Post for $11.7 million. It was an amount that led to a mixed reaction from Bandeen: "Hallelujah! As a taxpayer I weep, but as a Crown director, I'm happy." The clean-out at Datacrown that year included Michael Burns's firing of chief executive officer Richard Taylor. He was replaced by Duncan MacLachlan, a protégé of Harold Geneen, former chairman of ITT.

From a standing start in 1983, Crowntek, under MacLachlan, swallowed up Datacrown and $50 million in other acquisitions in its first year. Revenues in 1988 are expected to be at least $500 million and they could go to $1 billion. Employment will likely quadruple to 5,000 from 1984 levels of 1,200 as Crowntek spreads a wide net, looking for winners in the risky high-tech areas of software, communications, and retailing. MacLachlan's compensation package, including salary, bonus, and pension, approached $400,000 annually. Already a millionaire, MacLachlan hoped to own between 2 and 4 per cent of Crowntek by 1988. That plan ended in August 1985, when he resigned. Edward Cannon, a forty-five-year-old chartered accountant who had just joined Crownx in June, was named president and chief operating officer. After a high-flying start, Crowntek needed someone less entrepreneurial to manage the company on a daily basis, said Bandeen, adding: "I don't think [MacLachlan] enjoys that." Bandeen has high hopes for Crowntek. "We want to be among the sunrise, not the sunset, industries."

For Crownx, now that the company is extending its tentacles into all areas of financial services, the next step will be a new employee position—called account executive—who would become the customer's contact point. Each account executive would get to know the individual's financial situation and needs. Then, by relying on a number of back-up people within Crownx, the account executive could advise the customer in a number of areas—insurance, real estate, trustee functions, various deposit instruments, stocks and bonds—Bandeen's version of one-stop financial shopping.

In addition to the corporate acquisitions, Crownx, through Extendicare and Crown Life, has a number of other assets that are varied, pervasive, and little known. Plaza Hotels Inc. is a wholly owned subsidiary that operates four hotels across Canada: the Park Plaza and the Plaza II in Toronto; Plaza de la Chaudière in Hull, Que.; and the International Hotel in Calgary. Crownx Properties Inc. has land and real estate in Denver, Calgary, and Toronto. There is also a 28-per-cent interest in American Eagle Petroleums. As well, Crown assembled the land, developed, and built a building at 160 Bloor Street East in Toronto, then sold half of it to Royal Trustco in 1984 for $30 million. That left Crown with a 50-per-cent ownership for very little cost. The 15-storey, 365,000-square-foot building is clad in reflective curtain wall, enough glass to furnish every household in Toronto with a bathroom mirror. Prior to the sale, when the economy was still recovering and leasing was slow, the building was a sore point with Bandeen as he waited for tenants to fill up the building, thus bringing in revenue for Crown. At one point, VP Don Payne told Bandeen that things were looking better and said, "We've upped the tempo on 160." Bandeen smiled and cut him dead: "You've got two tenants instead of one?"

Payne, the first man hired to carry the acquisition function, didn't last long. Bandeen hired the former Bank of Montreal vice-president as executive vice-president for investment operations but he left after about a year, demonstrating that not all Bandeen's early moves were successful. "He was very competent on his own," says Al Morson of Payne, "but he's not a team player." Says his replacement, Bob Luba, who arrived in 1984 as executive vice-president for corporate finance, "When you get to that level, it's not a question of competence. We can all add up the sums in the same way. It's a question of emphasis. He lost the confidence of the people around here."

Another failure was the 1983 purchase, for US$9 million, of an interest in a California-based company called American Principals Holdings Inc. (APH), a developer of tax-sheltered housing investments. Some products were sold through a subsidiary, called Private Ledger, which had 650 brokers who sold the APH products. There were problems with the partnerships and some of the owners were ousted; an internal investigation followed. The U.S. regulatory body, the Securities and Exchange Commission, was notified and pushed APH into receivership. Crown's $9-million investment was in a debenture secured by shares of Private Ledger, so Crown realized on its security and, with court approval, took over Private Ledger in 1984. Because the brokers who work for Private Ledger all supply their own office space and cover their own expenses, Crown sees them as a low-cost distribution system for various investment products in the future.

The key man in Bandeen's future acquisition strategy is Bob Luba. Luba graduated with his MBA from the University of Western Ontario in 1967 and spent seventeen years with Labatt's just as that beer company was going through an expansion itself. When Luba joined Labatt's, 95 per cent of sales were beer. By the time he left, the company was so diversified that only about 40 per cent of sales came from beer. He was involved in the acquisition of Ogilvy Flour Mills and the sale by Labatt's of Laura Secord, Parnells, a food service business, and Mannings, the largest hospital contract food supplier in the western U.S. Luba knew how to both make and unmake deals. At Labatt's, he had been vice-president for finance, at twenty-nine. He was named vice-president for corporate finance at Crown, then when Payne was fired three months after Luba had arrived, Luba inherited investment operations and diversification. His job title became executive vice-president for corporate finance and invest-ment of Crown Life. In addition, he was executive vice-president and chief operating officer of Crown Financial Services, the arm through which Crown would expand.

Luba has the distinction of being one of the few members of the Young Presidents' Organization who work in the Canadian insur-ance industry. (Another is Larry Bourk, president and CEO of Constellation Assurance Co. of Toronto.) He had been asked to join while at Labatt's and retained the membership when he moved to Crown. YPO's main purpose is to be an educational and confidential idea exchange among members of local chapters. There is also, however, a social side. In June 1984, Luba joined ten other YPO members and their spouses on a bicycle tour of the wine country of France. Run by tour operators Blyth & Co., the tour was not a spartan affair. The group cycled from Mâcon to Dijon accompanied by a van driven by a repairman in case of breakdowns. There was also a car driven by a dignified lady, steeped in the lore of Burgundy, who acted as a tour guide. Days consisted of visits to wine châteaux such as Meursault, dining in fine restaurants, and visiting castles occupied by once-wealthy landowners. Luba brought back a 1971 Chambertin that cost about $20, one-quarter of its Canadian price—if it could be found here. He had been instructed to wait three months before drinking it so that the wine would settle down after travelling. That was too long for the action-oriented Luba. He managed to wait only three weeks.

In the early weeks at Crown, Luba felt the change from the beer business. The beer market is not growing, and three big companies slug it out for minor changes in the share of a stagnant market. "In the beer business," says Luba, "you can get the market share [figured out] down to two decimal points on a weekly basis. Here, it's much more volatile. I felt like I got on a merry-go-round at 100 miles an hour." Luba set up a working committee in Crown Financial and, after about six weeks on the job, went to Bandeen with his initial thoughts. Everything he suggested received an enthusiastic response. "Great," Bandeen would say. "Music to my ears. Go to it." Says Luba, "I couldn't believe his enthusiasm. I'd been used to much less flexibility. He wants to try things. A couple of things on my list were marginal. He knew that, but he created the illusion of 'Let's get on with it.' That's his real strength."

The first deal Luba struck was to buy 40 per cent of Beutel Goodman & Co. Ltd. (assets $3 billion), a Toronto firm that provides investment counselling to individuals and pension funds. Luba had asked several people who was the biggest and the best in the business. The answer he kept hearing was Beutel Goodman. No one, however, expected it was for sale. Luba's response: "Give 'em an opportunity to say yes." The initial contact was not auspicious. He phoned Austin Beutel and introduced himself. "I'm Bob Luba." Came the response: "Who?" After some explanations, Austin agreed to a lunch and the pitch began. Three months later, Luba had a handshake deal that was signed before the end of the year and closed in 1985. For Crown it meant an entrée into investment counselling, a key area for the one-stop approach.

As part of the Beutel deal, Crown also put $400 million of its investment portfolio with Beutel Goodman to be managed. The price Crown paid for 40 per cent of Beutel, $16 million, caused some raised eyebrows in the financial community. David Scott, president of Elliott & Page Ltd., the investment counselling firm owned by North American Life, says Luba paid a high price. The purchase price of an investment counselling firm, says Scott, is usually based on a multiple of the firm's gross income. Assuming that Beutel manages about $4 billion in funds and has a gross income of $16 million, then Luba paid about two and a half times gross for its 40 per cent. When Elliott & Page was purchased, North American paid about one times the gross, something less than $800,000 for 100 per cent of the firm, which managed about $250 million in funds at the time. "[North American president] Drew [McCaughey] looks after the pennies better than Bob Bandeen," says Scott.

In the end, if Bandeen is able to create a successful one-stop shop, any overpayment problems will fade. Luba thinks people have more confidence in a financial services institution if they buy two products, not just one—even more if they buy three. Says Luba, "We want to offer pools of financial excellence. We'll cover off what situations we can and where we can't, we'll send the customer elsewhere—whether we have an ownership position or not. We're going to be an institution offering innovative savings products. The protection element [life insurance] will be less and less. We're talking about building a financial services institution, not an insurance company. It's embryonic. The priorities are to solidify the turna-round at Crown Life and build on that strength. A consumer focus will give us a cohesive force."

There are stumbling blocks to overcome. Bandeen himself clearly became one. Respected in the company, he was not much liked. Stories that put him in a bad light abound. In Athens, in 1984, at Crown's tri-annual gathering for super-sellers, Bandeen threw a cocktail party in his suite at the Intercontinental. It was on the final night, after the closing dinner, and the gathering was meant to thank home office staff for their work in organizing the week and enter-taining the winners and spouses who attended. But it seems he can do no right: the event was seen by some as an event to celebrate Bandeen. Some attendees thought they should have been elsewhere. Sniffed one home office employee who thought he should have been off entertaining the winners in whose honour the conference was being held: "He thought this was a conference to make him look good. If he'd asked anybody, they would have told him that was not the time [to entertain home office]."

In August 1985, after a little more than three years on the job, Bandeen suddenly announced that he would take early retirement, at fifty-five, effective November 1. Michael Burns, who had hand-picked Bandeen to succeed Dowsett, named himself president of Crownx and installed David Hennigar as chairman. As the represen-tatives of the two major family owners, Burns and Hennigar had decided they wanted to become more involved in running the companies. For Bandeen, their decision meant there would be two people too many in the executive suite. "I find it very difficult to have shared responsibilities," said Bandeen. "One of us had to go and it wasn't likely to be the owners." Bandeen describes the financial settlement he received as "quite good" and while remaining a director, he talks of looking for a new challenge, perhaps in univer-sity education, a field that has long interested him. For Bandeen, as for his film counterpart, Gregory Peck, in *Twelve O'Clock High*, the "maximum effort" took its toll. The wars that made them both finally did them in.

CHAPTER FOURTEEN

LIES, DAMNED LIES, AND STATISTICS

A Day in the Life of a Claims Adjuster

K EN DAVIES is driving his new Ford Tempo down Riverside
Drive in Windsor, Ont. North across the Detroit River the
skyline of Detroit rears its head. Davies, forty-seven, is wearing a
blue hound's-tooth sports jacket and a ready smile, not a bad defence
against the lies policyholders tell him every day in his job as a claims
adjuster for Dominion of Canada General Insurance Co. Today, he is
worrying out loud about his image. His six-foot, 185-pound frame is
tucked behind the car wheel as he drives to talk to another insured
with a dented fender and a sore neck, two among the zillion
contingencies that an insurance policy is bought to cover.

As one of Dominion's claims adjusters in the company's eighteen
service offices across Canada, Davies must regularly deal with a
series of misconceptions by the public. Chief among them is the
view that all adjusters take kickbacks from body shops in return for
sending business their way. "It happens," he admits, "but it's not
widespread. There's a reputation that adjusters get kickbacks, but I
don't think it happens very often. I've never been approached."
Further, the system is changing. These days, the appraiser deals with
the repair shop, adjusters like Davies usually only deal with the
policyholder. Still, Davies knows there is some dishonesty as there is
in any system involving people. "There are going to be some
crooked operators—but most of us have enough problems. There are
more people taking advantage of the insurance system than there are
being taken advantage of by the insurance industry."

291

Davies works in what is known as a service office in Windsor. His office services the claims from policyholders who were sold their Dominion of Canada policies through about thirty insurance agents in Windsor, Essex County, and southwestern Ontario. When any policyholder (known as the insured) has a claim, the agent who sold the policy contacts Davies. In 1984 Dominion paid out $89 million in claims across the country—about $3.5 million through this office. With $150 million in income from policyholder premiums in 1983, Dominion ranks fifteenth out of the 170 property and casualty companies in Canada. Dominion of Canada has a little less than 2 per cent of the market, offering a range of property insurance against the sins of man and nature. It is Davies's job to make sure the coverage is in place, that the claim is reasonable, and that conflicting amounts are "adjusted" or adjudicated between someone's inflated idea of the value of the loss and a more realistic and equitable level.

He knows that some claims are outright frauds. "We pay fraudulent claims. I know that. But if you can't prove it, [knowing] doesn't really make any difference. You have to assume most people are honest and tell the truth—if you didn't you couldn't survive in this business." He estimates that perhaps 5 per cent of claims are fraudulent. Sometimes, however, he knows that in a certain area, the ratio must be higher. This fall a rash of motorcycle thefts was reported by policyholders of Dominion General. "Now this is the wrong time of year for that." Thieves are more likely to steal such a vehicle in the spring when there are months of good driving weather ahead. He knows that many of the thefts must have been engineered by the owners. "Maybe they've sold them for parts." With the insurance settlement, "they pay off the bank and have a little left over. Maybe they pay somebody $100 to make the theft." The police are unlikely to spend much time trying to track such thefts down. In most cases, the motorcycle is stripped and rendered unidentifiable anyway. Without firm proof of fraud, Davies has no choice but to pay the claim.

"If you took this business *too* seriously," he says, "it could get depressing. There's a lot of pressure. You're the man in the middle. You're trying to satisfy your insured, maybe another company, additional people, *and* your own company." Death claims are both difficult and easy. First, there is the emotion. "You try not to intrude; you let them know you're trying to help." Still, there is a finality that is tidy. "From an adjuster's point of view, it's easier to settle a claim when there is a death. It's cut and dried. An injury could go on and on."

A more broad concern to him is the ever-expanding value of settlements. Today, most policyholders have replacement value coverage. That means if a television set, say, is stolen, the policy pays for a new one—no matter the age or condition of the original. "Insurance used to indemnify you," he says, "it put you back where you were. Now, with replacement value, a TV set that's eight years old and ruined by a lightning strike will be replaced with a new one. Insurance coverage broadens as time goes on, it doesn't lessen." Contents coverage, part of most home-owner policies, includes replacement value coverage for a nominal sum, usually $20 a year. If a policyholder's building or house is covered to 80 per cent of its value, any loss is repaired or replaced with no depreciation charge. Structural repairs are made even if the cost comes to more than what the building is worth. "Some people end up better off than they were."

Claims seem to come in cycles. In the spring, there were three incidents where people had broken necks. He had seen none for the previous five years. When economic times are tough, there tend to be more burglaries, as people are driven to theft to make ends meet. Also, when the housing market in Windsor went sour earlier in the 1980s, there was a jump in the number of house fires. Many of them were caused by arson. Owners who had speculated on real estate as prices had risen got caught as interest rates soared and demand dropped. Still, he does not find that dishonesty has grown greatly in his more than twenty years in the business. "The public is simply more aware of what they're entitled to under policies. The agent is explaining more, that's one part of it, but people are just more aware. The majority of people are not out to rip the insurance company off. There may be a *few* more dishonest people than twenty years ago, but I don't think the percentage is that much greater."

A phone call to Davies's office can signal anything from a stolen bicycle to the report of an accident that may result in a lawsuit and disability payments running for years and totalling hundreds of thousands of dollars. The bumps and bruises of life are trotted to his door, from the tiny to the tragic. Because of its proximity to Detroit and the pervasive American attitude of going to court for every nickel, Windsor is a claims-conscious city. Windsor policyholders are more likely than most Canadians to call the claims office at the slightest hint that a loss can be covered by their policies. As a result, about 1,800 claims annually find their way to his busy fifth-floor downtown office. Three other employees toil with him there. One, Dave Saunders, is a field representative. He deals directly with the thirty agents, looking after their needs. Since each of them deals with several insurance companies, Saunders tries to get the agents to direct business to Dominion. He also offers advice on specific risks that an agent may be considering. Joan Mills is a claims examiner who handles claims that can be processed by telephone. The secretary is Evelyn Savage.

Mills is a long-time insurance employee—twenty-eight years for various firms. She approaches the whole business with a certain sense of humour. "The claims aren't crazy, it's the people. There are a lot of crazy people out there. And at some time or another, they all have claims. Some of them are just lonesome and want to talk to someone. You quickly move from the claim to [talking about] the children or the grandchildren." Today's oddball call involves a woman who fell asleep watching television and awoke at quarter to five in the morning to what she thought was the sound of someone trying to break down her front door. She called police, but no one was there when they arrived. This is not, she tells Mills, the first such incident. She lives alone and is convinced that a neighbour is hiring kids to come to harass her in various ways. She says she scared them away, but she wants a new and stronger door, one with a peephole to see who is doing these things to her. Mills handles about two-thirds of the calls, the ones that require little investigation or travelling outside the office. Davies looks after the rest.

Davies was born in Saskatchewan, left school after completing Grade Twelve, and moved to Ontario to find a job. After a few years in wholesale plumbing and finance company work, he joined a U.S. insurance firm as a claims adjuster in Detroit. He worked for two companies there for seven years, then moved to an independent adjuster, Morden & Helwig Ltd. in Windsor. Detroit, says Davies, "is a faster track." Too fast for him because it offered too little time for what he regarded as the proper job. "You really don't have too much time for people, and that's the way it has to be, or you wouldn't have time for anybody."

He joined Dominion of Canada in 1980. In all, he has spent twenty-one years in claims adjusting. He lives with his wife, an employee of CKLW radio, twenty miles outside Windsor in Belle

River. Their house, with its sand beach, backs onto Lake St. Clair, where he relaxes in his twenty-two-foot 170-horsepower cruiser on day trips or sails his Hobie 16. They have no children. Dominion offers the usual employee benefits—life insurance, disability, a dental plan, and three weeks' holidays after two years. The only additional perk is a savings on home and auto insurance. Because he buys direct from his employer, he saves the agent's commission, which ranges from 10 to 20 per cent, depending on the policy. There are no productivity awards or incentive programs like those found on the sales side. He makes $30,000 a year.

In his five years with Dominion of Canada General, he has never been to head office in Toronto. His direct supervision comes from London (one of ten branch offices in the company), and he travels there twice a year for seminars, usually on policy coverage or legal changes that affect his job. "The law is so complex," he says, "that it's hard to keep up with everything. You'd have to be a genius." When he began, for example, insurance payments to passengers covered only medical expenses. Anything else required gross negligence. Today, he points out, under Ontario's Family Law Reform Act, courts are awarding damages even to people who were not involved in the original accident. A claim on an injured child, for example, can include monetary damages for loss of love and affection by the child's grandmother.

The morning begins at eight-thirty with an eight-inch pile of files to be handled. They are among the 200 cases he has active at any one time. Some run as far back as 1980, usually not settled yet because lawyers and courts are involved. The files, some two inches thick, are choked with medical reports, police reports, appraisers' reports, statements taken from witnesses and the insured, correspondence with head office—all the supporting documentation that would be required if a case goes to court, as do about 5 per cent of his claims.

The files are stacked strategically around the office—on the desk, in his in-basket, on the dictaphone, on a nearby shelf—all at various stages of completion. He likes to split his day between the office and the field, checking out claims. He likes to get out because that's where the job is the most fun, where there is freedom from routine. Paperwork can be a chore—and more. "Paperwork can become a monster if you don't keep up with it. It can be boring. There are days when I say, 'What am I doing in this business?' But you know—you're helping people."

There can be excitement, too. "The thing is, you don't know when you're heading out what you're going to find at the other end. You prepare for it in your mind, but then what you thought about may not apply. Sometimes there are complications and you have to deal with them. It can be exciting." The excitement has never included a proposition from a female client. "You've heard about housewives coming to the door in negligées? Well, it doesn't happen. Sometimes you'll think you're getting the come-on, but you have to be careful. I often wonder what would happen if somebody phoned your company to complain. What would you do?"

Every claim comes with its legal-size manila file folder containing all the relevant documents. Most are white, but some are blue. The blue are "facility" files, drivers who cannot get insurance on a regular basis—because of earlier mishaps or misdemeanours—but must have insurance to drive under Ontario law. Premiums are paid by the driver into the Facility Association account. Dominion is one of twelve servicing carriers. Dominion, for example, would issue the cheque for a claims payment but money would be paid out of the Facility Association account. If there is a shortfall in the account, the industry makes it up on a prorated basis.

The first file this morning is a thin one. A phone call the day before from an agent had alerted Davies to an accident. An oncoming driver had made a left turn in front of a policyholder. The property damage is severe, although no one was hurt. If the vehicle had still been drivable, the owner could have taken it to one of the drive-in appraisal centres run by the industry. There are two in Windsor, sixty-three across the country. In this case, the car had been towed away and the appraiser called to take a look at the damages.

If passengers had suffered personal injuries or if a pedestrian had been struck, Davies likely would have investigated personally. Injuries mean that the insuring company's costs could skyrocket as medical claims and damages for pain and suffering are paid. If the Dominion's insured was impaired, his collision coverage wouldn't apply. He'd have to pay for damages to his car himself. A breathalyzer test is usually required as proof. Further, although the policy says impaired driving negates claim payment, in practice, a conviction is usually required before the company refuses to pay. Third-party coverage—for persons other than the insured who have been injured or suffered damages—is not affected. In other words, innocent victims are not penalized by the insurance company even if its policyholder was impaired. Sometimes, Davies will investigate himself. In the case of an injured pedestrian, for example, Davies would want to see where the actual damage occurred on the car. "Where did the pedestrian get hit—on the right or left of the vehicle? It can affect our liability, depending on how much time our insured had to react." If a pedestrian had stepped off a curb and been hit almost immediately by the front corner of the car, the insured would be less at fault than if the pedestrian had been crossing the road and was struck in the middle of the car. In this case, however, there was no injury, no need for Davies's personal attention, so an appraiser was hired.

The situation turns out to be cut-and-dried. Yesterday, he spoke to the adjuster representing the other insured's driver. The other company has accepted blame. That adjuster is a woman, one of a quickly growing number in the business. "Women were rare when I was breaking into the business," says Davies. "Even ten years ago. Now, they are very commonplace. In Windsor, it's probably fifty-fifty." Only among the independent adjusters, those who don't work as employees for a specific company, do males still predominate. In Windsor, among the dozen independents, there are only two women.

Davies has been given the file by secretary Savage, with the newly arrived appraiser's report included. It runs six pages, includes four Polaroid colour photos of the vehicle, and lists repairs that the appraiser says will cost $6,700. Also included are three quotes from used-car dealers showing that the same vehicle could be purchased from their lots for a similar amount. Clearly, the vehicle is a total write-off. It would cost as much to repair as to replace. As a result, the appraiser also includes three prices from junk-yards for the vehicle's scrap value—$1,500.

Davies accepts the appraiser's report without question and phones the agent who sold the policy. "It's a total loss," he reports. "[The appraiser] puts its value at $6,700 and sales tax. I don't know how that will go down with our insured." If the value is not accepted, the insured can hire his own recognized appraiser to do a second appraisal. The first appraisal, paid for by the company, cost $82. If the second valuation came in at a few hundred dollars more, that appraisal would be accepted. If the difference was much larger, say $1,000, the cost of a third appraisal would be shared by the insured and the company. Because the other driver has admitted fault, the damages will be paid by his insurance company. Rather than make the insured wait for payment, Dominion will pay its insured, then claim the amount (less salvage value) from the second company. Davies calls the insured; the $6,700 amount is agreeable. As soon as the insured signs a proof-of-loss form and sends in his ownership and the vehicle key, payment can be processed. Because payment is under $10,000, and therefore within Davies's authority, no approval is needed by his supervisor in London 120 miles away.

When the cheque is sent, the insured's banker will also be named on it, because the policy information shows that there was a loan on the vehicle. The insured presents the cheque for cashing, the bank takes its share and gives the rest to the insured—or may continue the loan, if the insured is buying another vehicle. Because fault was clearly established and the appraiser's views accepted, the matter is handled quickly and the insured will have a cheque in his hands within seventy-two hours of the accident. Davies's company will then go after the other driver's insurance company to reimburse itself. "That," says Davies, tossing the thin file into the out-basket, "is as simple as they come."

While he expects no problems in collecting from the other company because liability has been admitted by the other driver, not all companies pay quickly. "Some companies look at ways to *provide* coverage; others look at it differently. They ask: 'Is there some way of avoiding payment?'" He is reluctant to name specific companies—he has to work with them all—but he does tell two anecdotes. When he worked in Detroit, there was a body shop that had actually posted a sign reading: "We don't work for Allstate." Another time, he visited a body shop in Windsor. It had a guard dog. The owner said to Davies: "Say A-l-l-s-t-a-t-e." Davies couldn't understand why the owner had spelled out the word until he spoke it and the dog came bounding towards him, barking ferociously. He'd been trained to respond that way.

A phone call comes in on a long-running file. A woman missed the bottom three steps coming down an inside flight of stairs a year earlier. Dominion supplies liability insurance to the building's out-of-town owner. The stairs were well lit, carpeted, and in good repair, but the handrail ended three steps from the bottom. Her injuries have been slow to heal and may require plastic surgery. Although she had used the stairs many times, and should have known where the handrail ended, she is elderly and not agile. She hired a lawyer and is suing the building's owner. "The lawyer seems to think it's worth a lot of money," Davies is saying to the caller. "He's got his head in the clouds." The caller is the claims adjuster for another insurance company, which sold liability insurance to the tenant occupying the building, whom the woman was visiting when the accident happened. Adds Davies: "We agree that we should have some responsibility. How much we don't know yet."

The lawyer has asked for $29,000. The dispute is not just about the amount, but how to split it between the tenant she visited and the owner of the building, because under Ontario law both have responsibilities. The two insurance companies feel the woman was at some fault, too—called contributory negligence—because everything was in good repair. They recognize, however, that the rail should have run the full length of the stairs. To date, the adjuster for the tenant's insurance company has been handling the negotiations with the woman's lawyer on behalf of both insurance companies.

The two insurance adjusters agree, on behalf of their companies, to split a lesser settlement amount than demanded. Both independently have come up with an offer in the $10,000–$12,000 range. Davies has calculated general damages at $10,000, special damages at $5,500. Then he halved that figure to take her 50-per-cent contributory negligence into account. To that $7,500, he added the cost of medical reports supplied by her lawyer ($800), pre-judgment interest, and the lawyer's 15 per cent. He then divided that figure by two since Dominion would share it with the other company.

"We would be agreeable to contributing in the area of $5,000 to $6,000 to settle," says Davies, referring to Dominion's half. "There is an area of controversy. We may have a problem on contributory negligence. We may have to revise upwards, but [the lawyer] was too high to begin with." Davies is concerned that the matter not go to court. First, there is the cost of hiring a lawyer; second, who knows what a court might say about damages? He cautions the other adjuster to try for a settlement in the $10,000–$12,000 range they have discussed. "But if we're within $1,000," he adds, "let's not lose sight of that." The other adjuster will take the offer to the lawyer.

Davies knows if the matter goes to court the chances of the woman being found 50-per-cent responsible for the fall are slight. "When we say 50 per cent, we'll probably be fortunate to get away with it," he explains. "Courts are plaintiff-oriented. If they see an opportunity to supply her with something, they'll do it. I would doubt that it will settle for $12,000, but my sense is that another $1,000 or $2,000 will settle it." Davies wants to balance the proposed settlement off against what the court might find. The court may award more damages, the company costs will be higher—and the settlement may be a year or more finally reaching the woman. He blames the lawyers for the delay. Since the courts allow payment of pre-judgment interest, the lawyers are in no hurry. According to Davies, the lawyers say, "My client is getting interest on this money, so the value of the claim is always going up."

Davies does not want to go to court with this case or any other. Emotions can play a part when a jury decides on the size of the settlement. He shuddered, for example, at the end of *The Verdict*, starring Paul Newman, when the jury returned, found the hospital guilty, and wondered if the court set any limit on the amount of damages that could be assessed for the malpractice committed. The judge said there was no limit.

As with all claims, the first thing Davies did when he heard of the claim for the fall was to set up a reserve, an amount of money that the company sets aside when the claim is first presented so that funds are available when settlement occurs. In the case of the vehicle accident, he didn't establish a reserve because the claim was taken care of quickly. In the case of the woman on the stairs, he originally set a reserve of $5,000, a figure he knew was conservative, but he wanted to get something set aside. As he gathered information in the months since, he revised the reserve upwards. Now, under his worst-case scenario, it will go to court and she will be awarded $25,000. After cutting that by half for her contributory negligence, adding $4,000 for her legal fees and Dominion's, he has rounded off the reserve at $17,000. The figure is fed into the office computer, along with any other reserves taken that day, so that Dominion can make daily changes to its reserve requirements. (A few weeks later, the lawyer agrees to settle for $11,000. Dominion pays its share, $5,500, exactly where Davies hoped it would settle out.)

Joan Mills brings in a claim that has been telephoned in and looks interesting enough to pass on to Davies. She points to a particular box on the form and says to Davies, "Look at the time." The accident happened about a quarter to two in the morning. The immediate suspicion is that the driver may have been drinking. Davies phones for more information from the insured. The questions flow for about five minutes as Davies tries to reconstruct the accident on paper and discover what claims there might be from injured parties. Did the police investigate? Was anyone hurt? Were you wearing a seat-belt? Had there been any drinking? Have you been to the doctor? Will you be off work?

What he learns is this: the insured had been at a party all evening, stayed to help clean up, then drove a friend home. They decided to visit someone at one-thirty but passed the house, so the driver stopped the car on the right-hand side of the road and backed across the road while turning around to head back the way he had come. His vehicle struck a car parked on the other side. He is claiming significant damage to his own vehicle, but says there was none to the other. The owner of the other vehicle, who had been visiting nearby, happened along and agreed at the time that damage to his car wasn't sufficient to call police to the scene. The insured didn't call police himself for thirty-six hours. He was given a ticket for failing to report an accident. Davies arranges to visit the insured at his home, to see the car and get a statement.

Davies hangs up the phone, rubs his chin, and says of the tale, "That sounds a little peculiar. It rang a couple of bells." He ticks off the unusual circumstances. "It happened early in the morning. There was extensive damage to his car and none to the other. He didn't get the name of the driver of the other car. He's now claiming injuries to himself and his passenger." Injuries, says Davies, are unlikely when a car is backing up at low speed. Alcohol use could cancel claims payment, but there is no proof. "You're not going to get his friends at the party to say he was falling-down drunk. The potential problem is in the injury to the passenger."

Davies moves quickly to telephone the passenger. He wants a statement from him and arranges a meeting in the claims office later in the week. "He's saying he's shaken up and has a sore back. We want to talk to him before legal involvement—that could cost us more." Davies also listens carefully to the passenger's version of the incident. "The story is the same," he says afterwards, "but the words weren't identical." Precise phrase repetition could indicate they'd carefully rehearsed a version. "You look for key words," says Davies.

Another letter in his mail tidies up an old claim. A lawyer has written to discontinue an action against one of Davies's clients. A woman claimed she had swallowed an object in a soft drink bottle and became ill as a result. Dominion of Canada insured the local bottler. Tests had established that there was mould growth in the bottle. Asks Davies, "Who's to say something didn't get in the bottle after it was opened?" In fact, there was no firm proof either way. "We weren't there, but you have to assume there was some problem or she wouldn't have gone to all this trouble." Her lawyer had claimed $2,000 in damages; Davies countered that he would pay $500 "for its nuisance value." The lawyer suggested $1,000 and said he would recommend settlement to his client. She has accepted. Says Davies, adding the lawyer's letter to the file: "We try to exercise good judgment and good common sense."

A file at hand describes a year-old accident where there has been little activity. "This was a case where we rear-ended a car...," he begins as he tells the story, using, as he often does, the first-person plural—"we." It is an interesting usage. It is not the royal "we" that suggests some *noblesse oblige* view of life, where the rich and the poor alike are together, when in reality they are not. It is not the editorial "we" favoured by newspaper editors who try to imply that the view they are propounding is somehow shared by all. Nor is it a family "we," for not even the most eager corporate relations officer would make a case for such an extended family. There is a unity in the usage, however, the feeling that whatever happens to a policyholder happens to the company. After all, the company pays, it has a vested and financial interest in the actions and mishaps of its insureds. It is an involvement that goes beyond the contract, a tie that binds claimant, adjuster, and company together.

That does not mean, of course, that everyone's word in this union is accepted. The file describes an accident where a woman was injured and hired a lawyer, but has yet to file a claim. After time had passed with no word from the lawyer, Davies hired a private investigator at $40 an hour plus expenses to do what's known as an "activities report" and find out what was going on in the woman's life. "Maybe we've got a serious injury on our hands here," he argues by way of explaining his action. "Maybe we need to set up a higher reserve." The six-page report includes a list of people interviewed, a credit check, and details about her activities, ranging from hanging out the wash to visits to her chiropractor. Apparently she wore a collar for a while, but seems to have needed no further treatment, nor has she presented any disability claims. Davies is baffled as to why it is still outstanding. "She seems to have recovered quite well," he says. "The lawyer's attitude is the longer it takes, the more he seems to be doing for her."

He dictates a letter to the lawyer asking for a medical report and statement of claim. Davies also revises the reserve. It had been $6,500, close to the usual $4,000–$6,000 settlement for whiplash suffered for a year. Since this injury occurred almost fifteen months earlier, he assumes the settlement might run higher. He will await the lawyer's report. The activities report at least lets him know she is mobile and apparently carrying out her normal routines as a housewife. In this activities report, as with most, neighbours are a good source of information. "Neighbours will say a lot," says Davies. "It amazes me. Of course, sometimes they'll have an axe to grind, too. You have to be careful."

Davies sometimes makes check-up visits himself. He chuckles, then tells of such a stop the previous week. He arrived unannounced at the house of a woman on disability as the result of an accident. During the three months since her accident, Davies had urged her several times to retain a lawyer to handle her claim and negotiate a settlement. He knocked on the door, but there was no answer. As he began to leave, a woman who had apparently been visiting a neighbour came scurrying towards him. It was the woman he had gone to see. She told him she was not yet back to work. After their conversation, now that she knew who he was, she moved far more slowly. A few days later she phoned to say that she had gone back to work. The disability payments would no longer be needed.

Sometimes the search for information about a person on disability goes even further. In a recent case, the medical information supplied by a woman's lawyer didn't seem to corroborate the difficulty she said she was having with her arm. Davies hired Equifax Services Ltd. to carry out surveillance. They found that while receiving disability payments, she was also working elsewhere, in an outdoor location. Equifax produced a two-hour videotape that showed her bending, turning, and lifting—easily carrying out functions she had previously claimed were too difficult because of her condition. Because Davies has no video unit at the office, he took the tape home to view the evidence collected. Watching it made him a feel a little uneasy. "You almost feel guilty about observing someone who isn't aware of surveillance. It's a funny feeling." As a result, however, the disability payments were halted and a deposition taken from her, pending possible court action.

Disability claims seem to cause the most bizarre incidents. Once he visited an insured who had been injured on the job. "How many fingers did you lose?" asked Davies. The insured's hand was still bandaged. He replied, "They tell me I lost one. Would you like to see?" Davies couldn't figure out how he could say no. The insured produced a jar in which the finger had been preserved by the hospital.

The mail brings other news. A 1981 accident is finally going before the U.S. courts. The incident is being handled for Davies by a local independent adjuster in the state where the accident occurred. Davies's insured had caused an accident. The other driver had suffered injuries, including whiplash. A lawyer had been hired and was claiming damages of $8,000. The figure had seemed high to Davies, but not knowing well the settlement levels in that state, he was relying heavily on his hired adjuster. In the last conversation with him, Davies had suggested he try for a settlement in the $3,000–$4,000 range. He had given him the range so that the local adjuster could start at $3,000 and move up to $4,000—while the injured party's lawyer, he hoped, moved down from $8,000.

The report has arrived from the local adjuster. He has inexplicably offered to settle for $1,500. While the lowball offer did bring the claim down to $5,000 from $8,000, the lawyer is now threatening to issue a writ and take the matter to court. Davies does not want to go to court. He would then have to hire a local lawyer, at an estimated $1,000. Add that to the local adjuster's bill, already mounting at $40 an hour, and the value of the claim keeps going higher. Also, the amount the court might award is unpredictable.

Davies picks up the phone and calls the local adjuster. "We want to avoid litigation," he says. "We would be agreeable to paying $4,000. You make contact again. Since he's indicated he's issuing a writ, let's conclude things rather than go further. After the writ's served, it won't get cheaper. I'd appreciate it if you made contact and see if you can resolve it up to $4,000. It may be more than it's really worth but there's a practical side to it, too. If we give him the offer up front, maybe he'll come around."

After Davies gets off the phone, he wonders out loud about the local adjuster. "He seemed a bit lackadaisical. He didn't seem to be right on top of it." He scribbles a note in the file, outlining the content of the call. A full report, to be typed and included, will await the local adjuster's next report. (Within a few weeks, the incident is settled. The lawyer agrees to accept $3,000, fully $1,000 below Davies's ceiling. He is pleased that the local adjuster started lower than Davies originally proposed. ("He was wise to start at $1,500.")

The files he has been working on all morning are now spread around the office. Those to which he has added a memo are stacked on top of the dictaphone for the secretary, who will type out the additional material. Others rest on the credenza, awaiting further word that is expected soon. A third batch of files are in a desk tray to be refiled and brought forward again when further activity is expected. He gathers up another bundle to take with him for the afternoon of rounds. Half a dozen stops are planned. His days usually begin around eight-thirty, after a twenty-minute drive from his home. Most days are over by four-thirty, although there's the occasional evening when an event like a fire demands his presence. Another task that would entail working in an evening would be visiting a witness favourable to his cause who could not be interviewed at any other time. Weekends are usually free.

As he is about to leave today, a call comes regarding a claim he saw the day before. An institution suffered water damage after two summer rainstorms. Water poured in through the roof, requiring two days to clean up and painting worth $2,495. They claim that roofers working at the time damaged the roof when loading the material onto the roof, thus allowing rain to seep in. Because the claimants cleaned up the water themselves, they are making no claim for maintenance costs.

Davies had visited the site and concluded that there had been damage before as a result of leaks—that's why the roof-work was ordered. As a result, he doesn't feel that Dominion should pay for the full $2,495 paint job. He has offered $2,000. "If they insist on it," he said earlier, "I'll pay the $2,495. I could settle for $2,000 or I could settle for $2,495. Who's to say who's right? Only a court can decide. At this point, it's a question of judgment and common sense." They phone to say they will accept the $2,000 settlement. He has saved the company $495—but he doesn't think of it as a savings. "I could spend the $500 and no one [at head office] would criticize me, but I don't consider that I've saved the company $500. I just consider it's a just settlement in the circumstances. There was probably damage before."

This is the very centre of his work—trying to balance the claim with the reality, trying to reconstruct an event he did not see, an event for which there are often no witnesses, then pay out a compensating sum that is adequate. "You don't want to do something you couldn't live with from the point of view of your conscience. If you did that, the job would be too much of a drag. On the other hand, you don't want anybody to take advantage of you. I'm not a tough negotiator—but I'm no push-over, either." Some adjusters apply almost mathematical formulae to their claims. Windsor once employed such an adjuster. "He's dead now," says Davies, "but he used to split the difference on the claims." Whatever was claimed, whatever was offered, he simply came down the middle. "They called him 'fifty-fifty Charlie.'

"Someone might say to me, 'I'll settle for $500,' and I know they could get $1,000. I'm not going to offer them $1,000, because suddenly $1,000 is not enough [for them]. You've done your good deed and suddenly you've got a problem. Same thing with lawyers. One lawyer will settle a claim for $2,000, and another will settle the same claim for $2,500."

Among the stops that day is the site of a house fire that occurred two months earlier. The family is still not back in the house, awaiting repairs. Davies had been on the scene while the firemen were still there. His initial concern was how it got started. "We're always very interested in the cause. We want to make sure there's no mystery about the cause." In this case, there was no hint of arson. The house had been struck by lightning while the family was out. The fire had started in the electrical system. But his recollection is not just of detail and damages, there is an emotional memory still very much at the front of his mind as he describes the home-owner's reaction that night. "He's a big strong man, but he had tears in his eyes."

Damage was severe enough that the family moved out to allow repairs and renovations. Davies offered to pay up to $600 a month for an apartment while the work was being done, but they chose to stay close and live with neighbours. A living allowance of $150 a week (an amount arrived at by mutual agreement) is being paid to them anyway—no receipts required. He gave them an advance of $2,000 immediately and helped with contractor's estimates. Total costs may run to $20,000. All will be paid by their policy.

Renovations are coming along, but slowly. The family is still housed by neighbours, unlikely to return home for weeks yet. The place still reeks of smoke. The contractor didn't even show up for ten days earlier in the month, but work is under way now. The owner is worried about his swimming pool. It was undamaged by the fire, but because electricity was off for a time, there was no power to run the filter. The water is green with algae. The implication is that the pool clean-up will become part of the claim. Davies makes no commitment.

Down the street, he talks about the situation. Full damages are not yet known. "That loss isn't done with yet," he says. "We haven't gotten down to the hard negotiating areas." Cost of new kitchen cupboards is obvious, but furniture clean-up, for example, may not restore items to their original condition. There will be vigorous discussion about value. The pool, however, is a different matter. Davies doesn't feel a responsibility for its clean-up. Although the fire did shut off power for a while, Davies feels it was restored in the house in time to run an extension cord to the pool to run the ½-horsepower motor of the filter pump. "If he's going to pursue that, it might be a bit far-fetched." Damages suffered after an event are not as readily paid by a policy. "An insured has an obligation to protect his premises from further loss." Still, he is filled with admiration for the insured, for both their own efforts at clean-up and the attitude towards the time the work is taking. "I'm surprised that he's as patient as he is," says Davies. "I'm not sure I'd be that patient." (They moved in a month later; total pay-out by Dominion General ran to $30,000.)

There is a quick stop at another house to make sure that a pool liner has been installed. A $1,200 claim was paid after a tree branch fell in a windstorm, damaging the original liner. He wants to make sure that the money paid out was actually used for the purpose stated. While there, he eyeballs the house from the outside just to check that it's properly insured. His file shows that it is insured for $63,000. He estimates its size at 1,000 square feet plus the garage and concludes that the coverage is correct. If it had been insured for, say, $50,000, he would have passed word back through the system that the agent might want to re-evaluate it with the owner and increase the coverage. "If it was overinsured, say for $85,000, I wouldn't be as concerned as if it were too low," he says. The trouble comes when there isn't enough insurance to cover a loss. If the house looked to be in poor shape and was situated in a bad area, he might recommend when the policy came due that it not be renewed. "If it looked like a bad risk, I'd report it. If it's a high risk, from a purely selfish viewpoint, I don't need any [potential] problems like that."

While he's out, he stops in at a body shop. There, a parked car was damaged, the car's owner says, by tar that was being sprayed on the roof of the shop. The white convertible roof needs to be replaced. Davies's client is the roof contractor, who says that materials were brought up the back of the building and were nowhere near where the car was parked. Davies talks to a body shop employee who points out where the car was parked—about twenty feet west of the building. Davies cannot see how tar would fly that far. He decides to phone the local weather office to see which way the wind was blowing on the day his contractor client was working on the site. A west wind would have carried any tar overspray away from the car. "If the wind was blowing from the west, we'll have to resist a little bit, but if it was blowing from the east, there's a good possibility [we'll pay]." His call to the weather office confirms that the wind that day was blowing from the southeast and northeast at up to twenty kilometres per hour—sufficient to blow tar around and from the right direction to carry it west to where the car was parked. (In the end, Dominion compromises and agrees to pay half the cost of the damaged top.)

Next stop is at the house of the driver involved in the accident after the party. Davies sits at the kitchen table with the insured and his wife. He listens while the insured describes the evening and the accident, prodding him with questions, probing for more information. After forty-five minutes, Davies has written out a two-and-a-half-page handwritten statement. He reads it out loud, and the insured signs it. The insured is off work and has already seen a doctor about a sore back. Davies leaves him disability claims forms to complete. He also inspects the car and says an appraiser will come take a look, too.

Afterwards, as he drives down the street, he reflects on the story he has just been told. "I don't think I'm hearing it all. I suspect he got into this accident and didn't call police because he was drunk. I don't know if he was impaired, but I guess he didn't want to take the chance. And I guess if I was in the same situation, I might do the same thing." Reconstructing an event after the fact is one of the most difficult aspects of Davies's job. "It's very difficult to go into that room and find out what happened. I suspect drinking was involved. The area of real concern is the passenger. That's where our potential exposure would come from."

He will interview the passenger, but knows he is unlikely to say that the insured was drunk. A passenger has a responsibility not to get into a car if he feels that the driver is impaired. If the passenger sued and the insurance company was able to establish that the driver was impaired, the company's liability would be reduced. There are sometimes similar considerations regarding the passenger's use of a seat-belt. For a Dominion General insured who is the driver, however, not using a seat-belt doesn't affect his own disability, medical, or death benefits, even if expenses are higher as a result. If another driver is at fault, that driver's company might lessen the payment amount. For a passenger in a car driven by a Dominion General policyholder, the company will lower any liability payment if the passenger was not using a seat-belt.

There is another element to Davies's thinking. It is not all just suspicion that a story is incomplete. "If our insured is being truthful, you can't browbeat him. You have to treat the policyholder fairly unless there is strong evidence to the contrary." He would not, for example, set out to interview all the other party-goers to establish the amount that the insured drank that night. "You don't want to stir up a bunch of bad feelings and hurt somebody's reputation. You might have suspicions, but that's all they are.

"The reality," concludes Davies, "is that in the end we'll pay his collision claim, his disability claim, the passenger's disability, and something extra because he was injured." Davies will do some further checking with the person the insured stopped to see early in the morning, "just to make sure we're not dealing with a total fabrication. But if he was going to make up a story, this seems an unusual one to make up. I mean he could just say that somebody in the parking lot hit him in the ass end. Still, there are some odd circumstances. The police weren't called. It isn't your typical accident." (Over the next few days, Davies interviewed the person the insured was to visit and the passenger. The passenger said he suffered no injuries and would not be pursuing any claim against the insured. Everything checked out, so Davies paid the $1,500 collision claim.)

On the way to the next visit, the last one of the day, he passes a pair of snowmobiles sitting on a trailer in a driveway near the road. The owner's house is several hundred feet away. "There's a couple of snowmobiles parked out where they're easy to steal." He drives up to the home of a young man injured in an accident three years earlier. He hasn't worked since and will be in a wheelchair for the rest of his life. He has been receiving $140 a week in disability payment—the maximum allowed under an auto insurance policy. To date, his policy has paid out about $14,000 to cover medical bills, therapy, and a car fitted with hand controls. There is, however, a $25,000 limit in all policies (exclusive of the weekly disability payments), and that total must be claimed in the four years following the accident. Now that the medical expenses are nearly complete, he wants renovations done to his house to make it wheelchair-accessible. Davies approves $10,000 in expenses that will be included in the $25,000 amount. The visit is emotionally difficult. Davies is silent for a long while after leaving the house. On the one hand, he is pleased that the man's insurance policy is helping put his life into some order, but the impact of the insured's condition and his courage have a searing, emotional impact. Davies is drained.

At the end of this day, like all days, what Davies wants is simply his share of victories, times when he has made the system work for everyone. As for his own life-style, he knows that there would be more income for him in sales. He also knows, however, that the failure rate among sales agents is high. Still, income isn't everything; he likes claims adjusting, even though he knows he's not one of the most understood members of society. That Sunday, his wife had gone to church and reported to him that a claims adjuster figured in the sermon. According to the anecdote, the adjuster had a scam going in which he had agreed to pay out too much to contractors doing insurance work in return for a share of the ill-gotten gains.

Davies knows such a deal is illegal and he disapproves of it—yet he can almost understand. "I can identify with that," he says. "The public thinks we're deceitful, that we're pulling the wool over their eyes to save our company's money." For Davies, the charge hurts; he feels that he works for both the policyholder and the company. "There are occasions when I've been more generous than I needed to be." Those times, however, have been to the advantage of the claimant, not himself. "Sometimes I'll pay somebody more for one area than I know they deserve because I'm paying them less in another. I might pay for a rug that wasn't there before because I know that I'm making it up on contents. It all balances out. That's claims *adjusting*. It isn't an exact science. I know there are times when I've paid too much, and I know there are times when I've paid too little. You win some and you lose some. You like to think you win your share."

CHAPTER FIFTEEN

ALL IN THE FAMILY
The Mutual Life Assurance Co. of Canada

J OHN PANABAKER spins around in the hotel lobby, taking in all he can see with the skilled eye of a bell captain. Are all the guests being served? Is the brass on the mail chute brilliant enough? Is there any debris that should be cleared away? Shouldn't that visiting politician be greeted? Panabaker stretches himself to his full six-foot height and surveys with proprietorial pride the comings and goings at the Hotel Newfoundland in St. John's. As chairman of The Mutual Life Assurance Company of Canada, of Waterloo, Ont., he has a particular interest in the surroundings because Mutual owns 50 per cent of the hotel. Panabaker attended the sod-turning ceremony in 1980, but this is his first look at the finished product. He is clearly pleased with what he sees. Finally he takes a breath and says, "This is the first time I've stayed in a hotel I own half of. I feel like Conrad Hilton." The legendary hotel-owner could not have been prouder of the surroundings than Panabaker. As he pokes into the kitchen and visits the two squash courts, the night club, and the 150-year-old olive tree imported live from Jerusalem, a smile encircles his face and he grins like a child inspecting his Hallowe'en loot.

Opened in 1982, the hotel, managed by CN Hotels, overlooks St. John's Harbour where ferries, container ships, and fisheries research vessels are moored. Of the $28 million it cost, $22 million was put up by Mutual, $16 million in the form of a mortgage at 13.625 per cent for fifteen years and $6 million as an equity investment. The other investors are the CN pension fund and a local firm, Baine, Johnston & Co. Ltd., who put in $3 million each. The opening night in December 1982 got the hotel off to a dubious start. The fun began when Chief Justice Arthur Mifflin of the Newfoundland Supreme Court arrived by car. Mifflin was standing in as the Queen's representative because the province's lieutenant-governor was out of the city. The chief justice refused to get out of his car because the hotel's manager, Pat O'Callaghan, was not at curbside to meet him. O'Callaghan was in the Flag Deck room, where the receiving line was welcoming the 400 black-tie guests prior to the reception there and in the adjoining Garden Room. The protocol problem was solved when an assistant manager was dispatched to meet the chief justice and escort him and his party, an aide and their wives, to their reserved suite. The evening of tense incidents had only begun.

The chief justice sulked in the room, refusing to come down for a time because he had not been properly met. But there was an even worse slight to come. O'Callaghan had been told in advance by the province's protocol officer that while the chief justice would be representing the lieutenant-governor, he would not participate in the opening ceremonies. Accordingly, he was not seated at the head table. Instead, another table hard by the head table, one of the rounds of eight and ten set up for the dinner, was designated as his. When the chief justice came down and learned he was not to be at the head table, he became apopleptic.

O'Callaghan left the receiving line to greet him, and a heated discussion about the seating arrangements ensued. O'Callaghan explained the reason for the seating arrangement and said he would have the head table extended so the chief justice could be included. The chief justice refused, saying sniffily, "I've been poorly treated as the Queen's representative." Maurice LeClair, then president of Canadian National, joined the fray. The discussion continued until O'Callaghan, seeing that the chief justice was not to be mollified, made to leave, saying: "I've got other guests, I'm sorry if you're not prepared to have the head table extended. I can't really do anything more at this stage. The other guests must come first. The show must go on." "This is not the end of it," the Chief Justice retorted. "You'll hear from me." And he swept out to his car, never to return.

Next to come under fire were the speaking arrangements. Mutual had been taking a low profile on the occasion, and had sent president and chief operating officer Jack Masterman to represent the company officially. His dinner-time speech was a brief three minutes. Henry Collingwood, owner of Baine, Johnston & Co., spoke a little longer, about ten minutes. CN, however, with only a 25-per-cent interest, put up two speakers—LeClair and CN chairman Jack Horner. Each of them ran about ten minutes, Horner praising the virtues of railroads, an unpopular subject in Newfoundland, where passenger trains have been replaced by buses. Premier Brian Peckford had cancelled at the last minute, sending energy minister Bill Marshall in his place. O'Callaghan's instructions from the premier's office were that Marshall did not wish to speak. Marshall thought otherwise. After the dinner, he cornered O'Callaghan and tore strips off the already sore back of the manager. "Goddamn bunch of Liberals here," Marshall said. "There's no way a Conservative can get a word in." The evening ended just as it began, with a protocol kerfuffle. For Mutual Life the whole evening, with its lengthy speeches by lesser owners, was a little disconcerting. "I know we wanted to be low-profile," commented Masterman afterwards, "but that was ridiculous."

By contrast, this October 1984 visit to St. John's by Panabaker, chairman of Mutual, goes like clockwork. The trip is a self-proclaimed public relations tour. He will visit local agents, speak to a service club, inspect the hotel for the first time, visit the premier, and make a few other calls on local businesspeople. Panabaker is the missionary out thumping for his cause in the outposts of his vast parish. He doesn't just want their homage, he needs their hearts. The message is less than eternal life, but it does promise death without guilt towards unprovided-for loved ones.

To offer such heavenly promises, Mutual has to store up assets here on earth, some $6 billion of them, including $2.3 billion in bonds, $1.5 billion in mortgages, and $364 million in stocks. Annual income, tithed from the premiums of more than 550,000 policyholders and earned from investment interest, runs to $1.7 billion. Total life insurance in force is $45 billion, and $63 million is paid out every month to various policyholders. The hotel is only one of Mutual's recent acquisitions and investments. In addition, it owns 5 per cent of Canada Trustco (Mutual's 1 million shares give Panabaker a seat on the board along with Manufacturers Life chairman Syd Jackson). There is $200 million worth of real estate across Canada, including, for example, a $14-million seven-storey office building at the corner of 4th Avenue S.W. and 4th Street S.W. in Calgary, joint ownership in a two-tower office complex in Islington, Ont., worth $65 million, and a $22-million shopping plaza in Orleans, near Ottawa.

In some cases, Mutual places constraints on its investments not even required by law. In 1982, Mutual bought Association Life from International Harvester for $15.3 million. When Mutual bought the U.S. company as a beach-head for its U.S. operations, it had to provide written assurances to the superintendent of insurance that the company would operate in the U.S. just as it does in Canada. In other words, Mutual couldn't get fancy and set up a downstream holding company to get into areas of operations in the U.S. from which it was prohibited in Canada. Also understood, however, through the informal conversations was that if Mutual *asked* for more freedom to operate in the U.S., the request would be granted. Any restraint Mutual felt in the U.S., then, was really of its own doing. It was typical of the company and its Presbyterian missionary, John Panabaker, to work within narrowed confines of its own creation.

John Panabaker was born in 1928 in Preston, Ont., and never strayed far from home. He went down the road to Hamilton to attend McMaster University on scholarship; up the road to work during the summers at Mutual in Waterloo. In that first summer, 1947, he worked as a mortgage clerk in the great hall of Mutual, just inside the front door, steps away from his office as chief executive officer in the building's front corner twenty-five years later. On graduation, he won the chancellor's gold medal as the outstanding member of his class and joined Mutual in the investment depart-ment. In the early years at Mutual, he did graduate work extramur-ally and received his master's degree in political economy from McMaster in 1954. His thesis: "A Survey of Canadian Postwar Monetary Policy, 1946–1951." His career rise at Mutual was swift. By 1954 he was assistant treasurer; he became executive assistant in 1960, vice-president and treasurer in 1964, executive vice-president in 1969, and a director in 1971. Panabaker was named president and chief executive officer in 1973, chairman in 1982.

Panabaker is six feet tall, weighs 185 pounds, and has white hair in the tonsured style of a monk. His eyeglasses are the size of small saucers. Above them, his eyebrows protrude, incongruously black, bouncing in syncopation when he talks. His life-style is modest. He lives in a five-bedroom home in Kitchener. He has a company Buick and borrows someone from the mail room to be an occasional chauffeur. He earns $200,000 a year. "This company," he declares, "has not produced a fortune for anyone."

One of his main interests is post-secondary education. He has been on the board of governors of McMaster University and served as its chairman. At the end of 1984, he joined the Ontario Council on University Affairs, a body advising the minister of colleges and universities in Ontario. To do so, he quit his positions on the boards of McMaster and the Toronto School of Theology (where he served with Liberal leader John Turner) because of possible conflicts of interest. He is also one of twenty-five chief executive officers—along with twenty-five university presidents—on the Corporate Higher Education Forum, a group run by two Concordia professors.

Panabaker's penchant is doodling. He will sit at meetings, either at Mutual or outside the office, and doodle during discussions. These are not just ordinary squiggles; he carries graph paper with him just for the purpose. His artistic efforts have become well and widely known in the industry. Says Jack Lyndon, president of the Insurance Bureau of Canada, "There'd be something wrong if I didn't see Panabaker doodling at meetings." Elaborate geometric creations, using up to three different colours of ink, they cover half to two-thirds of the page with squares built upon rectangles upon rhomboids upon who knows what, some filled in, others empty. "It's like smoking," says Panabaker. "It gives me something to do with my hands." Although he downplays their significance, he does keep the doodles in a file in his desk. The file has grown to be three inches thick since he began saving them in 1970, representing an endless parade of captured meetings, frustrated afternoons and lost time. Most are dated, some even have accompanying descriptive phrases. One, for example, dated April 26, 1982, was created while waiting for a meeting with Allan MacEachen. Written at the bottom, in Panabaker's flowing hand, is the poignant question: "Where is the Minister of Finance?" Once, someone collected a sampling of them and showed them to a psychologist to see what they said about the depths of Panabaker's soul. The expert's response: "He just laughed," says Panabaker. Similarly, he keeps a daily journal, writing constantly with a stout black fountain pen, putting thoughts and occurrences into the leather-bound black book that he carries in his briefcase. Everything that happens is entered, from the rate of inflation announced that day to the weather, a permanent record of the status of the world and the state of his mind, nineteen years lined up ready to be reread at any time. Perhaps he intends an autobiography, illustrated by doodles of the day. Whatever the plans, he keeps them to himself, having decided that the artistic side of his temperament is not an asset in the insurance business.

Panabaker is a religious man, a practising Presbyterian; it is a faith whose spare, no-nonsense type of worship suits him. "It's part of me, it's part of the way I operate," says Panabaker. "I try to follow the Golden Rule. As a Presbyterian, I am conscious of the imperfection of things, the fact that no structure is ever going to function perfectly. I accept imperfection in others. I get very impatient with people who have found the one true way—on social policy, for example. You are very conscious of the dangers of untrammelled power anywhere in the system."

On his Newfoundland tour, Panabaker is the preacher for the modern age, the Presbyterian out among the believers and the non-believers alike. The executive at Mutual—Panabaker, Masterman, and vice-president for individual insurance André Anderson—try to visit twenty of the seventy-five sales offices among them each year. This visit by Panabaker is typical. The twenty-six agents (only one is a woman) are gathered at a U-shaped table awaiting his arrival. St. John's is a high-producing branch. In 1983, its $130 million in sales volume was fifth highest in the country. In 1984 the economy was off and individual sales reached only $99.4 million. Even so, more than one-third of the agents will qualify for membership in the Million Dollar Round Table.

All Mutual's agents are career agents: they sell only for Mutual, and no one else can sell Mutual products. Management and the agents who sell the products—life and disability insurance, annuities, and mutual funds—are a young group and are less likely to be rigid traditionalists. Of the 1,132 Mutual agents across Canada, 60 per cent are between twenty-five and forty-five; 72 per cent of the field managers are under forty-five. The more important figure, the one that Mutual flaunts in the industry, is its four-year retention rate of 36 per cent, about twice as high as the industry average. Mutual also claims the best conservation rate among policies sold. Ninety per cent of all policies sold are still on the books thirteen months later, slightly better than the industry average of 87 per cent.

The average annual income of a Mutual agent is $49,200 (among those with at least two years' experience and not including any agents over sixty-five still selling part-time). Twenty agents make more than $150,000 per year. In hiring, says André Anderson, "We look for a success pattern. People who are not nine-to-fivers, the moonlighters." They must score well on the aptitude test devised by a U.S. organization, LIMRA. The hour-and-a-half test is marked in the U.S. and has a possible top score of nineteen points. Mutual demands that an applicant receive at least twelve points before even being considered as an agent. Then Mutual spends $120,000 on training, support programs, and benefits over three years. (The figure is a total for the two and a half people it takes, on average, to produce one sales agent in three years.) If a Mutual agent leaves, he or she is not welcome back. Agents who have worked for other firms are rarely put under contract.

At the St. John's office Panabaker stands, turns his chair sideways, puts his foot on the chair, and begins to speak. He talks without notes for about fifteen minutes on a wide range of topics: government regulation, recruiting, results, and his own role. "During the past three to four years," he tells them, "I have spent more time on industry matters than on Mutual matters, so if you ask me why a certain commission is less than another, I won't know. I left things with Jack Masterman and others." It is the only area where he admits weakness. For the rest of the time, he speaks confidently and misses no questions, even raising a few new topics of his own when the questions lag momentarily.

Of all the Canadian life insurance CEOs, Panabaker is probably the best public speaker. "I enjoy public speaking. I guess I'm a ham actor," he says. "You can feel a lift in the room when you finish and you can sense how you're doing. You can tell by the applause—not the length, but the level. If you're not reaching [the audience], there's a constant rustle in the room. Once that starts, it's hard to get them back." He was a member of debating teams both at high school and at McMaster. There he was up against the likes of Robert Welch, later deputy premier of Ontario, and Robert Nixon, later leader of the Ontario Liberal party. He took a one-day speaking course offered by the industry association, the CLHIA. It involved practice sessions with videotape, a technique that Panabaker found helpful, but distasteful. "I hate watching myself on videotape, whether it's a speech or an interview. I can always think of the *mot juste* afterwards."

Panabaker wrote speech material for his superiors almost from the time he joined Mutual. He gave his first speech to agents at their convention in 1960. By 1969 he was an executive vice-president, and by 1971 Panabaker had an executive assistant, Don Coxe (now of

Gordon Capital Corp. in Toronto and a columnist with *Canadian Business*). Coxe drafted his speeches both then and later, when he was president at Mutual's investment arm, Mu-Cana Investment Counselling Ltd., and Panabaker's alter ego. "We would discuss a theme," says Panabaker, "he would go away and do a rough first draft. I would rewrite that, give it to him, and he would jazz it up, then give it to me, and I would jazz it down. By that time, we'd be close to a final version." Since Coxe left in 1983, Panabaker has been writing his own speeches, with some help from public affairs executive Mary McLaughlin, a former aide to Liberal cabinet minister Marc Lalonde. Panabaker works on a speech at home, using his Apple Macintosh computer to fool around with a draft McLaughlin has done. He can even call up his mail at home electronically and see what memos have been sent to him via the interoffice system known as DAX. Working at a keyboard comes naturally to him. He had a typewriter in his office until 1969, when he was made an executive vice-president and someone suggested that such a machine at the elbow of an executive wasn't very dignified.

The year's grandest occasion for speechifying comes at Mutual's annual meeting. For years, it was held in Waterloo in February, but in 1985 it was switched to March. The meeting began taking on special significance in the 1940s when the executives of the day started to invite investment dealers, other businessmen, and politicians for the pilgrimage. By the 1950s, 400 to 500 people were attending, and sales agents were bringing major clients for the social side and the chance to meet the executive. Various departments—investment, group insurance, and others—threw receptions, and the social event of the company's year was created. Today, it is a must event, and 1,000 people show up to pay their respects, see and be seen, and hear Panabaker's message. "You try to say something of significance, something that looks at public policy from a longer-term view."

Drafting the keynote speech is usually a two-month process. After an early version has gone through three drafts, it is circulated to the top four or five Mutual executives for comment. Often, there are two more drafts. When he is finally satisfied, Panabaker sits down with a typed version, marks up the words he wants to emphasize, and practises the speech out loud, working with a tape recorder to hear how he sounds so he can change his inflection and stress points, if necessary. "That doesn't bother me as much as watching." The taping process is repeated until he knows the speech intimately, but has not memorized it. Memorization, he knows, can create singsong cadences. "I want to know where the sentences are on the page."

Panabaker also fusses over the other speeches given at the meeting. Everyone's every word is considered. In 1978, before the annual meeting, Panabaker had given McLaughlin some material someone else had prepared for his own use at the annual meeting. She found it weak and said so. Panabaker stayed up all night reworking it and handed the rewrite to McLaughlin the next morning as they travelled to Toronto together in the back seat of Panabaker's limo. McLaughlin, who readily admits to being not too effusive before ten o'clock, read it and pronounced it "better". That weak praise wasn't good enough for Panabaker. Suddenly, his clenched fist came banging down on the briefcase on the seat between them. "Goddamn it, Mary," he shouted, "you're not much help." Every hair on the neck of the driver stood on end in surprise at the sound of the boss irate and swearing. He dined off the story for days. Panabaker and McLaughlin soon made up, and they worked on the draft together during the rest of the trip.

Panabaker's ire has been known to flare on other occasions. Once, while he was visiting Glenn Jenkins, an assistant deputy minister in the tax policy and legislation branch of the federal department of finance, the conversation became a bit strained. Again, Panabaker relieved his own tension and made his point by banging his fist down, this time on Jenkins's desk. The force of impact was hard enough for the bracelet on Panabaker's twenty-five-year presentation Omega to snap, sending the watch flying across the room.

There was also the time when planning had just begun on a national touring art exhibit of the works of William Kurelek. The initial budget was to be $100,000, but when it was handed over to McLaughlin to run, there was no advertising budget, no poster, and no French-language catalogue. She took the view that Mutual had to have all three if the show was to be a success and reflect some glory on Mutual. She drew up a budget of $250,000. Panabaker did not see the new figures until one day when they were flying back from Vancouver and McLaughlin took the opportunity to outline the new plans—and the cost—of an opening dinner for 100 and a reception for 500 people, visits to fourteen cities, and all the accompanying promotional material. He was irate.

The fight raged on at 35,000 feet with McLaughlin insisting that the exhibit needed this kind of support and Panabaker continuing to express displeasure. Even the flight attendant could barely interrupt them to take their drink orders. "Gin and tonic," he barked. "Bloody Mary," McLaughlin snapped. Finally, after several hours, Panabaker was convinced the budget was necessary. A few days later, when McLaughlin next saw Panabaker, he was even able to laugh about the whole scene. He was chuckling when she entered his office. "What are you laughing at?" she asked. "I was just thinking," he replied, "about the others on the plane last week. They must have been thinking, 'That marriage will never last.' " In the end, the fifty-canvas Kurelek exhibit was a great success. Opening in Kitchener in 1982, it visited all ten provinces and finished in the Art Gallery of Ontario early in 1985. In all, more than 200,000 people saw it.

When he speaks to agents, as in St. John's, he is frank. There had been concern about whether Mutual would change from its career agents system to another, where non-Mutual sales agents could sell Mutual products. It would have meant a reversal of the relationship that the company has always had with its agents. But the review took too long, agents in the field thought there must be changes coming. In the end, the decision was taken, earlier in 1984, to leave things the way they were, and the jungle drums in the company began to settle down. Change, what every employee fears most, wasn't coming after all. Panabaker knows the decision was too slow in coming. "We dithered for eighteen months—too long, in fact, about how we would market our products," he tells the group. Now that marketing methods are settled, other problems can be attacked: new products, rates, and recruiting. In the fast-changing financial services world, those eighteen months of dithering had been costly. Mutual's individual life sales, measured by volume, are down. "It's disturbing," admits Panabaker. "The cause is recruiting and the fact that we were not competitive in term [insurance] for part of the year."

There is some good news, however. Annuity sales have exploded, up 58 per cent year-over-year. (Total sales for 1984 were $508.4 million. On those sales, Mutual paid $10.2 million in commissions to its agents.) Further, an investment fund product is to be introduced. (It was launched in 1985.) Field force compensation is up 11 per cent, even though sales are down, and the bottom line looks healthy. "Our profits—that's a bad word for a mutual company, but we're more and more using it—operating income before taxes and extraordinary items have increased." There is also a new corporate symbol, new letterhead, and new advertising coming in the next few weeks, he tells them. "We haven't been 'just a life insurance company' for years, but our advertising reinforced the image that we were. Our ad campaign will try to break that in the minds of consumers."

The floor is open for questions. The first is about Trilon, the Bronfman empire's combination of life insurance (London Life), trust services (Royal Trust), and property and casualty insurance (Wellington). Asks the questioner: "Are we going to chase them?" Replies Panabaker: "We don't have the [legislative] powers to chase them. They're changing the marketplace, but there is limited proof yet that they have been successful at cross-selling [between the various Trilon companies]. We will be able to compete, perhaps not in a spectacular way, but in the way we can. One of the messages I get from the field is: 'Don't throw anything more at us. We can't take any more [new products].' One of the questions here is how fast can we move the system. Perhaps we're moving faster than we should."

Panabaker's foe, however, is elsewhere. "I worry more about the banks than I do about Trilon." Each of the three biggest banks is larger than the entire life insurance business, he says. "But the banks aren't necessarily staffed with people who are market-oriented." The other part of the problem is the unpredictable nature of the business. The public can put the company's cash flow up and down like a yo-yo on a string. He cites loans and surrenders, for example, the money borrowed against a policy plus the amount taken by policyholders cancelling their policies. In 1979, the annual amount was $106 million. In 1982, when interest rates went over 20 per cent, it rose to $213 million as policyholders found cheap money in their policies and cashed in the policies or took out loans at the interest rates of 6 or 13 per cent allowed under the rules of the policies. Even as rates fell, in 1984, loans still totalled $249 million. "We were really being drained," says Panabaker.

After saying that he would not talk about commissions, he does. A life policy makes no profit for the company in its first year because of administrative costs and high commissions. The only way to be profitable is for the policy to be kept on the books. And, Panabaker has concluded, the only way to ensure that is to give the sales agent a vested interest in keeping the policy alive. Panabaker is thinking that the first-year commission should be lowered and more of it spread out into the future. That would reduce first-year costs to the company and allow a policyholder to cancel without causing a loss. "The answer—and I hate to say this," Panabaker tells the agents, "is level commissions, to make your commission related more to business in force [than to business sold]."

The next question returns to a problem raised by Panabaker in his comments—falling recruitment. Because sales depend on the efforts of individuals, a life insurance office does not prosper by having fewer people work there, thus dividing up the territory among a smaller number of agents. In St. John's, where there are about 200 agents working for all the life insurance companies represented, there is pride at being the "hot shop." Right now, with Mutual's office running a few agents below its usual level, it doesn't feel like the hot shop. A couple of other companies have done some high-profile recruiting, taking agents away from other firms. What, the questioner asks, is Mutual going to do about poor recruiting levels?

Before Panabaker can reply, local manager Art Pearce interjects: "We're going to fire 80 per cent of our managers." There is a ripple of uneasy laughter around the table. Panabaker cites three recent problem areas. First: "We did tighten up our standards because recruiting is expensive. We may have overkilled." Second, the dithering about direction has cost. "There was a good deal of uncertainty earlier this year about the direction of our field force. There was a morale problem as a result. I hope that's over now." Third, there has been severe raiding, particularly in Quebec, of Mutual agents by other firms. Because of Mutual's policy that it will not hire other companies' agents, that method of building up staff is not available. Traditions, it seems, come with price tags.

Mutual is Canada's oldest mutual company and proudly so. The company was the idea of James McQueen, a school principal and town clerk in Fergus, Ont. He thought Canada should have an insurance company where the owners were the policyholders. So was born The Ontario Mutual Life Assurance Co. in 1868. (The current name was adopted in 1900.) Founders included all the key figures of the region at the time—a member of Parliament, a schoolteacher, a merchant, and a doctor, one J. W. Walden, who approved the doctors who then examined all of the applicants for insurance. He decided the 160 questions to be answered, including: "Is there any peculiarity in his configuration?" He earned 50 cents for each application passed. By 1870, 500 policies were written, most for $1,000. For that amount, the annual premium was $13.50. All policies were written by hand. Employees were hired with penmanship in mind.

The first death claims, four of them for a total of $3,250, occurred in 1872. Dr. Walden was called upon to assure the annual meeting that the cause of death in each instance could not have been foreseen in the medical exam. "One death," he reported, "resulted from apoplexy, caused by exposure while the assured was following his calling of auctioneer." Even with the death claims, however, the company was in a surplus position that year and declared a dividend to policyholders—the first of $383 million disbursed to policyholders over the next 100 years. Salaries for executives, however, were non-existent. The president and vice-president were not paid until 1875.

Life insurance was not an immediate success in the area. Many protested on religious grounds that it was unnecessary, citing Biblical references: the Lord shall provide. In rebuttal, life insurance sales agents pointed to Noah's Ark as insurance against disaster and Joseph's plan in Egypt to store up grain in the seven good years for the seven bad years to come. Even so, only thirty-three policies were issued in the early years in Waterloo, where the strict Mennonite religion was common. More successful were sales in Parkhill, eighty miles west, where fifty-six policies were sold. There was a widely held view in the industry that the mutual company would fail. It was sneeringly called "a little one-horse hole-and-corner affair run by a few irresponsible Waterloo Dutchmen." Mutual fought back, calling shareholders in stock companies no more "than barnacles on a ship." Amid the mud-slinging, sales grew, and by 1880, Mutual's annual sales had reached $1 million.

By the first decade of the twentieth century, new offices were needed. The building erected in Waterloo was a unique architectural confection. Designed by the Toronto firm of Darling and Pearson, it opened in 1912 on the corner of King and Union Streets. The land is surrounded by a wrought-iron fence behind which rises a two-storey building of light brown and yellow narrow Roman brick. There are panelled grey stone quoins at the building's corners, carved stone pediments over the windows, and stone carvings in a floral and leaf pattern under the cornice. Four Ionic columns frame the front door. Built on seven acres of land at a cost of $235,000, it has 16,000 square feet of office space and features eight kinds of Italian marble. Inside, a great hall served as a common working area with private offices around the perimeter. Above, there is a skylight, meant to reduce the need for lamps. The general manager of the day, according to company lore, stood inside the great hall, regarded the forty employees he could actually see of the sixty-five staff and said: "We'll never fill it up." He was wrong, of course, and six additions on the site have been required since—not to mention the two-storey underground computer installation. But the interior of the first building remains a gracious *grande dame* surrounded by late-comers to the ball. The building features foil paper, oak trim, hand-carved lintels, bronze busts, high ceilings, and marble fireplaces in many offices. These days, the glow, if not the warmth, is more likely to come from the IBM PCs that perch incongruously beside the desks.

When the building opened, it became the focus of Waterloo's business community. The grounds were planted in grass, flowers, and trees for noon-hour strolling. Five tennis courts and a full-size bowling green were installed for staff. The company served as social centre as well as employer. Still, there were obvious demands. A bell was installed to call lollygagging employees into the office. Charles Ruby, who worked at Mutual from 1884 to 1925 in various positions including general manager, would stand at the front door some days, his watch in hand, checking on late arrivals.

Walter Somerville, as general manager (then the equivalent to chief executive officer), brought Mutual through the Depression. A courtly and quiet gentleman, he was given the title executive vice-president in 1948—but he did not move out of the office he had occupied, the same one Panabaker used twenty-five years later. Eugene Pequegnat took over from Somerville as general manager, but Somerville remained a negative influence, parked in the symbolic office and living, as he did, directly across the street from the front entrance. He was convinced that the Depression would return after the Second World War and that Mutual should be prepared to hunker down and wait it out again.

In the 1950s, Somerville sat in on the finance committee meetings, where investment decisions were made. Memos proposing various activities would be presented to the group. Somerville would read the memo, toss it on the table, and scowl. His dark silences dampened any enthusiasm for aggressive investment. Next, Mutual went through two presidents, Harry Guy and Ed Rieder, in quick succession. Guy had been president for just a year when he died of cancer in 1959. Guy's death was so sudden, there hadn't even been time to have the traditional oil painting done to be hung with those of the previous presidents. Mutual had to make do by having a painting done from a photograph. Rieder, who succeeded him, developed Parkinson's disease less than two years after taking office. Those around him with sufficient experience were either too near retirement or seen as insufficiently competent to take over. Everyone else was too young. Panabaker, for example, the most likely candidate, was being groomed but at thirty-six it was too early for him to take command. Reider had no choice but to look outside the company. Among the people he phoned for names was Ken MacGregor, the federal superintendent of insurance. Asked Rieder: "Do you know anybody who'd be interested?" Well, *did* he. Rieder came to Ottawa and hired MacGregor in 1964 at $55,000, about twice what the public service was paying him after he'd worked in the Department of Insurance since 1930.

If ever a Christmas elf wore a three-piece blue pin-striped suit, he would look like Ken MacGregor—or Mr. Mac, as he is universally known around Mutual. Although he retired in 1983, he still has an office in the building. It is lined to the ceiling with bound copies of legislation, old superintendent's reports, and other printed memorabilia of the last fifty years of the business. Alive and alert at seventy-nine, he still comes into the office daily and knows, with the accuracy of a head librarian, the location of any document among the thousands he has stored around him.

When he joined the Department of Insurance as an actuary, there were sixty people on staff (there are now 250), and the practices of some of the companies were lax. As one company executive told MacGregor, "I keep the company money in one pocket and my money in the other." The department leaned on companies to do everything from sweep out the vault to safeguard commitments to policyholders. In addition to supervising the insurance companies operating in Canada, the department functioned as a policy incubator for government. Unemployment insurance was born in that office, and the staff did all the technical work that led to the Canada Pension Plan. MacGregor was also behind the 1957 federal legislation that allowed insurance companies to mutualize.

He became president in 1964. (He was not the only superintendent to go into the business. William McCabe, Canada's first superintendent, later worked for two U.S. firms and was named general manager of Confederation Life in 1871, then general manager of North American Life in 1879.) He was active for the next nineteen years—nine as president, nine more as chairman, and a further year as chairman of the executive committee. He had known Mutual from his days as a young member of the superintendent's staff in the early 1930s. It had a rather skinflint reputation. Says MacGregor, "If there was one company known for being economical, if not penurious, it was the Mutual." His arrival was like a load being lifted after years where morale was low and momentum non-existent. MacGregor put in place the planning for the 1969 addition to head office, started corporate strategic thinking, and set up a task force to study management organization. It was a drastic change from the former lacklustre ways. Recalls Panabaker, "The strategy was—well, we try to do a little better on sales, a little better on expenses, why do we need to plan?" As a result of MacGregor's notions, strategic planning was begun that was further refined by Panabaker. Now reports are presented to the board of directors three times a year. In November, economic and political forecasts are offered, in December, the operating plan, and in June, the overall strategy is considered.

But while strategy may have entered their lives, some things haven't changed since the early days. Just as the tennis courts and the grounds were the best around in 1912, current staff recreational facilities must be the most complete facilities of any insurance company in the country. Few private clubs have better. There are two billiard tables, a television room, four bowling lanes, a personal fitness centre for aerobics and yoga, two full-time fitness co-ordinators, a gym, sauna and whirlpool bath, stationary bicycles, rowing machines, and weights. Architecturally, no detail is spared in the other parts of the buildings. An interior garden contains papyrus, chinese evergreens, and stag-horn and bird's-nest ferns. A waterfall has chlorine carefully added to the water to prevent the growth of algae. There is even a day-care centre next door, in a building that was formerly a Baptist church, with space for about forty offspring of staff at $65 a week each.

Corporate concern for personal well-being goes beyond just the facilities. They take the whole person seriously. Once, when executive vice-president Bob Astley was making a presentation to the board of directors about insurance rates for non-smokers, director

William James, of Toronto, asked about the mortality rate among smokers as opposed to non-smokers. When he learned that non-smokers lived an average of seven years longer, he quit smoking cold turkey. Smoking was banned in all meetings at Mutual in September 1984. When someone inquired whether the ban included the boardroom during meetings of directors, Panabaker (who doesn't smoke) banned smoking there, too.

The environment where Mutualists (as they call themselves) work is just about as folksy as any in Canada. Some in the industry regard Mutual, sitting as it does in Waterloo, 120 kilometres west of Toronto, as an out-of-the-way place, serving mainly rural and small-town customers. It is even referred to by some as "R.R. 3." Says Drew McCaughey, chief executive officer of North American Life, "I think Mutual is the best company in the industry." But with the compliment comes the comment: "They're playing yesterday's game very well."

There are few lay-offs. Even during the recent recession, the only staff reductions came through attrition and early retirement; from 1982 to 1984 staff was reduced by about 200, to 2,143. There were no wholesale cut-backs as there were at many other firms. "We have benefitted," says executive vice-president Dunc Winhold, "from a bit more loyalty than others in the business. We were guilty of paternalism in the old days, thirty or forty years ago. That has changed. It's moved from the trustee concept to the entrepreneurial."

There is a board dining room used only for official entertaining, and the executive is more likely to be found in the company cafeteria, where 900 of the 1,400 employees at head office usually eat. Many, including some of the executive, also slip home for lunch. The informal atmosphere extends to reporting relationships. If chairman Panabaker wants to talk to an employee, he doesn't stand on ceremony and go through channels. "It's a relatively small city," he says. "I hope I can call up people in the organization without making them feel threatened. I can wander in and talk to the bond-traders, the datasystems people can come and talk to me." Many at head office and many agents call Panabaker by his first name. "That's not something I've cultivated and it doesn't bother me. It's just the way we are."

It is a successful family. In 1984 premium income was $1.1 billion, assets were $6 billion. Group insurance is big business. More than 1.2 million Canadians are covered by 6,000 different health plans run by Mutual. Over a million claims are processed annually—not a bad increase from the five claims processed, for a total of $2,469, when the business began in 1940. The group business is a fiercely competitive one, however, and as with all life insurance contracts, Mutual's profit margins can go below 1 per cent, depending on the competition. For smaller businesses, profit margins can reach 3 per cent. One of the big group contracts lost last year by Mutual was that of the Saskatchewan teachers. The contract covering group life insurance and accidental death and dismemberment for 13,000 persons had an annual premium of $1.8 million and went to Sun Life after three months of negotiation in 1984.

There is also an active investment division, known as Mu-Cana Investment Counselling, with more than $1 billion in assets in 1983. It was begun in 1973 to manage pension funds of Mutual clients. Included in the portfolio are funds from such local food-processing firms as J. M. Schneider Inc., a fund from the University of Waterloo, and the investment portfolio of the Gore Mutual Insurance Co. Funds in Mu-Cana increased by 45 per cent in 1983, 14 per cent in 1984. Included in the portfolio are real estate investments (such as the Hotel Newfoundland) and oil and gas through MLC Oil and Gas Ltd., with $17 million in assets in 1983, $24.2 million in 1984. MLC is involved in drilling and exploration in Alberta, in the Beaufort, and off the east coast. Mu-Cana also has a bond portfolio that is among the most active (along with ManuLife's and Confederation's) in the life insurance business.

Panabaker sees himself as just one of a team, one who listens to others. "I think of this company like a Japanese company," he says. "We're a consensus company. I distrust the corporate superman. Leadership is not necessarily giving orders. It can be prodding and poking and trying to keep people focussed. I think people view me as being more forceful than I am." In fact, in many ways, Panabaker has been an absentee landlord. From 1981 to 1984, he spent up to half of his time on industry association matters through the Canadian Life and Health Insurance Association. One year he was chairman. The other years, he was involved in representations to the government following the 1981 federal budget, which affected insurance. The time away has altered his relationship with employees. "I've become more remote than I want to be."

Mutual is somewhat remote itself, away from the mainstream of corporate Canada. But as much as it is marked by its surroundings as a company in a medium-sized centre, away from the bustle of commerce in the big city, Mutual has been shaped more by its mutuality, the fact that the policyholders actually own it. The stock companies tend to be scornful of mutuals, claiming that the shareholders in stock companies keep a closer watch on profit and on how management is doing. Says Bob Bandeen, chairman of Crown Life, a stock company: "If you want to get Panabaker, call him a socialist. He'll deny it, but I don't know what else to call him. There are no controls."

Panabaker becomes duly defensive to the charge. "Socialism implies government ownership," he says. "A co-operative enterprise is not necessarily socialistic in outlook. We manage as professionally as most companies in the industry and perhaps better than most. We watch the bottom line even though we cannot reward managers with ownership. Mutuals are funny organizations—funny-peculiar; they are strange animals because you cannot carve them up into ownership shares." From time to time, talk does occur about "demutualization," the process of putting the mutuals like ManuLife, Sun, Confederation, and Mutual up for sale through share issues to individuals and institutions. If the law did change, Panabaker for one would like a wealthy benefactor with whom he could live as controlling owner. "I would want to have a white knight at my elbow."

Still, mutuality, the core of the company, gets less attention these days. When a new mission statement was published in 1984, there were two noticeable differences from the 1968 statement. Mutuality was not even mentioned; profitability was. It was such a change that Panabaker felt he had to explain it to employees through the house organ, *Mutualist*. "We are still a mutual company. As I told the Annual Meeting, 'we exist to serve.' Unfortunately, the traditional concept of mutuality, in terms of participating insurance, has become very fuzzy in recent years. Many of our products, including the Accumulation Annuity, Life PRO, and Universal Life, are not 'participating' in the traditional sense. Other services, like Administrative Services Only (ASO), are not traditional at all. We felt we should not continue to use a concept which may limit people's vision of the role and ways in which we can serve our clients."

In interviews, however, he remains messianic about the mutuals.

"We have to treat the company as a kind of trust. We've gone outside for a president, we've changed as rapidly as the others—it took London Life [a stock company] a long time to appoint Earl [Orser]. The absence of a controlling shareholder is no more significant in our case than it is for a chartered bank, and I haven't heard them being called socialistic. A financial institution is not only an enterprise, it's a 'trust.' You are holding those funds as a trust for the policyholders. It's a little like a church. You keep the thing going because you are all making a contribution."

Keeping things going demands a succession plan. Panabaker's began early in the 1980s, as he picked his successor. There were really only two candidates. It was no contest: Jack Masterman, now fifty-five, easily won out over Dunc Winhold and was named president and chief operating officer in 1982. Winhold didn't really want the job and said as much. Winhold, who became senior vice-president, is a man of middle-class taste who dislikes things cultural. His views are so well known that once a couple of employees conspired to hoodwink him into attending a high-brow evening. A memo purporting to be from Panabaker was composed saying that the National Ballet was performing *Swan Lake*. According to the memo, both Panabaker and Masterman had to attend a board of directors event on a particular evening. Mutual, however, should be represented at the ballet. Would Winhold kindly go to the black-tie reception and performance? The memo was signed by Panabaker's secretary, who can do a more than passable imitation of her boss's flowing hand. Winhold was not pleased when he received it. He immediately phoned up the investment department and had them beat the bushes looking for clients he needed to have dinner with that same evening. Before any were found, however, the prank was revealed and Winhold laughed along with the rest. For his next birthday, his fiftieth, in 1982, Mutual's in-house artist drew a caricature for presentation. There was Winhold with hairy legs sticking out from below a ballerina's tutu.

For Masterman, Panabaker's choice was a lucky decision. Panabaker could just as easily have carried on as CEO for another five years, then found Masterman too old to take over. Like many at the top of life insurance companies, Masterman was trained at the University of Manitoba and joined Mutual in Winnipeg in 1953. By 1969 he was an executive officer, and he joined the board of directors in 1980. At six-foot-one and 210 pounds, Masterman has a jaw line that would be the envy of Brian Mulroney. He likely will have a ten-year run as CEO, then can pass the baton once more, probably to Bob Astley, forty, named an executive vice-president in the shuffle, who appears to be the next in line. Astley is another University of Manitoba graduate who joined Mutual in 1966, left to spend three years with the consulting firm of Towers, Perrin, Forster & Crosby, and returned in 1973 to create a computerized financial model of the company for planning. Until then, work had been done using an unsophisticated, manual method.

The computer update and succession were easier than the person-nel decisions with which Panabaker wrestled. The toughest was whether Mutual would change its historic association with career agents into some new distribution system. The study began at a two-day management meeting held away from the office. In the spring of 1983, the dozen members of top management met at the former estate of Lady Eaton, north of Toronto, now a live-in conference establishment. Panabaker pushed his colleagues to think about alter-natives to the system of career agents, a system as old as Mutual itself. He acted as an *agent provocateur*, stirring their thought processes by making them think he might even favour a change. "I didn't set out to make them think I wanted change," he says, "but I probably did, I came on so strong. I don't think they liked me when it was over."

After a year, later than he had intended, a consensus finally evolved. The result: things would stay just as they were. "We concluded it can continue to be an effective distribution system," says Panabaker. "We recognize there will be a market that will not want personal service but that there will be a sufficient market that will. The person who controls the distribution system controls the whole system. We decided not to become manufacturers who dis-tributed through someone else's system."

While the process may have taken longer than normal, the debate was typical of Panabaker's management style. He is no dictator and has let those under him run their areas more than MacGregor did. Says Dunc Winhold of the MacGregor era, "He wasn't trying to impose his will all the way down, but he kept his finger on everything." Panabaker has let go the reins. "We're democratically run," says Masterman. "Most important issues are discussed to the point of common agreement. You won't get unanimity on all questions, but we strive for it. Decisions seem to emerge, more than having someone saying, 'This is what we're going to do.'"

"I've opened it up a bit," says Panabaker of the decision-making process at Mutual. He delegated responsibility to try to increase the number of broad-brush executives because Mutual was thin at the top. One of Panabaker's first problems was depth of management. "When I became president [in 1973]," says Panabaker, "we were very vulnerable. If something had happened to me, we'd have been in the soup again." To change that, Panabaker made sure that other members of the executive were exposed to various aspects of the organization. Winhold, for example, an actuary, replaced Panabaker as head of the investment department. Don Post, vice-president for group insurance, has also worked in datasystems and personnel. Dave MacIntosh, vice-president for finance and treasurer, has been in corporate services and investments. Bob Astley, an actuary, has had experience in the actuarial department, as a line manager in the individual insurance division, and as vice-president for corporate planning and development.

There was widespread agreement in the firm, for example, that one-stop shopping was unlikely to sweep Canada's financial services or, indeed, even be demanded by consumers. "It's unlikely that the majority of consumers are going to go to one place for their financial services," says Astley. Instead, Mutual sees its competition as the other life companies, such as London Life, the firm that Panabaker particularly watches. The two companies are similar in size, both operate with career agents, and both are based in medium-sized cities in southern Ontario. Panabaker has watched how Earl Orser's arrival in 1978 has "increased the amount of competitive pressure." According to Panabaker, Mutual has responded with panache. "Ten years ago, the London was 37 per cent bigger than we were." By 1983, he notes, "it was a snick smaller" in assets.

Mutual has moved into accumulation annuities as a careful strategy. "The risk of death," says Bob Astley, "is becoming less and less significant to the financial plans of individuals. They are becoming more concerned about unemployment, disability, or coming to retirement with too little money." At the same time, life insurance became viewed less and less by the public as a place for savings dollars. In response, Mutual, along with the others, had to find another vehicle to satisfy the demand and offer competition to the trust companies' guaranteed investment certificates and the banks' term deposits. "We went on the basis that life insurance was for death benefit," says Panabaker, "and if you wanted [money] accumulation then you went into accumulation funds. We were very much afraid if life insurance was used too aggressively for savings, there would be tax consequences."

Those consequences were demonstrated in 1981 when the federal budget removed much of the tax advantage from the high-profile new money policies being written by some companies at the time. Maritime and Dominion Life were selling single-premium policies that were largely tax shelters to accumulate funds. Mutual had taken the safe route, separating death benefits and cash value, and it paid off. In 1984, $508 million was placed with Mutual in accumulation annuities, about fifty times the 1972 level of $10.6 million. From ninth position in 1972, Mutual now holds first place in annuities sales among the Canadian life insurance companies.

The public has become much more aware of the value of money in recent years. Mutual's daily interest account began in 1979 with about $388,000 on deposit. Within two years, when interest rates went to 20 per cent, the total invested had shot up to $250 million. In 1984, even though rates had gone down by almost half, there was $310 million in the account. "It's a money business, a savings and accumulation business now, to an extent that none of us foresaw," says Panabaker.

The business is also one of image. Policyholders need to feel confidence in the company. As Panabaker saw it, part of that public feeling could be created by such things as corporate logos. He oversaw, in 1961, the creation of a logo that served for the next two decades. The logo was an M in a box. Designed by Allan Fleming, who also did other well-known corporate logos, such as CN's, it replaced one with beavers and blind justice figures. The boxed M was in turn replaced in 1984 by a series of upright pillars in a diamond shape, designed by Andrew Csafordi and Karen Okada of Toronto. The logo was launched in September 1984, along with a $1.25-million television advertising campaign carried out by MacLaren Advertising, Mutual's Toronto-based agency. Television advertising took just under half the total budget. The campaign features a television ad with a rough diamond-shaped asteroid, meant to represent financial independence, floating through space.

Laser-like beams zap the asteroid to create a polished diamond while the voice of Orson Welles burrs in the background about financial services until the logo appears in the final seconds.

In St. John's, on that October 1984 visit, outer space is the farthest thing from Panabaker's mind. The missionary is doing a little listening as well. Among his other stops is the local office of the Canadian Petroleum Association, where regional director Kenneth Oakley briefs him on the offshore oil. It is a realistic appraisal, filled with none of the fanciful dreams that some have had about what oil will do for St. John's and Newfoundland. They talk of where the centre for supplies and services may be—Halifax or St. John's—and the changes the North Sea oil has wreaked on Aberdeen in Scotland. "So there won't be another Aberdeen?" asks Panabaker. "Hell, no," replies Oakley. In addition to the question of the size of the reserves off Newfoundland, there is debate about how they will be brought to shore. The Newfoundland government wants a fixed platform production system, Mobil is looking at a floating system. "When politicians get dug in," says Oakley, "it's hard to get change." Panabaker, himself no stranger to lobbying, laughs and says, "Over time they get worn down."

Oakley predicts that about $1.2 billion a year will be spent on east coast exploration. About 25 per cent of that is spent locally, the rest elsewhere. The message: there is no bonanza coming to St. John's immediately. Concludes Panabaker at the end of the briefing, "I think I have a somewhat more realistic view." "That's my job," replies Oakley, "to be realistic, so we're not blamed for the euphoria." Afterwards, Panabaker comments on the industry's changed stance. "Four years ago this place was going to boom. The industry was part of the euphoria." Still, for a local hotel owner, every snippet of economic information matters.

Next stop is a courtesy call on the premier of Newfoundland and Labrador, Brian Peckford. Peckford is late and keeps Panabaker cooling his heels in the reception area of his Confederation Building office for twenty minutes. Panabaker is impatient about the delay, but not surprised. As one who has visited a few legislators over the years, he's waited before. "I'm thinking of carrying a small silver cup in my pocket to present to the first politician who sees me on time," mutters Panabaker. "I'd call it the Panabaker Prize for Promptness."

Final call of the day is for an interview at radio station VOCM. A nervous Brian Madore is the reporter scheduled to meet Panabaker. Madore is carrying a tape recorder and begins: "I don't know too much..." Panabaker eases the anguish. "You want to be briefed." "I don't know much about life insurance," continues Madore, then offers hopefully, "but I do have a policy." Panabaker takes a minute to explain what he is doing in Newfoundland, Mutual's ownership of the hotel, and his scheduled speech to the Rotary the following day. Madore is feeling more relieved already. "You're not here selling policies?" "I'm not licensed to," says Panabaker.

Madore admits he is really only looking for a thirty-second clip for the newscast, turns on his tape recorder, and asks a few questions about Panabaker's trip, the hotel, and insurance legislation, the topics covered in Panabaker's "briefing." Panabaker concludes: "We think it's high time that the insurance legislation be updated. It's the kind of situation where you get frustrated as I know the people of Newfoundland will understand in *their* dealings with Ottawa." After a brief pause, Madore says: "That's about all I can think of." Panabaker smiles and says: "That should give you thirty seconds."

The next day begins with a tour of "his" hotel, conducted by executive assistant manager Joseph van Ulden. Included are the health club facilities, boiler room, bars, and kitchen. One of the failures is a solar heating system that was to have supplied energy to heat the water. The glass panels did not stand the rigours of St. John's winter gales. Also, the bar off the lobby didn't work well and has undergone $150,000 in renovations. Comments Panabaker: "I guess a hotel is like a machine. You have to let it run a bit no matter what the plans are."

In his later private meetings with agency management, Panabaker follows his usual practice of being non-committal when requests or ideas are put forward. Any hint of acknowledgement on his part could be taken as a go-ahead. "One of the things I've learned to do when I visit a branch is to nod and say nothing."

Lunch, the main event of the day, is a speech to the St. John's Rotary Club. About 100 local businessmen gather in a Hotel Newfoundland meeting room for a lunch of roast beef. The food is a cut above the usual fare in honour of Panabaker as an owner. Comments one attendee admiringly: "I haven't seen that much meat since Christmas." Once the lunch dishes are cleared away and coffee served, Panabaker is introduced. The head table is positioned midway along the long side of the rectangular narrow room so that lunch guests are stretched to his left and right while ahead of him there are few people. As he speaks, he has to swing his head from side to side as if he were watching a tennis match. The speech is rushed. Whether he is the hotel owner or not, the club organizers have repeatedly told him that the speech must end before two o'clock so that members can get back to work. Lunch, announcements, and the introduction mean that Panabaker isn't rising in his place to speak until 1:42. Eighteen minutes for an eleven-page speech entitled "No Business as Usual in Financial Services."

Panabaker moves to the podium, his wrist-watch moved down from his left wrist onto his hand, the face in the palm where he can see it. When he changes pages, he moves the watch to his right hand. At one point, he drops a page to save time as he talks about the revolution going on in the four pillars of Canadian financial services for the previous two decades. He is unsure whether legislation can keep up with the changing marketplace. "Time is not on the side of the bureaucracy and the politicians," he says. "Very powerful forces are at work in the marketplace which will be difficult—if not impossible—for them to control." The causes of change include inflation, which made all institutions worry more about short-term money; more services through technology; conglomerates, or non-regulated holding companies, allowing a single owner to have a stable of different firms; a jurisdictional split between the provinces and Ottawa that causes confusion; dithering by legislators; the growth of deposit insurance, which means the consumer is protected while some institutions can become less sound; and pressure from foreign-owned firms.

The results of these forces of change, Panabaker tells his audience, will include better deals for consumers because of increased competition, more convenient delivery of services, and the end of free services while margins grow narrow and firms are pressed to find ways to lower costs. He worries about the asset size of the banks, which are "larger, by a wide margin, than the combined assets of the Canadian trust and loan companies, the life companies, and the credit unions. Indeed the assets of the three largest Canadian banks are *individually* larger than the assets of all the Canadian life companies put together."

He is also worried about the conflicts of interest that may occur in the hands of the owners of the conglomerates as "the financial institution's resources are diverted to support their other enterprises." Conglomerates, he argues, will know all aspects of an individual's financial affairs. That, he believes, is a situation most Canadians do not want. "If Canadian financial services companies could ever be accused of being stodgy, that accusation will not survive much longer. The remaining unimaginative organizations will disappear into backwaters or, more likely, will be merged into larger, stronger, and more dynamic units."

Panabaker suggests that some life companies will specialize, others will combine their services, and "still others—like the company with which I am associated—will attempt to build on historic patterns of growth to provide an increasing range of related services to clients." He concludes with an appeal to governments: "The challenge to legislators is to create a new framework for regulation of these rapidly changing institutions. For the new federal government, this task commands the highest priority. The ice-floes are already moving, and the forces at work will not wait for still another leisurely review and investigation. Here is an opportunity for the new government to demonstrate clearly its foresight, its imagination, and its initiative."

He finishes the text at 2:03, right on schedule. As he concludes, he adds the local-interest announcement. Mutual Life will be participating with Esso Resources Canada Ltd. in an offshore exploration program 400 kilometres east of St. John's. Other participants include Mobil Oil Canada Ltd., Norcen Energy Resources Ltd., and Voyageur Petroleums Ltd. Total expenditure will be $100 million. Esso will establish an office in St. John's to manage the project, and 6,000 work-months of employment will result. Mutual (through its subsidiary MLC Oil and Gas Ltd.) has a 1.5-per-cent interest in the program, which consists of completion of approximately 1,800 kilometres of seismic exploration and drilling of two wells, one in 1985 and one in 1986. "MLC Oil and Gas will have a small participation. We're proud to be involved in investment in Newfoundland and have a part in the development of the offshore."

In fact, Esso has not yet made the announcement. A press conference is scheduled for two-thirty in the meeting room immediately opposite the Rotary meeting. Esso has agreed, however, that Panabaker can announce the participation in advance of the scheduled time. As his speech winds down, the noise in the hall grows, as Esso representatives and about twenty members of the media gather. Panabaker takes his seat to a round of applause. There is a brief flap when the Rotary realizes it doesn't have Panabaker's gift, the Rotary letter-opener, to give him. No matter, it will be sent, and the meeting closes with a rousing verse from "Ode to Newfoundland."

On the flight back to Toronto Panabaker grows reflective about his career and the transition to Masterman that is to occur shortly. Panabaker has seen enough bosses hang on too long to be aware of the potential problems. "I worried greatly when I took over as CEO that Ken MacGregor would stay on as *de facto* CEO—but he didn't. If I can do the same thing, I'll be very happy." Even as a summer student working at Mutual, he saw the negative influence of Walter Somerville's reluctance to let go of the reins.

As a result, when Jack Masterman became chief executive officer in 1985, Panabaker switched offices with Masterman, sending out a clear signal that a new boy was in charge. The decision to step aside was not easy. At the time, Panabaker was fifty-six years old, an unusual age to be passing on the title of chief executive officer to someone else. Most CEOs would probably wait until they were sixty, then make the change as they were winding down to retirement. Panabaker, however, had been CEO since 1973, and he felt he'd been in the post long enough. "I think a CEO should stay, plus or minus, ten years. Twenty years, which I could have stayed, causes blockage. I'm afraid I've seen enough cases where people are so 'indispensable' that no one else can make decisions. You create an environment where people stop aspiring. If we don't get some movement into the structure now, we're going to find ourselves in one helluva mess a few years out with nobody with experience in general management. And, finally, you sift the thinking of the company too long through one mind."

There was, however, another more personal reason to hand over the important CEO's title, a lack of energy beginning that previous spring. "I felt I had run into a wall," said Panabaker, "a lack of energy." Because he'd always had a ten-year term as CEO in mind, it was almost as if when he passed the ten years, he had no reserve left. "It was like a runner who trains for the 400-yard dash and can't run the 800," says Panabaker. In the summer of 1984, he spent six weeks at his three-bedroom cottage with its 200-foot lake frontage near

Minden, in the Haliburton region of Ontario, and decided that he had run his leg of the race and it was time to pass along the baton.

As chairman, Panabaker will continue to be involved in external relations for Mutual. He hopes to get back to his painting, and he says he will allow Masterman to run the place. Meanwhile, he has offered up the Presbyterian's final sacrifice: sometimes the only way to get ahead is to get out of the way.

CHAPTER SIXTEEN

DOING WELL BY DOING GOOD

The Co-operators Group Ltd.

W AYNE SCOTT, senior vice-president for general insurance, had been with The Co-operators Group Ltd., of Guelph, Ont., for twenty-five years before he finally had to fire someone in 1983. "It bothered me terribly. There was no question that it had to be done and I didn't like it very much. It may be that my bark is worse than my bite. In some ways—because of my size [he is six-foot-3½ and weighs 220 pounds], my manner, and some intensity— I may seem more intimidating than I really am."

If ever two unlikelier senior executives existed than Scott and chief executive officer Teunis Haalboom, they would be hard to find. Both are motorcycle enthusiasts and, in the parlance of ideologues, might be called bleeding hearts. Yet their company ranks as one of the most successful in the Canadian property and casualty business. It is at once the largest and the most unusual of the 300 or so companies operating in Canada.

To understand The Co-operators one needs to understand the co-operative movement. The movement is more than just a collection of people with mutual interests, it is the best attributes of a caring, unselfish community incarnate. The co-operative movement also serves as a captive market. Says Jack Lyndon, president of the Insurance Bureau of Canada, "They've got a natural and national community in the co-operative movement." The co-operative movement had its beginnings in Canada on the prairies with the formation of wheat pools in the 1920s to level seasonal fluctuations in wheat prices. Ontario, Quebec, and the Maritimes saw other co-operative movements grow out of the Depression of the 1930s. In many cases, the movement gained its strength in reaction to the big-city banks and insurance companies that left farmers and small-town folks to wither on the wind-blown land or waste away in the backwaters. Just as rural neighbours help out at harvest, after a crop failure or fire, the co-operative movement stepped in where far-off institutions had failed the locals. The movement, and The Co-operators, is like a corporate barn-raising.

The Co-operators is owned by thirty-five co-operative and credit union centrals, farm groups, and other co-operative associations in Canada. Some examples include the United Farmers of Alberta, B. C. Central Credit Union, Saskatchewan Wheat Pool, Canadian Brotherhood of Railway, Transport and General Workers, and the United Maritime Fishermen. In 1983 Co-operators General became the largest property and casualty company in the country. It passed British-owned Royal Insurance with earned premium income of $419 million. The Royal, long number one in the market, had slipped to $383 million from $441 million the year before. The Co-operators has 250 local service offices across Canada and the firm is a leading insurer of credit unions: a national pooling system spreads the risk over all the credit unions. But the bulk of the business comes from auto insurance.

At fifty-three, Haalboom is the $230,000-a-year chief executive officer at The Co-operators. With his five children grown and gone from home, he lives with his second wife in Elora, a town fifteen kilometres north of Guelph. Their rough cedar-clad home, complete with swimming pool, sits on an acre of land in the woods on the Grand River. Inside the house, there is more cedar and a minimum of walls and ceilings; the master bedroom is a loft. There is also an IBM terminal where Haalboom enjoys running spreadsheets on one of his favourite software systems, Lotus 1-2-3. His other hobby is repairing whatever goes wrong around the house. He is proud of the fact that no serviceman has been called in since he built the house six years ago.

At the office, neither he nor Scott is a high-profile performer. Haalboom leaves the insurance business largely to Scott. "He's a sleeping giant," says the IBC's Lyndon. "He's more involved in the [international] credit union and credit society. He is a titular head. The average property and casualty CEO is embarrassed at not really knowing what is going on in the shop." In 1984, Haalboom dropped off the IBC board of directors to carry out other duties in the co-operative movement, including becoming chairman and secretary of the Insurance Development Bureau (IDB) run by the International Co-operative Insurance Federation (ICIF). The ICIF is a world-wide voluntary association of eighty-seven co-operative insurers in thirty-three countries. The IDB is the vehicle through which the ICIF launches co-operative life and general insurance in the Third World.

In 1985 Haalboom spent about 20 per cent of his time on IDB business. He visited the U.S., Kenya, and Japan for IDB conferences, planning ways to help Third World countries establish their own insurance systems. Kenya, for example, has had its own co-operative company in place for four years now. Basic education and training began in the 1960s. That was followed by an agency and finally a company. Typically, the process takes ten to fifteen years and may involve exchanges. The Co-operators sent someone to Ghana for a year, for example, and has trained Third World people at Guelph head office. It is a process that can be interrupted by changing regimes. Training and education began in Uganda, for example, in 1962, but was abandoned under Idi Amin. When he fled the country, the help began anew with a shipment of used typewriters from IDB members. Now the organization has grown to a dozen employees writing insurance for their own account.

For The Co-operators, as for the other corporate members of the international organization (among Canadian firms are Assurance-vie Desjardins, of Lévis, Que., and Les Coopérants, société mutuelle d'assurance-vie, of Montreal), there is no financial reward. The purpose is to help the co-operative movement spread and give Third World countries their own insurance companies. "It's the co-opera-tive movement exemplified," says Haalboom. "It's important for Third World countries to have their own insurance companies. There's a lot of money flowing out of those countries that they cannot afford." Current estimates say that some $10 billion is leaving Third World countries to pay for insurance run from other countries. Running their own schemes keeps the business within their borders.

That same co-operative view marks the culture of The Co-operators, where there is less infighting than usual among execu-tives. "The competitive situation is not as heated as in most other organizations," says Haalboom. "People share a lot of information." Anyone in a Co-operators office across the country, for example, with access to the ubiquitous internal IBM systems can punch a few keys and read Haalboom's itinerary or memos being sent among various members of the executive in what is a very open system. While there is a confidential channel as well for some communication, it is little used.

The open system is intentional. "I'm not sure individual competitiveness is all that helpful," says Scott. "We've got 3,500 people. We can't waste time on competition. To a large extent, this organization depends on how well people work with each other, not how well they work for themselves. I'm a very competitive person. I don't like losing. The best way to get results is to be conscious of that. But I don't get anywhere without the support of others. Maybe the more competitive you are, the more you need others to succeed.

"Member-owners belong to a co-operative not for return on investments," says Scott, "but to have a voice in the quality of their co-op's product and services and to enjoy benefits of other forms of participation and mutual help. In addition to financial services, the principal benefit to our member-owners is our investments in other co-operative organizations, which total $246 million. The Co-operators is relatively lower-key, lower-profile in terms of the national and public image than the Royal. Royal Insurance, a few years ago, had as its president in Canada a man [Alan Horsford] who was doing everything, everywhere, all the time, judging from the insurance industry coverage in the press." Executives of The Co-operators mind the store and leave the communications within the company to work groups, where employees iron out problems with peers and superiors. The high-profile speech-making can be carried out by other companies. Says Scott, "Where the rubber meets the road, as they say in drag racing, is back home."

Even taking over in 1983 from Royal Insurance as the number one casualty company in the country (measured by premium income) does little for Haalboom. "It was more by default than anything else," he says modestly. "They made some terrible mistakes." In fact, the two companies are not in the same business. The Co-operators is a small, national, personal lines company. Royal is a large, international personal and commercial lines operation. There was, however, some pride in the accomplishment. "It was good for staff to feel part of something larger. For the co-operative movement, who feel very much the underdog in Canadian society, there were some positive aspects. Being biggest?" Haalboom shrugs and smiles. "It doesn't do much for me."

Haalboom has shown leadership in the industry, making changes few others would. Once, for example, he watched a public affairs show on television that took up the cause of the underinsured motorist. The show probed what happened if an individual was in a collision with another vehicle, and the other driver was at fault but had insufficient coverage to pay for ensuing damages or personal injuries. As Haalboom sat watching the show, spokesman after spokesman for the industry said nothing could be done. They specifically said that their own policyholders could certainly not make a claim against their own insurers because the company would have a conflict of interest.

Haalboom saw it differently. He instituted a clause in his firm's auto coverage saying that whatever third-party liability a Co-operators insured purchased (to cover claims against him by someone else), the insured had the same coverage on himself if the other driver was at fault and had no coverage. The Co-operators did what the industry said it could not do—pay claims by its own policyholders even if another person was at fault and had no coverage. Haalboom's thinking is simple. "When the industry says something can't be done, I'm not inclined to believe that," says Haalboom. "My tendency is to try a little harder. I probably have the same attitude within the company."

That attitude will mean more changes to come at the Co-operators. "Rather than having fewer organization changes, God help us, we're probably going to have more. We can't help people avoid change, if we're going to survive. What was more than adequate ten years ago is marginal today. So the bottom line is that we have to improve our productivity to keep pace with these increasingly higher standards and survive in an increasingly demanding market. Which means more changes. A sound organization cannot shelter its staff from change; it can only assist them to cope with more change."

Wayne Scott joined The Co-operators in Hamilton in 1958; he was appointed publications editor in 1962 and director of advertising in 1965. In 1971 he became marketing manager and in 1977 he moved to Calgary as vice-president for the western division. His current appointment came in 1983. He knows he is not as good with people as he should be. "A management profile questionnaire I completed once showed that I was oriented more towards goals than people. I think that's accurate." The only consolation he passes on to employees: "As I get older, I get more mellow." As with all senior executives, the staff perception of him makes him out to be a bit fearsome. A staffer was once told, "If you have an opportunity to have lunch with Wayne Scott, don't put salt on your food before you taste it because he'll judge you to be impulsive."

His views on life and on his capacity to change the world around him have changed, as they do with most people, as he grows older and more mature. Yet there is still the naive and youthful idealist inside, as captured in this rather rambling, yet revealing, description of himself. "When I was about seventeen or eighteen, I concluded that the world was a bit of a mess and that I should get it sorted out before too many years passed because I was obviously the guy to do the job. When I got to be about thirty, I had come to the conclusion that maybe there was more involved in terms of renewal than I was really going to get at. That I should perhaps limit myself to one organization and do a good job on it. More recently, within the last several years, I've come to the conclusion that I am probably able to change myself a little bit with great difficulty. And perhaps that's the best focus for me from now on—to see whether it's possible to do a good job on that.

"I think that everybody is capable of doing something significant. Some people are fortunate in the gifts that they have, or the environment in which they are able to function. But everybody, I think, has an obligation and responsibility to themselves and to their fellow-creatures to do what they can. If I can do that, then that's probably what it's all about. The final thing is that the purpose of life, in going through these years, is really to figure it out as best you can. You can read biographies, you can meet philosophers and talk to other people and get their ideas, but you really have to come to your own conclusions. If you do that, it's probably about time to call it quits. That's about as philosophical as I can get."

Haalboom and Scott are following a grand tradition at The Co-operators, one begun by Andrew Hebb. The basic change Haalboom, who inherited the top job from Hebb in 1971, has made is to remove himself from the day-to-day running of the firm and share responsibility with others. "He was an excellent guy to start the company," says Haalboom of Hebb, "but I'm not sure he could run it today."

The history of The Co-operators and the life of Andrew Hebb are inextricably tied together. For the first twenty-five years of the firm's existence he was the driving force behind it and perhaps the only reason it succeeded. Hebb was born in Chester, N.S., in 1905. He graduated in law from Dalhousie University but never practised. During his university days he was editor of the student newspaper, and after graduation he joined the Halifax *Daily Star* as a reporter. He went on to the Montreal *Star* and at twenty-five, in 1930, moved to Toronto. It was the Depression and there were no jobs. He worked as a farm labourer for the summer, then because it was the only thing he could find, went to work as a bonding underwriter at United States Fidelity & Guaranty Co., an insurance company, for eighteen months.

In 1932, he joined the Toronto *Star*, writing stories of the newspaper's Santa Claus Fund food distribution at Christmas. He saw anguish and despair among families that, added to the community-minded views of his mother as he grew up in Nova Scotia, radicalized him and formed his view of the world. In 1934, he married and bought the newspaper in a small town north of Toronto, the Newmarket *Era*. He paid $1,200 down on the total price of $7,800, which included the main-street building in which the newspaper was housed. He shocked the townspeople with his first action. He cut off those subscribers who had not been paying for the paper. He applied the same no-credit philosophy to local merchant advertisers, and the paper made money almost from the time of his arrival.

A local farmer, Leonard Harman, walked in one day offering to sell a column to Hebb. The result, called "Furrow's End," was eventually syndicated to a score of other weeklies, and the two became great friends. Harman became active in the co-operative movement, later rising to the position of general manager of United Co-operatives of Ontario. Hebb's background had prepared him for the fervour of the credit union movement, and his friends were beginning to draw him closer to it.

By 1944 he had sold the Newmarket paper (by then he had merged the *Era* with another local paper, the *Express*) and was editor of the *Rural Co-operator*, published by the United Farmers' Co-operative and the Ontario Federation of Agriculture. In 1946 A. C. (Bert) Savage, a veteran of the First World War and secretary of the Co-operative Union of Ontario, formed a mutual insurance group to provide bonding for the employees of co-operatives and credit unions who handled members' money. The insurance planned was mainly performance bonding for treasurers, for example, of credit unions. There was also blanket coverage of losses from robbery or misrepresentation of funds. The other founding group was the Ontario Credit Union League. The name of the new company: Co-operators Fidelity and Guarantee Association (CF&GA). The following year, the Ontario Federation of Agriculture became the third sponsor. Those on Savage's proposed list for membership on the board of directors were all farmers, however, and the Ontario regulators wanted some additional business expertise. Savage turned to Hebb, with his successful publishing career, law degree, and empathy for the co-operative movement. Hebb became a director of the CF&GA and would run it until 1970.

The name "Co-operators" was a compromise second choice. Ontario legislation in place at the time did not allow the name "Co-operative" to be used by an insurance company. There was only one company writing insurance on livestock being transported to market, so in response to farmers' pleas to bring some competition to that area, the Co-operators added coverage for animals in transit to market. Next, fire insurance was considered, but it was decided not to compete with farmers' mutuals already in business. The early years were not profitable. The summer of 1948 was hot, and every mail delivery to the Toronto office seemed to bring news of animals dying on the way to market. In 1949 automobile insurance was offered and 4,000 policies written. Again, the results were not auspicious—the Co-operators had an operating loss of $9,000 on its auto business.

With the losses came debate about who really owned and ran the company. The investors thought they should be in charge, but because the company was growing out of the co-operative movement, and because there were far more policyholders than investors, the policyholders thought they should have control. Because of the losses, however, the more important need was to inject more funds, more capital, to ensure that surpluses were built up. As a result, the United Co-operatives of Ontario put $75,000 into a new joint-stock company, in return for a half ownership, and the name was changed to Co-operators Insurance Association (CIA). The company was now owned by the various co-op movements.

The third employee to join was Margaret Chambers in 1948. With Savage, Hebb, and Bernard Shea, another early employee, she would help build the company. Chambers, then thirty-two, had graduated in 1938 from the University of Toronto. Then she worked in North American Life's actuarial department and at Dominion Securities, where she did bids and evaluations on bonds. She was hired by Co-operators at $50 a week. Hebb was still the newspaper editor, but she, Shea, Hebb, and two newpaper staffers were all in one room.

Chambers carried no job title in the early years. Shea was secretary-treasurer and Hebb became general manager. Hebb was quiet but demanding, and had an attitude towards employment that pre-dated human rights legislation. "He brought in coloured people," recalls Chambers, "which wasn't done too much in those days." He worked long hours, staying most nights until at least six, and many evenings and weekends as well. There was always the panic of the newspaperman about him as deadlines approached. Reports to the board, for example, would be lengthy, completed and finished only hours before they were to be presented. For years, Hebb would type them himself, pounding away on an old manual machine long after everyone else in the large general office that served everyone had switched to the more efficient electric models.

The main business came from farmers as the economic times improved. Many of them had neither owned a car nor carried insurance before. In the beginning, there was a policy fee in addition to the cost of the insurance. On a short-term policy, the fee meant the premium on a Co-operators policy was higher than on other policies. It was priced so that over a two-year period it would even out. The policies were sold direct to the policyholder (there was no agent in the middle charging up to the usual 20-per-cent commission), and claims were handled by independent adjusters to keep costs down. The sales agents were members of the various credit union staffs—at the telephone companies, steel plants, farm co-ops—who made applications available to members for no commission. Their only pay was a dinner sponsored from time to time by The Co-operators. Premiums were paid in cash; no costly credit was offered.

The combination of volunteer salespeople—the numbers grew quickly to 150—and the loyalty of customers caused the early growth. Right from the beginning there was great loyalty in rural Ontario. "People wouldn't shop around," says Chambers. The firm had sold policies only to members of the sponsoring organizations, but in 1951, that was changed so that anyone could purchase policies. As a result, over the next decade, farm automobile policies declined from 70 per cent of the total so that there was an even split in auto policies among farm policyholders, credit union members, and others. During that time, new types of coverage were offered: accident and sickness, family liability, and others.

One innovation instituted by The Co-operators persists across the industry today. When the premium notice is sent to a policyholder, the amounts under the various coverage sections are always rounded to the nearest dollar. There are no amounts including cents. The idea came at lunch one day when Chambers, Hebb, employee Ernie Moores, and some others were eating at a restaurant called The Diet Kitchen (famous in those days for its fruit salad) on Bloor Street near the company's Toronto offices. The discussion turned to the extra typing time in took to put in the cents in several places on every policy. There was talk of rounding it to every 10 cents, or every 25 cents, but Chambers pointed out that that would not save any time. There would still be two numbers to type. Why not, she suggested, round it to the nearest dollar? Amounts below 50 cents would be rounded down, amounts above, rounded up. There was immediate agreement and the rest of the industry soon followed. Policies are still billed this way.

They soon realized that agents needed more than just a casualty insurance product, so a fire insurance policy was introduced—but only for urban dwellers. The Co-operators did not want to compete with its brethren in the farm mutual fire business. Also added was medical coverage of injuries suffered in auto accidents. The Co-operators was among the first to offer it simply by putting a $2 charge (and a $1 policy fee) on the regular billing. Those who did not want the coverage could cross it off. Ninety per cent of the policyholders bought it.

Policyholders became so loyal to The Co-operators that in 1956, when policyholders were renewing their policies, they were also asked to make a $2 donation that would be a "gift to surplus" in order to strengthen the underlying financial position of the firm. The 56,500 policies in force produced "gifts"—of $1 or $2 each—totalling $49,573. Originally, the money was thought to be not subject to income tax in the hands of the company, but in 1961 the company paid a negotiated tax settlement of $8,868.

By the beginning of the 1960s, The Co-operators had 18,000 residential fire policies, 26,000 farm and urban liability policies, and 126,000 automobile policies in force. It had grown to second place among the 250 auto insurance companies in Ontario. Hebb had also discovered a way of keeping premiums low, by earning more money on investments in the stock market. Because dividends from Canadian tax-paying corporations were not taxable in the hands of the owner of the stock, CIA began investing heavily in Canadian stock as a way to both earn money and reduce tax annually by more than half. At first, stock ownership was 15 per cent of the total investment portfolio. That later grew to a 25-per-cent share. (By comparison, many life insurance companies today have less than 10 per cent of their investments in stock.)

Because stock investments fluctuate, such holdings were more risky than bonds or mortgages, where the return on investment is guaranteed. For The Co-operators, however, the risk paid off. "There were times when we weren't competitive," says Chambers. "We had to depend on loyalty—but there were [costly] policy lapses. In the 1960s, there was many a year when investment kept us in the black." In 1962, for example, income tax paid was $67,000. Without stock investments, it would have been $140,000, and the savings allowed a profit. There were certain stocks, however, that were not included in the portfolio. The Co-operators, for example, purchased no stock in any company that produced cigarettes or liquor because, it was argued, such products had a negative influence on claims.

The atmosphere in those early years was familial. The regular board meetings, for example, were held on Saturday because most of the directors were active in their local co-ops or credit unions the other five days of the week. When they came for the all-day meeting, the wives would come, too, do a little shopping together, and join their husbands at the end of the meeting, around three-thirty, for afternoon coffee and cookies. Hebb, who was no accomplished public speaker, would nonetheless go out to what were known as "policyholder-shareholder conferences," where the people who owned and used the company could complain about service or offer suggestions.

In 1959 a companion life company, Co-operators Life Insurance Association (CIA Life), was formed. Together the companies were known as Co-operators Insurance Associations of Guelph (CIAG). The two companies, the casualty company and the new life company, shared the same board of directors, sales force, staff, and offices. From the beginning, however, CIA Life was a weak sister because legislation prohibited it from receiving investment earnings from stocks and thus being able to reduce income taxes and keep premiums competitive. Still, as Hebb wrote in 1963, CIA had strength beyond the balance sheet. "The presidents of the three [sponsoring] organizations sit on the 1963–64 board of directors. A hundred or more sponsor committees join hands in an exciting project. City and country people, credit unionists and farmers, work together. Cooperation is both root and fruit."

In a firm that served so many farmers, it was only fitting that it was a farmer who succeeded Hebb. This farmer, however, had a degree in maths and physics. Teunis Haalboom was born in Holland in 1932, the son of a clergyman. He grew up with war around him. It was from Canadian soldiers who liberated the Netherlands that he learned about Canada. By 1951, he was through with his studies at the University of Amsterdam and the Dutch army was calling him for service in Indonesia. Haalboom concluded that he had seen enough war and decided to leave his family, including two sisters, to emigrate. His first choice was Australia, but the passage was too expensive. Canada was next on his list.

He visited the Canadian embassy only to discover that to get into the country, he had to pay his own way and agree to be a farm labourer for a year. He had passed a bit of time on the farms of relatives, but his experience was limited. Embassy officials knew he wasn't keen, but since that was the only route, he signed up. At nineteen, he sailed to Halifax, where he was put on an immigrant train for Toronto. The cars were ancient, equipped with wooden benches and stoves. The trip took five days. It was then that Haalboom began to get some idea of the immensity of Canada compared with his native land. "You do that for five days and you're only half-way across the country. You feel like you're being swallowed up."

In Toronto, he was shipped on to his farm destination in Mooretown, Ont., near Sarnia. There, he received room and board and $15 a week. Haalboom spent the first few months learning English and trying to adapt to his new home. He found the place primitive. He was confronted with an outhouse, wide open spaces, a country with few social programs, and a lot of people just struggling to get by.

By fall, the farm work was finished, the one-year obligation fulfilled. He went to work on a CNR section gang laying new track through an Indian reserve near Sarnia. Again he was plunged into a new learning experience. Language he was picking up from the gang, he realized, did not help him in polite company. Also, there were discrepancies all around him on the reserve. The railway was being laid to a new plant, part of the growing chemical valley development south of Sarnia. Cash payments had been made to each member of the band. The money had apparently all gone to luxuries. Outside the shacks sat Cadillacs and Lincolns.

Haalboom saw great social contrasts in Canada. As an immigrant, he was made to feel inferior by those in charge—the section gang superintendent, for example. "You don't feel part of society. People think you're stupid. I set out to prove them wrong." Next, he became a chemist in a lab at nearby Polymer Corp. He worked there from 1952 to 1954 until he discovered he was red-green colour-blind and couldn't identify test results accurately. The only other jobs open at Polymer were overseas. He did not want to leave Canada. He had something to prove.

His initial contact with The Co-operators came when his father, on a visit, was driving his son's car and got into an accident with a truck. It was the truck-driver's fault, but he was underinsured. Haalboom had no collision coverage, so his own insurance company could not pay for the damages. Because it was the fault of the other driver, Haalboom's insurance company, The Co-operators, did not even have a financial interest in the situation, under the thinking of the day. Once the damages to Haalboom's car were added up, the other company offered to pay half. The Co-operators urged him to accept. He was livid. The accident had not been his father's fault. There were no other witnesses, it was pointed out.

Haalboom became intrigued by the legal system that came into play and by the positions of the two companies. Although The Co-operators was prohibited from helping him by the lack of a financial interest, it did show him legal steps to take. He issued a writ against the other company, and a settlement was offered before the court date of the full amount. Haalboom was hooked. He wanted to know more. By that time, he was married and the father of two children. Going back to school to become a lawyer was out of the question, so he went into insurance—at The Co-operators.

At the time, the company was tiny. It was 1954, head office was in Toronto, and there were about forty employees. Premium income that year hit $1 million for the first time. (Current annual premium income is $441 million.) As a trainee, he did everything from answering the phones and filing to underwriting. In 1956 he became district manager in St. Catharines; in 1959 he was posted to Sault Ste. Marie to establish a northern Ontario district.

While the company had been getting some business from the area, mainly through credit unions, Haalboom had to start right from scratch, appointing agents, training people, and setting up service centres. Hebb, the autocratic general manager, left Haalboom alone except for twice-yearly reporting visits to Toronto. Haalboom revelled in the freedom. When he was finished, after seven years, he had built a district with seventy employees that wrote about 12 per cent of the company's overall business. Moreover, it was profitable at a time when many property and casualty companies were losing money in that area.

Head office moved to Guelph, about 100 kilometres west of Toronto. Haalboom moved to Guelph, too, where he was to run another district, central Ontario. Although he was not a head office employee, he was located in the same building. "Andrew Hebb had this model in his mind that you go where your support is," says Haalboom. And the support was outside Toronto, in the smaller communities and among farmers. Even today, The Co-operators has 12 per cent of the market in Ontario, but only 5 per cent of the Toronto market.

Guelph was not Hebb's first choice. Because of the early support of farmers and farm organizations in Grey County, he wanted to move the headquarters there. The Toronto staff rebelled. They were prepared to move out of Toronto, but they did not want to go to Owen Sound, where they felt education facilities were weak. Guelph, with its university, was a compromise. Hebb did, however, move the data-processing centre to Owen Sound. The company bought an old building in Guelph, formerly used by the YWCA. Only the bottom floor was usable. When it rained, there were floods upstairs. About seventy-five employees remained in Toronto, about sixty moved to Guelph. The bus depot was just down the street, and that was how papers, memos, and files were shipped between the two cities.

Throughout, there was only one boss—Andrew Hebb. He was a teetotaller and did not allow any drinking at company functions. Nor did he allow any gifts from suppliers, brokers, or claims adjusters. While he was autocratic and for years allowed no major decisions to be made without his approval, he also took an enlightened approach towards staff that went well beyond the usual paternalism of the time. He did personally hand out turkeys to staff at Christmas, but he also set up a variable annuity plan for employees—the first in Canada—to act as a pension scheme. Each employee put 3 per cent of his or her pay, via payroll deduction, into the plan. The company added a further 7 per cent (increasing to 12 per cent, depending on years of service) of the individual's salary. In profitable years, the company would contribute an extra amount. Hebb knew most of the employees by name and would keep people on after their usual retirement age of sixty-five, if they wanted to continue working to build up more pension benefits. Hebb also instituted the practice of posting all salaries in order to remove suspicion and staff rivalry. There were occasions when he wasn't even the top man on the list. His salary, even in his final year as boss, was $60,000. "He just didn't want more," says Margaret Chambers. "His salary demands were modest. The board always had to push him."

His attitude towards policyholders was unusual, too. In a case where a policy had lapsed, for example, and there was an accident, all a policyholder had to do was say he had intended to renew, pay the premium for the next year's coverage—and the claim for the accident would be paid. Before mandatory seat-belt legislation, the firm also paid a bonus to policyholders who were wearing their belts when involved in an accident and had thus reduced injuries. They tried to settle claims fairly and without going to court. The unspoken motto underlying everything done in the Hebb-run company was "Doing well by doing good."

In the 1960s, the firm was the first to computerize its operations. While other firms were still processing applications and claims by hand, The Co-operators kept expenses down by mechanization of much of the drudgery and paperwork. Even today, the computer centre in Meadowvale in the west Toronto suburbs is sufficiently advanced that it handles the needs of 700,000 credit union members in Ontario as well as its own policyholders' files.

Andrew Hebb signalled the end to his iron-fisted rule in 1968 when he posted a notice on a bulletin board one day saying that he would be retiring in 1970. He invited applications for his replacement as general manager, to be submitted for consideration by the board of directors. Haalboom wanted the job, but assumed it would go to Hebb's long-time second-in-command, Ernie Moores. Haalboom was not alone in his thinking. Many others on staff who saw Moores as a warmer person than Haalboom thought the same. At one point, Hebb had even sent Moores to university for a year, on full salary.

The day before applications closed, Hebb phoned Haalboom to urge him to apply. Haalboom told him that he thought the decision had already been made. "I don't think it's all that canned," said Hebb. Hebb told Haalboom he would put his name in. Haalboom was not hopeful. Even when he was telephoned at home the following day, he was a reluctant candidate. It was a Saturday; Haalboom was barbecuing for fifteen guests in his backyard. He really did not want to go in to the office for what he thought was just a charade before Moores was appointed. "I don't have to go through all this," he said. "I think you're going to appoint Ernie Moores. If you do, that's fine with me. But let's not waste my time." They persuaded him to be interviewed by the four-member board selection committee right then; he agreed to come in only if they'd let him show up in the shorts and T-shirt he was wearing that day.

It wasn't that he didn't want the job, but he didn't want to lunge and lose, he didn't want to put a strong effort forward if he didn't stand a chance. "I don't like losing," he says. "I'm not much of a gambler. I have to have fairly good odds. I wouldn't put my money in a ring with eight others unless it was on an even basis." A two-hour interview convinced him that this was no charade to crown Ernie Moores. He agreed, along with the other seven candidates, to undergo a day-long psychological test in Toronto—but only if he saw the full report submitted to the board. The results placed his intelligence level among the top 2 per cent of the population. While it also indicated he could get along with people, it said that he was impatient with those who couldn't keep up with him and had a drive to succeed that could hurt others.

A few days later, he headed out on a Friday on a family camping holiday in northern Ontario. Hebb had failed to tell him that a decision was possible the following day. The board chose Haalboom for the job and then couldn't find him. Messages were flashed out through the offices in the hopes he might call in at an office to say hello to old friends on his way through. Monday, he phoned from Sault Ste. Marie. Hebb told Haalboom that he had been picked as heir apparent. Years later, Haalboom realized that it was in the cards all along. "I guess what I didn't realize was that he wanted me to succeed him. He would have let the board come to that decision—but if they hadn't, he would have persuaded them."

As heir apparent, he would be deputy general manager and become general manager in 1970 when Hebb stepped down as previously announced. There was a new wrinkle, however; two of the other hopefuls were being appointed assistant deputy managers (for finance and administration) under Haalboom. They were Ernie Moores and Bob Power. Hebb wanted Haalboom to accept on the spot. Haalboom was still playing the reluctant heir. Haalboom deferred, saying he wanted to think about it during his vacation and talk to Moores and Power on his return. Hebb agreed. After Haalboom had returned, Moores told him that he had never expected the job to come to him. He was happy as assistant general manager. Haalboom accepted.

Nothing changed immediately. Hebb continued to run the place single-handed. Haalboom was supposed to be in training, sitting at the feet of Hebb, getting ready to take over. But Hebb let few tasks pass out of his hands. Finally, in order to speed the transition, Hebb gave up the general manager's job a few months earlier in 1970 than originally intended. Haalboom took over soon thereafter. Hebb ran investments for a year, then retired in 1971. At his going-away party, they gave him a silver tray and a copy of *Alice in Wonderland*, a book from which he had quoted at many an annual meeting.

When he became general manager in 1970, at thirty-eight, Haalboom set out to put his own stamp on the place. He consulted Hebb from time to time in the early going, but it was not his style to do that after Hebb had left. Among the first innovations he put in place was a change to cover policyholders who found themselves in the same position as his father twenty years earlier. Contingent collision coverage ensured that if another company's insured struck a policyholder of The Co-operators and was at fault—and The Co-operators policyholder had no collision coverage—The Co-operators would pay for repairs on its policyholder's vehicle, then seek reimbursement from the other insurance company. The policyholder of The Co-operators was not out of pocket for damages that weren't his fault, nor did he have to force payment, the way Haalboom had had to do twenty years earlier by threatening court action.

Haalboom oversaw expansion through a merger that began in 1972. The shareholders of the two companies in Ontario and Saskatchewan approved a study of a merger. The two companies were then known as Co-operators Insurance Associations of Guelph and CIS Ltd. CIS was a holding company that co-ordinated both Regina-based companies, Co-operative Fire and Casualty Co. (formed in 1952) and Co-operative Life Insurance Company, known familiarly as Co-op Life. Co-op Life had been formed by the directors of the Saskatchewan Wheat Pool in 1945. Co-op Life had similar beginnings to the Ontario company's—unhappiness with old-line companies. In the Depression of the 1930s, many prairie farmers lost everything, including life insurance policies, when they could no longer pay the premiums. The response was to form insurance mutuals. At the end of each year, members got a rebate if there was money left over, or paid in more premiums to balance the books.

As the 1970s passed, union between the firms in Regina and Guelph continued to be explored. In 1974 a committee of six, including Haalboom, was formed to explore ways of co-operating with each other. In 1976 the Co-operators Insurance Associations of Guelph merged with Co-operative Insurance Services of Regina to form The Co-operators (renamed The Co-operators Group Ltd. in 1978), with Haalboom as chief executive officer. The merger caused considerable turn-over. By 1980 only four of the original vice-presidents remained, only two of them in the same roles. The organization was highly decentralized, even disorganized. Although much of the accounting function was carried out in Regina, the treasurer and the chief financial officer were in Guelph. There were three field divisions, eight regions, forty-two districts—and no chief operating officer directly responsible for day-to-day operations.

Problems were beginning to develop. Between 1976 and 1981, for example, policies per staff member (a key measure of productivity) decreased 17 per cent, despite increased computerization. Market share had begun to decrease and the expense ratio was climbing considerably. Expense per policy had doubled, from $35.87 in 1976 to $72.28 in 1981. The place needed to be brought up short. A committee of vice-presidents had begun in December 1980 to look at ways of gaining new levels of productivity. In a 1982 report, the committee reported: "One of our corporate objectives is to provide security of employment. This does not mean we guarantee that everyone will remain in his or her present job, but it does mean that we will not have lay-offs for short-term financial gains for the company."

There was a down side to the decision, however. Salary raises in 1983 were tied to productivity improvement and an even more fundamental change occurred at the senior management level. With the departure of Hebb, one-man rule had been replaced by the consensus approach. Senior management arrived at major decisions as a group. That had to change. The individual responsibility of the manager was increased and senior management cut its meetings from eight or nine a year to two. A smaller group of vice-presidents advised Haalboom, and two senior vice-presidents, Wayne Scott at Co-operators General and Blair Roland at Co-operators Life, were appointed to head the two insurance companies as management focussed around the specific operations.

Non-sales staff were reduced by attrition beginning in July 1982. Within twelve months, 230 fewer employees were on the payroll— a reduction of 6.2 per cent. Voluntary work-sharing programs allowed staff to take jobs in other departments during peak load times. The number of part-timers was reduced as a result. An early retirement plan for non-sales staff over fifty-five was introduced. On the sales side, staff was increased by 25 per cent. Commissions were improved and overall costs went up only slightly because the non-sales staff savings were transferred to the sales side.

With the staff reductions came productivity improvement, and as a result, staff received a lump-sum payment equal to 6 per cent of their salary. The expense ratio, which had grown from 23.1 in 1976 to 31.2 in June 1982, began to fall, reaching 27.3 in March 1985. The ratio of policies in force per non-sales employee was 460 in 1981 and 553 in March 1985.

The improvements, toughest the company ever had to make, were only possible because of the corporate culture, argues Haalboom. "There is a strong sense among senior managers that they are part of the co-operative movement, that policyholders are people—believe it or not. There is a strong sense that we are not in business for one group of stakeholders. We're not here just to make a buck for those who supply the capital. There must be a balance between policy-holders and shareholders. What one person does reflects upon the others."

That doesn't mean Haalboom won't admit to feeling personal satisfaction at his success. That section gang superintendent who scoffed at his English and sneered at his understanding of the country would have to sit up and take notice now. Haalboom admits that he has felt some surge within that he has proved such people wrong. "Initially, it's defensive: I'll show these guys. I wasn't conscious of it at the time. It's only on reflection. I'm a prouder Canadian than a native-born Canadian. Once you get the feeling that you do belong, all the rest leaves you."

CHAPTER SEVENTEEN

"RIDING ON A SMILE AND A SHOESHINE"

The Duel Between Agent and Client

THERE ARE a dozen of us gathered in the downtown Toronto office meeting room on a winter night, all drawn by a small newspaper announcement promising a career and riches in the life insurance business. Arthur Balfour, sales manager of the University Avenue branch of Sun Life, is telling us just how easy the whole process really is. "We're not involved in selling at all," he says. "We're consulting and advising." As for finding those people to "advise"— well, it's a snap. All it takes is talking to people you know. "If you've been a nurse, then you've met a lot of people during your life—other nurses, doctors, pharmacists, the guy at your local Becker's, the dry cleaners you've been going to for the last fourteen years." To hear Balfour tell it, the world is full of prospects just waiting for a call.

Or so those gathered desperately want to believe. Among the group looking for the easy life are a couple of computer programmers, a white-haired man from the property and casualty insurance business, a film distributor, a housewife, and assorted others who don't identify themselves, including me. Balfour is looking for new recruits for his branch, where there are already twenty agents in an office that stands tenth in Sun's sales rankings even though some branches have three times as many agents. A night like this, a combination Tupperware party and psychologist's couch, is one way he finds new talent.

For Balfour, nothing is more important than life insurance sales. "We grease the wheels of industry," he tells the group. "We help businesses run. Nothing out there can happen without our being involved." But for all that, he admits, life insurance and its agents are not seen for the godsend that they are. "We still have to go out there and tell people. It's the most frustrating thing. They should be queuing at the door and around the corner." Further, as if the product wasn't enough in itself, there's the fact that the price of insurance has even been dropping relative to other items, he says.

He talks about the process of sales, how well educated the consumer has become, and how, in response, insurance sales agents have had to become increasingly professional. After an introductory session with a client at which information is gathered, the agent makes a return visit to close the deal. It's easy, maintains Balfour. "You go back with information that's fact, it's true, it's not Mickey Mouse." The housewife is not convinced. "How do I, a forty-one-year-old housewife, talk to my neighbour, a doctor, a lawyer, about what to do about investments etc.?" Balfour is nothing if not confident. "We'll have you doing it in three weeks." "Do some people contact you?" someone asks. "Not very much," Balfour admits.

Insurance sales, like most other products, is a numbers game. If an agent carries out such a fact-finding talk with two people a day, that's ten people seen in a week. Perhaps three agree to a second visit; one buys. "You have to live with the turn-downs every day," says Balfour. "You've got to be hungry for achievement. You've got to be able to dream. You've got to want it so much—without trampling on people—that the problems you face won't faze you." There is independence, too, away from office routine and demanding managers. "You don't have to ask anybody for a raise. You don't have to worry about anyone liking you."

Then he gets to the best part: the money. Balfour talks of an agent he knows who spends four months a year lolling in Mexico. The agent owns two cars and has a cottage with four boats. After the cold reality of rejection, the group begins to warm to the tales Balfour spins, imagining their own life-style after a few successful years in the business. He skips over the grungy details of joining Sun—the two-hour aptitude test, two to four months' training, the payroll subsidy system—because soon the sky's the limit. Two recruits last year each made $35,000 in their first twelve months on the job. "In the fifth year, you should be making $60,000 and up," he says. The training Sun gives is important, but not as important as the individual's talent and motivation. "The real entrepreneur will do well no matter how we train them. They'll run over us."

Arthur Balfour is doing what every manager must do: recruiting new agents. For every twenty-five he talks to, eight will take the aptitude test, five will pass, and one will be successfully recruited. Sales is a numbers game for him, too. Of all the strange things being sold in this world, life insurance must rank with the most bizarre. Think about it. Some agent comes round to your house, gives you a spiel you don't understand, signs you up to send in cheques for something you not only will never see but will have to die to collect. Even those in the industry itself realize that life insurance selling is a difficult proposition. "We're asking people to turn money over to us that they will never see in their lifetime," admits John Gardner, senior vice-president and executive officer of Sun Life.

Some of the methods used to sell the product are equally bizarre. Everyone in the business has a favourite among the worst lines used. Example: an agent phones up a prospect, makes the pitch to both the husband and wife, and then concludes by saying to the wife, "Why don't you sleep on it, and if Mel wakes up in the morning, you can let me know your decision."

To be fair, not every insurance agent is the pushy, won't-take-no-for-an-answer person of lore. It's no fun being an agent, either. First, there is the image problem. Even Woody Allen, whose fixation with death is the theme of many of his movies, has this to say: "After all, there are worse things than death. Have you ever spent an evening with a life insurance agent?" Still, it can't be easy for the sales agent hearing prospects say no all day. The old saw in the business goes: "There's no one with endurance like the man who sells insurance." The constant rejections drive many from the business because some agents take them personally. All sales agents regularly go through periods when the fear of rejection paralyzes them. They can't make telephone calls, they can't knock on doors, they drive around the block several times before approaching a house. The disease has various names: "hot doorknobs" is a favourite.

Brian Wrixon, superintendent of agencies for training and development at Confederation Life, regularly sees the effects of rejection first-hand. Once, after he had spent two hours showing one agent-trainee how to make a phone call to a prospect, the lesson still had not achieved the required effect. The trainee's hands trembled, sweat poured down his face, and he simply could not pick up the phone.

Wrixon spent another twenty minutes coaxing and cajoling, finally convincing him to place his first call. A woman answered, and the trainee asked to speak to the man whose name was on his list. The man, he was told, had died two days earlier. The trainee never made another sales call.

The high rate of rejection and the lowly image combine to cause a huge turn-over in sales agents. After Sun's Arthur Balfour has churned through twenty-five people to find just one new agent, most of them still don't last. Of every hundred agents who start, eighty-two are gone after four years. In the industry, they turn that number around and refer to the four-year "retention" rate, and the average is eighteen. Still, in any given year, new agents are coming along, clamouring to try a sales career. In 1984 there were 21,500 agents in Canada. Eighty-five per cent of all individual life insurance sold is sold by career agents, agents tied to one company. In the U.S., the figure drops to 65 per cent and the situation is more competitive. More agents are able to compare and sell the policies of several companies rather than just the one they happen to work for.

While the vast majority of sales agents, 91 per cent, are male, at least one company has made an effort not only to employ women, but to sell to them as well. Imperial Life Assurance opened a Women's Financial Planning Centre in 1983 in Toronto. The Centre is staffed by women, all of them university graduates, and it reaches many of its female prospects through financial planning seminars. Not everyone uses such subtle techniques to sell insurance. Toronto broker Arnold Freeman mails out dollar bills—$1,500 a month—to attract attention to his North City Insurance Agency. He has also experimented with cassette tapes containing a four-minute spiel by a professional announcer.

For all the bad press salespeople have received, however, they occupy a pivotal role in modern life. In George Orwell's *Coming Up for Air*, the narrator says: "What are the realities of modern life? Well, the chief one is an everlasting, frantic struggle to sell things. With most people it takes the form of selling themselves—that's to say, getting a job and keeping it." The world that Orwell describes applies to two plays that span thirty-five years of theatre, Arthur Miller's 1949 *Death of a Salesman* and David Mamet's 1984 play *Glengarry Glen Ross*. In Miller's play, Willy Loman's self-delusions take him a long way from reality. Mamet's crew is more practical as they trick unsuspecting clients into buying Florida swampland.

The salesmen presented in both plays live on their spiels, however, and bemoan what's happened to the profession of sales and to their individual place in the world. Says Loman, "Today it's all cut and dried, and there's no chance for bringing friendship to bear—or personality." Complains one of Mamet's characters: "We are the members of a dying breed." The salesman is, in fact, at the heart of society's dreams, as Miller wrote: "He's a man way out there in the blue, riding on a smile and a shoeshine. And when they start not smiling back—that's an earthquake. And then you get yourself a couple of spots on your hat, and you're finished... A salesman is got to dream, boy. It comes with the territory." And society buys those dreams. From the preacher, eternal life. From the insurance sales-man, your loved ones' eternal gratitude. For the preacher, there are souls to convert at whatever the cost. For the insurance salesman, that next client might be a biggie, the one that will help win the toaster or the exotic vacation.

What motivates the super-seller? A 1984 article in *Psychology Today* cited a number of requirements for what the author termed "the fire within." The first was status. "They enjoy power and authority, and are strongly aware of image and reputation." Second, control. They like people, "but they seldom care deeply whether others like them, a trait which enables them to use emotion without falling prey to it." Super-sellers also are honest, believe in the product, and need stimulation. "They have more physical energy than most of us." Respect and routine are also important, as is accomplishment. All-time top insurance salesman Ben Feldman admits, "Money loses its ability to inspire you." New and impossible sales goals are the answer for him.

In the early going, of course, pay can be peanuts for insurance sellers. At the top, however, a high-flying sales agent can make $400,000 a year. Notes André Anderson, Mutual of Canada's vice-president for individual insurance: "The highest-paid person in the company is an agent, the lowest-paid person in the company is an agent. The two qualities required are imagination and guts." Imagi-nation is needed for prospecting—finding potential new clients. The guts are needed to make the approach. "When you get to the door," says Anderson, "the handle is pretty hot. Many don't have the audacity to turn the handle. You can't teach an agent all the situa-tions he'll face, but if he's got a good imagination, he'll do it. It's pretty lonely out there. And you don't get paid unless there's a sale."

Although the money can be good, that can't be the only driving force, says Jack Brindle, president of Sun Life. "If you really belong in the life insurance business, you become a crusader. Life insurance has to be sold, and if you really believe a man should have the protection for his family, the successful ones are not in it for the money." For many, the crusade becomes religious. "The strongly religious people make good insurance salesmen," says Brindle. "The link is internal with them." The internal link, of course, is to the eternal. In the movie *Love at First Bite* George Hamilton, as the modern-day Dracula, is making his move on an unsuspecting Susan St. James. "I can promise you eternal life," he says. "Oh no," comes her reply, "not another life insurance salesman."

One of the attractions of the business is that an individual can become a sales agent, with all the entrepreneurial freedom that brings, with no initial capital investment required. Unlike most businesses, where there are start-up costs, overhead, inventory, and a host of other expenses, getting into insurance sales costs nothing. It's like buying a car with no money down. Companies train agents and the largest—Sun, London, Confederation, and a few others—tend to train everyone because the smaller companies simply cannot afford good programs.

Prospective agents at London Life are told to telephone ten people they know well and ten they don't to try to line them up as possible insurance clients. From those twenty people, they have to obtain another thirty names. After fifty calls, they know if this is the kind of work they want to do. Another early task for a new agent is to deliver a cheque to a widow in order to experience her gratitude and be motivated by both the utility and the emotional rewards of the product. After the initial training, the agent must pass a provincial licensing exam, then can proceed through courses offered by the Life Underwriters Association of Canada, as well as a Chartered Life Underwriter (CLU) course, a university-level program that takes five years.

In the first few months, most companies put new agents on a monthly draw so that some money is paid to them when sales are slow. Mutual has one of the best financing programs, helping Mutual to attract good salespeople and keep them, thus maintaining the high retention rate. One such person is Philip Moller, thirty-eight, who was vice-president of a book publishing company. After thirteen years in publishing, he decided to go into insurance sales. His financing plan at Mutual provided him with $3,600 a month against earnings.

He didn't need much help. He joined Mutual in June 1982 and grossed $88,000 in his first full year. In 1985, his fourth year with Mutual in Toronto, he will gross $150,000 and net $115,000 after expenses. Business is so good that his wife, Candy, has left her publishing job to join him. "I'm in the business," says Moller, "because whatever agent came to see me never asked me about my problems. They just went into their product and the features. Whatever income level I was at, the answer to my problems was always $50,000 whole life." He felt he could empathize with clients more closely and solve their problems. "A career in insurance offered me the opportunity to go into business for myself using the only capital I had, talent and energy. I wanted to make a comfortable living and to satisfy the needs of my clientele." He felt that, with his sales background, he could sell circles around most in the business. He was right. In his first year, his total sales were high enough to gain membership in the Million Dollar Round Table.

In 1983 he sold ninety-six individual insurance policies with a volume of more than $14 million and a premium income of almost $67,000. He also sold sixty-six annuities with a premium of over $750,000 and five group policies with a premium of $87,000. Mutual named him "Recruit of the Year." The company wanted him to participate in a forty-five-minute video explaining his technique so that others could learn from him. His initial explanation of his success: "I probably had the highest mortgage of anybody you recruited that year—$95,000."

In his four years, he has seen some sales tactics that make him weep for his profession. Early on, he heard a tale from another agent about a salesman who actually brought a miniature coffin on sales calls and placed it in front of the prospect to remind him of his mortality. The industry calls such theatrics "backing the hearse up to the door." One of Moller's clients had suffered through just such an approach when he was pitched by an agent from another life insurance company out doing cold calls. The other agent's pitch included a mini-slide projector with transparencies of auto accidents, complete with mangled guard-rails and crumpled cars. He flashed about a dozen slides in all until, as Moller describes the scene, he felt he had created "the appropriate emotional atmosphere."

Moller's rival was following an ancient and honourable tradition. An 1879 London Life manual declared: "It is an awful thing for a man on his death-bed to consider, that, ere his corpse grows cold, his widow may be haggling with the undertaker for the price of his coffin, and his family may hunger and thirst to provide him with a decent sepulchre." A 1900 North American Life diary was filled with homilies such as: "Will your widow dress as well as your wife does? Have you paid your premium?" And this from an early Mutual Life pamphlet: "The husband who during his life neglects to provide for his family robs his last sad hours on earth of one of their grandest consolations—the comforting and peace-inspiring thought that those loved ones he must leave behind will not be exposed to the ruthless pinch of poverty or be thrown upon the cold charity of a pitiless world."

Not only do most modern-day sellers use different techniques, but the results, at least for the top agents, are easier to reach. Cam Leamy, senior vice-president for marketing at Sun Life, began as a salesman in Montreal in October 1953. In 1954 he earned $2,012. By 1973, he was heading Sun's agency in Houston, Tex., and by 1980 he was making $150,000. Don't believe, he insists, the sales image of "some poor SOB who gets fifteen nos for every yes. The successful sales-man who has 500 clients never has to deal with a stranger again." In April 1981 he was promoted to head office in Toronto. The pitch was irresistible when it was pointed out to him that, as a sales rep, he had probably criticized the company. Now, he was being offered a chance to change things at the top. "With what licence," the question went, "will you be able to criticize Sun ever again?" Admits Leamy: "That's when they tripped the ego of the salesman."

Lloyd Kirk, today a senior vice-president at North American Life, took a similar route to the top. Kirk was born in Thunder Bay, Ont., and started to work as a young man for a local tycoon, Frank Murphy, owner of Murphy Coal & Fuel Co. Kirk wasn't out of university two years when Murphy died. Even with his apparent wealth—a home in Thunder Bay, a cottage outside the city, another home in the south—Murphy's only liquid asset was $50,000 worth of shares in Inco and a small amount of cash. The business and some apartment buildings had to be sold to pay estate taxes. Kirk saw firsthand what a life insurance policy would have meant to the family.

In 1958 Kirk joined Great-West Life as an agent, then became a general agent in 1962, selling life as well as property and casualty insurance. From the beginning, life insurance had more appeal for him. "It did something important. A $3,000 car accident claim is a heck of a lot different than a death in the family."

In his early days as an agent, he found other potent examples of life insurance's social worth. At one point, he was working on two clients. One bought a policy and the other didn't. Within months, both were dead. The widow of the man who hadn't bought a policy had to sell everything to carry on. The other woman received a cheque from Great-West for $80,000 and wept for gratitude. "I had a story to tell," recalls Kirk.

He also spent time during his career teaching others, taking young agents out and watching them use one of the seller's favourite devices, the "fatal alternative." An agent makes his pitch, then presents two policies to the client and asks the client to choose one of them. An agent never asks, "Do you want a policy or don't you?" That would give the client a chance to say, "No sale." Today, sitting at the top of the management ladder, Kirk's pleasure can only be vicarious. "I look at the [death claim] numbers and think those are people enjoying something that the company has done for them. Each of them has a story."

Being a member of management also means that some in sales can and do earn more than he does. At North American, there are 850 agents in the field force and about 250 broker-agents. Out of these 1,100, about one-fifth earn $50,000 a year or more and about 300 win a week-long incentive trip paid for by the company. In 1984 the destination was Monte Carlo, all expenses paid, for the agent and spouse. In 1986 North American's gathering will be in London, England. In addition to trips, money is also a powerful incentive. A top career agent at North American will earn $110,000, and a top general agent (who has other agents working in his office) will earn $300,000. Many of the Canadian companies—Crown and North American are two examples—use independent general agents in the U.S. They sell policies themselves and wholesale policies through other agents and can often make millionaires of themselves.

Some agents rebel against the company systems and go on their own. Julian Wise and Carole MacDonald, of Toronto, met in 1976 when they went through the three-week London Life training program in London. Wise, a former special projects manager at the *Financial Post*, and MacDonald, a former emergency-room nurse, were drawn to life insurance—as many are—by the idea that independence was possible without any capital outlay.

The course was a shock to both their systems. "It was like a revival meeting of the Pentecostals, almost the Moonies," says MacDonald. "You were *theirs*. They were Mother." The course was structured to make participants think owning insurance was vital for almost everyone in society. "Not just selling insurance," says Wise, "but *permanent* life insurance with London Life. And if they couldn't afford it, you convinced them they could." Further, Wise noted, they were encouraged to own some first. "You can't sell it yourself unless you own some. Then you go and proselytize."

Both were successful in the early months and both made the London Life weekly sales bulletins, the "hit parade," by reaching a certain sales level in a given week. In the first year, commission income was a reasonably good $12,000–$14,000. But each was finding many things wrong with the system—even though they were succeeding within it. It bothered them that London Life regarded them as professionals after such minimal training. "They wanted us to talk to professionals as 'instant professionals,'" says MacDonald. Worse, however, the product seemed too high-priced, difficult to justify, and outdated compared with the new money products some firms were offering as interest rates shot up. Although she was doing reasonably well selling clients, she found herself asking: "Is there something wrong with me, is there something wrong with them, or is there something wrong with the system?" Both fled London Life, Wise in 1977 after one year, MacDonald in 1978 after eighteen months.

Wise joined North West Life, where new money policies were selling for one-third as much as whole life plans from old-line firms such as London Life. At the time, North West had no one in Ontario promoting the product, and there was some early consumer resistance. Says MacDonald, "People didn't want to buy it because they thought something was wrong." Wise became a managing general agent for North West, trying to get other agents interested in the product so they, in turn, would sell it to the public. The other agents, however, were slow to respond because they were happy with the conventional whole life products, where there were cash values building slowly. They didn't really want to move out of their comfortable ruts. It did not help that commissions on new money products were lower than on conventional products and no commission at all was paid on renewals.

The old-line firms buttressed the agents' view that there was something wrong with the interest-sensitive policies. One of the ways such policies were sold was by persuading the customer to cash in a current whole life and use the money to buy a new money product. This technique is an example of twisting and Wise became such a master that he jokingly says his theme song was the Chubby Checker hit from the 1960s "Let's Twist Again." And why not? He could get his clients three times the insurance coverage for the same premium. Old-line companies, of course, claimed these "twisters" were sent by the devil, and they feared for their profits. One insurance company executive told Wise they didn't even know how profitable whole life policies had been over the years. "It's been so profitable we haven't had to figure out how profitable," he was told. Wise argued that all he was doing was acting in the best interests of his clients, getting them the best, and least expensive, deal.

New money policies shook up the business. Some firms, such as London Life, rather than responding with similar products immediately, tried other fighting methods first. When it received requests for information about cash values in policy, London Life assumed the policyholder was considering switching to a new money policy and dragged its corporate feet before supplying the information, in the hopes of deterring the sale and keeping the policy on its own books instead.

In 1979 Wise and MacDonald (who had gone into real estate for a time) joined to run an agency together. They called themselves Wise, Hutton, MacDonald Insurance Agencies Inc. (Hutton is Carole MacDonald's maiden name) because they liked the sound of the three names. They formed a partnership in which Wise does most of the selling and MacDonald administers the office, does the books, deals with underwriters at the insuring company, and does some selling by phone. Wise's idea was to take new money policies one step beyond individual sales, and in 1978 he approached the Ontario Medical Association. The OMA did not want life insurance sales done door to door in the doctors' offices but did agree to a direct mail campaign that would allow those doctors who were interested to let Wise know. Three hundred doctors responded to the initial mailing, and Wise called on them all; he sold policies (backed by North West Life, then Gerling Global Life) to 280 of them, with an average death benefit of $200,000.

While the backing company has changed to ManuLife since the business was first set up, the thinking has remained the same: take the benefits of group—lower cost, reduced medical requirements—to individuals. Today MacDonald, forty-six, and Wise, thirty-eight, split about $150,000 in gross income annually. They have about 300 active clients and a further 150 who have been sold at some point. They are probably in the top 1 per cent of agents. One year, Wise reached the Top of the Table at the Million Dollar Round Table.

The fight between old-line companies and new money policies is over. But there are still problems in the system, according to Wise and MacDonald. When an agent leaves, as many do, any commission paid on policy renewals put in place by the agent reverts to the company. If a new agent takes over those policies, known as "orphans," the agent only receives a commission on a new sale, not for keeping policies on the books. The savings to the companies are unknown, but not inconsequential. The companies, then, need not really care about high turn-over rates. All those policies that stay in place—even after the agent who sold them is long gone—cost nothing in terms of commission.

Sales training is insufficient, they argue. "The business requires five to ten years before a person is competent," says MacDonald. "Training should be out of the hands of the company." Instead, the industry relies on half a dozen companies to do all the training in a few weeks, then expects the agents to perform professionally on behalf of clients. But the agent may not really be acting for the client. Because the agent's income will increase if business is placed with one company, the agent will hardly spread business around trying to give the client the most competitive deal.

One central training course would raise the level of training, MacDonald and Wise say, and an articling process, similar to legal articling, after some university training would also benefit a beginner. When training is in the hands of the individual companies, new agents don't know what other products exist for comparison. Only through such broad changes will the industry lift its image and be able to offer top service to clients. Says MacDonald, "It's tough to sell integrity in a business where there hasn't been a history of much integrity."

Sometimes, in insurance, it's hard to tell the difference between the successes and the failures. Don Smith is an independent agent in Calgary. Before he started selling insurance in Vancouver in 1975, he was a high-flying badminton ace. He had twice lost out in the Canadian badminton championship finals when his game fell apart under pressure.

Smith's hope was that his insurance career would be the success that wiped away past failures and realized new dreams. His new playing ground was the homes of prospective clients. "I traded away the badminton court for the kitchen table—and this time, I wasn't going to lose." By 1981 his success seemed assured, his annual sales reached $14.6 million. Trouble was that two-thirds of that total was in income averaging annuity contracts (IAACs). They had been popular with clients because they spread income out over a number of years into the future and reduced income tax payable.

The federal budget of November 12, 1981, ended some popular IAACs sold by insurance companies. "Two-thirds of my production was gone. It's tough to grow and be strong when you're crying," he told an audience of life insurance agents three years later. He switched his business to estate and business planning. In the past, he had found his clients by culling various street directories and other lists. He was able to go back to those he'd sold IAACs, help them plan their estates under the new rules, and gain more referrals in the process. His success was immediate again. He made the Top of the Table again the next year, 1982. "I have the vision." In badminton, "I didn't quite reach the stars." He intends to do so in insurance. And when he does, "I'm going to learn how to say 'I made it' in Chinese." Insurance offers him a chance to redeem himself. "We have the opportunity to be in total control of our lives. Let's all dare to dream big dreams because big dreams have the power to move mountains." For Smith, life insurance is a blood sport.

There are few better at the sales performance tap-dance than Lewis Warke, Jr., thirty-nine, of Edmonton. He runs the Warke Agency from the renovated red-brick Lemarchand Mansion, five minutes from his home in prestigious Belgravia. He has about 450 clients and a gross income of $545,000 a year. After expenses, he says, he nets "about $150,000." Most years, he will add about forty new clients, touching base with the old ones through birthday and Christmas cards. Every other year, he sits down and reviews each client's insurance program.

He is deeply religious and his beliefs are almost a sales tool. Warke fervently believes in God, and he likes to give something of himself before he takes something from a client. "A person really has to know how much you care before he cares how much you know." That's where the religion comes in, almost as an ice-breaker. "Number one in my life is God and my relationship with Jesus Christ, my saviour."

Most people go through life thinking God and the government will provide, says Warke. He is here to tell you that that isn't enough. Along with his argyle sweater, his baby face, and his pitch about his product, there is also a little of that old-time religion. "A successful person has to believe in the product. He's always wanting to grow. Every successful person has to come to grips with his success and his faith. God made no failures. He made you and I to be successful in whatever we choose to do."

Warke has certainly been successful. In 1983 one of the companies he works for, North American Life, declared him president of its President's Club, the company's top personal-production honour. He has $39 million in insurance in force with North American. He took the award with a grain of salt. "Our industry," he says, "is going to be the demise of the walnut tree. We get so many plaques. You get a plaque just for coming to work on Monday." The product, of course, is what's special, according to Warke. That's why he can sell it. "God has provided life insurance so that you can provide for people you care about. He provides for the birds of the air, but he doesn't throw the seed into the nest."

Warke was born in Ireland and moved to Canada with his family in 1948. His father was a minister, first a Presbyterian, later a Baptist. The family moved often and lived in five provinces, latterly Camrose, Alta., where Warke went to high school and sang with a rock group called The Xtatix. He still enjoys singing; at life insurance dinners at head office, he will remove his jacket, loosen his tie, and do "When Irish Eyes Are Smiling" after only the slightest provocation. He also sings at weddings, including the marriage of Edmonton Eskimo footballer Dan Kepply.

After he graduated from high school, he attended the Prairie Bible Institute in Three Hills, Alta., for one year. He was so lonely, he wrote away to the travel bureaus of various countries just to get the return mail. He attended Northern Alberta Institute of Technology at night and participated in a management training program with the Bay and became a ladies' dress buyer. In 1969 he joined New York Life and by 1979 he was ready to go on his own as a broker. Now he sells group insurance for Travelers, Dominion, Great-West, Manufacturers, Sun Life, and North American, as well as disability insurance for Paul Revere and Provident. He books 90 per cent of his individual life policies with North American. He keeps four staff, a tax accountant, and five underwriters busy. Three other brokers place their business through him.

Most of his business, selling individual life insurance policies, comes from referrals. Contented clients give him the names of others who might benefit from Warke's services. "Most insurance agents spend 90 per cent of their time looking for new clients; we spend 90 per cent of our time working with clients." When selling to individuals, he tries to concentrate on those who have annual incomes greater than $30,000. Prospects receive a letter from Warke offering estate planning, not life insurance. He waits three weeks, in the hopes that the prospect sees the friend who recommended Warke and Warke gets a favourable mention, then he telephones the prospect. After he has established that the letter has arrived and has worked in the name of the recipient's friend, the opening gambit is always the same: "Did you throw it in the garbage before you read it, or after you read it?" The line usually gets a laugh, the prospect is put at ease, and the "total-need service" is mentioned. A meeting is set, usually for coffee at a convenient restaurant.

Having morning coffee with Warke is like attending a Billy Graham prayer breakfast. On his first meeting with a new client, Warke hands over his calling card. On one side, his name and telephone number are in tiny print. In larger print, in the middle, is this phrase from Philippians: "I can do all things through Christ which strengtheneth me." Then the added epithet, again in small print: "Try faith and watch what happens." On the other side of the card, the small print asks: "What do you see?" The formless shapes below, when viewed properly, spell out Jesus. At the bottom, more small print: "The above is the answer to all your problems."

Warke then gives the prospect his "total-need service coffee-break appraisal" pamphlet with its thirty-two questions covering personal and business information. Warke likes to leave the prospect alone while the questionnaire is completed. He makes himself scarce, usually heading for the washroom. When he returns, he reads the responses and can tell whether a sale is likely. He is a hugger and a toucher. "If I haven't touched you in the first five minutes there's something wrong."

After the coffee meeting, the client is invited to Warke's office for a further half-hour exploration of assets and hopes. Warke produces a six-to-eight-page report worked out by his accountant and a computer on the client's financial position, estate planning, and insurance needs. A meeting is arranged that will include the spouse. Baby-sitting service is provided if the meeting is at Warke's office. Throughout, his message is simple: "I'm trying to help you get what you want, then I can get what I want."

Warke has certainly bought his own product. He pays $6,000 a month in premiums for a total of $2.5 million in coverage for himself, his family, and his business. Included is a $400,000 policy on his wife, Valerie, and $100,000 on his daughter, Katy-Joy, twelve, a competitive gymnast.

The business has its perks. He travels six to eight weeks a year, sometimes at the expense of some company's incentive plan or out on the speaking circuit. "Insurance companies have carrots," he admits. During the last six years, he has been to Hawaii, Arizona, Portugal, Spain, Paris, London, Monte Carlo, Switzerland, Italy, Palm Springs, and Mackinac Island. While the companies know how to treat their sales agents, the industry needs to change the image. "Many see agents as pressure salespeople. I'd like to see the insurance companies emphasize the value of what an agent can do. North American paid out $396 million in disability, retirement, and death benefits last year. We do a lot more than the lotteries. They're a tax on the ignorant."

People who buy insurance are special, says Warke. "It takes a lot of character to buy our product. The guy who is out partying doesn't buy it—unless it's to ease his conscience." For his part, he believes in tithing. He gives 10 per cent of his income to his Baptist church and donates sums to other charities as well. That's because God is a partner in the agency. "My business is run by the Lord and sometimes I get in the way. I give God all the credit and he gives me all the commission." Will he ever leave the life insurance business? "Why," he asks, "and leave the stage?"

Kanwar D. Singh, forty-two, signed a contract to sell life insurance for Crown Life on March 1, 1984. During the next three and a half months, he made a phenomenal 259 sales, most of them in the first six weeks on the job. In a business where two sales a week is tops, even for a seasoned agent, Singh was selling at the rate of thirty policies a week. Because he leapt to the lead in a sales contest Crown was running, he quickly came to the attention of Bob Reynolds, Crown's vice-president of marketing for Canadian individual insurance. The new superstar aroused suspicion. "My God," Reynolds remembers asking himself, "what's happening?" When they checked Singh's applications more closely, there were striking similarities, the pattern was too neat. Few applicants required medicals; most policies were for amounts that didn't need credit checks. Reynolds cut off Singh's commission payments. With the flow of company money halted, Singh lost not only his source of income, but also the support structure for the ingenious rebating scam he was running at Crown's expense.

Singh was not the only agent involved in the scam. In Hindi, "singh" means lion, and since the scam seemed to be focussed in Toronto's East Indian community, the investigation was called Operation Lion by the Ministry of Consumer and Commercial Relations, the Ontario government watch-dog on insurance agents. When Crown phoned to report Singh, ministry investigators were already on to some fifty agents across the province, most in the Toronto area, doing $20 million in business with twenty-three companies. While there have been some similar sting operations in Vancouver, Toronto seems to be the centre. Singh has already lost his licence; others will follow. In addition, the anti-rackets squad of the Ontario Provincial Police and the Metro Toronto Police fraud squad are investigating.

Singh's operations were typical of how rebating works. Singh's associate beat the bushes, largely among the East Indian community in Toronto, saying that he had a friend who could arrange a year's free life insurance. Once an interested person was found, Singh would arrive and draw up a policy, being careful to assure the company underwriters that the applicant was in good health and keeping the policy value in the $125,000 range so it wouldn't trigger a credit check on the buyer. Often Singh sold other members of the family on the same visit. The buyer would pay Singh the first year's premium, and Singh would immediately refund the policyholder an equivalent amount.

That he could afford to give refunds and still make money is both the heart and the heartache of the life insurance sales system. While most insurance policies pay an agent about 80 per cent of the first year's premium in commission, a good sales agent can increase the remuneration to 140 per cent through various incentive payments received for achieving certain sales volume. Further, most life insurance companies decide the commission level to be paid to an agent by projecting one month's volume over the next twelve months. In that way, an agent who sells at a good clip for one month will be paid for that month as if the same rate will be maintained over a year. Thus his first month's commission will be at the 140-per-cent-rate, giving him enough money to rebate the policy buyer the full amount of the premium paid—and still leave enough for himself. On a typical policy costing $600 in annual premium, for example, the company would pay $840. The buyer gets his money back, the agent gets to keep $240.

The companies, of course, lose out because few of these policies are renewed. The buyer has had his free year and usually can't afford to pay for the second. The agent moves on because rebating works only on new policies; second-year commissions drop to 15 per cent of premium paid. Commissions paid and administrative costs are far from recouped in the first year. Still, when Ontario superintendent of insurance Murray Thompson first told the industry about the extent of rebating, "there was a certain element of disbelief," says Thompson. The industry just wanted to keep quiet and hope that the whole thing faded away; they did not want any bad publicity about the rogues among agents whose pushy public image was already low.

The sales system, to state the obvious, is geared to make agents sell. High commission structures, microwave ovens, and trips to Monte Carlo are all meant to spur sales. A top sales agent can make $300,000 a year. In some cases, first-year commission rates can reach ludicrous heights. Until recently, Crown had a policy called "whole life protector." If an agent sold $35 million worth in a year to families who wanted coverage for a newborn baby, commission rates could reach 480 per cent. On a typical policy with a premium of $300, the first-year commission would be $1,440. And, just to ensure that the system was open to abuse, the commission was paid immediately.

In addition to providing a tempting commission system, the companies don't share enough information about bad agents. When ministry investigators caught up with Singh, he admitted that he had been rebating since 1981. Crown hadn't been his only victim. Before Crown, it had been Empire Life Insurance Co.; after Crown it was Standard Life Assurance Co. Standard apparently did not even think it was curious that his contract had been cancelled by Crown so swiftly, and although Crown alerted the ministry, no mechanism existed to tell other companies. Over four years, Singh was able to submit in excess of $500,000 in premiums through the three companies, including $350,000 in one nine-month period with Standard; up to 80 per cent of that $500,000 was rebated.

When Superintendent Thompson ordered an open hearing under the Insurance Act in March 1985, Singh didn't even bother to defend himself. Investigators who interviewed a sampling of Singh's clients found families where the applicant, spouse, and one or two children had signed on for policies costing up to $8,000 a year in premiums. Not content just to receive the amount of commission over 100 per cent, in some cases Singh asked the policyholders to pay some portion of the "free" insurance and he would pocket that payment as well.

For his part, Singh blames the whole insurance system. "All the licences should be revoked," he told investigators. "As long as these licences remain it is like eating a bone. There is no meat on the bone but the dog still chews it all night, so all these guys are just like that; they're chewing the bone and they will keep on chewing as long as they have a licence." While the ministry is unlikely to ban insurance, some 13,500 insurance policies sold by the fifty agents most suspect are also being inspected for forged signatures, rebating schemes, and just plain fake deals. One particular apartment showed up, for example, as the address for five different families all supposed to be the clients of an agent.

Widespread rebating could weaken the whole insurance system and hurt honest policyholders and agents alike. Says Phil Yakubovich, deputy director of the investigation branch of the Ontario ministry's financial institutions division, who spent eight years investigating organized crime for the RCMP: "If the insurance companies are being gaffed, they're going to raise all premiums. Individually, this is not big-time, but collectively it is." The problem goes beyond the individual losses to the company's financial strength. If a company suffers excessive rebating, its solvency will be weakened; a collapse, although unlikely, would be hurtful to other policyholders. Because rebated policies are unlikely to be renewed, costs are high and profits reduced, thus companies can afford rip-off artists only by raising rates for everyone.

There are other repercussions. One company has demanded that a Toronto broker pay back $50,000 in commissions paid through him to an agent carrying out a rebating scheme—even though the broker was unaware his agent was rebating. Another broker, faced with a similar demand, was unable to repay the company the amount it said he owed, and he went bankrupt. Says Yakubovich, "This is not a victimless crime."

The immediate victims, the industry, set up an eight-member task force in November 1984 to recommend ways to end rebating. Under chairman Donald Elliott, president of Empire Life of Kingston, Ont., the committee made its recommendations in April to the Canadian Life and Health Insurance Association, which represents 117 of the 170 companies operating in Canada. Some of the recommendations were that companies should not project commission based on early sales without evidence of bona fide customers; that privileged information on bad agents should be released by a company when asked; and that commission payments should be monitored to nab rebaters. The committee did not recommend any change in the commission structure. "It hasn't been a problem," insists Elliott. "An accident has occurred that has caused an emergency. Why reduce commission when you can get the job done another way?" Elliott sees the problem as a limited one. "In Toronto we've got an ethnic group who said, 'Let's rip off the system.' I don't conclude that the commission system is bad. The monitoring system is bad; the information system is bad."

Ministry investigators, however, note that rebating is not isolated within one ethnic group; it cuts across many. If first-year commission rates were reduced below 100 per cent, there would be no money for the scam artists to run the scheme. The industry committee did not recommend that, however, for fear that agents would rebel. Yet if a multi-company committee does not make such a recommendation, when will action ever be taken? Certainly no individual company is going to do it and risk losing good agents to companies that are still paying 140 per cent. "You wouldn't want to be the first," admits Elliott.

While rebating does not appear to be widespread in North America, there are U.S. jurisdictions, notably New York state, where first-year commission is kept to 50 per cent by law. Canadian provinces should invoke a similar rule. Currently, agents can receive up to 160 or 175 per cent over two years. To maintain income, but stretch it out over two years, the amount could be divided equally between the first and second years. In order to protect the income levels of current agents further, yet put the ceiling into play, the rule could be applied just to new agents. At the rate agents leave the business, it wouldn't be long before the vast majority of agents would be operating under a new system that would snuff out rebating forever without monitoring, release of privileged information, or any registry of scam artists. Operation Lion could yet bell the cat.

William Sutton was among the special guests at a dinner in Prague during the 1985 world hockey championships. The dinner, hosted by international hockey guru Alan Eagleson, was nicely under way when a Czech police officer burst into the room and made to arrest one of the other Canadian guests for trading currency on the black market. The conversation became quite heated and the room hushed at the thought of the international incident that was brewing. After three or four minutes of realistic dialogue, the truth was revealed. The "policeman" was the maître d' in a borrowed coat. The "lawbreaker" was Air Canada area manager for sports Aggie Kukulowicz. Both were part of an event staged by Eagleson, the master puppeteer.

Bill Sutton isn't usually fooled so easily. His fancy handle is special risk underwriter and his firm, William J. Sutton & Co. Ltd. of Toronto, is one of three in North America selling insurance to pro sports stars. As such, he is a combination of New York bodyguard, Hollywood press agent, and Zurich gnome in a business involving $750 million in face values on policies that have been sold to teams and individuals in the National Hockey League, the National Basketball Association, and the two U.S. pro football leagues, the National Football League and the United States Football League.

"The average person can buy disability insurance easily," says Sutton. "Not so the professional athlete."

Of course, the average person doesn't need as much coverage. Among the high-risk, high-coverage players Sutton handles is Edmonton Oiler superstar Wayne Gretzky, with a $5-million policy against the day he is injured and can't play or fulfil his product endorsement contracts, including one with an insurance company, Travelers Canada. Some of the baseball players, with their recently signed $10-million lifetime contracts, are putting even higher coverage in place. "Gretzky," laughs Sutton, "is a pauper compared to those guys."

The sports insurance business began in the 1960s when hockey players' salaries began to jump, as the World Hockey Association raided the NHL to stock its new teams, thus bidding up the salaries of eligible players. Insurance agent Robert Bradshaw knew Toronto lawyer Eagleson, who acted for a number of players, and was the man who started the business. As salaries rose, teams moved to protect the drawing cards in the franchises and companies began worrying about the health of players who were advertising their products. Hockey star Bobby Orr, for example, required a policy for $600,000 to cover all his contract commitments. Thus the sports insurance business was born in Toronto; it is still centred there.

In the 1960s, few insurance companies would cover athletes, certainly not in the amounts that were becoming necessary among at least some of the 3,500 pros in North America. Firms offering such business included two U.S.-based firms, Employers Reinsurance Corp. and American Re-Insurance Co., as well as Lloyd's of London. Originally, premiums were based on the companies' experience with the entertainment business, insuring such important items as Betty Grable's legs and Jimmy Durante's nose. Bradshaw's step was to combine American Re and Lloyd's to push coverage ceilings for athletes to as high as $1.5 million, far higher than before. Bradshaw was able to arrange Orr's coverage with Lloyd's, which, until then, was more familiar with Bob Hope and the Rolling Stones.

Sutton, forty-six, a chartered accountant by profession, was with the firm Ernst & Whinney in the 1960s, then joined Bradshaw in 1974 until their arrangement came apart in 1978. Sutton had come to like the people he dealt with, and he had built up a credibility with Lloyd's of London, so he decided to set up his own business. "I'm not a typical entrepreneur," he says. "I'm much more a technocrat than a marketing person." In September 1974, he opened up shop with just himself and a secretary. Today he has thirteen employees and takes in $7.5 million in annual premium income. About 40 per cent of his business is in sports insurance (about three-quarters of that in disability), 25 per cent in conventional personal accident coverage (such as corporate plans); 15 per cent is reinsurance for domestic life insurance companies, and 20 per cent comes from NHL group administration plans, kidnap coverage, and other miscellaneous policies.

In sports coverage, hockey and football players are at the high end of the premium scale; baseball, golf, and tennis professionals get cheaper rates, in a range from $6.50 per $1,000 to $14 per $1,000 for coverage on contract liability payments to a player who can no longer play. Because the pro football and baseball leagues have no league-wide disability plans, the teams buy disability coverage separately. Sutton handles eight football teams, six in the USFL and two in the NFL. As well, he deals with three baseball teams, Toronto Blue Jays, New York Yankees, and Chicago Cubs.

Team coverage extends beyond contract liability. They also buy catastrophe coverage against the single accident that kills all the players. The need became apparent as early as 1958 when a plane crashed near Munich killing eight players from Manchester United, an English pro soccer team. Today, rates for such coverage are $1 per $1,000 of coverage for a year. For $10 million in coverage, then, the premium is $10,000. In addition, most leagues have so-called re-stocking clauses, which mean that each team would supply, say, three players from its roster to the team that suffered the disaster. The largest coverage amount available from the underwriters is $32 million. "They just don't want to take any more," says Sutton.

Most of the insurance Sutton sells is put through Lloyd's, where eighty syndicates handle the policies and spread the risks among them. While teams have insurance on the players, many players add their own coverage. Team-owners in the NHL, for example, offer $100,000 in disability insurance for each player, and the players' association kicks in another $75,000. On average there are five disability claims a year within those amounts. To date, there have been comparatively few large pay-outs. When they do occur, how-ever, they can be sizeable. A decade ago New York Knickerbocker basketball player Willis Reed suffered a knee injury that led to a

$600,000 payment. Other awards have included $400,000 to Pittsburgh Penguin Bob Stewart for a knee injury. The largest award to date was to Bill Walton of the NBA San Diego Clippers, who collected $1.1 million for a broken bone in his foot.

In addition to coverage on sports, Sutton can also arrange coverage for ransom demands on kidnapped businessmen. Amounts up to $1 million are common, but policies as high as $5 million are also available. For a small or medium-sized company, coverage for all employees and their immediate families (assuming no travel outside North America) would cost $2,500 for a $1-million limit. Three trips a year by policyholders to South America would add an additional $1,000 to the premium. Buyers include the banks, oil companies, and breweries insuring their top executives.

Football remains the area offering Sutton the greatest number of potential new clients each year. Owners have plenty of eager college players from whom to choose and don't need to worry about insurance on the current crop. Says Sutton, "There are three times the number of players required in football. They are seen as interchangeable parts." As long as that is the case, sports insurance will remain a growing business.

The visitors had been gathering for days in Fort Simpson in the Northwest Territories. The town's usual population of less than a thousand souls had been swollen by guests all hoping to receive the blessings of the Pope during his flying three-hour visit in September 1984. The ceremonies with their sacred fires, drums, and dancing began three days before the Holy Father arrived. The Canadian Conference of Catholic Bishops had encouraged the Pope to visit the north, and it took little convincing for him to add the stop to see Canada's original peoples on the banks of the Mackenzie River.

As with many of the other events scheduled during the eleven-day tour, the turn-out was smaller than expected. An estimated 4,000 people gathered, when tens of thousands had been expected. Worse was to come. The morning of His Holiness's arrival, fog rolled in and visibility was reduced to a few yards, not clear enough for the public celebration of mass and certainly too dangerous for the Pope's plane to land. Rescheduling was impossible, given the Pope's other commitments.

In addition to the disappointed members of the Dene nation and native groups, there were some anxious southern eyes trained on the cancelled event. The worst fears of Jack Keough, vice-president of Reed Stenhouse Ltd., the broker who put the insurance into place for the Pope's tour, had just been realized. Among the coverage the bishops had bought was cancellation and no-show insurance against just such an eventuality. Fortunately, the no-show turned out to be the only sizeable claim. "A lot of people breathed a sigh of relief [when the Pope left Canada]," said Keough, "particularly the underwriters, who had a lot on the line."

Insurance planning for the papal visit began sixteen months before the tour. The potential for problems was immense. There had already been two attempts on the Pope's life, including one in St. Peter's Square in 1981. At the time insurance was being considered for Canada, the Pope was visiting South Korea and New Guinea, where there was further concern about injury not just to the Holy Father, but also to innocent bystanders who might then sue organizers. The Canadian hosts, the Canadian Conference of Catholic Bishops, needed protection against such eventualities, and Keough took on the task of devising an insurance plan. The firm's London branch had long been the broker for numerous Roman Catholic dioceses and religious communities, including most of the dioceses in Ontario and many other parts of Canada.

Keough's first step was to survey insurance that had been put in place for papal visits to other countries. The closest parallel to the Canadian situation was in the U.S., but coverage there had been put in place regionally or by city as was seen fit. In the U.K. a countrywide policy had been used, and Keough decided that such a global approach was better. "We recommended that the insurance plan be written on a global basis to cover the entire papal visit right across Canada," says Keough. "In this way, the aim would be to provide an adequate and uniform level of protection." The Conference agreed and in December 1983, a questionnaire was sent to all the dioceses that would be visited by the Pope. The survey asked for information about planned activities, construction, numbers of persons expected, how parking and food concessions would be handled, and whether buses or other vehicles would be leased or operated. "The purpose," says Keough, "was to try to find out the numbers of persons who might be in one place at one time, and whether there was a danger of a catastrophe or bodily injury liability situations. The most obvious insurable exposure was in the area of liability for injury to persons or damage to property of others. Because of the large numbers of persons who would be attending these events, there was concern that agitators or terrorists might seize the opportunity to try to promote their own ends."

Following the survey, Keough estimated the risks and recommended that total coverage be $300 million. The broad policy he had in mind included liability, all-risks property insurance, blanket crime including fidelity bonding (of employees, for example), comprehensive boiler and machinery insurance (for power supply and distribution systems at outdoor masses), and cancellation or nonappearance insurance in case the Pope didn't come. Other special extensions included libel, slander, and defamation; non-owned watercraft and aircraft; tenants' all-risks; copyright infringement; medical malpractice (when first aid was applied); advertisers' liability; and auto insurance for the two popemobiles. (After the visit, one popemobile was donated to the Museum of Science and Technology in Ottawa; the other was given to the Vatican for its use.) There was no coverage either on the Pope's life or for any kidnap and ransom insurance. While Keough offered to cost out such coverage, the bishops said that whatever coverage the Vatican normally carried on the Pope would be sufficient.

All the insurance coverage was put in place April 1, 1984, more than six months before the visit, in order that claims during the preparations were covered as well. Those covered were the Conference itself, all dioceses and religious communities, clergy, employees, and volunteers, as well as parish officers and members and the general public. In addition, there was coverage for buildings and refreshment booths as well as religious paraphernalia right down to vestments, chalices, ciboria, candelabra, statuary, and altar cloths.

The company serving as the primary insurer was Royal Insurance Canada. Fireman's Fund Insurance Co., one of the few companies offering cancellation insurance, wrote that particular policy because of its experience in this type of coverage for celebrities and special events. The amount insured was $10 million, a sum that Keough describes as "just an arbitrary figure, plucked out of the air. If the [entire] trip had been cancelled, the actual costs would have been higher." The premium for the $10-million policy was in excess of $100,000. The premium charged by Royal on the global policy was approximately $150,000.

Royal then spread the full $300 million at risk among a further eleven companies. If there had been a major claim, each would have paid in proportion to its coverage. Of the first $100 million coverage, Royal took the first $25 million and $23 million of the next $75 million. Also sharing the next $75 million were Scottish & York Insurance Co. Ltd., $27 million; Chubb Insurance Co., $15 million; New Hampshire Insurance Co., $10 million. The next $200 million was shared among Royal, $45 million; Fireman's Fund, $40 million; INA Insurance Co. of Canada, $25 million; First State Insurance Co., $25 million; Home Insurance Co., of New York, $20 million; Chubb, $15 million; U.S. Fire Insurance Co., $15 million; Halifax Insurance Co., $10 million; Kansas General Insurance Co., $5 million.

In the end, in typically cautious Canadian style, the trip was grossly overinsured. In total, there were fifty claims, totalling about $100,000 (separate from the no-show claim). The fifty included fewer than ten minor bodily injury claims due to falls and similar incidents. None of the claims went to court for litigation. The other claims involved lost, missing, or damaged property such as electrical cables, chairs, and various other pieces of equipment, ranging from a wheelchair worth less than $100 to combined values at other locations ranging from $2,500 up to $15,000. The most bizarre theft involved the disappearance of 150 portable toilets from the mass site in St. John's. The one major claim yet to be settled remains the no-show in Fort Simpson. Under the policy wording, the insurance will pay for "net ascertained loss," meaning the expenses of the organizing committee less any revenues they collected. The team who investigated the claim included an adjuster from New York and an accountant from Los Angeles.

Because the number of claims was much smaller than expected, the Conference will receive a refund, likely 25 per cent on the premium it paid. There was, however, no insurance against small turn-outs. "This was a first in Canada," says Keough. "There were estimates of sizeable crowds that scared a lot of people away." In Toronto, where up to 1.1 million were expected at the Downsview service, only 400,000 showed. Nor was there any coverage against weather. One mass in Quebec was conducted in a sea of mud.

There are just some acts of God that no pacts by man will cover. Insurance, unlike the Pope, is not infallible.

APPENDIX A

The Top Twenty Life Insurance Companies in Canada (1984)

Rank by assets	Assets (thousands $)	Premium Income (thousands $)	Company (head office)
1	13,550,253	2,497,112	Manufacturers Life Insurance Co. (Toronto) (1)
2	12,957,804	2,172,092	Sun Life Assurance Co. of Canada (Toronto)
3	9,066,866	2,003,204	Great-West Life Assurance Co. (Winnipeg)
4	6,032,779	1,112,341	Mutual Life Assurance Co. (Waterloo, Ont.)
5	5,884,293	1,164,734	Canada Life Assurance Co. (Toronto)
6	5,654,100	881,534	London Life Insurance Co. (London, Ont.)
7	5,225,741	1,268,369	Confederation Life Insurance Co. (Toronto)
8	4,846,127	1,457,989	Crown Life Insurance Co. (Toronto)
9	3,629,328	366,188	Standard Life Assurance Co. (Montreal) (2)
10	3,332,932	560,649	Metropolitan Life Insurance Co. (Ottawa) (2)
11	2,965,767	418,034	North American Life Assurance Co. (Toronto)
12	2,594,100	394,927	Imperial Life Assurance Co. of Canada (Toronto)

13	2,146,359	388,610	Prudential Insurance Co. of America (Toronto) (2)
14	1,770,251	469,702	Prudential Assurance Co. (Montreal) (2)
15	1,516,307	372,869	Aetna Canada (Toronto) (2)
16	1,353,133	207,574	Maritime Life Assurance Co. (Halifax)
17	1,291,120	266,260	Industrial Life Assurance Co. (Quebec City)
18	866,716	185,458	National Life Assurance Co. of Canada (Toronto)
19	789,841	222,922	Assurance-vie Desjardins (Lévis, Que.)
20	611,839	110,074	Alliance Mutual Life Insurance Co. (Montreal)

(1) Includes assets of Dominion Life Assurance Co. (Waterloo, Ont.), purchased in 1985.
(2) Foreign-owned.

APPENDIX B

The Top Fifteen General Insurance Companies in Canada (1984)

Rank by premium income	Premium income (thousands $)	Revenue (thousands $)	Company (head office)
1	441,151	503,122	Co-operators General Insurance Co. (Guelph, Ont.)
2	397,210	488,934	Royal Insurance Co. (Toronto) (1)
3	360,985	392,158	Lloyd's of London (Montreal) (1)
4	248,392	287,292	Wawanesa Mutual Insurance Co. (Winnipeg)
5	245,903	286,377	Economical Group (Kitchener, Ont.)
6	245,457	287,259	Allstate Insurance Co. (Toronto) (1)
7	237,000	273,000	Commercial Union Assurance Group (Toronto) (1)
8	233,477	233,688	General Accident Assurance Co. (Toronto) (1)
9	233,428	260,312	Travelers Canada (Toronto) (1)
10	211,960	198,715	Laurentian Group General Insurance Cos. (Quebec City)
11	209,550	250,219	Prudential Assurance Group (Montreal) (1)

12	205,704	250,281	Phoenix Continental Insurance Cos. (Toronto) (1)
13	197,969	230,535	State Farm Group (Toronto) (1)
14	190,648	224,252	Zurich Insurance (Toronto) (1)
15	170,259	212,911	Dominion of Canada General Insurance Co. (Toronto)

(1) Foreign-owned.

INDEX

B.C. Central Credit Union, 341
Beatty, Gordon, 35
Bégin, Robert, 188-91
Beightol, Dick, 112
Bell, Walter, 159
Belli, Melvin, 141
Belton, Ted, 143, 145
Belzberg, Sam, 174
Bennett, Jalynn, 172, 181, 182
Bernier, Jean-Pierre, 14
Beutel, Austin, 289
Beutel Goodman & Co. Ltd., 263, 289
Bill 75 (Quebec), 135, 136, 137, 138-9
Boeckner, Bob, 267
Booz, Allen, Hamilton, 254
Borden, Robert, 8, 273
Borland v. Muttersbach and Royal Insurance Group, 21
Bourassa, Robert, 132
Bourk, Larry, 288
Bourke, George, 38-9
Bowell, Mackenzie, 8
Bowie, George, 186-91, 193-6, 198
Boyd, Ty, 93
Bradford, William, 272
Bradshaw, Robert, 381
Bradshaw, Thomas, 102
Brady, I.P., 212
Brascade Resources, 199
Brascan Ltd., 199-200, 201-3, 207, 208, 218
Bratton, D.A., 212
Breen, Maurie, 193-7
Brindle, Jack (John Arthur), 14, 26, 29, 30, 41, 43, 44-6, 54, 365
British America Assurance Co., 246
British Pacific Life Insurance Co., 19

Bronfman, Edward, 5, 199, 201-2
Bronfman, Peter, 5, 199, 201-2
Brown, E.J.S., 274, 275
Brown, Ron, 190, 194
Bruneau, Claude, 127, 136
Bryce, Robert, 52
Buckley, Paul, 78, 79, 92
Bullock, Kathy, 196
Buntin, Alexander, 34
Burns, Charles, 274, 275
Burns, Herbert, 274
Burns, Michael, 261, 263-4, 266, 275, 276, 279, 281-2, 285, 290
Burns, Pat, 14, 285
Burns, Sue, 273
Burns family, 261
Bussières, Pierre, 156

Campbell, Alistair, 27, 39, 40, 47, 48, 49, 51, 52
Campbell, William, 247, 248, 254, 256
The Canada Life Assurance Co., 6, 7-8, 10, 20
Canada Pension Plan, 325
Canada Trustco Mortgage Co., 180-1, 313
Canadian and British Insurance Companies Act, 10, 151, 158, 180, 378
Canadian Brotherhood of Railway, Transport and General Workers, 341
Canadian Conference of Catholic Bishops, 383, 384, 385, 386
Canadian Foundation Co. Ltd., 100, 106, 112, 124

Canadian General Life
Assurance Co., 267
Canadian Life and Health
Insurance Association Inc.
(CLHIA), 5, 6, 14, 32-3, 68,
135, 201, 220, 262, 284, 317,
328, 379
Canadian Life Insurance
Association, 40. *See also*
Canadian Life and Health
Insurance Association Inc.
Canadian Marconi Co., 97, 99
Canadian National, 261, 268,
271, 311
The Canadian Provident-
General, 133
Canadian Provident-Life
Insurance Co., 133
Canagex, 133, 139
Cannon, Edward, 286
Can West Capital Corp., 104-5,
106, 107-8, 109, 110
Capitol Bankers Life Insurance
Co., 112-14, 121, 123
captives, 142
Cardinal Insurance Co., 144
Carlile, J.B., 165
Carruthers, Douglas, 248
Carten, Michael, 194
Carter, J.A. (Bob): appearance
and life-style, 184-6; morals
charges, 184, 186, 197, 198; at
Northern, 191, 192-8; in oil
business, 191-2
Carter, Sheila, 185, 196
Cascade Group, 198
Castonguay, Claude, 14, 49,
188; background, 130, 131-2,
134; and industry, 136, 137; as
Laurentian CEO, 125-6, 129,

135-7, 139-40; management
style, 127, 135-6, 139-40; in
politics, 126, 132; salary, 136
Castonguay, Mimi, 131
Castonguay, Pouliot, Guerard &
Associates Inc., 131
Cecil-Stuart, Wendy, 199
Chambers, Margaret, 347-8,
349, 350, 354
Charron, André, 190-1
Cherry, Zena, 285
Chrétien, Jean, 51
Christie, Gayle, 159
Chubb Insurance Co., 386
Churchill, Winston, 2
CIS Ltd., 357
Citibank, 4
Clark, Ken, 207
Clarke, George, 23, 26-7, 32,
40, 41-2, 46, 48, 52, 54-5
Clarke, John, 172, 176, 179,
182-3
Clarke, Larry, 205, 206, 219
Clarkson, Gordon & Co., 99,
205, 207, 218
Clifford Lawrie Bolton Ritchie
Architects, 166
Cockwell, Jack, 202, 203
Cohen, Mickey, 249
Cohen, Reuben, 59
Cohen, Susan, 200, 203
Colander Publications, 146
Collingwood, Henry, 312
Colonia, 68
Commercial Union, 100
commissions. *See* insurance sales
Confederation Life Insurance
Co., 4, 5, 14, 17, 20, 25, 165,
174, 175, 281, 284-5, 326,
328, 362, 365

Excelsior Life Insurance Co., 68, 69
Extendicare Ltd., 106, 263, 275-6, 286
Eyton, Trevor, 202

Facciani, Rudy, 276, 277
Facility Association, 296
Family Law Reform Act (Ontario), 147, 295
Fauteux, Gaspard, 131
federal budget (1981), 70-1, 137, 328, 333, 372
Feldman, Ben, 84-7, 92-3, 93-4, 364
Ferguson, George Howard, 273
Ferguson, Peter, 11-12
F.H. Deacon Hodgson, 200
financial services sector: competition within, 4-6, 11, 12-15, 125-6, 135, 137, 264, 336; federal advisory committee and discussion paper, 12, 19, 127, 200, 204, 218-9, 249, 263; "four pillars", 4. See also insurance industry, financial services offered by; one-stop financial shopping
Finlayson, Jock, 26
Fireman's Fund Insurance Co. of Canada, 200, 385, 386
First Atlantic Assurance Co., 151, 152, 155, 156, 157
First Boston Corp., 43
First Choice, 181, 200
First City Financial, 174
First State Insurance Co., 386
Fleming, Allan, 333
Fonyo, Steve, 185

"four pillars" of financial services, 4
Frazee, Rowland, 264
Freedman, Adele, 11
Freeman, Arnold, 363
Freeman, Russ, 228

Galt, Alexander, 30
Galt, George (father of Thomas), 30-31
Galt, George (son of Thomas), 31
Galt, John, 30
Galt, Sir Thomas, 30
Galt, Thomas Maunsell: appearance and character, 30, 31-3, 52; background, 30-1, 47; and industry, 32-3; life-style, 31-2; management style, 27, 33, 38, 44, 47, 53-4; salary, 47; as Sun chairman, 26-7, 36, 37-8, 41, 43, 44, 46, 48, 52, 53-4, 55-6; as Sun president, 28, 39, 47-8, 50-2
Gardner, John, 29, 56, 362
Garneau, Raymond, 133
Gault, Mathew Hamilton, 34
Gaver, Don, 32, 50
general insurance. See property and casualty insurance companies
Geoffrion, Leclerc Inc., 126, 139
Gerling Global Life, 68, 371
Gibbons, Anne, 91
Gordon, Peter, 26, 36
Gore Mutual Insurance Co., 328
Gowdy, Jim, 39
Graham, Michael, 203
Great Lakes Group Inc., 200

373; staff, 104, 109, 116, 120;
U.S. operations, 98, 100, 102,
112-4, 119-23, 368
North American Security Life,
120, 121
North Canadian Trust Co., 283
North City Insurance Agency, 363
The Northern Life Assurance
Co. of Canada, 133, 184,
185-98; assets, 187, 188, 197;
directors, 190-1, 194-6;
expenses, 193; history, 187-8;
insurance in force, 188; losses,
197; offices, 187, 189;
owners, 185, 187, 188, 189,
192, 198; staff, 187, 189, 193,
197; U.S. operations, 188
Northern Union, 155
North West Life Assurance Co.
Ltd., 68, 127, 188-9, 190,
369, 371

Oakley, Kenneth, 334
Oatman, Jim, 193-7, 198
O'Callaghan, Pat, 312, 313
Occidental Life Insurance Co.
of Canada, 19
O'Donoghue, Paul, 143, 145
Okada, Karen, 333
Olympia & York, 102, 200
Olympic team (Canadian), 263
one-stop financial shopping, 5,
33, 125, 136, 138, 201, 262-3,
264, 286, 289-90, 332, 337.
See also financial services sector
Ontario Credit Union League, 347
Ontario Federation of
Agriculture, 346, 347
Ontario Medical Association,
370-1

Ontario Mutual Life Association
Co., 21
The Ontario Mutual Life
Assurance Co., 322
Operation Lion, 376
Oronhyatekha, 9
Orr, Bobby, 381
Orser, Earl Herbert, 13-14, 97,
124, 138-9, 221, 270, 330,
332; appearance and
character, 204-5; background,
205-6; and industry, 203,
204, 212, 218, 220; as London
CEO, 201, 209-20; as
London consultant, 205-6,
207-8; management style,
211, 213, 214-6, 219; salary,
212; at Trilon, 203, 217-8
Osler, Gordon, 31
Osler, Justice, 19

Palk, Edward A., 188
Panabaker, John, 33, 137, 138,
173, 218, 282, 284;
appearance and character,
314-6, 319; background, 314,
325; and industry, 33, 284,
317, 321, 328, 336-7;
life-style, 314, 316, 338-9;
management style, 328,
331-2, 338; as Mutual
chairman, 311, 313, 314,
318-22, 326, 327, 329-33,
335; public relations efforts,
313, 317, 334-7, 339; salary,
314; as speaker, 317-9, 336
papal visit to Canada, 383-6
Paragon Insurance Co., 133
Parizeau, Jacques, 125, 126, 127,
135, 137

State Farm, 242
Stephens, Durham, 154-5
Stephenson, Herbert Roy, 273-4
Stewart, Bob, 383
Stormont, Allan, 38
Strathcona, Lord, 187
Strathcona General Insurance
   Co., 144, 150
Suitter, Nicole, 22
Suncor Inc., 148
Sun Life Assurance Co. of
   Canada, 11, 14, 20, 23, 26-57,
   125, 360, 361, 365, 367;
   assets, 3, 12, 28, 29, 162;
   corporate culture, 28-9, 32,
   33-4, 36, 38, 48, 53-4, 56-7;
   directors, 26, 34; executives,
   26-7, 30, 38, 39, 47, 56;
   financial performance, 28,
   29, 30-1, 42, 43, 44, 49, 52-3;
   head office moved from
   Montreal, 27-8, 48-53;
   history, 34-5, 38-41;
   insurance in force, 29;
   international operations, 29,
   34, 46; investments, 29-30,
   35, 36; marketing, 29, 39,
   42-3, 55; offices, 30, 34-5,
   36-8, 50, 53; planning and
   organization, 39-40, 41, 43,
   46, 48, 54-6; salaries and
   benefits, 47; sales agents, 29,
   53, 55; staff, 29, 36, 47; U.S.
   operations, 29, 39, 43, 48
The Sun Mutual Life Insurance
   Co., 34
superintendents of insurance, 8,
   13, 150, 253, 325-6, 377,
   378; in Pitts failure, 151,
   153-60. *See also* Deparment

of Insurance
supermarket concept. *See*
   one-stop financial shopping
Sutton, William, 380-3
Symons, Alan, 154
Syncrude Canada Ltd., 1, 141

Tanenbaum, Larry, 111
Tardif, J.A., 128, 129
Taylor, J. Allyn, 208
Taylor, Richard, 285
Tellinghast, Nelson & Warren
   Inc., 69, 193
term insurance. *See* life
   insurance policies
Thomas, Art, 279
Thompson, Harold, 108, 112, 115
Thompson, Murray, 377, 378
Thomson, Richard, 207
Thorne Riddell, 153, 158
Thorne Stevenson & Kellogg,
   196, 267
Tingey, George, 18
Tonti, Lorenzo, 9
Top of the Table, 77, 371, 372.
   See also Million Dollar Round
   Table
Toronto-Dominion Bank, 156,
   200, 201, 202, 207
Tory, John, 26, 40
Touche Ross, 207
Traders Group, 190
Travelers Canada, 6, 381
Tremblay, Marcellin, 127
Trilon Financial Corp., 5,
   200-1, 203, 207, 213, 218,
   219, 283, 321
Trizec Corp., 202
Trollope, Robert Woodland,
   151-9

Trudeau, Pierre, 51, 52
Trust Général du Canada, 137
Tupper, Charles, 8, 273
Turner, John, 273
"twisting", 68, 220, 370

unemployment insurance, 325
United Co-operatives of
Ontario, 346, 347
United Farmers of Alberta, 341
United Maritime Fishermen,
341
United States Fidelity &
Guaranty Co., 346
universal life. *See* life insurance
policies; new money products
Universal Protection, 130
University of Manitoba
graduates, 31, 112, 131, 165,
170, 330, 331
University of Waterloo, 328
U.S. Fire Insurance Co., 386

Vancouver Whitecaps, 198
van Ulden, Joseph, 335
variable life. *See* life insurance
policies; new money products
Vrysen, John, 120, 121

Walden, J.W., 322-3
Walker, Gordon, 249, 250, 251
Walsh, John, 198
Walton, Bill, 383
Warke, Katy-Joy, 375
Warke, Lewis, Jr., 372-6
Warke, Valerie, 375
Warke Agency, 372-6
Warren, Lloyd, 165
Watkins, Lyndon, 204
Webster, Lorne C., 188

Wellington Insurance Co., 5,
200, 201
Westbury Life Insurance Co., 152
Whole life insurance. *See* life
insurance policies
Wilkinson, George, 1, 141
William J. Sutton & Co. Ltd., 380
William M. Mercer Ltd., 113,
195, 265
Williams, Arthur C., 275
Williams, Dave, 279
Wilson, Barry, 249, 252
Win-Bar Insurance Brokers
Ltd., 91
Winhold, Dunc, 327, 330, 331,
332
Winters, Robert, 273
Wise, Julian, 369-71
Wise, Hutton, MacDonald
Insurance Agencies Inc.,
370-1
Witten, Mark, 31
women in insurance, 76, 77, 91,
181-2, 219, 221, 224-5, 297,
316, 318, 363
Wood, Arthur, 27, 38-9
Workman, Thomas, 34, 56
World Wildlife Fund Canada, 6
Wright, Bill, 274
Wrixon, Brian, 25, 362-3
Wyatt Co., 145

Xerox Canada Realty Inc., 103

Yakubovich, Sam, 378-9
Young Presidents' Organization
(YPO), 186, 288

Zukerman, Barry, 117